Lecture Notes in Computer Science 9514

Commenced Publication in 1973
Founding and Former Series Editors:
Gerhard Goos, Juris Hartmanis, and Jan van Leeuwen

Naofumi Homma · Marcel Medwed (Eds.)

Smart Card Research and Advanced Applications

14th International Conference, CARDIS 2015
Bochum, Germany, November 4–6, 2015
Revised Selected Papers

Springer

Editors
Naofumi Homma
Tohoku University
Sendai
Japan

Marcel Medwed
NXP Semiconductors
Gratkorn
Austria

ISSN 0302-9743   ISSN 1611-3349   (electronic)
Lecture Notes in Computer Science
ISBN 978-3-319-31270-5   ISBN 978-3-319-31271-2   (eBook)
DOI 10.1007/978-3-319-31271-2

Library of Congress Control Number: 2016933118

LNCS Sublibrary: SL4 – Security and Cryptology

This Springer imprint is published by Springer Nature
The registered company is Springer International Publishing AG Switzerland

Preface

The 14th Smart Card Research and Advanced Application Conference was held in Bochum, Germany, during November 4–6, 2015. The conference was organized by the Horst Görtz Institute for IT-Security (HGI) and held at the Ruhr University Bochum (RUB).

Since 1994, CARDIS has been the foremost international conference dedicated to smart card research and applications. Smart cards and secure elements are the basis for many secure systems and play a decisive role in ID management. Established computer science areas such as hardware design, operating systems, system modeling, cryptography, verification, and networking have adapted to this fast growing technology and investigate emerging issues resulting from it. Unlike events devoted to commercial and application aspects of smart cards, CARDIS conferences gather researchers and technologists who focus on all aspects of the design, development, deployment, validation, and application of smart cards and secure elements in secure platforms or systems.

CARDIS 2015 received 40 submissions from 18 countries. Each paper was reviewed by at least three independent reviewers. The selection of 17 papers to fill the technical program was accomplished based on 158 written reviews. This task was performed by the 29 members of the Program Committee with the help of 69 external reviewers. The technical program also featured two invited talks. The first invited speaker, Brecht Wyseur, from Nagra, Switzerland, presented "White-Box Cryptography and Smart Cards: Friend or Foe?" The second invited speaker, Sebastian Faust, from Ruhr University Bochum, Germany, gave a talk on "Leakage Resilient Masking Schemes."

We would like to thank the Organizing Committee chairs, Tim Güneysu, Amir Moradi, and Christof Paar, for their excellent conference management. Furthermore, we would like to thank Aurélien Francillon for his valuable advice and help. We are also grateful for the excellent local arrangements organized by Irmgard Kühn. Besides the organizers of the conference and the venue, we would also like to express our sincere thanks to the people who enabled the technical program to have such high quality. These are most prominently the members of the Program Committee and the external reviewers, but also the invited speakers and the authors. Finally, we would also like to acknowledge the Steering Committee for giving us the privilege of serving as program chairs of CARDIS 2015. In particular, we thank the Steering Committee chair, François-Xavier Standaert, for his help and guidance throughout the process.

November 2015

Naofumi Homma
Marcel Medwed

Organization

CARDIS 2015 was organized by Horst Görtz Institute for IT-Security (HGI) at Ruhr University Bochum (RUB).

Organizing Committee Chairs

Tim Güneysu	University of Bremen, Germany
Amir Moradi	Ruhr University Bochum, Germany
Christof Paar	Ruhr University Bochum, Germany

Conference Program Co-chairs

Naofumi Homma	Tohoku University, Japan
Marcel Medwed	NXP Semiconductors, Austria

Program Committee

Guillaume Barbu	Oberthur Technologies, France
Guillaume Bouffard	ANSSI, France
Kim-Kwang Raymond Choo	University of South Australia, Australia
Christophe Clavier	University of Limoges, France
Elke De Mulder	Cryptography Research France, France
Thomas Eisenbarth	Worcester Polytechnic Institute, USA
Wieland Fischer	Infineon Technologies, Germany
Aurelien Francillon	EURECOM, France
Benedikt Gierlichs	KU Leuven, Belgium
Christophe Giraud	Oberthur Technologies, France
Sylvain Guilley	Telecom-ParisTech and Secure-IC, France
Tim Güneysu	University of Bremen, Germany
Johann Heyszl	Fraunhofer AISEC, Germany
Michael Hutter	Cryptography Research US, USA
Lanet Jean-Louis	University of Limoges, France
Ilya Kizhvatov	Riscure, Netherlands
Yuichi Komano	Toshiba Corporation, Japan
Victor Lomne	ANSSI, France
Stefan Mangard	TU Graz, Austria
Amir Moradi	Ruhr University Bochum, Germany
Svetla Nikova	KU Leuven, Belgium
Elisabeth Oswald	University of Bristol, UK
Axel Poschmann	NXP Semiconductors GmbH, Germany
Francesco Regazzoni	ALaRI - USI, Switzerland

François-Xavier Standaert	UCL Crypto Group, Belgium
Takeshi Sugawara	Mitsubishi Electric Corporation, Japan
Yu Yu	Tsinghua University, China

Additional Reviewers

Josep Balasch
Valentina Banciu
Georg T. Becker
Molka Ben Romdhane
Shivam Bhasin
Begül Bilgin
Cees-Bart Breunesse
Samuel Burri
Cong Chen
Jean-Michel Cioranesco
Jean-Sebastien Coron
Thomas De Cnudde
Kurt Dietrich
Quang Do
Baris Ege
Benoit Gerard
Gilbert Goodwill
Karin Greimel
Vincent Grosso
Zheng Guo
Patrick Haddad
Helena Handschuh
Ray Hunt
Gorka Irazoqui
Elif Bilge Kavun
François Koeune
Thomas Korak
Julien Lancia
Hélène Le Bouder
Liran Lerman
Junrong Liu
José Lopes-Esteves
Florian Lugou
Mark Marson
Steven Murdoch

Yusuke Naito
Tsunato Nakai
Ventzi Nikov
Tsukasa Omino
David Oswald
Eric Peeters
Peter Pessl
Rodrigo Portella do Canto
Guillaume Rambaud
Pablo Rauzy
David Rennie
Oscar Reparaz
Sebastien Riou
Cyril Roscian
Minoru Saeki
Pascal Sasdrich
Falk Schellenberg
Martin Schläffer
Tobias Schneider
Dave Singelee
Daisuke Suzuki
Mostafa Taha
Philippe Teuwen
Mike Tunstall
Thomas Unterluggauer
Jasper van Woudenberg
Rajesh Velegalati
Vincent Verneuil
Weijia Wang
Mario Werner
Antoine Wurcker
Sen Xu
Tomoko Yonemura
Yu Yu

Sponsoring Institutions

Cryptography in Ubiquitous Computing (UbiCrypt)
European Competence Center for IT Security (eurobits)
Robert Bosch GmbH
Brightsight
Infineon Technologies AG

Contents

Side-Channel Attacks

Side-Channel Attacks on SHA-1-Based Product Authentication ICs

David Oswald$^{(\boxtimes)}$

The University of Birmingham, Birmingham, UK
d.f.oswald@cs.bham.ac.uk

Abstract. To prevent product counterfeiting, a common practice is to cryptographically authenticate system components (e.g., inkjet cartridges, batteries, or spare parts) using dedicated ICs. In this paper, we analyse the security of two wide-spread examples for such devices, the DS28E01 and DS2432 SHA-1-based authentication ICs manufactured by Maxim Integrated. We show that the 64-bit secret can be fully extracted using non-invasive side-channel analysis with 1,800 and 1,200 traces, respectively. Doing so, we present the, to our knowledge, first gray-box side-channel attack on real-world devices employing an HMAC-like construction. Our results highlight that there is an evident need for protection against implementation attacks also for the case of low-cost devices like product authentication ICs.

Keywords: Side-channel analysis · SHA-1 · Product authentication · Anti-counterfeiting · Real-world attack

1 Introduction

Counterfeit electronic products have become an immense problem for manufacturers. According to a report of the United Nations Office on Drugs and Crime [20], the market for counterfeit goods had a value of USD 250 billion in 2012. Approximately 8 % of all counterfeit products are electrical or computer equipment (based on the number of counterfeit seizures made at the European borders in 2008). Hence, protecting products against being "cloned" is a necessity for a manufacturer today.

Devices that consist of several components of different complexities appear to be a profitable target for counterfeit in particular: For example, while fake printers are relatively rare, there is a huge variety of compatible ink cartridges for all brands, presumably because cartridges are easy to produce and in constant demand. The same holds for similar low-cost items like accessories for mobile phones (e.g., chargers, batteries, etc.) and also for more expensive equipment like medical sensors or extension modules for network infrastructure. To ensure

---

D. Oswald—Part of this work was carried out while the author was at the Chair for Embedded Security, Prof. Dr.-Ing. Christof Paar, Ruhr-University Bochum, Germany.

© Springer International Publishing Switzerland 2016
N. Homma and M. Medwed (Eds.): CARDIS 2015, LNCS 9514, pp. 3–14, 2016.
DOI: 10.1007/978-3-319-31271-2_1

that such components are genuine, various commercial solutions based on cryptographic authentication are available. Usually, an additional IC is placed on the device to be authenticated. The host (e.g., a printer or a mobile phone) then executes an authentication protocol with the IC to verify that the component (e.g., an inkjet cartridge or a battery) is genuine. The cryptographic algorithms commonly encountered in this area range from AES [1] and SHA-1 [12] over SHA-2 to Elliptic Curve Cryptography (ECC) [9]. Commonly, the authentication is unilateral, i.e., the device is authenticated to the host, but not vice versa.

Being often relatively low-cost products, devices protected with such ICs are easily available to a potential adversary for detailed analysis. Hence, the question about the physical security arises. In this paper, we focus on the SHA-1 EEPROM product line of Maxim Integrated, analysing two specific ICs from a side-channel point-of-view, the DS28E01-100 [12] and the older DS2432 (which is not recommended for new designs). These devices enable the unilateral authentication of a component to the host using a shared 64-bit secret in a challenge-response protocol based on SHA-1 as the main cryptographic primitive. Note that more expensive invasive and semi-invasive attacks (e.g., microprobing, circuit modification with a Focused Ion Beam (FIB), laser Fault Injection (FI), etc.) are outside the scope of this paper. Instead, we focus on Side-Channel Analysis (SCA) that can be performed using relatively low-cost oscilloscopes (in the range of a few thousand EUR) or even cheaper, specialised acquisition hardware.

1.1   Related Work

In contrast to standard block ciphers, implementation attacks on SHA-family hash functions have to our knowledge so far mostly been studied theoretically or for prototypical implementations: In [10], an FI attack on the SHA-1-based cipher SHACAL-1 is proposed, which is extended to also apply for a standard SHA-1 Hash-based Message Authentication Code (HMAC) in [8]. With respect to SCA, McEvoy et al. described a Correlation Power Analysis (CPA) on their own implementation of a SHA-2 HMAC on an FPGA [13], also covering suitable countermeasures against this type of attack. In [7], template attacks on HMACs are studied. The authors of [2] generalize and improve the ideas of [13].

With regard to real-world targets, in a presentation at the 27th Chaos Communication Congress [4], a sophisticated FI-based attack on an older SHA-1 device, the Dallas iButton, was described. The author also disclosed information on the authentication protocol, which is similar to that of our Device Under Test (DUTs). The attacks of [4] are based on partially overwriting the secret (achieved using FI) and may also apply to the DS2432 or the DS28E01 analyzed in this paper. However, the attacks could be rather easily prevented by setting the corresponding write-protect flag for the memory storing the secret.

1.2   Contribution

As the main contribution, we present the—to our knowledge—first real-world SCA of SHA-1-based authentication ICs. In doing so, we devise a method to further reduce the attack complexity (in terms of the number of targeted rounds), using properties of the way the SHA-1 is employed in the given context. This paper is partially based on the research done for the author's PhD thesis [15].

The remainder of this paper is structured as follows: In Sect. 2, we describe the authentication protocol used by the DS28E01 and DS2432. Section 3 outlines a basic attack, which is subsequently extended to exploit certain properties of the W-schedule of SHA-1. The described methods are then applied in practice to the DUTs in Sect. 4. Finally, we conclude in Sect. 5, covering future work, responsible disclosure, and potential countermeasures.

2 Authentication Protocol

As an initial step, based on the full datasheet for the older DS1961S iButton (which has a similar protocol) and source code for the communication with the DS2432 found on the Internet, we understood and implemented the full communication protocol with the DS28E01 and DS2432. It turned out that the protocol for the DS28E01 only differs in details from that of the DS2432.

On the electrical level, the DUTs use Maxim's 1-wire interface [11]. A single supply/data pin (IO) is at the same time used for delivering the operating voltage and bidirectional communication. This is achieved by connecting the supply voltage via a small pull-up resistor (in the range of $1\,\mathrm{k\Omega}$) to IO and actively pulling the line low for data communication in an open-drain configuration. In addition, the interface requires a ground connection, hence, technically, two wires are used.

The 1-wire interface allows bit rates of $15.3\,\mathrm{kBit/s}$ ("regular speed") and $125\,\mathrm{kBit/s}$ ("overdrive speed"), respectively. For each bit, the interface uses a separate time slot. The duration for which the data line is pulled low determines whether a one or zero is sent. For reading data, the host issues a "read" slot and then disconnects its driver to bring the data line its default (high-impedance) state. To send a zero, the DUT then pulls IO low for a certain duration, otherwise, for a one, IO is left at a high level.

Both the DS28E01 and the DS2432 employ a straightforward challenge-response protocol to prove the authenticity of the device. To this end, the host writes a 5-byte (for the DS28E01) or 3-byte (for the DS2432) challenge to an internal buffer ("scratchpad memory") of the device and sends a ReadAuthPage command. The DUT then computes a slightly modified SHA-1 hash over the data stored in the addressed memory page, the Unique Identifier (UID) of the DUT, the challenge, certain constants, and the 64-bit secret k. The result is returned to the host as response. For both DUTs, the function SHA-1' follows the standard [14], except for the fact that only one block is hashed and the addition of the final $H_0^{(i-1)}, \ldots$ is omitted (cf. [14, p. 19, step 4]). The overall protocol is shown in Fig. 1.

The function f is essentially a simple concatenation: the input to the SHA-1 is constructed as shown in Table 1, whereas k_i ($0 \leq i \leq 7$) are the eight bytes of the secret, P_i ($0 \leq i \leq 31$) the bytes of the addressed page of the DUT's

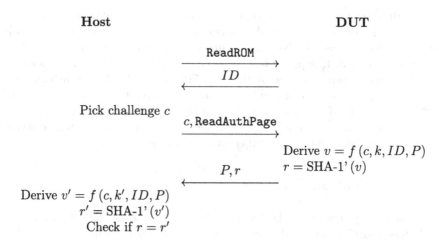

Fig. 1. Simplified protocol for authenticating DS28E01/DS2432 to host

memory, M a value derived from the page address, ID_i ($0 \le i \le 6$) the UID, c_i ($0 \le i \le 4$) the 5-byte challenge, and x_i ($0 \le i \le 10$) fixed constants. For the DS2432, the first two challenge bytes c_0 and c_1 are set to 0xFF, because the challenge has a length of only three byte for this device.

Incidentally, the length of 3 byte is short enough that an adversary could get the full dictionary of challenge-responses pairs (for one particular device) in reasonable time: for setting up a challenge and receiving the response, 296 bit are

Table 1. Input to the SHA-1 for the `ReadAuthPage` command of the DS28E01 (similar for DS2432)

Word	Byte 3	Byte 2	Byte 1	Byte 0
W_0	k_0	k_1	k_2	k_3
W_1	P_0	P_1	P_2	P_3
W_2	P_4	P_5	P_6	P_7
		$\cdots$		
W_8	P_{28}	P_{29}	P_{30}	P_{31}
W_9	c_0	c_1	x_0	x_1
W_{10}	M	ID_0	ID_1	ID_2
W_{11}	ID_3	ID_4	ID_5	ID_6
W_{12}	k_4	k_5	k_6	k_7
W_{13}	c_2	c_3	c_4	x_2
W_{14}	x_3	x_4	x_5	x_6
W_{15}	x_7	x_8	x_9	x_{10}

exchanged between host and device, which leads to approximately 19.2 ms in normal mode (65 μs per bit) and 2.4 ms in overdrive mode (8 μs per bit) in the ideal case. Additional delays for start-up and the SHA-1 execution add another 3 ms, resulting in an overall best-case figure of 5.4 ms per challenge-response pair. Hence, to obtain all 2^{24} pairs, approximately 1 day of communication with the DUT and 368 MB of storage would be required. In contrast, obtaining the full dictionary for the DS28E01 would take approximately 188 years under the above conditions.

Note that we did not thoroughly analyse the mathematical security of the employed protocol. However, for the given application where only one block is hashed and hence length-extension attacks [16] do not apply, using the SHA-1 without a proper HMAC construction [3] (which would require two SHA-1 executions) seems to be "secure enough".

3   Side-Channel Analysis of SHA-1

In contrast to block ciphers like AES or DES, SHA-1 involves mostly linear operations and does not have separate, constant subkeys combined with varying input. Instead, for the present DUT, the secret key is part of the input. Hence, in order to apply SCA to extract the secret in the given situation, a dedicated attack procedure had to be devised.

3.1   Basic Approach

Based on the SCA on a SHA-1 HMAC proposed in [13], we first started with a basic attack (which is a similar to the method independently proposed in [2] for SHA-2). This method was subsequently extended to reduce the number of targeted rounds and hence lower the computational complexity and reduce the susceptibility to errors. In the present case, the output of the SHA-1 (after 80 rounds) is available to the adversary, while only part of the input (the challenge) can be chosen. Hence, our attack first targets and undoes the final round and is then repeated for prior rounds until enough information to recover the secret is available.

In the following, we denote the value of the SHA-1 32-bit state registers after round i as A_i, B_i, C_i, D_i, and E_i, respectively. Hence, the output of the SHA-1 available to the adversary is $(A_{79}, B_{79}, C_{79}, D_{79}, E_{79})$. From this, the four state words A–D after round 78 can be directly computed as $A_{78} = B_{79}$, $B_{78} = \text{rrot}_{30}(C_{79})$, $C_{78} = D_{79}$, and $D_{78} = E_{79}$. In contrast, to compute the remaining register E_{78}, the knowledge of the (unknown and secret-dependent) value W_{79} is required:

$$E_{78} = A_{79} - K_{79} - W_{79} - \text{lrot}_5(B_{79}) - F_{79}(C_{79}, D_{79}, E_{79})$$

Note that W_{79} depends on the challenge and hence cannot be directly recovered using CPA. However, by construction of the W schedule of SHA-1, W_{79} can be written as a XOR combination of a known (and challenge-dependent) value

W_{79}^{known} and an unknown value W_{79}^{secret} depending on the secret. Thus, considering all candidates for W_{79}^{known} and identifying the correct value with CPA, E_{78} can be fully recovered and the complete round be inverted. Since W_{79}^{known} is a 32-bit value, 2^{32} candidates would have to be tested with SCA, which is possible but could be undesirable in certain cases. However, using partial correlations for 8-bit parts (starting at the least-significant byte) as suggested in [13], the number of candidates can be reduced at the cost of a higher trace complexity. Having recovered W_{79} and inverted the final round, the attack now identically repeats for round 78, 77, and so on. Following [2,8], to fully undo the W schedule and recover the complete input including the secret, the sixteen values $W_{79}, \ldots, W_{64}$ are sufficient. In total, this attack hence requires $16 \cdot 4$ CPAs with 2^8 candidates each, or alternatively 16 CPAs with 2^{32} candidates each.

3.2   Improved Attack on Final Two Rounds

While the basic method is fully practical for the present DUT, it has the shortcoming that a single error in one round will affect all subsequent rounds and make the attack fail. Since we target relatively linear operations (addition modulo 2^{32}), the occurrence of such errors is more likely compared to non-linear S-boxes, especially for earlier rounds where the leakage is partially lower than for the final rounds. However, in the following we show that (for the way the input is constructed for the DUT) the knowledge of W_{79}^{secret} and W_{78}^{secret} is sufficient, i.e., only the final 2 rounds have to be targeted.

First, note that when fully unrolling the W schedule, W_{78}^{secret} and W_{79}^{secret} are linear combinations of several rotated instances of W_0 and W_{12}. The question arises if W_0 and W_{12} can be uniquely recovered from W_{78}^{secret} and W_{79}^{secret}. To this end, we express left-rotation by j positions as polynomial multiplication with x^j modulo $x^{32} + 1$ [17] and denote the polynomial representation of a word in $\mathbb{F}_2[X]/(x^{32} + 1)$ with the same letter in lower case. Then,

$$
\begin{aligned}
w_{79}^{\text{secret}} &= \left(x^{22} + x^8\right) \cdot w_0 + \left(x^{18} + x^{14} + x^{12} + x^8 + x^6\right) \cdot w_{12} \\
&= a_1 \cdot w_0 + b_1 \cdot w_{12} \\
w_{78}^{\text{secret}} &= \left(x^{20} + x^{18} + x^{15} + x^8 + x^7\right) \cdot w_0 + \left(x^{15} + x^{11} + x^8\right) \cdot w_{12} \\
&= a_2 \cdot w_0 + b_2 \cdot w_{12}
\end{aligned}
$$

This linear equation system is solvable if the inverse d^{-1} of the determinant

$$
d = \det \begin{pmatrix} a_1 \ b_1 \\ a_2 \ b_2 \end{pmatrix}
$$

exists. This is the case for the given scenario, with $d^{-1} = x^{29} + x^{26} + x^{24} + x^{23} + x^{21} + x^{20} + x^{16} + x^{13} + x^{12} + x^{11} + x^{10} + x^8 + x^4 + x^2 + x$. Then, we obtain

$$
\begin{aligned}
w_0 &= \left(w_{79}^{\text{secret}} \cdot b_2 + w_{78}^{\text{secret}} \cdot b_1\right) \cdot d^{-1} \\
w_{12} &= \left(w_{79}^{\text{secret}} \cdot a_2 + w_{78}^{\text{secret}} \cdot a_1\right) \cdot d^{-1}
\end{aligned}
$$

Note that this method also applies when only one round is inverted by means of SCA. Then, one exhaustively tests all 2^{32} candidates for W_{78}^{secret}, applying the above method to obtain w_{12} and w_0, and checking the resulting secret with one SHA-1 output.

4 Practical Results

For evaluating the practical applicability of the above attack to the DUTs, we implemented the 1-wire protocol on a custom device (based on an FPGA) for precise control over the protocol execution. We then built simple test fixtures to access the pins of the DUT and insert a measurement resistor into the ground line ($490\,\Omega$ for the DS28E01, $50\,\Omega$ for the DS2432). Note that the DS28E01 continued to function correctly even though a relatively high resistor value was chosen. We used a Picoscope 6402 C to record the voltage drop over the measurement resistor at a sample rate of 625 MSPS. We digitally downsampled the resulting traces by a factor of 5, leading to a sample rate of 125 MSPS, and furthermore lowpass-filtered the traces with a cutoff frequency of 8 MHz (DS28E01) and 5 MHz (DS2432), respectively. These parameters were determined heuristically by observing the correlation for a known secret in the profiling phase (Sect. 4.1). We found that the SHA-1 is executed after the 32-byte page data, one constant byte `ff`, and the (inverted) 2-byte Cyclic Redundancy Check (CRC) has been read. Hence, we triggered the trace acquisition on the final bit of the CRC being read.

4.1 Profiling

Using the described setup, we recorded 3,000 traces each for a fixed, known secret, using uniformly distributed, random challenges. We then performed CPAs for various intermediate values and leakage models. Experimentally, we found that the leakage of both DUT follows the Hamming Distance (HD) between

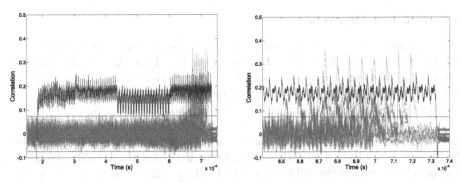

Fig. 2. DS28E01: correlation for HD between states of E in final 8 rounds after 3,000 traces (grey); average trace (blue, not to scale). Left: overview, right: zoomed on final rounds (Color figure online)

the SHA-1 state registers in subsequent rounds, suggesting a complete hardware implementation. Figures 2 and 3 depict the correlation for the DS28E01 and the DS2432 for the pairwise HD between the final eight states of E, i.e., $HD(E_{78}, E_{79})$, $HD(E_{77}, E_{78})$, and so on. The average trace (amplitude not to scale) is overlaid in blue. The red horizontal lines indicate the expected noise interval of $\pm 4/\sqrt{\#\text{ traces}}$. For the DS28E01, the correlation for the final two rounds reaches approximately 0.35, while for the DS2432, a value of approximately 0.49 is observed. This is likely due to the DS2432 using an older process technology with higher current consumption, leading to a higher overall Signal to Noise Ratio (SNR)—even with a much lower measurement resistor value.

In the average traces, the 80-round structure of the SHA-1 is clearly visible, and even the different boolean functions are discernible. For instance, at approximately 450 μs (for the DS28E01), the shape of the trace changes significantly. This region comprises the execution of rounds 40 to 59, in which $F_i = (B\,\&\,C)\mid(B\,\&\,D)\mid(C\,\&\,D)$.

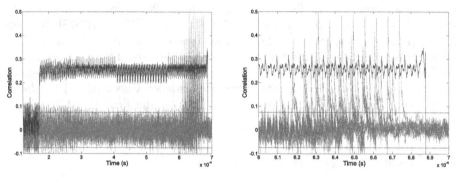

Fig. 3. DS2432: correlation for HD between states of E in final 8 rounds after 3,000 traces (grey); average trace (blue, not to scale). Left: overview, right: zoomed on final rounds (Color figure online)

4.2   Full Key Recovery

Before applying the attack procedure of Sect. 3 to the traces acquired for the DUTs, we estimate the expected correlations based on the profiling results (Sect. 4.1). When recovering the Least Significant Byte (LSByte), 8 out of 32 bit are predicted, hence, we expect a correlation of $0.35 \cdot \sqrt{8/32} = 0.175$ (DS28E01) and 0.245 (DS2432), respectively [5].

Carrying out the actual key recovery, we obtained correlations that closely match the expected values, for instance, values between 0.175 and 0.177 for the LSByte in case of the DS28E01 and 0.268 to 0.279 for the DS2432. We then successfully recovered the full key for both DUTs attacking the final two rounds.

To more precisely estimate the amount of required traces, we computed the average Partial Success Rate (PSR) for single bytes and the Global Success Rate (GSR) [19] for the recovery of the full secret for 16 sets of 3,000 traces each for the DS28E01 (with 16 different random secrets).

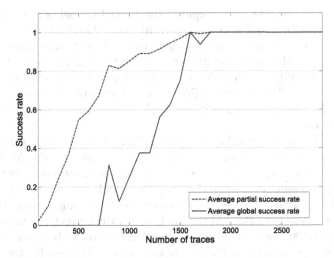

Fig. 4. Average GSR and average PSR for DS28E01, 16 experiments

The results are depicted in Fig. 4. The average PSR is computed for each byte in round 78 and 79 separately. Note that in contrast to block ciphers, however, a failure in correctly recovering a single byte will cause all subsequent bytes to fail as well. Hence, the GSR is a more appropriate metric in this case, as it only "accepts" secrets that were recovered completely. A stable GSR of 1 is reached after 1800 traces, with only a single experiment failing at 1700 traces. The acquisition of 1800 traces took approximately 40 min. with our setup. However, note that the rate was mainly limited due to the oscilloscope and PC storage (not the operation of the DUT) and could be significantly optimized further (e.g., by choosing a lower sample rate, acquiring only the relevant part of

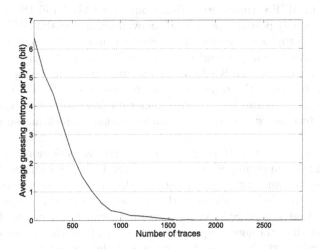

Fig. 5. PGE in bit per byte for DS28E01, 16 experiments

the traces, and so on). We also computed the Partial Guessing Entropy (PGE) (over both rounds for 4 byte each) as shown in Fig. 5. The PGE falls below 1 bit (i.e., the correct candidate has an expected rank of 1 or 2) after approximately 700 traces. This would mean that after recovering the LSByte with a CPA with 2^8 candidates, 2 candidates remain on average. These two candidates can then be checked with two 2^8-candidate CPAs for the next byte and so on, leading to in total $2^8 + 2 \cdot 2^8 + 2^2 \cdot 2^8 + 2^3 \cdot 2^8 = 15 \cdot 2^8 = 3840$ candidates to be checked with CPA per round.

Note that due to the similarity to the DS28E01, we did not compute the success rate over many experiments for the DS2432. However, due to the larger leakage, the key recovery can be expected to require even less traces in this case. We verified this assumption by performing the attack for one fixed key on the DS2432, and found that the correct candidate reached rank 1 after 500 traces for 7 of 8 byte—only for byte 2 in the final round, the correct candidate moved to rank 2 after 1,100 traces, requiring at least 1,200 traces to be stable at rank 1. Based on this experiment and the higher correlation obtained for the DS2432, we hence assume a value of 1,200 traces to be a good upper-bound estimate for the security of this DUT.

5   Conclusion and Outlook

In this paper, we presented successful key recovery attacks on Maxim's DS28E01 and DS2432 product authentication ICs. The methods allow to fully extract the 64-bit secret with approximately 40 min. for the trace acquisition. The employed SCA techniques have relatively low requirements with respect to the measurement equipment (sample rate 125 MSPS) and the trace complexity (1,800 and 1,200 traces, respectively). Hence, it is conceivable that the attacks could also be carried out using low-cost tools, e.g., the GIAnT or the ChipWhisperer, both featuring ≥ 100 MSPS Analog to Digital Converter (ADCs) [6, 18].

Hence, SCA may pose a serious problem even given that the DUTs are a low-cost solution to provide some protection against counterfeiting and are of course not intended to replace high-security smartcard ICs. We had a brief look at newer SHA-2-based authentication ICs from two manufacturers, including Maxim Integrated. Figure 6 depicts the respective side-channel traces: for DUT 1 (left), we measured the Electro-Magnetic (EM) emanation (due to certain properties of the available test board), while we acquired normal current measurements for DUT 2.

Although we did not perform a thorough analysis as demonstrated for the DS28E01/DS2432, applying SCA to these newer DUTs appears to be complicated by a higher amount of noise both in the signal amplitude and timing. However, more precisely analyzing SHA-2-based devices with regard to their level of protection against SCA is an interesting point for future work.

Apart from that, the general question on how to appropriately protect against the demonstrated attacks arises. For existing designs using the analysed ICs, certain steps on the system level to mitigate the consequences of a successful

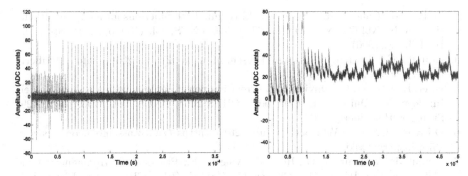

Fig. 6. Part of example traces for SHA-2 ICs from different manufacturers, left: EM, DUT 1, right: power, DUT 2

key recovery should be taken: First of all, it should be ensured that there are no system-wide secrets (stored on every ICs) and that secure key diversification (e.g., based on the UID of the DUT) is in place. Otherwise, a single successful attack on a single device would render all other devices insecure. In this regard, note that also the counterpart on the host must be protected, especially if it stores a system-wide diversification key.

Checking the UID (and using it for key diversification) on the host also ensures that an adversary cannot use a real DS28E01/DS2432 IC for a cloned product by simply copying the recovered secret and memory contents. Instead, since the UID is factory-programmed, he would have to create a custom emulator, e.g., using a microcontroller or a custom ASIC. This increases the complexity and cost of counterfeiting, possibly to a point where the cloning becomes unprofitable.

In the long run, ICs like the DUTs analysed in this paper should include side-channel countermeasures to at least prevent low-cost SCA techniques and raise the bar in terms of trace and measurement equipment complexity. Adapting common countermeasures (e.g., randomization of timing, masking, etc.) to the specific requirements for product authentication ICs (in particular low cost and hence low chip area) is an interesting problem.

Finally, having discovered the security problems, as part of a responsible disclosure process, we contacted the vendor Maxim and informed them about our investigations. Maxim acknowledged our result and is exploring ways to mitigate the security issues. We would also like to note that the more recent products of Maxim are not directly vulnerable to the methods presented in this paper.

References

1. Atmel. ATAES132A 32K AES Serial EEPROM Specification. Datasheet, July 2015. http://www.atmel.com/Images/Atmel-8914-CryptoAuth-ATAES132A-Data sheet.pdf
2. Belaid, S., Bettale, L., Dottax, E., Genelle, L., Rondepierre, F.: Differential power analysis of HMAC SHA-2 in the hamming weight model. In: SECRYPT 2013, Reykjavik, Iceland. Scitepress, July 2013

3. Bellare, M., Canetti, R., Krawczyk, H.: Keying hash functions for message authentication. In: Koblitz, N. (ed.) CRYPTO 1996. LNCS, vol. 1109, pp. 1–15. Springer, Heidelberg (1996)

4. Brandt, C.: Hacking iButtons. Presentation at 27C3 (2010). http://cribert. freeforge.net/27c3/ibsec.pdf

5. Brier, E., Clavier, C., Olivier, F.: Correlation power analysis with a leakage model. In: Joye, M., Quisquater, J.-J. (eds.) CHES 2004. LNCS, vol. 3156, pp. 16–29. Springer, Heidelberg (2004)

6. O'Flynn, C.: ChipWhisperer, July 2015. https://www.assembla.com/spaces/ chipwhisperer/wiki

7. Fouque, P.-A., Leurent, G., Réal, D., Valette, F.: Practical electromagnetic template attack on HMAC. In: Clavier, C., Gaj, K. (eds.) CHES 2009. LNCS, vol. 5747, pp. 66–80. Springer, Heidelberg (2009)

8. Hemme, L., Hoffmann, L.: Differential fault analysis on the SHA1 compression function. In: Proceedings of the Workshop on Fault Diagnosis and Tolerance in Cryptography - FDTC 2011, pp. 54–62. IEEE Computer Society, Washington, DC (2011)

9. Infineon. ORIGA SLE95200. Datasheet, July 2015. http://www. infineon.com/dgdl/ORIGA2_SLE95200_Product_Brief_v1+00.pdf? fileId=db3a30433580b3710135a50170336cd8

10. Li, R., Li, C., Gong, C.: Differential fault analysis on SHACAL-1. In: Proceedings of the Workshop on Fault Diagnosis and Tolerance in Cryptography - FDTC 2009, pp. 120–126. IEEE Computer Society, Washington, DC (2009)

11. Maxim integrated. 1-Wire, July 2015. http://www.maximintegrated.com/en/ products/comms/one-wire.html

12. Maxim integrated. DS28E01-100 1 Kb Protected 1-Wire EEPROM with SHA-1 Engine, July 2015. http://www.maximintegrated.com/en/products/digital/memo ry-products/DS28E01-100.html/tb_tab0

13. McEvoy, R., Tunstall, M., Murphy, C.C., Marnane, W.P.: Differential power analysis of HMAC based on SHA-2, and countermeasures. In: Kim, S., Yung, M., Lee, H.-W. (eds.) WISA 2007. LNCS, vol. 4867, pp. 317–332. Springer, Heidelberg (2008)

14. NIST. FIpPS 180–4 Secure Hash Standard (SHS). http://csrc.nist.gov/ publications/fips/fips180-4/fips-180-4.pdf

15. Oswald, D.: Implementation attacks.: from theory to practice. Ph.D. thesis, Ruhr-University Bochum, September 2013

16. Preneel, B., van Oorschot, P.C.: MDx-MAC and building fast MACs from hash functions. In: Coppersmith, D. (ed.) CRYPTO 1995. LNCS, vol. 963, pp. 1–14. Springer, Heidelberg (1995)

17. Rivest, R.L.: The invertibility of the XOR of rotations of a binary word. Int. J. Comput. Math. **88**(2), 281–284 (2011)

18. Sourceforge. GIAnT (Generic Implementation ANalysis Toolkit), April 2013. https://sf.net/projects/giant/

19. Standaert, F.-X., Malkin, T.G., Yung, M.: A unified framework for the analysis of side-channel key recovery attacks. In: Joux, A. (ed.) EUROCRYPT 2009. LNCS, vol. 5479, pp. 443–461. Springer, Heidelberg (2009)

20. United nations office on drugs and crime. Counterfeit Goods - A Bargain or a Costly Mistake? Fact Sheet (2013). http://www.unodc.org/documents/toc/factsheets/ TOC12_fs_counterfeit_EN_HIRES.pdf

Enhancing Dimensionality Reduction Methods for Side-Channel Attacks

Eleonora Cagli[1,2,4]($\boxtimes$), Cécile Dumas[1,2], and Emmanuel Prouff[3,4]

[1] Univ. Grenoble Alpes, 38000 Grenoble, France
[2] CEA, LETI, MINATEC Campus, 38054 Grenoble, France
{eleonora.cagli,cecile.dumas}@cea.fr
[3] ANSSI, Paris, France
emmanuel.prouff@ssi.gouv.fr
[4] UPMC Université Paris 06, Équipe POLSYS, LIP6, 75005 Paris, France

Abstract. Advanced Side-Channel Analyses make use of dimensionality reduction techniques to reduce both the memory and timing complexity of the attacks. The most popular methods to effectuate such a reduction are the Principal Component Analysis (PCA) and the Linear Discriminant Analysis (LDA). They indeed lead to remarkable efficiency gains but their use in side-channel context also raised some issues. The PCA provides a set of vectors (the *principal components*) onto which project the data. The open question is which of these principal components are the most suitable for side-channel attacks. The LDA has been valorized for its theoretical leaning toward the class-distinguishability, but discouraged for its constraining greed of data. In this paper we present an in-depth study of these two methods, and, to automatize and to ameliorate the principal components selection, we propose a new technique named *cumulative Explained Local Variance (ELV) selection*. Moreover we present some extensions of the LDA, available in less constrained situations than the classical version. We equip our study with a comprehensive comparison of the existing and new methods in real cases. It allows us to verify the soundness of the ELV selection, and the effectiveness of the methods proposed to extend the use of the LDA to side-channel contexts where the existing approaches are inapplicable.

Keywords: Side-channel attacks · Dimensionality reduction · Principal components analysis · Components selection · Linear discriminant analysis · Explained local variance · Small size sample problem

1 Introduction

The measurement of the power consumption or of the electromagnetic irradiations during the execution of cryptographic algorithms in constrained electronic devices can reveal information about sensitive variables (*e.g.* cryptographic keys). The side channel traces are usually acquired by oscilloscopes with a very high sampling rate, which permits a powerful inspection of the component behaviour, but, at the

© Springer International Publishing Switzerland 2016
N. Homma and M. Medwed (Eds.): CARDIS 2015, LNCS 9514, pp. 15–33, 2016.
DOI: 10.1007/978-3-319-31271-2_2

same time, produces high-dimensional data, that spread the sensitive information over a (sometimes) huge number of time samples. Reducing the dimensionality of the data is an important issue for Side-Channel Attacks (SCA). Considering the side channel traces as column vectors $\mathbf{x}$ in $\mathbb{R}^D$, the compressing phase might be seen as the application of a function $\varepsilon\colon \mathbb{R}^D \to \mathbb{R}^C$, called *extractor* in this paper.

The present work focuses on the so-called *projecting extractors*, *i.e.* those methods that provide extractors ε whose image components are linear combinations of the original data, or equivalently, expressible *via* a matrix multiplication:

$$\varepsilon(\mathbf{x}) = A\mathbf{x} \text{ with } A \in M_{\mathbb{R}}(C, D) \;, \tag{1}$$

where $M_{\mathbb{R}}(C, D)$ denotes the set of real-coefficient matrices of size $C \times D$. In particular we effectuate an in-depth study and a comprehensive comparison between the PCA and the LDA methods [10,11], and we investigate their exploitability in Side-Channel context. Indeed, PCA and LDA are classical statistical procedures, but the way they have been inherited in SCA domain is somehow ambiguous and opened some issues and questions.

The PCA has been applied both in an *unsupervised* way, i.e. on the whole data [2,14], and in a *supervised* way, i.e. on traces grouped in classes and averaged [1,7–9,22]. The second way implies that, during the training phase, the attacker is able to choose, or at least to know, the secret parameters of the implementation under attack (or a perfect copy of it). As already remarked in [9] and not surprisingly, the complete knowledge assumed in the supervised approach hugely raises performances; we will highlight it in our experiments, and we will concentrate on this powerful kind of approach, leaving the unsupervised case for further studies. The main competitor of PCA in the supervised context is the LDA, that thanks to its class-distinguishability asset, is known to be more meaningful and informative [4,22] than the PCA method for side channels. Nevertheless, the LDA is often set aside because of its practical constraints; it is subject to the so-called *Small Sample Size problem (SSS)*, i.e. it requires a number of observations (traces) which must be higher than the dimension (size) D of them. In some contexts it might be an excessive requirement, which may become unacceptable in many practical situations where the amount of observations is very limited and the traces size is huge.

One of the open issues in PCA concerns the choice of the components that must be kept after the dimension reduction: as already remarked by Specht et al. [21], some papers declare that the leading components are those that contain almost all the useful information [1,8], while others propose to discard the leading components [2]. In a specific attack context, Specht et al. compares the results obtained by choosing different subsets of consecutive components, starting from some empirically chosen index. They conclude that for their data the optimal result is obtained by selecting a single component, the fourth one, but they give no formal argumentation about this choice. Such a result is obviously very case-specific. Moreover, the possibility of keeping non-consecutive components is not considered.

Our main contribution consists in proposing a new selection methodology, called *cumulative ELV selection*. We will argue about the generality and the soundness of this methodology and show that it can raise the PCA performances, making them close to those of the LDA, even in the supervised context. This makes PCA an interesting alternative to LDA in those cases where the LDA is inapplicable. The reasonning behind the ELV selection methodology is essentially based on the observation that, for secure implementations, the leaking information, if existing, is spread over a few time samples of each trace. This observation has already been met by Mavroeidis et al. in [17], where the authors also proposed a components selection method. As we will see in this paper, the main difference between their proposal and ours is that we do not discard the information given by the eigenvalues associated to the PCA components, but we synergistically exploit such information and the observation met. For the sake of comparison, we also analyse many propositions to circumvent the SSS problem that have been made in literature, especially by Pattern Recognition and Face Recognition communities [3,6,13,24]. The gain given by these techniques does not outperform the PCA method equipped with our ELV selection.

The paper is organised as follows: in Sect. 2 we fix notations, recall preliminaries and formalize the context. Section 3 presents the PCA, and handles the choice of components problem, introducing the ELV selection method. In Sect. 4 the LDA method is presented, together with different methodologies to avoid the SSS problem. Experiments and comparisons are showed in Sect. 5, while conclusions and perspectives follow in Sect. 6.

2   Preliminaries and Formalization

2.1   Preliminaries

In the following, bold block capitals $\mathbf{M}$ denote matrices and Greek or Latin bold lower cases, $\boldsymbol{\alpha}$ or $\mathbf{x}$, denote real column vectors. The i-th entry of a vector $\mathbf{x}$ is indicated by $\mathbf{x}[i]$.

A side-channel key recovery adversary, being inspired by the model proposed by Standaert et al. [23], corresponds to a 5-tuple $\mathcal{A} = (A, \tau, m, N', N)$, where A is an algorithm or a procedure with time complexity τ and memory complexity m, that takes as input two sets of measurements of respective sizes N' and N. The algorithm A returns a vector of key candidates. Since the goal of the attack is to distinguish the right key $k^\star$ in a set $\mathcal{K}$ of candidates, the output vector, called *guessing vector* $\mathbf{g}$, sorts such candidates in decreasing order with respect to their likelihood:

$$A \colon \left((\mathbf{x}_i)_{i=1,\ldots N'}, (\mathbf{y}_j)_{j=1,\ldots N} \right) \mapsto \mathbf{g} = [\mathbf{g}[1], \ldots, \mathbf{g}[|\mathcal{K}|]] \ . \tag{2}$$

The first set of input traces $(\mathbf{x}_i)_{i=1,\ldots N'}$, here called *profiling set*, is optional, and corresponds to measurements obtained from a profiling device, identical to the device under attack but with full access to the public and secret parameters. The second set of traces $(\mathbf{y}_j)_{j=1,\ldots N}$, called *attack set*, corresponds to measurements acquired from the device under attack, parametrized by a key which will be the target of the attack.

An interesting tool to assess the soundness of an adversary is given by the *guessing entropy* [16] and by the asymptotic guessing entropy, respectively defined as

$$\mathrm{GE}_{\mathcal{A}(N)} = \mathbb{E}\left[i\colon \mathbf{g}[i] = k^\star\right] \quad \text{and} \quad \mathrm{GE}_{\mathcal{A}}^\infty = \lim_{N\to\infty} \mathrm{GE}_{\mathcal{A}(N)} , \qquad (3)$$

where $\mathcal{A}(N)$ denotes the adversary $\mathcal{A}$ with its fifth parameter fixed to N.

A trace $\mathbf{x}$ can be seen as an element in $\mathbb{R}^D$, and its size or dimension D, that depends on a lot of factors (e.g. the instruments setup or the cryptographic algorithm under attack), usually ranges between some thousands and some hundreds of thousands. Nevertheless, only few points of the trace depend on the secret target key. A preliminary step of an attack therefore generally consists in the extraction of the so-called Points of Interest (PoI) from the rough traces. By definition, the latter points are those which depend on both the secret target parameter and on some given public data (a necessary condition to perform *differential* attacks). This extraction represents a non-trivial concrete obstacle for the practical performances of an attack.

2.2   Formalization: Extractors and Fundamental Property

To formalize the problem of the research of PoIs, we remark that in general an attack is composed of four fundamentally different phases:

1. Instruments calibration and traces acquisitions (to build the profiling and attack sets)
2. [Optional] trace pre-processing
3. [Optional] profiling (useful to model the leakage function)
4. Key discrimination: a statistical test, or a statistical distinguisher, is processed over the traces to discriminate key candidates

In this scheme the research of PoI is part of the traces pre-processing. We will formalize it as the application of a function, called *extractor* (by analogy to the notion of randomness extractor [18]):

Definition 1. Let $\mathbf{x} \in \mathbb{R}^D$ represents an observation. An *Extractor* is any function of the form:

$$\varepsilon_C\colon \mathbb{R}^D \to \mathbb{R}^C \quad \text{with } C \leq D$$
$$\mathbf{x} \mapsto \varepsilon_C(\mathbf{x}) .$$

Notation 1. *The dimension C of an extractor will be omitted if there is no ambiguity or if it is not needed in the context.*

Example 1. A special family of extractors that is widely studied in last years, is the one constituted by the *linear* or *projecting* extractors, *i.e.* those for which each sample in the reduced space $\mathbb{C}$ is a linear combination of samples of the original space. By analogy to (1), such extractors can be defined as $C \times D$ matrices, whose rows are the coefficients to use for the C linear combinations.

Obviously, not any extractor ε is suitable to soundly realise the traces pre-processing of an attack; for example the restriction over a random coordinate, i.e. $\varepsilon(\mathbf{x}) = x[r]$, r being random, is hardly a good candidate for an extractor. For this reason an adversary might aim to only consider extractors that satisfy the following fundamental property:

Property 1 (Effective Extractors). Let $\mathcal{A}$ be an adversary and $\text{GE}_{\mathcal{A}(N)}$ be its guessing entropy, when no trace processing phase is effectuated. Let ε be an extractor, and $\mathcal{A}'$ be an adversary that coincides with $\mathcal{A}$ but whose algorithm A is fed with the sets $\left((\varepsilon(\mathbf{x}_i))_{i=1,\dots N'}, (\varepsilon((\mathbf{y}_j)))_{j=1,\dots N} \right)$, i.e. an adversary that applies ε as traces pre-processing phase. The extractor ε is an *effective extractor with respect to N* only if, for any $T \geq N$, we have:

$$\text{GE}_{\mathcal{A}'(T)} \leq \text{GE}_{\mathcal{A}(T)} . \tag{4}$$

In practice this property guarantees that the application of ε does not discard the informative parts of the traces, those that make $\mathcal{A}$ achieve its guessing entropy.

3   Principal Component Analysis

3.1   Principal Component Analysis, the Classical Statistical Tool

The Principal Component Analysis (PCA) [10] is a statistical technique for data dimensionality reduction. It looks for the so-called *Principal Components* (PCs for short), which are vectors that form an orthonormal basis for $\mathbb{R}^D$ (*i.e.* these vectors have norm equal to 1 and are orthogonal to each other). Such PCs are computed as the eigenvectors of the empirical covariance matrix of data: given a set of data $(\mathbf{x}_i)_{i=1,\dots,N}$, the empirical covariance matrix is given by:

$$\mathbf{S} = \frac{1}{N} \sum_{i=1}^{N} (\mathbf{x}_i - \bar{\mathbf{x}})(\mathbf{x}_i - \bar{\mathbf{x}})^\mathsf{T} , \tag{5}$$

where $\bar{\mathbf{x}}$ is the empirical mean of data. Let us denote by r the rank of S and by $\alpha_1, \dots, \alpha_r$ and $\lambda_1, \dots, \lambda_r$ its eigenvectors and the corresponding eigenvalues, respectively. We assume that the α_i are listed in the decreasing order of the values λ_i. It can be shown that each λ_i equals the empirical variance of the data projected onto the corresponding PC α_i. Since the data variability is associated to the amount of information, transforming data over the basis provided by the PCs leads to a dimensionality reduction that reinforces the information: such a dimensionality reduction is obtained by projecting the data onto the C-dimensional subspace of $\mathbb{R}^D$ spanned by the C leading PCs, or equivalently by constructing the matrix A of (1) storing as rows the C leading PCs, transposed.

3.2   Principal Component Analysis, the *Class-Oriented Version*

In SCA context, the useful information part contained in data is the one that allows to discriminate observations linked to different intermediate computations. Let us denote by $Z = e(P, K)$ the target intermediate variable, that depends on both a secret variable K and on a public one P, and that takes values $z \in \mathcal{Z}$. The side-channel attack efficiency depends on the ability of the involved extractor to amplify the distinguishability between traces associated to different z.

During the profiling phase the attacker is assumed to know the value z of the sensitive variable handled during each acquisition. He can therefore assign the *class* z to each profiling trace (in analogy with the pattern recognition terminology), obtaining the labelled profiling set $(\mathbf{x}_i^z)_{i=1,\dots,N_z}$, where N_z is the number of traces belonging to the class z. This knowledge is very useful to construct a good class-distinguishing extractor, but the classical PCA does not exploit it. For this reason in SCA literature [1,7–9,22] a *class-oriented* version of PCA is often used instead of the classical one. Let $\overline{\mathbf{x}}^z$ be the empirical mean of traces belonging to the same class z. The class-oriented version of the PCA consists in applying the PCA dimensionality reduction to the set $(\overline{\mathbf{x}}^z)_{z \in \mathcal{Z}}$, instead of applying it directly to the traces $\mathbf{x}_i^z$. This implies that the empirical covariance matrix will be computed using only the $|\mathcal{Z}|$ average traces. Equivalently, in case of *balanced* acquisitions (N_z constant for each class z), it amounts to replace the covariance matrix $\mathbf{S}$ of data in (5) by the so-called *between-class* or *inter-class scatter matrix*, given by:

$$\mathbf{S_B} = \sum_{z \in \mathcal{Z}} N_z (\overline{\mathbf{x}}^z - \overline{\mathbf{x}})(\overline{\mathbf{x}}^z - \overline{\mathbf{x}})^{\mathsf{T}} . \tag{6}$$

Remark that $\mathbf{S_B}$ coincides, up to a multiplicative factor, to the covariance matrix obtained using the class-averaged traces.

Performing PCA (or LDA as we will see in next section) always requires to compute the eigenvectors of some symmetric matrix $\mathbf{S}$, essentially obtained by multiplying a matrix $\mathbf{M}$ with its transposed (e.g. for class-oriented PCA we have $\mathbf{M} = [\sqrt{N_{z_1}}(\overline{\mathbf{x}}^{z_1} - \overline{\mathbf{x}}), \sqrt{N_{z_2}}(\overline{\mathbf{x}}^{z_2} - \overline{\mathbf{x}}), \dots]$). Let $\mathbf{M}$ have dimension $D \times N$, and suppose $N \ll D$ (which occurs for example in class-oriented PCA , since $N = |Z|$). Then, the matrix $\mathbf{S} = \mathbf{M}\mathbf{M}^{\mathsf{T}}$ has rank at most N. Moreover, rows of $\mathbf{M}$ are often linearly dependent (as in our example since they are forced to have zero mean), so the rank of $\mathbf{S}$ is actually strictly less than N, giving us at most $N - 1$ eigenvectors.

A practical problem when D is large, which happens e.g. when attacking RSA, is represented by the computation and the storage of the $D \times D$ matrix $\mathbf{S}$. Archambeau et al. [1] proposed a method that circumvents this issue, allowing computing the eigenvectors of low-rank big-dimensional symmetric matrices without computing and storing such matrices. In Sect. 4 we will observe in which cases such a method can be applied to LDA and for which LDA variants.

3.3   The Open Question: Choosing the Components to Keep

The introduction of the PCA method in SCA context (either in its classical or class-oriented version) has raised some important questions: *how many* principal components and *which ones* are sufficient/necessary to reduce the trace size (and thus the attack processing complexity) without losing important discriminative information?

Until now, an answer to the questions above has been given in [8], linked to the concept of *explained variance* (or *explained global variance*, EGV for short) of a PC $\boldsymbol{\alpha}_i$:

$$\mathrm{EGV}(\boldsymbol{\alpha}_i) = \frac{\lambda_i}{\sum_{k=1}^{r} \lambda_k} , \tag{7}$$

where r is the rank of the covariance matrix $\mathbf{S}$, and λ_j is the eigenvalue associated to the j-th PC $\boldsymbol{\alpha}_j$. $\mathrm{EGV}(\boldsymbol{\alpha}_i)$ is the variance of the data projected over the i-th PC (which equals λ_i) divided by the total variance of the original data (given by the trace of the covariance matrix $\mathbf{S}$, *i.e.* by the sum of all its non-zero eigenvalues). By definition of EGV, the sum of all the EGV values is equal to 1; that is why this quantity is often multiplied by 100 and expressed as percentage. Exploiting the EGV to choose among the PCs consists in fixing a wished *cumulative explained variance* β and in keeping C different PCs, where C is the minimum integer such that

$$\mathrm{EGV}(\boldsymbol{\alpha}_1) + \mathrm{EGV}(\boldsymbol{\alpha}_2) + \cdots + \mathrm{EGV}(\boldsymbol{\alpha}_C) \geq \beta . \tag{8}$$

However, if the adversary has a constraint for the reduced dimension C, the EGV notion simply suggests to keep the first C components, taking for granted that the optimal way to chose PCs is in their natural order. This assumption is not always confirmed in SCA context: in some works, researchers have already remarked that the first components sometimes contain more noise than information [2, 21] and it is worth discarding them. For the sake of providing a first example of this behaviour on publicly accessible traces, we applied a class-oriented PCA on 3000 traces from the DPA contest v4 [20]; we focused over a small 1000-dimensional window in which, in complete knowledge about masks and other countermeasures, information about the first Sbox processing leaks (during the first round). In Fig. 1 the first and the sixth PCs are plotted. It may be noticed that the first component indicates that one can attend a high variance by exploiting the regularity of the traces, given by the clock signal, while the sixth one has high coefficients localised in a small time interval, very likely to signalize the instants in which the target sensitive variable leaks.

To the best of our knowledge, a single method adapted to SCA context has been proposed until now to automatically choose PCs [17] while dealing with the issue raised in Fig. 1. It is based on the following assumption:

Assumption 1. *The leaking side-channel information is localised in few points of the acquired trace.*

In the rest of the paper, we conduct our own analyses under Assumption 1 that we think to be reasonable in SCA contexts where the goal of the security developers is to minimize the number of leaking points. Under this assumption, the authors of [17] use for side-channel attack purposes the *Inverse Participation Ratio* (IPR), a measure widely exploited in Quantum Mechanics domain (see for example [12]). They propose to use such a score to evaluate the eigenvectors *localization*. It is defined as follows:

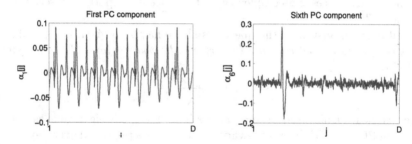

Fig. 1. First and sixth PCs in DPA contest v4 trace set (between time samples 198001 and 199000)

$$\text{IPR}(\boldsymbol{\alpha}_i) = \sum_{j=1}^{D} \boldsymbol{\alpha}_i[j]^4 \ . \tag{9}$$

The authors of [17] suggest to collect the PCs in decreasing order with respect to the IPR score.

The selection methods provided by the evaluation of the EGV and of the IPR are somehow complementary: the former is based only on the eigenvalues associated to the PCs and does not consider the form of the PCs themselves; the latter completely discards the information given by the eigenvalues of the PCs, considering only the distribution of their coefficients. One of the contributions of the present paper is to propose a new selection method, that builds a bridge between the EGV and the IPR approaches. As we will argue, our method, based on the so-called *explained local variance*, does not only lead to the construction of a new selection criterion, but also permits to modify the PCs, choosing individually the coefficients to keep and those to discard.

3.4   The Explained Local Variance Selection Method

The method we develop in this section is based on a compromise between the variance provided by each PC (more precisely its EGV) and the number of time samples necessary to achieve a consistent part of such a variance. To this purpose we introduce the concept of *Explained Local Variance* (ELV).

Let us start by giving some intuition behind our new concept. Thinking to the observations $\mathbf{x}^{\mathsf{T}}$, or to the class-averages $\bar{\mathbf{x}}^{\mathsf{T}}$ in class-oriented PCA case, as realizations of a random variable $\mathbf{X}^{\mathsf{T}}$, we have that λ_i is an estimator for the variance of the random variable $\mathbf{X}^{\mathsf{T}} \cdot \boldsymbol{\alpha}_i$. Developing, we obtain

$$\lambda_i = \hat{\text{var}}\left(\sum_{j=1}^{D} \mathbf{X}^{\mathsf{T}}[j]\boldsymbol{\alpha}_i[j]\right) = \sum_{j=1}^{D}\sum_{k=1}^{D} \hat{\text{cov}}(\mathbf{X}^{\mathsf{T}}[j]\boldsymbol{\alpha}_i[j], \mathbf{X}^{\mathsf{T}}[k]\boldsymbol{\alpha}_i[k]) \tag{10}$$

$$= \sum_{j=1}^{D} \boldsymbol{\alpha}_i[j] \sum_{k=1}^{D} \boldsymbol{\alpha}_i[k]\hat{\text{cov}}(\mathbf{X}^{\mathsf{T}}[j], \mathbf{X}^{\mathsf{T}}[k]) = \sum_{j=1}^{D} \boldsymbol{\alpha}_i[j](\mathbf{S}_j^{\mathsf{T}} \cdot \boldsymbol{\alpha}_i) \tag{11}$$

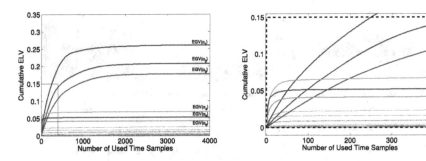

Fig. 2. Cumulative ELV trend of principal components. On the right a zoom of the plot on the left. Data acquisition described in Sect. 5.

$$= \sum_{j=1}^{D} \alpha_i[j]\lambda_i\alpha_i[j] = \sum_{j=1}^{D} \lambda_i\alpha_i[j]^2 \tag{12}$$

where $\mathbf{S}_j^\mathsf{T}$ denotes the j-th row of $\mathbf{S}$ and (12) is justified by the fact that α_i is an eigenvector of $\mathbf{S}$, with λ_i its corresponding eigenvalue. The result of this computation is quite obvious, since $\| \alpha_i \| = 1$, but it evidences the contribution of each time sample in the information held by the PC. This makes us introduce the following definition:

Definition 2. The *Explained Local Variance* of a PC α_i in a sample j, is defined by

$$\mathrm{ELV}(\alpha_i, j) = \frac{\lambda_i \alpha_i[j]^2}{\sum_{k=1}^{r} \lambda_k} = \mathrm{EGV}(\alpha_i)\alpha_i[j]^2 . \tag{13}$$

Let $\mathcal{J} = \{j_1^i, j_2^i, \ldots, j_D^i\} \subset \{1, 2, \ldots, D\}$ be a set of indexes sorted such that $\mathrm{ELV}(\alpha_i, j_1^i) \geq \mathrm{ELV}(\alpha_i, j_2^i) \geq \cdots \geq \mathrm{ELV}(\alpha_i, j_D^i)$. It may be observed that the sum over all the $\mathrm{ELV}(\alpha_i, j)$, for $j \in [1, \ldots, D]$, equals $\mathrm{EGV}(\alpha_i)$. If we operate such a sum in a cumulative way following the order provided by the sorted set $\mathcal{J}$, we obtain a complete description of the trend followed by the component α_i to achieve its EGV. As we can see in Fig. 2, where such cumulative ELVs are represented, the first 3 components are much slower in achieving their final EGV, while the 4th, the 5th and the 6th achieve a large part of their final EGVs very quickly (*i.e.* by adding the ELV contributions of much less time samples). For instance, for $i = 4$, the sum of the $\mathrm{ELV}(\alpha_4, j_k^4)$, with $k \in [1, \ldots, 30]$, almost equals $\mathrm{EGV}(\alpha_4)$, whereas the same sum for $i = 1$ only achieves about the 15 % of $\mathrm{EGV}(\alpha_1)$. Actually, the EGV of the 4th, the 5th and the 6th component only essentially depends on a very few time samples. This observation, combined with Assumption 1, suggests that they are more suitable for SCA than the three first ones. To validate this statement, it suffices to look at the form of such components (Fig. 3): the leading ones are very influenced by the clock, while the latest ones are well localised over the leaking points.

Operating a selection of components *via* ELV, in analogy with the EGV, requires to fix the reduced space dimension C, or a threshold β for the cumulative

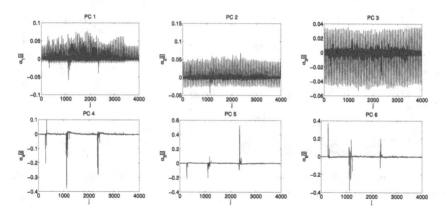

Fig. 3. The first six PCs. Acquisition campaign on an 8-bit AVR Atmega328P (see Sect. 5).

ELV. In the first case, the maximal ELVs of each PC are compared, and the C components achieving the highest values of such ELVs are chosen. In the second case, all pairs (PC, time sample) are sorted in decreasing order with respect to their ELV, and summed until the threshold β is achieved. Then only PCs contributing in this sum are selected.

We remark that the ELV is a score associated not only to the whole components, but to each of their coefficients. This interesting property can be exploited to further remove, within a selected PC, the non-significant points, *i.e.* those with a low ELV. In practice this is done by setting these points to zero. That is a natural way to exploit the ELV score in order to operate a kind of *denoising* for the reduced data, making them only depend on the significant time samples. In Sect. 5 (scenario 4) we test the performances of an attack varying the number of time samples involved in the computation of the reduced data, and showing that such a denoising processing might impact significantly.

4   Linear Discriminant Analysis

Linear Discriminant Analysis (LDA) [11] is another statistical tool for dimensionality reduction, which is theoretically more appropriate than PCA for classification problems, such as SCA, as already observed in [4,22]. Indeed it seeks for linear combinations of data that characterize or separate two or more classes, not only spreading class centroids as much as possible, like the class-oriented PCA does, but also minimizing the so-called *intra-class variance*, i.e. the variance shown by data belonging to the same class.

Description. Applying LDA consists in maximizing the so-called *Rayleigh quotient*:

$$\alpha_1 = \text{argmax}_\alpha \frac{\alpha^\mathsf{T} S_B \alpha}{\alpha^\mathsf{T} S_W \alpha} , \tag{14}$$

where $\mathbf{S_B}$ is the *between-class scatter matrix* already defined in (6) and $\mathbf{S_W}$ is called *within-class* (or intra-class) *scatter matrix*:

$$\mathbf{S_W} = \sum_{z \in \mathcal{Z}} \sum_{i=1}^{N_z} (\mathbf{x}_i^z - \overline{\mathbf{x}}^z)(\mathbf{x}_i^z - \overline{\mathbf{x}}^z)^\mathsf{T}. \tag{15}$$

Remark 1. Let $\mathbf{S}$ be the global covariance matrix of data, also called *total scatter matrix*, defined in (5); we have the following relationship between $\mathbf{S_W}, \mathbf{S_B}$ and $\mathbf{S}$:

$$\mathbf{S} = \frac{1}{N}(\mathbf{S_W} + \mathbf{S_B}) . \tag{16}$$

It can be shown that the vector $\boldsymbol{\alpha}_1$ which maximizes (14) must satisfy $\mathbf{S_B}\boldsymbol{\alpha}_1 = \lambda \mathbf{S_W}\boldsymbol{\alpha}_1$, for a constant λ, *i.e.* has to be an eigenvector of $\mathbf{S_W^{-1}S_B}$. Moreover, for any eigenvector $\boldsymbol{\alpha}$ of $\mathbf{S_W^{-1}S_B}$, with associated eigenvalue λ, the Rayleigh quotient equals such a λ:

$$\frac{\boldsymbol{\alpha}^\mathsf{T}\mathbf{S_B}\boldsymbol{\alpha}}{\boldsymbol{\alpha}^\mathsf{T}\mathbf{S_W}\boldsymbol{\alpha}} = \lambda . \tag{17}$$

Then, among all eigenvectors of $\mathbf{S_W^{-1}S_B}$, $\boldsymbol{\alpha}_1$ must be the leading one.

The computation of the eigenvectors of $\mathbf{S_W^{-1}S_B}$ is known under the name of *generalized eigenvector problem*. The difficulty here comes from the fact that $\mathbf{S_W^{-1}S_B}$ is not guaranteed to be symmetric. Due to this non-symmetry, $\boldsymbol{\alpha}_1$ and the others eigenvectors do not form an orthonormal basis for $\mathbb{R}^D$, but they are anyway useful for classifications scopes, as in SCA. Let us refer to them as *Linear Discriminant Components* (LDCs for short); as for PCs we consider them sorted in decreasing order with respect to their associated eigenvalue, which gives a score for their informativeness, see (17). Analogously to the PCA, the LDA provides a natural dimensionality reduction: one can project the data over the C first LDCs. As for PCA, this choice might not be optimal when applying this reduction to side-channel traces. For the sake of comparison, all the selection methods proposed for the PCA (EGV, IPR and ELV) will be tested in association to the LDA as well.

In the following subsection we will present a well-known problem that affects the LDA in many practical contexts, and describe four methods that circumvent such a problem, with the intention to test them over side-channel data.

4.1   The Small Sample Size Problem

In the special case in which the matrix $\mathbf{S_B}$ is invertible, the generalized eigenvalue problem is convertible in a regular one, as in [22]. On the contrary, when $\mathbf{S_B}$ is singular, the simultaneous diagonalization is suggested to solve such a problem [11]. In this case one can take advantage by the singularity of $\mathbf{S_B}$ to apply the computational trick proposed by Archambeau et al., see Sect. 3.2, since at most $r = \mathrm{rank}(\mathbf{S_B})$ eigenvectors can be found.

If the singularity of $\mathbf{S_B}$ does not affect the LDA dimensionality reduction, we cannot say the same about the singularity of $\mathbf{S_W}$: SCA and Pattern Recognition literatures point out the same drawback of the LDA, known as the *Small Sample Size problem* (SSS for short). It occurs when the total number of acquisitions N is less than or equal to the size D of them.[1] The direct consequence of this problem is the singularity of $\mathbf{S_W}$ and the non-applicability of the LDA.

If the LDA has been introduced relatively lately in the SCA literature, the Pattern Recognition community looks for a solution to the SSS problem at least since the early nineties. We browsed some of the proposed solutions and chose some of them to introduce, in order to test them over side channel traces.

Fisherface Method. The most popular among the solutions to SSS is the so-called *Fisherface* method[2] [3]. It simply relies on the combination between PCA and LDA: a standard PCA dimensionality reduction is performed to data, making them pass from dimension D to dimension $N - |\mathcal{Z}|$, which is the general maximal rank for $\mathbf{S_W}$. In this reduced space, $\mathbf{S_W}$ is very likely to be invertible and the LDA therefore applies.

$\mathbf{S_W}$ Null Space Method. It has been introduced by Chen et al. in [6] and exploits an important result of Liu et al. [15] who showed that Fisher's criterion (14) is equivalent to:

$$\alpha_1 = \operatorname{argmax}_\alpha \frac{\alpha^\mathsf{T}\mathbf{S_B}\alpha}{\alpha^\mathsf{T}\mathbf{S_W}\alpha + \alpha^\mathsf{T}\mathbf{S_B}\alpha} . \tag{18}$$

The authors of [6] point out that such a formula is upper-bounded by 1, and that it achieves its maximal value, *i.e.* 1, if and only if α is in the null space of $\mathbf{S_W}$. Thus they propose to first project data onto the null space of $\mathbf{S_W}$ and then to perform a PCA, *i.e.* to select as LDCs the first $|\mathcal{Z}| - 1$ eigenvectors of the between-class scatter matrix of data into this new space. More precisely, let $Q = [\mathbf{v}_1, \ldots, \mathbf{v}_{D-\mathrm{rank}(\mathbf{S_W})}]$ be the matrix of vectors that span the null space of $\mathbf{S_W}$. [6] proposes to transform the data $\mathbf{x}$ into $\mathbf{x}' = QQ^\mathsf{T}\mathbf{x}$. Such a transformation maintains the original dimension D of the data, but let the new within-class matrix $\mathbf{S}'_\mathbf{W} = QQ^\mathsf{T}\mathbf{S_W}QQ^\mathsf{T}$ be the null $D \times D$ matrix. Afterwards, the method looks for the eigenvectors of the new between-class matrix $\mathbf{S}'_\mathbf{B} = QQ^\mathsf{T}\mathbf{S_B}QQ^\mathsf{T}$. Let U be the matrix containing its first $|\mathcal{Z}| - 1$ eigenvectors: the LDCs obtained via the $\mathbf{S_W}$ null space method are the columns of $QQ^\mathsf{T}U$.

Direct LDA. As the previous, this method, introduced in [24], privileges the low-ranked eigenvectors of $\mathbf{S_W}$, but proposes to firstly project the data onto the rank space of $\mathbf{S_B}$, arguing the fact that vectors of the null space of $\mathbf{S_B}$ do

---

[1] It can happen for example when attacking an RSA implementation, where the acquisitions are often huge (of the order of 1,000,000 points) and the number of measurements may be small when the SNR is good, implying that a good GE can be achieved with a small N.

[2] The name is due to the fact that it was proposed and tested for face recognition scopes.

not provide any between-class separation of data. Let $D_B = V^\mathsf{T}\mathbf{S_B}V$ be the diagonalization of $\mathbf{S_B}$, and let $V^\star$ be the matrix of the eigenvectors of $\mathbf{S_B}$ that are not in its null space, $i.e.$ whose eigenvalues are different from zero. Let also $D_B^\star$ denotes the matrix $V^{\star\mathsf{T}}\mathbf{S_B}V^\star$; transforming the data $\mathbf{x}$ into $D_B^{\star 1/2}V^{\star\mathsf{T}}\mathbf{x}$ makes the between-class variance to be equal to the $(|\mathcal{Z}|-1) \times (|\mathcal{Z}|-1)$ identity matrix. After this transformation the within-class variance assumes the form $\mathbf{S'_W} = D_B^{\star 1/2}V^{\star\mathsf{T}}\mathbf{S'_W}V^\star D_B^{\star 1/2}$. After storing the C lowest-rank eigenvectors in a matrix $U^\star$, the LDCs obtained via the Direct LDA method are the columns of $V^\star D_B^{\star 1/2}U^{\star\mathsf{T}}$.

$\mathbf{S_T}$ **Spanned Space Method.** The last variant of LDA that we consider has been proposed in [13] and is actually a variant of the Direct LDA: instead of removing the null space of $\mathbf{S_B}$ as first step, this method removes the null space of $\mathbf{S_T} = \mathbf{S_B} + \mathbf{S_W}$. Then, denoting $\mathbf{S'_W}$ the within-class matrix in the reduced space, the reduced data are projected onto its null space, i.e. are multiplied by the matrix storing by columns the eigenvectors of $\mathbf{S'_W}$ associated to the null eigenvector, thus reduced again. A final optional step consists in verifying whether the between-class matrix presents a non-trivial null-space after the last projection and, in this case, in effectuating a further projection removing it.

Remark 2. Let us remark that, from a computational complexity point of view (see [13] for a deeper discussion), the least time-consuming procedure among the four proposed is the Direct LDA, followed by the Fisherface and the $\mathbf{S_T}$ Spanned Space Method, that have a similar complexity. The $\mathbf{S_W}$ Null Space Method is in general much more expensive, because the task of removing the $\mathbf{S_W}$ null space requires the actual computation of the $(D \times D)$-dimensional matrix $\mathbf{S_W}$, $i.e.$ the computational trick proposed by Archambeau et al. [1], see Sect. 3.2 is not applicable. On the contrary, the other three methods take advantage of such a procedure, reducing drastically their complexity.

5   Experimental Results

In this section we compare the different extractors provided by the PCA and the LDA in association with the different techniques of components selection. Defining an universal criterion to compare the different extractors would not make sense since the latter one should encompass a lot of parameters, sometimes opposite, that vary according to the context (amount of noise, specificity of the information leakage, nature of the side channel, etc.). For this reason we will choose to split our comparisons according to four contexts depending on the final goal pursued by the attacker:

1. *Minimize N*: achieve $\mathrm{GE}_{\mathcal{A}'} \leq \beta$ with the minimal number of attack traces, with β a fixed threshold, common to the four goals
2. *Minimize N'*: achieve $\mathrm{GE}_{\mathcal{A}'} \leq \beta$ with the minimal number of profiling traces
3. *Minimize C*: achieve $\mathrm{GE}_{\mathcal{A}'} \leq \beta$ reducing as much as possible the size of the extracted traces
4. *Minimize #PoI*: achieve $\mathrm{GE}_{\mathcal{A}'} \leq \beta$ exploiting the minimal number of original trace points.

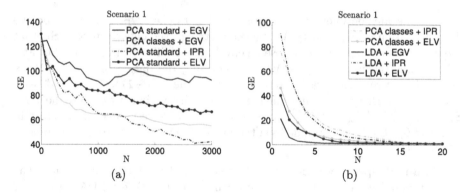

Fig. 4. Guessing entropy as function of the number of attack traces for different extraction methods. All Guessing Entropies are estimated as the average rank of the right key over 100 independent experiments.

An attack scenario has been defined for each of the goals above: in each one, three of the four parameters $N, N', C, \#PoI$ are fixed and one varies. For those in which N' is fixed, the value of N' is chosen high enough to avoid the SSS problem, and the extensions of LDA presented in Sect. 4.1 are not evaluated.[3] This choice of N' will imply that the LDA is always performed in a favourable situation, which makes expect the LDA to be particularly efficient for these experiments. Consequently, for the scenarios in which N' is high, our goal is to study whether the PCA can be made almost as efficient as the LDA thanks to the component selection methods discussed in Sect. 3.3.

The Testing Adversary. Our testing adversary attacks an 8-bit AVR microprocessor Atmega328P and acquires power-consumption traces via the Chip-Whisperer platform [19].[4] The target device stores a secret 128-bit key and performs the first steps of an AES: the loading of 16 bytes of the plaintext, the AddRoundKey step and the AES Sbox. It has been programmed twice: two different keys are stored in the device memory during the acquisition of the profiling and of the attack traces, to simulate the situation of two identical devices storing a different secret. The size D of the traces equals 3996. The sensitive target variable is the output of the first Sbox processing, but, since the key is fixed also during the profiling phase, and both Xor and Sbox operations are bijective, we expect to detect three interesting regions (as those high-lighted by PCs 4, 5 and 6, in Fig. 3): the reading of the first byte of the plaintext, the first AddRoundKey and the first Sbox. We consider an *identity classification* leaking function (i.e. we make minimal assumption on the leakage function), which implies that the 256 possible values of the Sbox output yields to 256 classes. For each class we assume that the adversary acquires the same number N_p of traces, *i.e.* $N' = N_p \times 256$. After the application of the extractor ε, the trace size

---

[3] This study is let open for an extended version of this paper.

[4] This choice has been done to allow for reproducibility of the experiments.

is reduced to C. Then the attacker performs a Bayesian Template Attack [5], using C-variate Gaussian templates. This choice comes from the information-theoretic optimality of such an attack which, exploiting the maximum likelihood parameters estimation, yields to an unbiased comparison between the extractors.

Scenario 1. To analyse the dependence between the extraction methods presented in Sects. 3 and 4 and the number of attack traces N needed to achieve a given GE, we fixed the other parameters as follows: $N_p = 50$ ($N' = 50 \times 256$), $C = 3$ and $\#PoI = 3996$ (all points are allowed to participate in the building of the PCs and of the LDCs). The experimental results, depicted in Fig. 4(a)–(b), show that the PCA standard method has very bad performances in SCA, while the LDA outperforms the others. Concerning the class-oriented PCA, we observe that its performance is close to that of LDA when combined with the selection methods ELV (which performs best) or IPR.

Scenario 2. Now we test the behaviour of the extraction methods as function of the number N_p of available profiling traces per class. The number of components C is still fixed to 3, $\#PoI = 3996$ again and the number of attack traces is $N = 100$. This scenario has to be divided into two parts: if $N_p \leq 15$, then $N' < D$ and the SSS problem occurs. Thus, in this case we test the four extensions of LDA presented in Sect. 4.1, associated to either the standard selection, to which we abusively refer as EGV,[5] or to the IPR selection. We compare them to the class-oriented PCA associated to EGV, IPR or ELV. The ELV selection is not performed for the techniques extending LDA, since for some of them the projecting LDCs are not associated to some eigenvalues in a meaningful way. On the contrary, if $N_p \geq 16$ there is no need to approximate the LDA technique, so the classical one is performed. Results for this scenario are shown in Fig. 5. It may be noticed that the combinations class-oriented PCA + ELV/IPR select exactly the same components, for our data, see Fig. 5(e) and do not suffer from the lack of profiling traces. They are slightly outperformed by the S_W Null Space method associated with the EGV, see Fig. 5(d). The Direct LDA (Fig. 5(b)) method also provides a good alternative, while the other tested methods do not show a stable behaviour. The results in absence of the SSS problem (Fig. 5(f)) confirm that the standard PCA is not adapted to SCA, even when provided with more profiling traces. It also shows that among class-oriented PCA and LDA, the class-oriented PCA converges faster.

Scenario 3. Let C be now variable and let the other parameters be fixed as follows: $N = 100, N_p = 200, \#PoI = 3996$. Looking at Fig. 6, we might observe that the standard PCA might actually well perform in SCA context if provided with a larger number of kept components; on the contrary, a little number of components suffices to the LDA. Finally, keeping more of the necessary components does not worsen the efficiency of the attack, which allows the attacker to choose C as the maximum value supported by his computational means.

---

[5] It consists in keeping the C first LDCs (the C last for the Direct LDA).

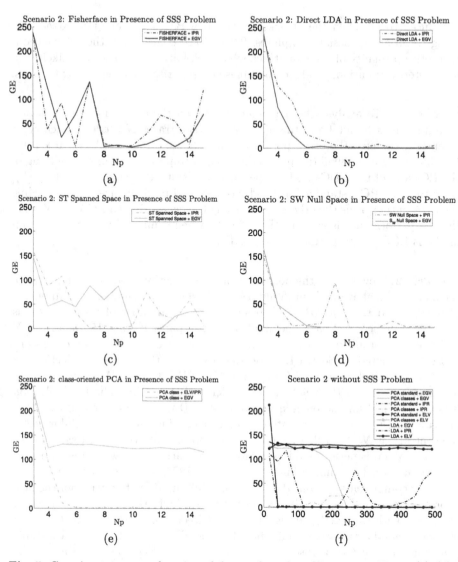

Fig. 5. Guessing entropy as function of the number of profiling traces. Figure (a)–(d): methods extending the LDA in presence of SSS problem; Fig. (e): class-oriented PCA in presence of the SSS problem; Fig. (f): number of profiling traces high enough to avoid the SSS problem.

Remark 3. In our experiments the ELV selection method only slightly outperforms the IPR. Nevertheless, since it relies on more sound and more general observations, *i.e.* the maximization of explained variance concentrated into few points, it is likely to be more robust and less case-specific. For example, in Fig. 5(f) it can be remarked that while the class-oriented PCA + ELV line keeps constant on the value 0 of guessing entropy, the class-oriented PCA + IPR is sometimes higher than 0.

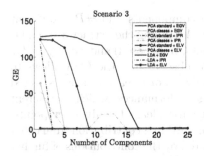

Fig. 6. Guessing entropy as function of the number of the traces size after reduction

Table 1. Overview of extractors performances in tested situations.

Method	Selection	Parameter to minimize			
		N	N' (SSS)	N' ($\neg$SSS)	C
PCA standard	EGV	-		-	-
PCA standard	ELV	-		-	-
PCA standard	IPR	-		-	+
PCA class	EGV	-	-	-	-
PCA class	ELV	+	★	★	+
PCA class	IPR	+	★	+	-
LDA	EGV	★		+	★
LDA	ELV	+		+	★
LDA	IPR	+		+	★
S_W Null Space	EGV		★		
S_W Null Space	IPR		+		
Direct LDA	EGV		★		
Direct LDA	IPR		+		
Fisherface			-		
S_T Spanned Space			-		

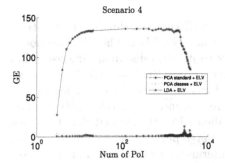

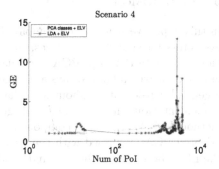

Fig. 7. Guessing entropy as function of the number of time samples contributing to the extractor computation.

An overview of the results of our comparison in scenarios 1, 2 and 3 is depicted in Table 1: depending on the adversary purpose, given by the parameter to minimize, a ★ denotes the best method, a + denotes a method with performances close to those of the best one and a − is for methods that show lower performances. Techniques introduced in this paper are highlighted by a grey background. For example we remark that the class-oriented PCA takes advantage of the association with our ELV selection of components, achieving optimal performances when the goal is to minimize the number of profiling traces N'. As expected, when there are no constraints over N', the LDA outperforms the other methods; however, even in this case which is very favourable to the LDA, the class-oriented PCA equipped with the ELV selection has an efficiency which is close to that of the LDA.

Scenario 4. This is the single scenario in which we allow the ELV selection method to not only select the components to keep but also to modify them, keeping only some coefficients within each component, setting the other ones to zero. We select pairs *(component, time sample)* in decreasing order of the ELV values, allowing the presence of only $C = 3$ components and $\#PoI$ different times samples: *i.e.*, we impose that the matrix A defining the extractor (see (1)) has $C = 3$ rows (storing the 3 chosen components, transposed) and exactly $\#PoI$ non-zero columns. Looking at Fig. 7 we might observe that the LDA allows to achieve the maximal guessing entropy with only 1 PoI in each of the 3 selected components. Actually, adding PoIs worsen its performances, which is coherent with the assumption that the vulnerable information leaks in only a few points. Such points are excellently detected by the LDA. Adding contribution from other points raises the noise, which is then compensated by the contributions of further noisy points, in a very delicate balance. Such a behaviour is clearly visible in standard PCA case: the first 10 points considered raise the level of noise, that is then balanced by the last 1000 points.

6   Conclusions

In this paper we studied and compared two well-known techniques to construct extractors for side-channel traces, the PCA and the LDA. The LDA method is more adequate than the PCA one, thanks to its class-distinguishing asset, but more expensive and not always available in concrete situations. We deduced from a general consideration about side-channel traces, i.e. the fact that for secured implementations the vulnerable leakages are concentrated into few points, a new methodology for selecting components, called ELV. We showed that the class-oriented PCA, equipped with the ELV, achieves performances close to those of the LDA, becoming a cheaper and valid alternative to the LDA. Being our core consideration very general in side-channel context, we believe that our results are not case-specific. Finally, among other alternatives to the LDA in presence of SSS problem proposed in Pattern Recognition literature, we showed that the Direct LDA and the $\mathbf{S_W}$ Null Space Method are promising, as well.

References

1. Archambeau, C., Peeters, E., Standaert, F.-X., Quisquater, J.-J.: Template attacks in principal subspaces. In: Goubin, L., Matsui, M. (eds.) CHES 2006. LNCS, vol. 4249, pp. 1–14. Springer, Heidelberg (2006)
2. Batina, L., Hogenboom, J., van Woudenberg, J.G.J.: Getting more from PCA: first results of using principal component analysis for extensive power analysis. In: Dunkelman, O. (ed.) CT-RSA 2012. LNCS, vol. 7178, pp. 383–397. Springer, Heidelberg (2012)
3. Belhumeur, P.N., Hespanha, J.P., Kriegman, D.J.: Eigenfaces vs. fisherfaces: recognition using class specific linear projection. IEEE Trans. Pattern Anal. Mach. Intell. **19**(7), 711–720 (1997)
4. Bruneau, N., Guilley, S., Heuser, A., Marion, D., Rioul, O.: Less is more. In: Güneysu, T., Handschuh, H. (eds.) CHES 2015. LNCS, vol. 9293, pp. 22–41. Springer, Heidelberg (2015)
5. Chari, S., Rao, J.R., Rohatgi, P.: Template attacks. In: Kaliski Jr., B.S., Koç, Ç.K., Paar, C. (eds.) CHES 2002. LNCS, vol. 2523, pp. 13–28. Springer, Heidelberg (2003)

6. Chen, L.-F., Liao, H.-Y.M., Ko, M.-T., Lin, J.-C., Yu, G.-J.: A new LDA-based face recognition system which can solve the small sample size problem. Pattern Recogn. **33**(10), 1713–1726 (2000)
7. Choudary, O., Kuhn, M.G.: Efficient stochastic methods: profiled attacks beyond 8 bits. IACR Cryptology ePrint Archive (2014)
8. Choudary, O., Kuhn, M.G.: Efficient template attacks. In: Francillon, A., Rohatgi, P. (eds.) CARDIS 2013. LNCS, vol. 8419, pp. 253–270. Springer, Heidelberg (2014)
9. Eisenbarth, T., Paar, C., Weghenkel, B.: Building a side channel based disassembler. In: Gavrilova, M.L., Tan, C.J.K., Moreno, E.D. (eds.) Transactions on Computational Science X. LNCS, vol. 6340, pp. 78–99. Springer, Heidelberg (2010)
10. Fisher, R.A.: The statistical utilization of multiple measurements. Ann. Eugenics **8**(4), 376–386 (1938)
11. Fukunaga, K.: Introduction to Statistical Pattern Recognition, 2nd edn. Academic Press Professional Inc, San Diego (1990)
12. Guhr, T., Müller-Groeling, A., Weidenmüller, H.A.: Random-matrix theories in quantum physics: common concepts. Phys. Rep. **299**(4), 189–425 (1998)
13. Huang, R., Liu, Q., Lu, H., Ma, S.: Solving the small sample size problem of LDA. Pattern Recogn. **3**, 29–32 (2002)
14. Karsmakers, P., Gierlichs, B., Pelckmans, K., De Cock, K., Suykens, J., Preneel, B., De Moor, B.: Side channel attacks on cryptographic devices as a classification problem. Technical report, COSIC technical report (2009)
15. Liu, K., Cheng, Y.-Q., Yang, J.-Y.: A generalized optimal set of discriminant vectors. Pattern Recogn. **25**(7), 731–739 (1992)
16. Massey, J.L.: Guessing and entropy. In: 1994 Proceedings of the IEEE International Symposium on Information Theory, p. 204. IEEE (1994)
17. Mavroeidis, D., Batina, L., van Laarhoven, T., Marchiori, E.: PCA, Eigenvector localization and clustering for side-channel attacks on cryptographic hardware devices. In: Flach, P.A., De Bie, T., Cristianini, N. (eds.) ECML PKDD 2012, Part I. LNCS, vol. 7523, pp. 253–268. Springer, Heidelberg (2012)
18. Nisan, N., Zuckerman, D.: Randomness is linear in space. J. Comput. Syst. Sci. **52**(1), 43–52 (1996)
19. O'Flynn, C., Chen, Z.D.: ChipWhisperer: an open-source platform for hardware embedded security research. In: Prouff, E. (ed.) COSADE 2014. LNCS, vol. 8622, pp. 243–260. Springer, Heidelberg (2014)
20. TELECOM ParisTech. DPA contest 4. http://www.DPAcontest.org/v4/
21. Specht, R., Heyszl, J., Kleinsteuber, M., Sigl, G.: Improving non-profiled attacks on exponentiations based on clustering and extracting leakage from multi-channel high-resolution EM measurements. In: Mangard, S., Poschmann, A.Y. (eds.) COSADE 2015. LNCS, vol. 9064, pp. 3–19. Springer, Heidelberg (2015)
22. Standaert, F.-X., Archambeau, C.: Using subspace-based template attacks to compare and combine power and electromagnetic information leakages. In: Oswald, E., Rohatgi, P. (eds.) CHES 2008. LNCS, vol. 5154, pp. 411–425. Springer, Heidelberg (2008)
23. Standaert, F.-X., Malkin, T.G., Yung, M.: A unified framework for the analysis of side-channel key recovery attacks. In: Joux, A. (ed.) EUROCRYPT 2009. LNCS, vol. 5479, pp. 443–461. Springer, Heidelberg (2009)
24. Yu, H., Yang, J.: A direct LDA algorithm for high-dimensional data with application to face recognition. Pattern Recogn. **34**, 2067–2070 (2001)

A Semi-Parametric Approach for Side-Channel Attacks on Protected RSA Implementations

Guilherme Perin and Łukasz Chmielewski$^{(\boxtimes)}$

Riscure BV, Delftechpark 49, 2628 XJ Delft, The Netherlands
{Perin,Chmielewski}@riscure.com

Abstract. Side-channel attacks on RSA aim at recovering the secret exponent by processing multiple power or electromagnetic traces. The exponent blinding is the main countermeasure which avoids the application of classical forms of side-channel attacks, like SPA, DPA, CPA and template attacks. Horizontal attacks overcome RSA countermeasures by attacking single traces. However, the processing of a single trace is limited by the amount of information and the leakage assessment using labeled samples is not possible due to the exponent blinding countermeasure. In order to overcome these drawbacks, we propose a side-channel attack framework based on a semi-parametric approach that combines the concepts of unsupervised learning, horizontal attacks, maximum likelihood estimation and template attacks in order to recover the exponent bits. Our method is divided in two main parts: learning and attacking phases. The learning phase consists of identifying the class parameters contained in the power traces representing the loop of the exponentiation. We propose a leakage assessment based on unsupervised learning to identify points of interest in a blinded exponentiation. The attacking phase executes a horizontal attack based on clustering algorithms to provide labeled information. Furthermore, it computes confidence probabilities for all exponent bits. These probabilities indicate how much our semi-parametric approach is able to learn about the class parameters from the side-channel information.

To demonstrate the power of our framework we attack the private exponent d_p of the 1024-bit RSA-CRT implementation protected by the SPA, 32-bit message blinding, and 64-bit exponent blinding countermeasures; the implementation runs on a 32-bit STM32F4 microcontroller.

Keywords: RSA · Modular exponentiation · Side-channel attacks · Horizontal attacks · Unsupervised learning · Clustering algorithms · Leakage assessment

1 Introduction

RSA [1]-based cryptosystems are frequently used in credit cards and e-commerce applications. Running on embedded systems, it is a common target of side-channel attacks. The main goal of these attacks is to recover the private key which is directly employed in the modular exponentiation phase – the main

© Springer International Publishing Switzerland 2016
N. Homma and M. Medwed (Eds.): CARDIS 2015, LNCS 9514, pp. 34–53, 2016.
DOI: 10.1007/978-3-319-31271-2_3

RSA operation. Countermeasures like uniformity of modular operations execution as well as message and exponent blinding render classical side-channel attacks (SPA [5,10], DPA [6], CPA [7], collision [8,11], template [15]) unfeasible against RSA implementations. These attacks require a fixed exponent for all measured power (or electromagnetic) traces. The main protection relies on the full randomization of intermediate data, including input message, exponent and modulus, during the execution of an exponentiation [9,12,13].

Horizontal attacks [16–24] are emerging forms of side-channel attacks on exponentiation-based algorithms. Their methodology allows recovering the exponent bits through the analysis of individual traces. Therefore, horizontal attacks are efficient against exponent blinding even when combined with message and modulus blinding[1]. A basic requirement of horizontal attacks is the knowledge of the modular exponentiation algorithm. Afterwards, the attacker may choose between different common distinguishers: SPA, horizontal correlation analysis [17], or clustering [22,23], among others.

Most forms of horizontal attacks require advanced trace preprocessings, characterization and leakage assessment before the application of distinguishers. The main problem of the horizontal attacks is: extracting the leakage from a single trace is limited by noise and unlabeled information. In particular, common leakage assessments, like [30] or t-test [35], require labeled samples and that is not possible due to exponent blinding. Therefore, we have decided to investigate semi-parametric models based on unsupervised learning [31,33,34].

The only horizontal solutions, to the above problem to the best of our knowledge are [22,23]. The first paper [22] proposes to apply a clustering classification to a single trace to allow labeling specific classes operations; this method works well for low noise measurements and requires an EM station composed of multiple probes. The authors of [23] considered a heuristic approach based on difference-of-means for the points of interest selection, which can have large complexity. Furthermore, both solutions use a single trace leakage assessment, which may be affected by a large amount of noise. We discuss horizontal attacks with respect to RSA countermeasures in Sect. 2.1.

Another approach to horizontal attacks is horizontal cross-correlation for elliptic curve scalar multiplication [32][2]. This approach exploits collisions in subsequent additions of a scalar multiplication algorithm using a single trace. Identifying points of interest is not considered in [32].

Contributions. In this paper, we propose a generic framework that aims at solving the aforementioned leakage assessment problem by combining multiple traces even if the device is protected with exponent blinding. The framework

---

[1] Note that message and modulus blinding affect only the exponentiation input, but not the algorithm itself. Therefore, since horizontal attacks exploit the exponentiation algorithm structure, the aforementioned countermeasures are expected to be ineffective.

[2] Horizontal cross-correlation has not been yet successfully applied to RSA to the best of our knowledge.

assesses the leakage on blinded RSA implementations from multiple traces without access to any labeled information; in particular, it does not require a fully controlled device on which we can reprogram or learn the blinded exponent. Our framework builds and improves on the work from [22,23] by employing information from multiple traces and by implementing a wide range of leakage assessment methods and statistical classifiers. A direct practical application of our framework is a side-channel ICC EMVCo smart card evaluation [38] since in such an evaluation a fully controlled device is not available.

The framework is divided in two main parts, i.e., learning and attacking phases. This parallel with template attacks comes from the fact that the first phase tries to learn the class parameters from the traces using unsupervised learning and horizontal attacks. During this learning phase, we propose a new leakage assessment based on unsupervised learning which can precisely identify the leakage location by returning the class parameters from mixture of distributions. Points of interest are identified during the leakage assessment and used as the input for a clustering-based horizontal attack [22,23]. The latter's output is an approximate exponent for each single exponentiation trace. The attacking phase considers the approximate exponent results to re-compute the class parameters and horizontally applies them to the same set of traces using parametric and multivariate attacks. This second phase returns probabilities indicating how much the class parameters are correctly learned from the non-profiled side-channel information.

The presented framework allows the attacker to verify if a protected RSA implementations provides side-channel information even in the presence of blinding countermeasures. The basic assumption is that the device leaks some partial SPA information. We demonstrate that although in attacking phase the horizontal attack is performed on a single trace, we can use clustering algorithms in the learning phase to process multiple traces (which represent randomized exponentiations) to precisely identify the leakage location.

We present the effectiveness of our framework by attacking the private exponent d_p of 1024-bit RSA-CRT implementation protected by SPA countermeasures (like regularity between squares and multiplications), message blinding and exponent blinding. For the sake of simplicity we implement the square-and-multiply exponentiation[3]. The implementation is run on a 32-bit STM32F4 microcontroller. We apply both parts of our framework consecutively and we achieve error rate of 1.27%; it means that for a 512-bit d_p, randomized with a 64-bit value, our framework commits approximately 11 errors.

The above result (11 errors) implies that a brute-force attack is feasible to recover the correct exponent assuming that an attacker can determining the locations of possible errors. Our frameworks outputs not only the recovered exponent bits but also confidence probabilities of the correct guesses (where

---

[3] Observe that our framework can be also used to attack another exponentiation algorithms, square-and-multiply always [12], for instance. In this case, however, the framework needs to be applied to the whole exponentiation iteration at once and not to single modular multiplications.

0.5 denotes a random guess, for example). These probabilities can be used as a reference for the exponent bits selection with respect to a brute-force attack. In our experiment there are less than 20 bit with the probabilities between 0.45 and 0.55. A known-key analysis, for this specific case, confirmed these 20 bits contain all 11 errors. Furthermore, brute-forcing 20 bits of the RSA key is practical since it can take up to a few hours on a modern PC. The details of the error correction are presented in Sect. 4.2.

Organization of the Paper. This paper is organized as follows. We briefly describe preliminaries, in particular we introduce horizontal attacks on exponentiations and unsupervised learning in side-channel attacks, in Sect. 2. Section 3 presents the device under test and our measurement setup. Subsequently, the attack framework is presented in Sect. 4. Finally, Sect. 5 summarizes our contribution, presents future work, and concludes the paper.

2 Preliminaries

Notations. Let x be the realization of a random variable X. A sample from X is denoted by x_i. The term $p(X)$ defines the probability mass function when X is discrete and $p(X|Y)$ is the conditional probability of X given Y. Given a set of class parameters θ defining a univariate normal distribution $\mathcal{N}(\mu, \sigma^2)$ with mean μ and variance σ^2. Here, $g(x \mid \theta)$ is the function of x defined up to the parameters θ. The term $\mathcal{L}(\theta|X)$ is the likelihood of parameters θ on the sample X.

Trace Characterization. The n-th measured side-channel trace, which represents the power consumption (or electromagnetic emanation - EM) of a cryptographic device over the time domain, is denoted by the uni-dimensional $(1 \times aL)$ vector $\mathbf{t}^n = \{O_1^n, O_2^n, ..., O_{aL}^n\}$. Here, we consider a trace $\mathbf{t}^n$ as being the side-channel information of a modular exponentiation composed by a fixed number aL of modular operations. The factor a depends on the exponentiation algorithm and L is the bit-length of the RSA private key. The trace $\mathbf{t}^n$ can be described by a set of ℓ-sized sub-vectors:

$$\mathbf{t}^n = \{O_1^n, O_2^n, ..., O_{a.L}^n\} = \{(t_{1,1}^n, ..., t_{1,\ell}^n), (t_{2,1}^n, ..., t_{2,\ell}^n), ..., (t_{a.L,1}^n, ..., t_{a.L,\ell}^n)\} \tag{1}$$

where $t_{i,j}^n$ is the j-th element of each sub-vector O_i^n. The element $t_{i,j}^n$ can also be viewed as a sample in the time domain from the side-channel trace $\mathbf{t}^n$. The set $\{t_{i,j}^n\}$, $i = 1..aL$, refers to a set of samples where each element $t_{i,j}^n$ is extracted from one modular operation O_i^n for a fixed j (e.g., $\{t_{i,10}^n\}$ contains aL samples, each element $t_{i,10}^n$ is selected from the 10th sample of each sub-trace O_i).

Statistical Model. Let us consider a set of side-channel traces $\mathbf{T}$. It represents the power consumption of N modular exponentiation executions. We assume a modular exponentiation trace $\mathbf{t}^n$ as a data set composed by k classes or sets of parameters θ_k. Each class is statistically defined by a univariate normal distribution $\mathcal{N}(\mu_k, \sigma_k^2)$ and the set of aL samples $\{t_{1:aL,j}^n\}$ (for a fixed j) is drawn from a multivariate normal distribution, or a mixture of Gaussians, $\mathcal{N}_d(\mu, \Sigma)$. Because the statistical model is built from RSA implementations, the classes can be understood as squares and multiplications or even exponent bits zeros or ones.

2.1 Horizontal Side-Channel Attacks on Exponentiations

Exponent blinding [6,12] is the main RSA countermeasure against side-channel attacks. During decryption or singing, this countermeasure changes the sequence of exponent bits for every execution of the algorithm. Therefore, power (or electromagnetic emanation) traces cannot be aligned and processed together to reduce the noise from a set of measurements. Horizontal attacks [16–24] were proposed as an alternative methodology to extract the private key bits from a single trace.

By applying side-channel attacks in a horizontal setting, the n-th trace $\mathbf{t}^n$ must be split in sub-traces, $O_i^n = \{t_{i,1:\ell}\}$, each one representing a particular iteration from the ring of the exponentiation. The sub-trace O_i^n might be the set of samples representing one modular operation or the processing of one exponent bit. This splitting procedure is illustrated in Fig. 1.

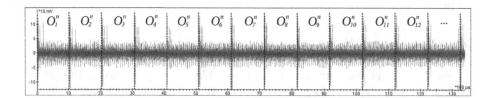

Fig. 1. Modular exponentiation trace.

A basic assumption for the horizontal attacks is the knowledge of the modular exponentiation algorithm (for instance, square-and-multiply always [12], sliding window exponentiation, Montgomery ladder [14], etc.). After, the attacker may choose between different distinguishers: SPA, horizontal correlation analysis [17], Euclidean distance [16], horizontal collision-correlation [18–21] or clustering [22,23]. The encryption or verification with a public-key can be performed with the same set of instructions used for decryption and signing. In this case, the classes parameters could be learned using the public key and applied as templates on single traces using the private key [24]. However, in this work we assume that this scenario is not possible. Therefore, we decided to investigate semi-parametric models based on unsupervised learning [31,33,34] for the horizontal attacks.

2.2   Unsupervised Learning in Side-Channel Attacks

Before entering in the context of unsupervised learning methods for side-channel attacks, it is worth to establish a parallel between supervised and unsupervised learning when attacking exponentiations. Profiled template attacks [15] are a classical example of supervised learning approaches. In this case, a cryptographic device having a fixed or known key is used to learn the statistics (for instance, mean and variance) related to the processing of known exponent bits. Other attacks (e.g., SPA, CPA) that are efficient on non-randomized exponent devices do not consider a learning phase and they are able of breaking the device by statistically processing a set of measurements. Thus, noise contained in the traces can be sufficiently eliminated, enabling the key recovering with the application of specific distinguishers (difference-of-means [6], correlation [7], mutual information [26,27]).

In a situation when the secret exponent is a random value for each measured trace, and of course, in the absence of a known-key device, multiple traces cannot be conventionally processed together. Thus, as we present in the Sect. 4, unsupervised learning is the methodology that can still provide leakage assessment if the appropriate leakage or statistical model is defined for the set of traces. Clustering methods allow learning the mixture parameters from unlabeled data.

Considering that a set of samples $\{t_{i,j}^n\}$, where $i = 1..aL$ and j is fixed, is characterized by a mixture density:

$$p(t_{i,j}^n) = \sum_{k=1}^{K} p(t_{i,j}^n | \mu_{k,j}^n, \sigma_{k,j}^{2(n)}) \mathcal{N}(\mu_{k,j}^n, \sigma_{k,j}^{2(n)}), \tag{2}$$

where $p(t_{i,j}^n | \mu_{k,j}^n, \sigma_{k,j}^{2(n)})$ is the probability density of $t_{i,j}^n$ with respect to the class parameters $(\mu_{k,j}^n, \sigma_{k,j}^{2(n)})$. The number of parameters K should be defined beforehand. Given a set of samples $\{t_{i,j}^n\}$ extracted from a single exponentiation trace t^n, learning corresponds to estimating the component densities and proportions. We assume the samples obey a parametric model and that we need to estimate their parameters: the mean $\mu_{k,j}^n$ and variance $\sigma_{k,j}^{2(n)}$ for each class k on each sample j.

Let us first define $r_{i,j}^n$ as a parameter defining whether a sample belongs to a specific group or distribution $\mathcal{N}(\theta_{k,j}^n)$. Therefore, $r_{i,j}^n = 1$ if the sample $t_{i,j}^n$ belongs to class k and $r_{i,j}^n = 0$ otherwise. In a supervised setting, $r_{i,j}^n$ is known and we compute the class parameters according to:

$$\mu_{k,j}^n = \frac{\sum_{i=1}^{aL} r_{i,j}^n t_{i,j}^n}{\sum_{i=1}^{a.L} r_{i,j}^n} \qquad \sigma_{k,j}^{2(n)} = \frac{\sum_{i=1}^{aL} r_{i,j}^n (t_{i,j}^n - \mu_{k,j}^n)(t_{i,j}^n - \mu_{k,j}^n)^T}{\sum_{i=1}^{a.L} r_{i,j}^n} \tag{3}$$

In this work, the analysis is unsupervised and the values of $r_{i,j}^n$ are unknown. The **k-means** algorithm [31] can label the data sample by iteratively computing the means for k classes using the distance between samples and means. First, the means $\mu_{k,j}^n$ are randomly initialized by receiving, at random, one element of $\{t_{i,j}^n\}$. The values of $r_{i,j}^n \in \{0,1\}$ are them defined as being:

$$
r_{i,j}^n = \begin{cases} 1 & \text{if } |t_{i,j}^n - \mu_{k,j}^n| = \underset{c}{\mathrm{argmin}} \, |t_{i,j}^n - \mu_{c,j}^n| \\ 0 & \text{otherwise} \end{cases}
$$

Following, new means $\mu_{k,j}^n$ are computed using Eq. 3. The process continues iteratively with the re-definition of $r_{i,j}^n$ and the respective re-computation of means $\mu_{k,j}^n$ till convergence. Usually, the convergence is verified when the current and the previous means are equal.

Fuzzy k-means [31,33] is an extension of k-means and compute the probability of a sample $t_{i,j}^n$ to belong to a cluster k. Now, the cluster parameter, or probabilities, are $p(t_{i,j}^n|\mu_{k,j}^n) \in [0,1]$. They are initialized at random, with random probabilities inside the interval $[0,1]$ such that $\sum_k p(t_{i,j}^n|\mu_{k,j}^n) = 1$, $\forall i$, and initial means $\mu_{k,j}^n$ are computed as following:

$$
\mu_{k,j}^n = \frac{\sum t_{i,j}^n \cdot (p(t_{i,j}^n|\mu_{k,j}^n))^{\frac{2}{\eta-1}}}{\sum (p(t_{i,j}^n|\mu_{k,j}^n))^{\frac{2}{\eta-1}}} \tag{4}
$$

where η is free parameter and usually set to 2. Different choices for η depend on the sample set features (e.g., size, noise, etc.). The algorithm computes new probabilities with the following equation:

$$
p(t_{i,j}^n|\mu_{k,j}^n) = \frac{1/(|t_{i,j}^n - \mu_{k,j}^n|^{\frac{2}{\eta-1}})}{\sum_{c=1}^{K} 1/(|t_{i,j}^n - \mu_{c,j}^n|^{\frac{2}{\eta-1}})} \tag{5}
$$

and, respectively new means $\mu_{k,j}^n$. It continues iteratively till convergence, i.e., when the previous and current means remain unchanged. The fuzzy k-means has the cluster centers, or means, and the probabilities as class parameters.

The **Expectation-Maximization (EM) algorithm** [34] is a probabilistic approach which includes the covariance in the set of parameters. Given a Gaussian mixture, the EM algorithm can model the class parameters and maximize the likelihood function with respect to these parameters. Firstly, the means $\mu_{k,j}^n$, covariances $\Sigma_{k,j}^n$ and mixing coefficients $\pi_{k,j}^n$ are initialized. The mixing coefficients must satisfy $0 \le \pi_{k,j}^n \le 1$ together with $\sum_{k=1}^{K} \pi_{k,j}^n = 1$. Following, the algorithm alternates between E-step and M-step:

1. E-step: evaluate the responsibilities using the current class parameter values:

$$
\lambda_{i,k}^n = \frac{\pi_{k,j}^n exp(-\frac{1}{2}(t_{i,j}^n - \mu_{k,j}^n)\Sigma_{k,j}^{-1(n)}(t_{i,j}^n - \mu_{k,j}^n)^T)}{\sum_{c=1}^{K} \pi_{c,j}^n exp(-\frac{1}{2}(t_{i,j}^n - \mu_{c,j}^n)\Sigma_{c,j}^{-1(n)}(t_{i,j}^n - \mu_{c,j}^n)^T)}
$$

2. M-step: re-estimate the class parameters using the responsibilities computed in the E-step:

$$
\mu_{k,j}^{new(n)} = \frac{1}{L_{k,j}^n} \sum_{i=1}^{a.L} \lambda_{i,k}^n t_{i,j}^n \tag{6}
$$

$$\Sigma_{k,j}^{new(n)} = \frac{1}{L_{k,j}} \sum_{i=1}^{aL} \lambda_{i,k}^n (t_{i,j}^n - \mu_{k,j}^{new(n)})(t_{i,j}^n - \mu_{k,j}^{new(n)})^T \qquad (7)$$

$$\pi_{k,j}^{new} = \frac{L_{k,j}^n}{aL} \quad L_{k,j}^n = \sum_{i=1}^{aL} \lambda_{i,k}^n \qquad (8)$$

3. Verify the convergence by verifying the log-likelihood:

$$\mathcal{L}(\theta|\mathbf{t}^n) =$$

$$\sum_{i=1}^{aL} \log \left\{ \sum_{c=1}^{K} \pi_{c,j}^{new(n)} exp(-\frac{1}{2}(t_{i,j}^n - \mu_{c,j}^{new(n)}) \Sigma_{c,j}^{-1(new)(n)}(t_{i,j}^n - \mu_{c,j}^{new(n)})^T) \right\}$$
$$(9)$$

The E and M steps are recursively repeated till a convergence criteria is satisfied.

The three aforementioned clustering methods can be used to model the class parameters from a measured trace $\mathbf{t}^n$ and the contained set of sampled $\{t_{i,j}^n\}$. Section 4 demonstrates how the unsupervised learning can be used to learn the class parameters (μ, σ, Σ) and identify points of interest for horizontal side-channel attacks on protected exponentiations. First, Sect. 3 gives details about the target implementation and measurement setup.

3 Device Under Test and Measurement Setup

The target under evaluation is a software 1024-bit RSA-CRT implementation. The design runs on a training target for side channel analysis and fault injection testing – piñata board[4]. The board is based on a 32-bit STM32F4 microcontroller with an ARM-based architecture.

Given the RSA private key d and the respective modulus $M = pq$. RSA-CRT algorithm solves the modular exponentiation by using a set private parameters $d, p, q, d_p = d \mod (p-1), d_q = d \mod (q-1)$ and $i_q = q^{-1} \mod p$. This protocol provides a decrypted or signed value $s = CRT(s_p, s_q) = s_q + q(i_q(s_p - s_q) \mod p)$, where: $s_p = y^{d_p} \mod p \quad s_q = y^{d_q} \mod q$.

The modular exponentiation is computed with the left-to-right square-and-multiply algorithm. The implementation features SPA and DPA countermeasures like regularity between squares and multiplications and exponent/message randomization. Algorithm 1 shows the exponentiation method and countermeasures regarding the CRT exponentiation related to prime p. It returns the result s_p. The computation of s_q can be done with the same method.

The random numbers r_1 and r_2 are 32-bit and 64-bit values, respectively. The target of the present evaluation is the exponentiation $y^{d_{p_r}=d_p+r_2(p-1)} \mod p$. Here, the size of RSA prime p is 512 bits and the random exponent d_{p_r} is, in average, 576 bits. Therefore, we consider L as being 576 and the parameter a as being 1.5. Therefore, the average number of modular operations aL in an exponentiation trace is $1.5 \times 576 = 864$. From this amount, we expect to have,

---

[4] https://www.riscure.com/security-tools/hardware/pinata.

Algorithm 1. Protected left-to-right square-and-multiply

Data: y, p, $d_p = (d_{L-1}...d_1 d_0)_2$.

Result: $s_p = y^{d_p} \bmod p$

1 $y_r \leftarrow y + r_1 p$
2 $d_{p_r} \leftarrow d_p + r_2(p-1)$
3 $A \leftarrow 1$
4 **for** $i = L - 1$ **to** 0 **do**
5      $\quad A \leftarrow A^2 \bmod p$
6      $\quad$ **if** $d_{p_r}(i) = 1$ **then**
7          $\quad\quad |\ A \leftarrow A \times y_r \bmod p$
8      $\quad$ **end**
9 **end**
10 Return A

---

in average, $l_0 = 576$ squares and $l_1 = 288$ multiplications for every execution of the exponentiation. Once the randomized exponent d_{p_r} is recovered, the method proposed in [28] can be adopted to recover p.

The measurement setup is composed by the STM32F4 evaluation board, a current probe, an oscilloscope and a power computer to communicate with the equipment and store the acquired traces. The power traces were measured at a sampling frequency of 500MS/sec.

4   Attack Framework

This section describes a new methodology for the application of side-channel attacks on protected RSA implementations. The attack framework is presented in Fig. 2. All stages of the framework are described in the remaining part of this section.

The framework combines the concepts of unsupervised learning, horizontal attacks, maximum likelihood estimation and template attacks. The first phase aims at learning the class parameters which are supposed to be protected due to the embedded countermeasures. The second phase follows the principles of maximum likelihood estimation and template attacks. The output is given in terms of probabilities and provides an indicative of how much the class parameters were learned from the protected device.

4.1   Learning Phase

The first phase of our methodology concentrates its efforts in the learning of the class parameters contained in a set of N measured power traces. The analysis starts by assessing the contained leakage in order to identify points of interest. In this work, a point of interest is defined as the sample index $j \in \{1, \ell\}$ where the corresponding sample set $\{t_{i,j}^n\}$, for $i = 1 : aL$, has an observable difference

---

1. **Learning Phase** executes:
   (a) **Unsupervised Learning for Leakage Assessment** takes as input a set of traces $\{t^n\}$, and returns points of interest;
   (b) **Horizontal Attack** takes as input the points of interest, the set of traces, and for each trace t^n returns an approximate exponent;
   (c) **Optimizing the Points of Interest Selection** takes as input the set of traces, the approximate exponents, and executes:
      i. Using the approximate exponents, determines refined points of interest using T-test;
      ii. Repeats the **Horizontal Attack** using the refined point of interest and outputs improved approximate exponents.
2. **Attacking Phase** to recover the correct exponent executes:
   (a) **Computing Final Probabilities** takes as input the set $\{t^n\}$, the improved approximate exponents, and returns final probabilities; for a modular operation, its final probability is the probability of that operation being a square;
   (b) **Error Detection and Correction**, for a single trace, it takes as input an improved approximate exponent and the final probabilities; it returns a correct exponent or reports a failure.

Fig. 2. Attack Framework

between its class parameters μ_k, σ_k, Σ_k, $k \in \{0,1\}$ (since the goal is to identify squares and multiplications, we consider only two possible classes). Therefore, in a single trace t^n, the maximum amount of points of interest is ℓ, which is exactly the amount of samples in a modular operation interval. The question here is: which are the points that leaks confidential information according to a pre-defined leakage model? To identify the points of interest, the leakage model is defined as the samples containing observable difference between squares and multiplications (conditional branches, address-bit). These points of interest are the entry for the horizontal attack that provides an approximate exponent for each trace t^n. Finally, the approximate exponents are used to refine the points of interest selection. The horizontal attack might then be repeated to reduce the error rate in the approximate exponents.

Unsupervised Learning for Leakage Assessment. Leakage assessment techniques determine if a cryptographic device is leaking side-channel information according to a specific algorithm and leakage model. Welch t-test is a statistical method which can assess the presence of leakage in cryptographic devices. In the context of public-key algorithms, the document presented in [30] shows a case study of leakage assessment from RSA implementations.

In [29], the authors demonstrate how t-test and mutual information analysis identify the leakage location in time domain. The authors of [27] considered mutual information as a tool to identify the leakage location in the frequency domain and, consequently, the frequency bands in RSA EM traces which contain

larger differences between squares and multiplications. Once the leakage is identified, points of interest can be selected for the application of different forms of
side-channel attacks with appropriate distinguishers.

An RSA implementation protected with exponent blinding provides random
sequences of exponent bits at every execution of the algorithm. The aforementioned application of t-test and mutual information becomes unfeasible since the
operations cannot be initially grouped in different and labeled classes. Recent
publications addressed the use of unsupervised learning method to exploit the
leakage from symmetric and asymmetric cryptographic algorithms [22,23,25].
In [25], the authors considered a device with a fixed key, which is not our case.
The approaches presented in [22,23] do not demonstrate how to precisely identify points of interest. The authors of [23] considered that a heuristic approach
based on difference-of-means for the points of interest selection, which can be
very complex in some cases. [22] proposes to apply a clustering classification to a
single trace which allows labeling the operations in specific classes. The method
works better for low noise measurements and requires a EM station composed
by multiple probes.

To suppress this gap in terms of points of interest location from randomized exponentiations, we demonstrate that we can combine multiple traces for
the leakage assessment even if the device is protected with exponent blinding.
Additional and optional software countermeasures like message and modulus
randomization has no influence against this unsupervised leakage assessment.

As specified in Sect. 3, the terms l_0 and l_1 refer to the amount of squares
and multiplications, respectively, in a single trace $\mathbf{t}^n$. The proportion l_0/l_1 is
approximately constant for every exponentiation. Due to the exponent blinding
countermeasure, the order of squares and multiplications varies from trace to
trace. However, the clustering algorithm classifies samples in k groups taking
into account the amplitude of these samples. The samples are discrete values
represented by an amplitude value, given in volts, and come from the oscilloscope
quantization features (resolution, sampling rate). The position of squares and
multiplications inside the exponentiation loop is irrelevant for the clustering
mechanism. We make the following assumptions:

Assumption 1: At the trace $\mathbf{t}^n$, the mean value for the set of samples $\{t_{i,j}^n\}$ (at
   sample j) for squares and multiplications are, respectively, $\mu_{0,j}^n + \gamma_{0,j}^n$ and
   $\mu_{1,j}^n + \gamma_{1,j}^n$, where $\gamma_{k,j}^n$ is the random noise having Gaussian distribution for
   the class k.

Assumption 2: The means $\mu_{k,j}^n$ are constant values for all traces $\mathbf{t}^n$.

Let us consider the n-th trace represented as a set of samples according to
Eq. 1. We apply a clustering algorithm to each set of samples $\{t_{i:l_0+l_1,j}^n\}$ at a
fixed sampling time j. The clustering returns two centers $c_{0,j}$ and $c_{1,j}$ and two
groups of clustered samples $\{g_{0,j}\}$ and $\{g_{1,j}\}$ containing $p_{0,j}$ and $p_{1,j}$ elements,
respectively, where $p_{0,j} + p_{1,j} \approx l_0 + l_1$.

Now, for every trace $\mathbf{t}^n$, we have a set of parameters $c_{0,j}^n$, $c_{1,j}^n$, $\{g_{0,j}^n\}$, $\{g_{1,j}^n\}$,
$p_{0,j}^n$ and $p_{1,j}^n$ ($j \in \{1,..,\ell\}$) that can be used for the leakage assessment. We

provide results for four different techniques: difference-of-means (DoM), sum-of-squared differences (SOSD), sum-of-squared t-values (SOST), and mutual information analysis (MIA). Because, we expect $p_{0,j}^n \approx l_0$ and $p_{1,j}^n \approx l_1$, we define the following ratio parameters:

$$r_{k,j}^n = \begin{cases} p_{k,j}^n/l_k & \text{if } l_k \geq p_{k,j}^n \\ l_k/p_{k,j}^n & \text{if } l_k \leq p_{k,j}^n \end{cases}$$

The ratio parameters $r_{k,j}^n$ are considered as a multiplication factor in the equations for difference-of-means, SOSD and SOST which are given by:

$$\delta_j = \left(\prod_{k=0}^{1} r_{k,j}^n \right) \left(\frac{1}{N} \sum_{n=1}^{N} |c_{0,j}^n - c_{1,j}^n| \right) \quad \text{(DoM)} \quad (10)$$

$$\varsigma_j = \left(\prod_{k=0}^{1} r_{k,j}^n \right) \left(\frac{1}{N} \sum_{n=1}^{N} |c_{0,j}^n - c_{1,j}^n|^2 \right) \quad \text{(SOSD)} \quad (11)$$

$$\tau_j = \left(\prod_{k=0}^{1} r_{k,j}^n \right) \left(\frac{1}{N} \sum_{n=1}^{N} \left(\frac{|c_{0,j}^n - c_{1,j}^n|}{\sqrt{\frac{\sigma_{0,j}^{2(n)}}{p_{0,j}^n} + \frac{\sigma_{1,j}^{2(n)}}{p_{1,j}^n}}} \right)^2 \right) \quad \text{(SOST)} \quad (12)$$

Considering $\sigma_j^{2(n)}$ as the variance for the sample set $\{g_{0,j}(n)\} \cup \{g_{1,j}(n)\}$, the mutual information value υ_j at each sample index j is computed by deriving the differential entropy [27] for each set of samples according to:

$$\upsilon_j = \sum_{n=1}^{N} \log \sqrt{\frac{1}{p_{0,j}^n + p_{1,j}^n - 1} \sigma_j^{2(n)}} + \sum_{k=0}^{1} (-1)\varrho^k (1-\varrho)^{1-k} \log \sqrt{\frac{1}{(p_{1-k,j}^n) - 1} \sigma_{1-k,j}^{2(n)}} \quad (13)$$

where $\varrho = \frac{p_{0,j}^n}{p_{0,j}^n + p_{1,j}^n}$. The values of υ_j can also be multiplied by the factor $\prod_{k=0}^{1} r_{k,j}^n$ in order to improve the results. Note that the four leakage assessment methods are a sum of individual leakage assessments for each individual trace. The application of clustering algorithms provide an estimation for the mean values $\mu_{k,j}^n$. Due to the aforementioned assumptions on the mean values and due to the summations from equations for SOSD, SOST, DoM and MIA, the noise $\gamma_{k,j}^n$ is eliminated if the number of processed traces is sufficiently large. Figure 3 shows the leakage assessment results for the four aforementioned methods. The time interval represented in this figure is a modular operation interval. The larger peaks in the leakage assessment results indicate the presence of a mixture of distributions with observable difference between its class parameters. A flat line means that the clustered set of samples are drawn from a normal distribution.

Horizontal Attack. The horizontal attack methodology we adopted is based on unsupervised learning approaches [22,23]. The main goal is to create one

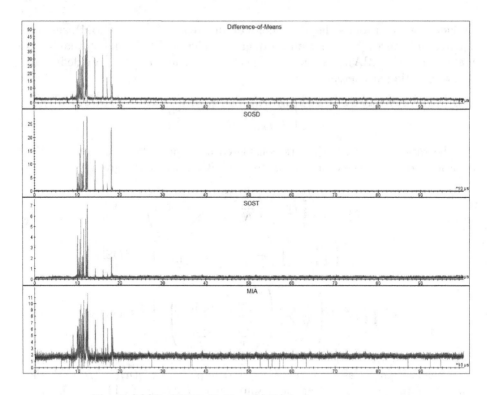

Fig. 3. SOSD, SOST, DoM and MIA leakage assessments.

approximate exponent for each trace $\mathbf{t}^n$. We particularly adopted the method presented in [23], which is divided in four main steps:

1. Trace preprocessings: an exponentiation trace is organized as a set of samples, following Eq. 1.
2. Points of interest selection: for this, we considered the proposed unsupervised learning for leakage assessment, as detailed in the last subsection.
3. Cluster classification of set of samples: the basic idea is to consider a fixed amount of points of interest J_{poi} and apply a clustering algorithm (k-means, fuzzy k-means or EM algorithm) over each set of samples $\{t_{i,j}^n\}$, $i = 1 : aL$ having a fixed $j \in \{1, ..., J_{poi}\}$. A reference point of interest is necessary to associate clusters with classes. The output of this step are exactly J_{poi} clustered sets, grouped into squares and multiplications.
4. Final exponent estimation: the authors of [23] proposed different approaches to provide an approximate exponent for a single trace. Step 3 returns clustered data for J_{poi} sets of samples. It means that J_{poi} candidates for the exponent are given for a single trace. These candidates are combined into one final exponent $\lambda_i^n \in \{0,1\}$, $i = 1..aL$, using statistical classifiers (majority rule, likelihood estimation and Bayes's estimator).

As described in [23], an optimized selection of points of interest is required by this horizontal attack.

Optimizing the Points of Interest Selection. After one approximate exponents is found for each exponentiation trace $\mathbf{t}^n$, we use these outputs to develop a second leakage assessment step which allows us to refine the points of interest selection.

Now, considering the whole set of N measured exponentiation traces and their respective approximate exponents $\lambda_i^n \in \{0,1\}$, $i = 1..aL$, new means and variances are obtained:

$$\mu_{0,j} = \sum_{n=1}^{N} \frac{\sum_{i=1}^{aL}(1 - \lambda_i^n)t_{i,j}^n}{\sum_{i=1}^{aL}(1 - \lambda_i^n)} \qquad \mu_{1,j} = \sum_{n=1}^{N} \frac{\sum_{i=1}^{aL}\lambda_i^n t_{i,j}^n}{\sum_{i=1}^{aL}\lambda_i^n} \tag{14}$$

$$\sigma_{0,j}^2 = \sum_{n=1}^{N} \frac{\sum_{i=1}^{aL}(1 - \lambda_i^n)(t_{i,j}^n - \mu_{0,j})^2}{\sum_{i=1}^{aL}(1 - \lambda_i^n)} \qquad \sigma_{1,j}^2 = \sum_{n=1}^{N} \frac{\sum_{i=1}^{aL}\lambda_i^n(t_{i,j}^n - \mu_{1,j})^2}{\sum_{i=1}^{aL}\lambda_i^n} \tag{15}$$

Having the class parameters (means and variances) and assuming they are drawn from a mixture of Gaussian distributions, the analysis should infer the difference between these distribution parameters and be able to decide whether they lead to observable dissimilarities.

A t-test calculation is a proper solution for this case. Results presenting important peaks indicate that the classes (e.g., squares and multiplications) have observable difference with respect to their distribution parameters. The new t-values τ_j^{new} are obtained with the following equation:

$$\tau_j^{new} = \frac{|\mu_{0,j} - \mu_{1,j}|}{\sqrt{\frac{\sigma_{0,j}^2}{h_{0,j}} + \frac{\sigma_{1,j}^2}{h_{1,j}}}} \qquad h_{0,j} = \sum_{n=1}^{N}\sum_{i=1}^{aL}(1 - \lambda_i^n) \qquad h_{1,j} = \sum_{n=1}^{N}\sum_{i=1}^{aL}\lambda_i^n \tag{16}$$

Figure 4 compares the first and second leakage assessment using t-test. This figure highlights only the part of the modular operation that showed distinct peaks during the first assessment. The optimization step presents more distinct peaks, which are selected as the new points of interest.

After the refinement of points of interest selection, *the horizontal attack is repeated* and supposed to produce new set of approximate exponents $\lambda_i^{new(n)}$ with lower error rates. Table 1 presents examples of error rate results for the approximate exponents before and after the points of interest optimization. All the results were obtained from the same trace set and are provided for all possible combinations of clustering algorithms, leakage assessment method and statistical classifier during the horizontal attack. All combinations of techniques provide fairly similar results. However, the decision for specific methods and algorithms depends on the trace and target features.

4.2   Attacking Phase

The second phase, the attacking phase, aims at recovering the full correct blinded exponent from a single trace.

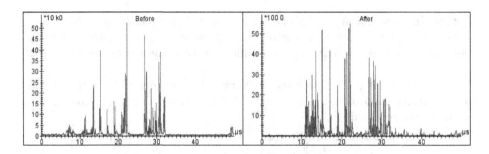

Fig. 4. T-test results before and after the optimized selection of points of interest.

Computing Final Probabilities. In this section, we create a metric to estimate how much the class parameters (mean, variance) were correctly learned
from the blind RSA implementation. The input for the attacking phase is a set
of N traces $\mathbf{t}^n$ labeled with approximate exponent values λ^n. The output of this
phase are so-called final probabilities; for each modular operation O_i^n a final
probability indicates the probability O_i^n is square. Analogously, this part of the
attack framework follows the same methodology of template attacks [15].

Initially, new class parameters $(\mu_k, \sigma_k^2, \Sigma_k, k \in \{0,1\})$ are built (they can
be seen as templates) from the set of labeled traces. We acquired 10000 power
traces from the target device. Therefore, in average $10000 \times 576 = 5.76M$ squares
and $10000 \times 288 = 2.88M$ multiplications are used to build templates. Following,
we apply parametric and multivariate attack models on the same sets of traces.
We compute the likelihood $\mathcal{L}(\theta_k|O_i^n)$ that each modular operation O_i^n belongs
to a specific class θ_k. The likelihoods are used to estimate the final probability
for each modular operation O_i^n.

A *parametric model* is the univariate model where the class parameters are
the mean and the variance. After the determination of the class parameters
for squares $(\mu_{0,j}, \sigma_{0,j}^2)$ and multiplications $(\mu_{1,j}, \sigma_{1,j}^2)$ over the set of points of
interest $j \in \{1, .., J_{poi}\}$, the log-likelihood of a set of parameters for the operation
O_i^n is determined by:

$$\mathcal{L}(\theta_{k,j}|O_i^n) = \mathcal{L}(\mu_{k,j}, \sigma_{k,j}^2|O_i^n) = \sum_{j=1}^{J_{poi}} \log p(t_{i,j}^n|\mu_{k,j}, \sigma_{k,j}^2) \qquad (17)$$

where $p(t_{i,j}^n|\mu_{k,j}, \sigma_{k,j}^2)$ is the probability density function based on the Gaussian
normal density. The *multivariate model* involves the mean vector $\boldsymbol{\mu}_k = \{\mu_{k,j}\}$,
for $j \in \{1, .., J_{poi}\}$, and the covariance Σ_k in the computation of the probability
density function. The log-likelihood is given by:

$$\mathcal{L}(\theta_k|O_i^n) = \mathcal{L}(\mu_k, \Sigma_{k,j}|O_i^n) =$$

$$\log \left(\frac{1}{\sqrt{2\pi^{J_{poi}}|\Sigma|}} exp(-\frac{1}{2}(O_i^n - \boldsymbol{\mu}_k)\Sigma_k^{-1}(O_i^n - \boldsymbol{\mu}_k)^T) \right) \qquad (18)$$

Table 1. Error rate before and after the optimized selection of points of interest.

Clustering Algorithm	First Leakage Assessment Method	Horizontal Attack (Statistical Classifier)	Error rate before optimization	Error rate after optimization
K-MEANS	SOSD	Majority Rule	13.29 %	2.35 %
		Log Likelihood	13.01 %	2.31 %
		Bayes Estimation	12.96 %	2.27 %
	SOST	Majority Rule	11.46 %	2.31 %
		Log Likelihood	11.52 %	1.91 %
		Bayes Estimation	12.96 %	2.38 %
	DoM	Majority Rule	13.06 %	2.34 %
		Log Likelihood	12.46 %	2.36 %
		Bayes Estimation	12.90 %	2.34 %
	MIA	Majority Rule	14.81 %	2.77 %
		Log Likelihood	14.05 %	2.68 %
		Bayes Estimation	14.27 %	2.71 %
FUZZY K-MEANS	SOSD	Majority Rule	10.15 %	1.61 %
		Log Likelihood	10.28 %	1.48 %
		Bayes Estimation	11.37 %	1.83 %
	SOST	Majority Rule	9.45 %	2.11 %
		Log Likelihood	9.33 %	1.27 %
		Bayes Estimation	9.35 %	1.41 %
	DoM	Majority Rule	10.41 %	2.12 %
		Log Likelihood	10.33 %	2.31 %
		Bayes Estimation	10.44 %	1.91 %
	MIA	Majority Rule	10.98 %	1.65 %
		Log Likelihood	10.77 %	1.99 %
		Bayes Estimation	10.40 %	1.85 %
EM ALGORITHM	SOSD	Majority Rule	11.27 %	2.23 %
		Log Likelihood	12.04 %	2.27 %
		Bayes Estimation	11.95 %	2.19 %
	SOST	Majority Rule	10.01 %	1.75 %
		Log Likelihood	9.88 %	1.66 %
		Bayes Estimation	9.97 %	2.12 %
	DoM	Majority Rule	11.98 %	2.47 %
		Log Likelihood	12.01 %	2.43 %
		Bayes Estimation	12.15 %	2.47 %
	MIA	Majority Rule	12.70 %	2.33 %
		Log Likelihood	12.29 %	2.44 %
		Bayes Estimation	12.34 %	2.37 %

The final probability that an operation O_i^n is a square can be given by:

$$p(O_i^n \mid \theta_0) = \frac{\mathcal{L}(\theta_0|O_i^n)}{\mathcal{L}(\theta_0|O_i^n) + \mathcal{L}(\theta_1|O_i^n)} \tag{19}$$

Error Detection and Correction. Due to noise and other aspects that interfere the side-channel analysis (misalignment, clock jitter, etc.), the derivation of the final exponent for a single exponentiation trace may contain errors. If the amount of wrong bits is sufficiently small, a brute-force attack is still feasible to finally recover the correct exponent. However, the attacker needs a metric to indicate the location of the possible wrong bits in the recovered exponent. The final probabilities can be used as a reference for the exponent bits selection with respect to a brute-force attack.

Note that in Table 1, in the column "errors after optimization", the best result, with smallest error rate 1.27 %, is achieved for fuzzy k-means, SOST, and Log Likelihood. Furthermore, for any clustering algorithm used with SOST and Log Likelihood, the error rates are less than 2 %. We are uncertain why the combination of fuzzy k-means, SOST, and Log Likelihood provides the best result, but we suspect the that the reason is target-specific.

Observe that the 1.27 % error rate implies that only $864 \cdot 1.27\% \approx 11$ modular operations are identified incorrectly. In general brute forcing 11 bits is easy, however, the following problem arises: which modular operations are recognized incorrectly? The localization of wrong bits in the recovered exponent is based on calculated likelihood using parametric or multivariate attacks; the probabilities $p(O_i^n|\theta_0)$ are computed for each modular operation. The obtained results indicate less than 20 wrong bits in the exponent if the probabilities interval between 0.45 and 0.55 is considered as the wrong bits interval. A known-key analysis, for this specific case, confirmed that exponent bits with final probabilities between 0.45 and 0.55 contain all wrong guesses. Brute-forcing 20 bits of the RSA key is practical since it can take up to a few hours on a modern PC. Therefore, we confirm that our attack framework recovers the exponent successfully.

5   Conclusions and Future Work

In this work, we presented an attack framework for side-channel attacks on protected RSA implementations. The methodology combines the concepts of unsupervised learning, horizontal attacks, maximum likelihood estimation and template attacks in order to recover the exponent bits.

We proposed an unsupervised learning approach to assess the side-channel leakage even in the presence of exponent and message blinding. We demonstrate that the order of the modular operations inside each exponentiation trace is irrelevant for the leakage analysis; therefore, multiple traces can be processed together in order to find class parameters. If the device leaks SPA-related information, a horizontal attack is able to produce approximate exponents for each exponentiation trace. We demonstrate how these approximate exponents can be used to optimize the leakage location and, finally, refine the determination of approximate exponents. As a final step, the attacker can recover the error bits through the computation of final probabilities for the exponent bits.

To demonstrate the power of our approach we attacked the 1024-bit RSA-CRT implementation protected by the SPA, message blinding, and exponent blinding countermeasures, running on a 32-bit STM32F4 microcontroller. In our experiment the error rate was 1.27 %.

As a future work we consider extending our framework to ECC-based cryptographic protocols [3, 4]; we believe that it should be possible due to similarities between ECC and RSA. Another interesting future work is applying our framework in the frequency domain; the goal would be to check whether it is possible to lower the error rate by using side-channel attacks in the frequency domain instead of the time domain. Furthermore, we believe that our framework can be further improved by recovering error bits faster than by using "brute-force", for example, approaches from [36, 37] can be incorporated into the framework.

References

1. Rivest, R., Shamir, A., Adleman, L.: A method for obtaining digital signatures and public key cryptosystems. Commun. ACM **21**(2), 120–126 (1978)
2. Koblitz, N.: Elliptic curve cryptosystems. Math. Comput. **48**, 203–209 (1987)
3. Miller, V.S.: Use of elliptic curves in cryptography. In: Williams, H.C. (ed.) CRYPTO 1985. LNCS, vol. 218, pp. 417–426. Springer, Heidelberg (1986)
4. Montgomery, P.L.: Speeding the Pollard and elliptic curve methods of factorization. Math. Comput. **48**(177), 243–264 (1987)
5. Kocher, P.C.: Timing attacks on implementations of Diffie-Hellman, RSA, DSS, and other systems. In: Koblitz, N. (ed.) CRYPTO 1996. LNCS, vol. 1109, pp. 104–113. Springer, Heidelberg (1996)
6. Kocher, P.C., Jaffe, J., Jun, B.: Differential power analysis. In: Wiener, M. (ed.) CRYPTO 1999. LNCS, vol. 1666, pp. 388–397. Springer, Heidelberg (1999)
7. Brier, E., Clavier, C., Olivier, F.: Correlation power analysis with a leakage model. In: Joye, M., Quisquater, J.-J. (eds.) CHES 2004. LNCS, vol. 3156, pp. 16–29. Springer, Heidelberg (2004)
8. Fouque, P.-A., Valette, F.: The doubling attack – *why upwards is better than downwards*. In: Walter, C.D., Koç, Ç.K., Paar, C. (eds.) CHES 2003. LNCS, vol. 2779, pp. 269–280. Springer, Heidelberg (2003)
9. Bajard, J.-C., Imbert, L., Liardet, P.-Y., Teglia, Y.: Leak resistant arithmetic. In: Joye, M., Quisquater, J.-J. (eds.) CHES 2004. LNCS, vol. 3156, pp. 62–75. Springer, Heidelberg (2004)
10. Courrège, J.-C., Feix, B., Roussellet, M.: Simple power analysis on exponentiation revisited. In: Gollmann, D., Lanet, J.-L., Iguchi-Cartigny, J. (eds.) CARDIS 2010. LNCS, vol. 6035, pp. 65–79. Springer, Heidelberg (2010)
11. Homma, N., Miyamoto, A., Aoki, T., Satoh, A., Shamir, A.: Comparative power analysis of modular exponentiation algorithms. IEEE Trans. Comput. **59**(6), 795–807 (2010)
12. Coron, J.-S.: Resistance against differential power analysis for elliptic curve cryptosystems. In: Koç, Ç.K., Paar, C. (eds.) CHES 1999. LNCS, vol. 1717, pp. 292–302. Springer, Heidelberg (1999)

13. Dupaquis, V., Venelli, A.: Redundant modular reduction algorithms. In: Prouff, E. (ed.) CARDIS 2011. LNCS, vol. 7079, pp. 102–114. Springer, Heidelberg (2011)
14. Joye, M., Yen, S.-M.: The Montgomery powering ladder. In: Kaliski Jr., B.S., Koç, Ç.K., Paar, C. (eds.) CHES 2002. LNCS, vol. 2523, pp. 291–302. Springer, Heidelberg (2003)
15. Chari, S., Rao, J.R., Rohatgi, P.: Template attacks. In: Kaliski, B.S., Koc, C.K., Paar, C. (eds.) CHES'02. LNCS, vol. 2523, pp. 13–28. Springer, Heidelberg (2002)
16. Walter, C.D.: Sliding windows succumbs to big mac attack. In: Koç, Ç.K., Naccache, D., Paar, C. (eds.) CHES 2001. LNCS, vol. 2162, pp. 286–299. Springer, Heidelberg (2001)
17. Clavier, C., Feix, B., Gagnerot, G., Roussellet, M., Verneuil, V.: Horizontal correlation analysis on exponentiation. In: Soriano, M., Qing, S., López, J. (eds.) ICICS 2010. LNCS, vol. 6476, pp. 46–61. Springer, Heidelberg (2010)
18. Clavier, C., Feix, B., Gagnerot, G., Giraud, C., Roussellet, M., Verneuil, V.: ROSETTA for single trace analysis. In: Galbraith, S., Nandi, M. (eds.) INDOCRYPT 2012. LNCS, vol. 7668, pp. 140–155. Springer, Heidelberg (2012)
19. Bauer, A., Jaulmes, E., Prouff, E., Wild, J.: Horizontal and vertical side-channel attacks against secure RSA implementations. In: Dawson, E. (ed.) CT-RSA 2013. LNCS, vol. 7779, pp. 1–17. Springer, Heidelberg (2013)
20. Bauer, A., Jaulmes, É.: Correlation analysis against protected SFM implementations of RSA. In: Paul, G., Vaudenay, S. (eds.) INDOCRYPT 2013. LNCS, vol. 8250, pp. 98–115. Springer, Heidelberg (2013)
21. Bauer, A., Jaulmes, E., Prouff, E., Wild, J.: Horizontal collision correlation attack on elliptic curves. Reasearch Gate (2014)
22. Heyszl, J., Ibing, A., Mangard, S., Santis F., Sigl, G.: Clustering algorithms for non-profiled single-execution attacks on exponentiations. IACR Cryptology ePrint Archive, vol. 2013, p. 438, 2013 (2013)
23. Perin, G., Imbert, L., Torres, L., Maurine, P.: Attacking randomized exponentiations using unsupervised learning. In: Prouff, E. (ed.) COSADE 2014. LNCS, vol. 8622, pp. 144–160. Springer, Heidelberg (2014)
24. Bauer, S.: Attacking exponent blinding in RSA without CRT. In: Schindler, W., Huss, S.A. (eds.) COSADE 2012. LNCS, vol. 7275, pp. 82–88. Springer, Heidelberg (2012)
25. Batina, L., Gierlichs, B., Lemke-Rust, K.: Differential cluster analysis. In: Clavier, C., Gaj, K. (eds.) CHES 2009. LNCS, vol. 5747, pp. 112–127. Springer, Heidelberg (2009)
26. Batina, L., Gierlichs, B., Prouff, E., Rivain, M., Standaert, F.X., Charvillon, N.V.: Mutual information analysis: a comprehensive study. J. Cryptology **24**(2), 269–291 (2011)
27. Meynard, O., Réal, D., Flament, F., Guilley, S., Homma N., Danger, J.L.: Enhancement of simple electro-magnetic attacks by pre-characterization in frequency domain and demodulation techniques. In: Proceedings of Design, Automation and Test in Europe (DATE), pp. 1004–1009. IEEE (2011)
28. Krämer, J., Nedospasov, D., Seifert, J.-P.: Weaknesses in current RSA signature schemes. In: Kim, H. (ed.) ICISC 2011. LNCS, vol. 7259, pp. 155–168. Springer, Heidelberg (2012)
29. Mather, L., Oswald, E., Bandenburg, J., Wójcik, M.: Does my device leak information? An *a priori* statistical power analysis of leakage detection tests. In: Sako, K., Sarkar, P. (eds.) ASIACRYPT 2013, Part I. LNCS, vol. 8269, pp. 486–505. Springer, Heidelberg (2013)

30. Jaffe, J., Rohatgi, P., Witteman, M.: Efficient side-channel testing for public key algorithms: RSA case study, report (2011)
31. Alpaydin, E.: Introduction to Machine Learning, 3rd edn. The MIT Press, London (2014)
32. Hanley, N., Kim, H.S., Tunstall, M.: Exploiting collisions in addition chain-based exponentiation algorithms using a single trace. In: Nyberg, K. (ed.) CT-RSA 2015. LNCS, vol. 9048, pp. 429–446. Springer, Heidelberg (2015)
33. Duda, R.O., Hart, P.E., Stork, D.G.: Pattern Classification, 2nd edn. Wiley-Interscience, New York (2001)
34. Bishop, C.M.: Pattern Recognition and Machine Learning (Information Science and Statistics). Springer, USA (2007)
35. Goodwill, G., Jun, B., Jaffe, J., Rohatgi, P.: A testing methodology for side channel resistance validation. In: Non-Invasive Attack Testing Workshop – NIAT (2011)
36. Bauer, S.: Attacking exponent blinding in RSA without CRT. In: Schindler, W., Huss, S.A. (eds.) COSADE 2012. LNCS, vol. 7275, pp. 82–88. Springer, Heidelberg (2012)
37. Heninger, N., Shacham, H.: Reconstructing RSA private keys from random key bits. In: Halevi, S. (ed.) CRYPTO 2009. LNCS, vol. 5677, pp. 1–17. Springer, Heidelberg (2009)
38. EMV, EMVCo Security Evaluation Process, Security Guidelines, Version 0.5, March 2005

Java Cards

seTPM: Towards Flexible Trusted Computing on Mobile Devices Based on GlobalPlatform Secure Elements

Sergej Proskurin[1], Michael Weiß[2(✉)], and Georg Sigl[1]

[1] Technische Universität München, Munich, Germany
{sergej.proskurin,sigl}@tum.de
[2] Fraunhofer Institut AISEC, Garching, Germany
michael.weiss@aisec.fraunhofer.de

Abstract. Insufficiently protected mobile devices present a ubiquitous threat. Due to severe hardware constraints, such as limited printed circuit board area, hardware-based security as proposed by the Trusted Computing Group is usually not part of mobile devices, yet. We present the design and implementation of seTPM, a secure element based TPM, utilizing Java Card technology. seTPM establishes trust in mobile devices by enabling Trusted Computing based integrity measurement services, such as IMA for Linux. Our prototype emulates TPM functionality on a GlobalPlatform secure element, which allows seamless integration into the Trusted Software Stack of Linux-based mobile operating systems like Android. With our work, we provide a solution to run Trusted Computing based security protocols while supplying a similar security level as provided by hardware TPM chips. In addition, due to the flexible design of the seTPM, we further increase the security level as we are able to selectively replace the outdated SHA-1 hash algorithm of TPM 1.2 specification by the present KECCAK algorithm. Further, our architecture comprises hybrid support for the TPM 1.2 and TPM 2.0 specifications to simplify the transition towards the TPM 2.0 standard.

1 Introduction

The shift from the era of primitive mobile devices to full-blown general purpose smart phones significantly affected the importance of mobile security. Becoming omnipresent, the mobile market turned out to be very attractive for cyber-criminals: The continuously rising computing power, management of personal information, as well as the potential interoperability with corporate networks and services present an ideal base for various cyber-attacks. Software security hardening solutions, such as antivirus products, try to mitigate the stated issues. However, there is no guarantee that software-based security hardening measures themselves cannot become victims of cyber-attacks and thus be intentionally misused by malware. Because of this, software-based security hardening solutions alone cannot always provide trust.

For this purpose, hardware supported security hardening measures are needed. Therefore, modern embedded systems rely on the concepts of *Trusted*

© Springer International Publishing Switzerland 2016
N. Homma and M. Medwed (Eds.): CARDIS 2015, LNCS 9514, pp. 57–74, 2016.
DOI: 10.1007/978-3-319-31271-2_4

Computing [1] integrated into isolated, hardware supported, environments such as *Trusted Platform Modules* (TPMs) [2,3] and *Trusted Execution Environments* (TEEs) [4,5]. A TPM presents a dedicated microprocessor that is utilized to establish trust between communication partners. It comprises secure storage capabilities for cryptographic keys and cryptographic co-processors to provide reliable integrity measurement and remote attestation services. On the other hand, a TEE is usually part of the main processor and provides an isolated execution environment for *Trusted Applications* (TAs), which can be executed concurrently to a rich operating system. The *Trusted Computing Group* (TCG) and the *GlobalPlatform* jointly elaborated a TPM 2.0 Mobile architecture [6] that can be implemented as a TA [7]. However, TEE-based solutions cannot provide the same isolation as TPMs, e.g., concerning side-channel vulnerabilities. Although a dedicated *Mobile Trusted Module* (MTM) [8] has been specified, it has not yet been accepted within the world of mobile devices. One reason for this is that mobile devices suffer from severe hardware constraints, such as printed circuit board area. Another reason is that usually a dedicated security chip is already deployed in most modern smartphones for other purposes like secure payment.

Our work introduces a TPM implementation for GlobalPlatform specified *secure elements* (SEs) providing flexibility of software- and tamper resistance of hardware supported approaches without the need for additional circuit area. We based our work on the software TPM emulator for Linux [9]. In contrast to this software-only solution, our implementation has been designed to run on Java Card technology [10] based SEs. In short, the seTPM presents a highly portable and tamper resistant TPM emulator that can be easily integrated in modern mobile architectures. Our contributions comprise the following features:

- The seTPM extends the idea of a portable TPM emulator in [9] in a way that it becomes applicable to virtually every platform being able to interface with GlobalPlatform specified secure elements.
- The seTPM software architecture enables transparent integration into Trusted Computing applications like *Integrity Measurement Architecture* (IMA) [11].
- We show that the seTPM can be functionally extended according to individual requirements. Our implementation extends the TPM 1.2 specification [12] on demand, by exchanging the SHA-1 with the KECCAK [13] hash algorithm.
- We provide a KECCAK implementation for Java Card to further increase the security level compared to modern hardware TPM chips.
- We present an architecture of a hybrid system combining the TPM 1.2 and TPM 2.0 standards.
- Further security enhancement is discussed by facing hardware reset attacks.

The rest of this paper is organized as follows: After providing related work in Sect. 2, we present background information in Sect. 3. The architecture and design of seTPM is described in Sect. 4. We discuss and evaluate our implementation in Sect. 5. Finally, we conclude the paper in Sect. 6.

2   Related Work

Strasser and Stamer [9] introduce a software-based TPM emulator. Their implementation presents a Unix-platform independent realization of the TPM 1.2 specification [12] in software, providing a perfectly suitable environment for testing, research, and educational purposes. seTPM adopts the concepts of the TPM emulator within the context of Java Card technology based SEs. Thus, seTPM extends capabilities of the TPM emulator by providing a hardware supported, isolated, execution environment.

Costan et al. [14] introduce a concept called *Trusted Execution Module* (TEM), providing a secure and tamper resistant execution environment in form of a Java Card applet. The execution environment of a TEM comprises a virtual machine executing user provided execution primitives, called closures. In contrast to seTPM, TEM does not focus on system integrity measurement and attestation capabilities but rather provides a general-purpose execution environment that is similar to TEEs of modern processors.

Portable TPM (PTM) has been presented by Zhang et al. [15]. Similar to seTPM, PTM has been implemented for Java Cards providing TPM-like functionality. Unlike seTPM, Zhang et al. follow a user centric approach by binding the PTM to users. This concept establishes trust between users and remote challengers and provides the flexibility of being able to be utilized across different platforms. However, the PTM requires migratable Storage- and Attestation Root Keys, managed by additional TPMs on the respective platforms.

Within the context of multi-application smartcard environments, Akram et al. [16] present the *Trusted Environment and Execution Manager* (TEM) that acts as a TPM for smartcards. Hence, TEM introduces the concepts of Trusted Computing directly into secure elements ensuring trustworthiness of the individual smart card applications.

With vTPM, Berger et al. [17] integrate their own TPM implementation into a Xen-hypervisor providing a software-based trusted environment for virtual machines. This way, Berger et al. establish a flexible multi-context TPM, providing TPM functionality to multiple virtualized environments. Similar to vTPM, given sufficient memory resources, the isolation capabilities of Java Card applets in SEs may manage multiple instances of seTPM, providing similar functionality.

3   Background

To maintain the property of trust, the TCG defines a *Trusted Computing Base* (TCB) to be a part of the system. The TCB comprises so called *roots of trust* that are considered as inherently trustworthy: These are the *Root of Trust for Measurement* (RTM), *Root of Trust for Storage* (RTS) and *Root of Trust for Reporting* (RTR). Usually RTS and RTR are represented by a TPM. A TPM symbolizes a *trust anchor* simplifying detection of potentially malicious code and protection of cryptographic keys from physical theft and distribution.

3.1 TCG Software Architecture

The TCG software architecture provides a modular design that distributes tasks across layers in user- and kernel space (Fig. 1). Every layer of the TCG architecture provides an abstract interface towards its upper layer. The user space components, also referred to as the *TCG Software Stack* (TSS), comprise the *TCG Device Driver Library* (TDDL), *TCG Software Stack Core Services* (TCS), *TCG Service Provider* (TSP), and an application making use of these layers. In short, the TPM device driver establishes a communication with the TPM, providing an interface towards the user space layers. The TDDL layer maintains a uniform and operating system independent interface towards the TCS layer. The TCS layer yields core services, such as key-, credential- and context-management. The TSP layer comprises a C-library, utilized by Trusted Computing applications. On Linux-based devices, the open source TrouSerS library [18] provides the TSS of the platform, which is accessed through the *tcsd* user space daemon. As shown in Fig. 1, the user space layers of the TSS-2.0 differ entirely from its TSS-1.2 counterpart. The *System API* (SAPI) replaces the TDDL and thus directly interfaces and communicates with the TPM device driver via raw byte commands. The upper layers – *Feature API* and *Extended System API* (ESAPI) – serve as abstraction layers. The *Resource Manger*, *TPM Access Broker* (TAB), and *TPM Command Transmission Interface* (TCTI) layers are optional, transparent, layers providing further features such as the scheduling of multiple TPM sessions and TPMs in user space. For further reading on TSS-2.0, we refer to [19].

3.2 Java Card Technology

The Java Card technology provides a uniform platform, implemented on various SE architectures. Its specification comprises a *Java Card Virtual Machine* (JCVM), a *Java Card Runtime Environment* (JCRE), and a *Java Card API* [10]. These components represent the actual Java Card platform. The JCVM and JCRE enable hardware abstraction and provide a universal API for Java Card applet developers. The communication between the host and the Java Card is established via a message passing based protocol, exchanging *Application Protocol Data Units* (APDU) [20]. An APDU represents a self-contained message

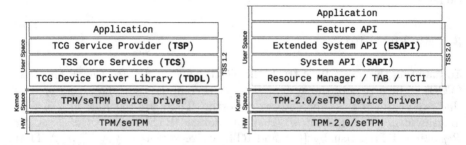

Fig. 1. TCG software interfaces and services to communicate with a TPM-1.2 [1] and TPM-2.0 [19]. Highlighted layers present modifications of the TCG architecture.

enclosing either command- or response-information. A command APDU comprises a header and a body. The header contains information, specifying the instruction class and type (CLA and INS) and instruction parameters (P1 and P2). The body of a command APDU indicates the size of the data to follow (Lc) and the maximum number of bytes of the response APDU to receive (Le). The Response APDU comprises a body, including the response information, and a trailer, indicating the status of the processed instruction.

Shareable Interface. A Java Card application comprises multiple Java Card applets associated with a single package. In other words, applets belonging to the same package share a joint object space, also referred to as a context. The applet firewall enforced by the JCRE strictly constrains the access to data belonging to another context. To permit communication and data sharing throughout the applet firewall and thus between different contexts, applets have to implement the *Shareable* interface of the Java Card API. This way, so called server applets may share selected functionality with chosen client applets from different contexts. To acquire access to this functionality an applet has to request a reference of the particular *Shareable Interface Object* (SIO) through defined system calls.

4 Architecture and Design of seTPM

The idea behind seTPM is a transparent integration into Trusted Computing based applications and the ability to functionally extend the emulated TPM according to individual requirements. These characteristics present an inherent component of the seTPM architecture. Figure 2 gives an overview of our system architecture, which integrates Trusted Computing applications into mobile devices using a GlobalPlatform defined secure element, e.g., in form of a microSD card. Due to its popularity and open source character, our architecture particularly targets mobile devices running the Android operating system. In general, applications communicate with the seTPM by setting off TPM commands. TPM commands traverse the entire TSS before they are forwarded by the Data Transfer Management System to the seTPM applets running on the GlobalPlatform SE. Our architecture introduces a switchable hashing engine allowing to choose between the SHA-1 and the KECCAK algorithm. The KECCAK algorithm can produce hash values of arbitrary sizes, and thus can be seamlessly integrated into the TPM 1.2 specified protocol. Further, to ease the transition towards the TPM 2.0 standard, we propose a hybrid system supporting both TPM specifications by two interacting seTPM applets residing on the same SE and sharing key resources by means of a server applet.

4.1 Hardware Design

The conceptual hardware design of our project comprises three main components: a *host*, a *card acceptance device* (CAD), and a *secure element*. Within the context of seTPM, the host represents an Android mobile device, such as a smart

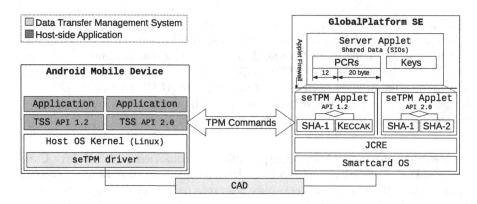

Fig. 2. seTPM system architecture

phone or tablet. The employed SE supports Java Card technology with cryptographically relevant functions. The CAD bridges the interface between the host and SE by transparently forwarding requests and replies in form of APDUs. A CAD should be seen as a means for the purpose of provisioning a communication medium and can be realized, e.g., by conventional card readers.

4.2 Software Design

The software design of seTPM has been adopted from the TCG software architecture [1] being presented in Sect. 3.1. Along with security aspects, seTPM has been designed with flexibility concerning the scope of application and ease of extensibility in mind. To meet these goals, the software architecture of seTPM is divided into three isolated components, which can be incorporated into TCG-compliant systems: These comprise a *host-side application*, a *data transfer management system*, and a *secure element based Trusted Platform Module*. They are described in detail in the following.

Host-Side Application. The host-side application basically combines all user space TCG components, namely the TSS and the actual application making use of the TSS layers (Fig. 1). It is conceivable to extend the TDDL and the SAPI (TSS 2.0), respectively, in order to preprocess and forward APDUs to and from the seTPM device driver. This way, the TDDL/SAPI layer would be able to directly communicate with the seTPM and simultaneously maintain its initial functionality comprising abstraction of the underlying hardware implementation towards its upper layers. However, the kernel should be able to start measuring integrity of the underlying system before userspace is initialized and the associated libraries are loaded. Therefore, we shifted the TCG architecture adjustments to the lower levels residing in kernel space (highlighted layers in Fig. 1). Thus, the initial behavior of the user space components of the TCG architecture remains unchanged. This allows to transparently incorporate the seTPM into existing Trusted Computing applications without the need for additional user space libraries.

Secure Element Based Trusted Platform Module. Our Java Card technology based SE needs to implement the TPM 1.2 [12] and the TPM 2.0 command specification [21] as two isolated applets, each with its own *Application Identifier* (AID). The idea is to share resources, such as *Platform Configuration Registers* (PCRs) and root keys, between both instances using the *Shareable* interface [22] of the underlying Java Card API, as being discussed in Sect. 3.2. This interface allows to share objects throughout the applet firewall in form of so called SIOs. Our server applet manages the creation of and the access to these SIOs. In terms of compatibility, the size of PCRs must be increased from 20 to 32 bytes. The lower 20 bytes can be used by the TPM 1.2 protocol whereas the upper 12 bytes are additionally utilized by the TPM 2.0 implementation. Thus, TPM 2.0 compliant integrity measurements utilizing the SHA-256 hash algorithm can be assured. In short, this approach meets SE related hardware constraints and additionally allows to support a set of Trusted Computing applications implementing different TPM protocols. For instance, in the event of a legacy trusted boot process, the seTPM may measure integrity and extend its PCR values by applying the original TPM 1.2 functionality. Further integrity measurements may, however, appropriately pad and extend the stored 160 bit values by utilizing the specified SHA-256 hash algorithm. For this, the associated remote attestation party needs to consider this chain of events or simply maintain valid hash values to preserve anonymity. In addition, our design implements an explicit hash algorithm switch inside the TPM 1.2 applet. For legacy/backward compatibility or if not explicitly specified by the host we make use of the SHA-1 algorithm. The host may issue a switch command to change the hash engine to KECCAK at any time by providing owner credentials. However, in that case, a reset is necessary to get consistent PCR states.

Data Transfer Management System. The data transfer management system presents a kernel module in form of a device driver. The general idea is to enable a communication between the host-side application and seTPM so that the integrity measurement services provided by seTPM are transparently made available to both, kernel- and user space applications. As a result, not only user space applications but also the operating system kernel can perform integrity measurements, e.g., of kernel modules, security-critical system configuration, and certain applications, even before user space components have been initialized. The seTPM device driver hides details concerning low level communication between the host and seTPM. This way, it is possible to communicate with a particular seTPM via different communication standards, such as PC/SC[1].

For the actual communication, we define a protocol that wraps incoming TPM requests into case-4 command APDU messages, which are then forwarded to the seTPM (left part of Fig. 3). To simplify the interpretation of incoming APDUs on the seTPM side, individual TPM request meta information fields are mapped to command APDUs as shown in Table 1. The command APDU entry

---

[1] Personal Computer/Smart Card (PC/SC) specifies the communication between a host computer and a smartcard.

Table 1. TPM request header to APDU header mapping

APDU header	TPM 1.2	TPM 2.0
CLA	0xB0 | CLA xor 0x01	
INS	TAG[0]	
P1	ORDINAL[3]	TPM_CC[1]
P2	ORDINAL[0]	TPM_CC[0]
Lc	PARAMSIZE[0] | MAX_APDU_PAYLOAD	

Lc, representing APDU size, is limited to $min(\texttt{MAX\_APDU\_PAYLOAD}, 255)$ byte. This limitation is explained by vendor specific maximum APDU sizes of the Java Card. In case a TPM request exceeds this size, the APDU entry CLA signalizes data to follow with a set *chaining bit* – the chaining bit is the least significant bit of the CLA header entry. Chained TPM requests reuse the header of the first transmitted command APDU. The end of a TPM request chain is identified by a clear chaining bit. Besides, only two bytes (MSB and LSB) of ordinals within TPM requests carry significant information. Thus, remaining bytes are left out of the mapping, as shown in Table 1. The same applies to TPM 2.0 specified command codes. Only the first two bytes are relevant as shown in [21]. The format of TPM responses embedded in response APDU messages is visualized in the right part of Fig. 3. Received response APDU messages contain TPM responses, which are extracted and subsequently passed to the TDDL/SAPI layer of the TCG architecture (Fig. 1). TPM responses exceeding the limit of $min(\texttt{MAX\_APDU\_PAYLOAD}, 256)$ byte are divided into multiple chained response APDUs. Chained response APDU messages are detected by analyzing the actual size of the TPM response embedded within the body of the respective APDU. In case of a chained response, the data transfer management system needs to assemble the complete TPM response before forwarding it to the TDDL or the SAPI layer, respectively.

4.3   Extension of TPM 1.2

The TPM 1.2 specification utilizes the SHA-1 algorithm for hash values and as part of the *Message Authentication Code* (MAC) computation. The SHA-1 cryptographic hash algorithm generates 160-bit (i.e. 20 bytes) hash values from

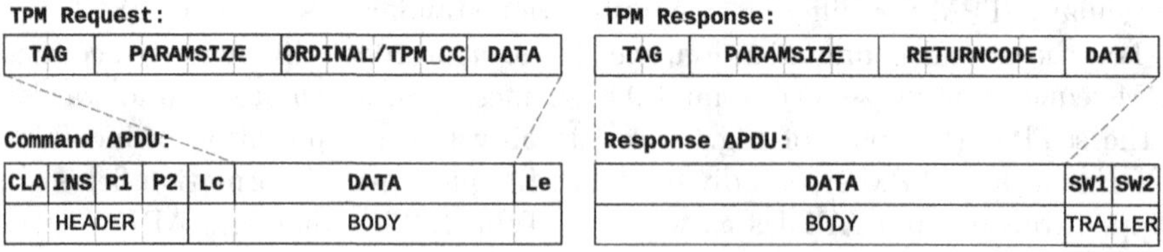

Fig. 3. Integration of TPM requests and extraction of TPM responses from APDUs.

messages of arbitrary sizes. To find a collision using a brute force method, one would need to calculate hash values of about 2^{80} random messages. However, Wang et al. [23] showed that for the SHA-1 algorithm collisions can be found with complexity of only 2^{69}. To increase the collision-resistance of the SHA-1 hash algorithm and simultaneously to maintain the field lengths of the TPM protocol according to the TPM 1.2 specification, our design introduces the KECCAK hash algorithm [13]. The KECCAK hash algorithm belongs to the *sponge function* family being able to produce hash values of any desired length and is the algorithm behind SHA-3, the latest successor of SHA-1. Because NIST specified SHA-3 by limiting arbitrary hash lengths to four values, namely to 224, 256, 384, and 512 bit [24], we decided to utilize the original KECCAK algorithm to generate hashes of 160 bit and simultaneously provide collision-resistance of the strength of 2^{160}. As specified in [13], the KECCAK sponge function makes use of the parameters KECCAK$[r,c,d]$ with *bitrate r*, *capacity c*, and *diversifier d* [25]. The bitrate r presents the block size, meaning the maximum number of bits that are processed at every iteration step. The capacity c can be seen as a security parameter. KECCAK claims to be resistant against collision-attacks with complexity of $2^{c/2}$ and against preimage-attacks with complexity of 2^c although the output length N may be higher. The diversifier d is meant to make two KECCAK instances utilizing equal parameters r and c to produce different results. KECCAK applies so called KECCAK-f permutations on its internal state with the width of $b = r + c$ bit, whereas the state width b is limited to the values $b \in \{25, 50, 100, 200, 400, 800, 1600\}$. The state represents a three-dimensional $5 * 5 * w$ bit array. To achieve best performance, w may be chosen similarly to the word size on the CPU with $w \in \{1, 2, 4, 8, 16, 32, 64\}$ (i.e. 16 bit CPUs should use the parameter $w = 16$). Consequently, seTPM supports KECCAK $[80,320,0]$, providing maximum security for the resulting $N = 160$ bit hash values.

4.4 Countering Reset Attacks

Earlier TPM 1.1b [26] specified chips were prone to so called *reset attacks* [27]. In this scenario, the weakest link was given by the *Low Pin Count* (LPC) bus connecting TPMs with the southbridge of their host system. Kauer [27] showed that a TPM can be reset through an induction of the *LRESET#* signal without restarting the system. A subsequent invocation of TPM_Startup(TPM_CLEAR) puts the TPM and its PCRs in a default state. Ergo, an attacker can extend the PCRs to reproduce a consistent state despite system integrity manipulations.

The TPM 1.2 specification approached this issue by introducing the concept of *Locality*. Apart from Legacy Locality, this concept classifies execution entities, such as the RTM, trusted OS, and trusted hardware, on the basis of five Locality levels. These levels represent a certain level of trust that is encoded into the address of the LPC start cycle. Thus, upon command reception, a TPM 1.2 specified chip identifies the active level of trust and regulates access, especially reset, to certain PCRs. The Locality level of 4 is applied only within the context of special CPU instructions such as those introduced by Intel *Trusted eXecution Technology* (TXT) and AMD *Secure Virtual Machine* (SVM) (SENTER/SKINIT).

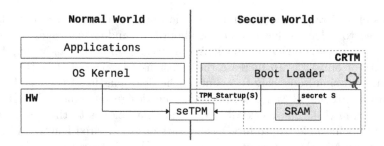

Fig. 4. seTPM grants state resets originated only from the CRTM.

Consequently, illegal attempts to reset the associated dynamic PCRs (PCR17–22) by software are detected resulting in a prevention of reset attacks. Yet, Winter et al. [28] manage to hijack the LPC bus to effectively emulate Locality level 4 interactions so that it becomes possible to reset the TPM state.

In mobile devices, SEs in form of SD cards can be physically accessed by potential adversaries and even reset by software at any time. This way, all volatile state of SE applications gets lost. Since the design of seTPM maintains PCR values in persistent memory (EEPROM), a volatile state loss is not a concern. On the other hand, the Java Card framework cannot distinguish between hardware and software card resets. Within the context of seTPM, hardware resets are tolerated. Software induced card resets through special APDUs must be intercepted to prevent reset attacks. This leads to the question how to determine when the TPM_Startup command is allowed to reset the PCR values of seTPM.

To face reset attacks on smartcards that cannot distinguish between hard and soft reset, we propose a hardware-assisted solution that can be realized with modern mobile device architectures, such as ARM *TrustZone* (TZ) [29]. A simplified architecture is shown in Fig. 4. In general, ARM TZ introduces the concept of two strongly isolated worlds: The *secure* and the *normal world*. The normal world executes a rich *operating system* (OS), whereas the secure world hosts trusted applications. ARM TZ provides among others secure SRAM for key storage. Access to the secure SRAM is regulated by the so called *TrustZone Memory Adapter* (TZMA), whereas the access is granted only when the CPU is in a privileged mode called secure world. We propose to use an immutable, signed, boot loader or locked flash memory as the *Core Root of Trust for Measurement* (CRTM). As shown in Fig. 4, the boot loader is placed inside of the high-privileged secure world and starts the OS kernel in the less-privileged normal world. Our design assumes the boot loader to generate a random secret that is stored in the secure, persistent memory. Due to the flexibility of seTPM, we are able to parametrize the TPM_Startup command so that the generated secret can be persistently stored inside of seTPM. Section 4.5 discusses the individual steps required for a secure secret transfer. During the seTPM initialization, the TPM_Startup handler of seTPM determines when the TPM state must be reset.

1. The initial setup of seTPM is determined by a missing secret. In this case, the TPM_Startup command initializes the secret on the SE and sets its state to default values, respectively.
2. Further setup attempts compare the maintained secret with the provided secret value of the TPM_Startup command. In case the compared values match, the seTPM continues setting its state to default values. Otherwise, the command is aborted keeping the old PCR values.

This method assures that only the boot loader is able to reset the seTPM state. Reset attack attempts could be reported through custom seTPM commands.

4.5   Secure System Initialization

As being discussed in Sect. 4.4, it is the task of the immutable boot loader to generate a secret that is shared between the mobile host and seTPM. To prevent potential abuse, the secret must be maintained on both sides in a secure way so that it cannot be accessed by adversaries. Thus, on the mobile host side, the secret is stored within the secure SRAM that can be accessed only from the secure world. The seTPM side provides tamper resistant capabilities preventing illegal access. Yet, the communication channel between the host and seTPM can be attacked. Thus, the secret must be delivered in a way that provides integrity, confidentiality, and prevents eavesdropped messages from being replayed.

As shown in Fig. 5, to provide integrity and confidentiality, the bootloader must encrypt the generated secret and its hash value with a public key of seTPM. For this, the bootloader can make use of a crypto co-processor that is often part of the ARM architecture. Since the bootloader is signed, the cryptographic functionality must already be part of the code base and can be reused for our purposes. Replay attacks can be prevented by interpreting the secret value as a counter. After initial transfer of the secret towards seTPM, the associated TPM_Startup handler will reset the TPM state only on reception of the value secret+1. In case the adversary manages to inject a crafted TPM_Startup request into the communication channel before the host, she could take over control of seTPM. Because of this, we suggest to bind seTPM to the associated mobile device as part of a device pairing process in a physically secured environment.

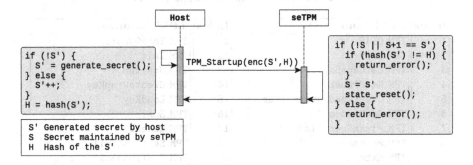

Fig. 5. Tasks performed by the mobile host and seTPM on TPM_Startup invocation.

5   Prototype Implementation

The software implementation of seTPM comprises a host-side application, a data transfer management system, and a Java Card applet representing the seTPM. The host-side application may represent any Trusted Computing application utilizing the services provided by a conventional TPM. TrouSerS [18] provides a set of *tpm-tools* which enable the use of basic TPM services on Linux-based systems. These tpm-tools employ the TrouSerS library providing the TSS (Fig. 1). To demonstrate the seamless integration of seTPM into Trusted Computing environments, we utilized tpm-tools to provide a TSS 1.2 compliant implementation of the host-side application. As being discussed in Sect. 4.2, the data transfer management system manages the communication between the host-side application and the seTPM. This part is implemented as a device driver maintaining a PC/SC connection with the SE. The last bit of our implementation concerns the seTPM Java Card applet providing TPM 1.2 functionality. Our current implementation supports 20 commands as specified by [12]. The supported commands are listed in Table 2. Every TPM command processes incoming data and subsequently generates a TPM response. If the TPM response exceeds the maximum number of bytes that can be embedded into a response APDU, the message is split up into chunks. Thus, the host's data transfer management system becomes responsible to request the remaining chunks of the TPM response.

5.1   Challenges

For our prototype implementation, we had to cope with various challenges which are discussed in the following. Severe resource constraints of SEs generally present one significant difficulty. As a result, the use of SEs with higher resource capacities may solve issues that might have affected earlier implementations.

Memory Management. Java Card technology based secure elements utilize RAM and EEPROM for different purposes. Volatile RAM is used for temporary computations, whereas EEPROM is used to persistently store code and data of

Table 2. TPM commands supported by seTPM.

Index	TPM Command	Index	TPM Command
1	TPM_OIAP	11	TPM_TakeOwnership
2	TPM_OSAP	12	TPM_Init
3	TPM_GetCapability	13	TPM_Startup
4	TPM_ReadPubek	14	TPM_CreateWrapKey
5	TPM_OwnerReadInternalPub	15	TPM_LoadKey
6	TPM_GetRandom	16	TPM_Seal
7	TPM_FlushSpecific	17	TPM_Unseal
8	TPM_PcrRead	18	TPM_SelfTestFull
9	TPM_Extend	19	TPM_ContinueSelfTest
10	TPM_OwnerClear	20	TPM_GetTestResult

Java Card applets. Dynamic object construction allocates memory in EEPROM. However, access to EEPROM is typically about 30 times slower than access to volatile data in RAM. Due to the limited amount of RAM and dramatically slow access of dynamically allocated memory in EEPROM, our implementation handles temporary values in RAM and stores only the data that must survive power loss in EEPROM. Yet, the Java Card technology does not support allocation of arbitrary data structures in RAM but rather manages data in form of transient byte arrays. Therefore, the state of the seTPM is managed by dedicated wrappers maintaining data structure elements in transient byte arrays. This way, temporary computations of arbitrary data structure elements can be performed in RAM, thus limiting the number of accesses to EEPROM.

Key Encryption. The TPM command TPM_Create_WrapKey initiates the generation of an asymmetric key pair that can be stored as an encrypted blob on the host side. To bind the key to the TPM, the TPM specification 1.2 [12] states that the newly created key pair should be encrypted by means of the non-migratable *Storage Root Key* (SRK). Therefore, essential parameters, which are used to restore the key at a later point in time, are encrypted with the SRK and sent to the host. However, the asymmetric key representation in CRT form used by the Java Card API requires more than 1024 bytes (the size of the utilized asymmetric key length). Since the asymmetric encryption is not capable of encrypting more bytes than the asymmetric key size, our implementation shifts towards a merged architecture combining the TPM 1.2 and TPM 2.0 specifications: The TPM 2.0 specification supports the encryption of asymmetric keys by means of a symmetric encryption algorithm (AES). As a consequence, keys of various lengths can be encrypted. Therefore, we introduce an additional non-migratable symmetric *Key Encryption Key* (KEK), which is generated during the installation process. As discussed in Sect. 4, our future implementation of a TPM 2.0 compliant seTPM applet can share the KEK with its TPM 1.2 counterpart.

Garbage Collection. Automatic memory reclamation is usually not part of the JCRE. To prophylactically prevent running out of memory at run-time, all objects need to be allocated during the applet installation and initialization stage. Thus, the allocated objects need to be made globally available to the rest of the implementation. Static object instances would meet this requirement. However, to additionally ensure uniqueness of these instances, we have decided to apply the Singleton pattern to globally used objects.

Stack Frames. Method invocations and utilization of try-catch blocks create overhead concerning memory consumption through the dynamic generation of stack- and exception frames. This needs to be considered during implementation as the number of invoked methods may lead to memory shortage.

5.2   Evaluation

We evaluated our prototype by measuring the execution time of five of the most critical TPM commands from two different host systems (Freescale i.MX6 development board and a Lenovo Thinkpad X220) and compared the results with performance measurements of a TPM natively built into a notebook (Lenovo Thinkpad X220). Our measurements consider the time required to traverse the entire TCG stack beginning from the TSP interface (TSPI) down to the seTPM/TPM (Fig. 1). Therefore, we measured the time needed for invocations of the TSPI functions. The utilized SE implements the Java Card specification 2.2.2 and contains 4 kB of volatile RAM and about 80 kB of non-volatile EEP-ROM. The communication is established through a conventional card reader with PC/SC support. The following presents our evaluation results. However, the data transfer overhead caused, e.g., by a slow card reader needs to be considered: An internal card reader might result in a smaller transmission overhead.

- Figure 6(a) presents a non linear timing behavior in both seTPM setups and the native TPM. One explanation is that the `TPM_CreateWrapKey` command generates an asymmetric key pair on the seTPM/TPM and hence needs to

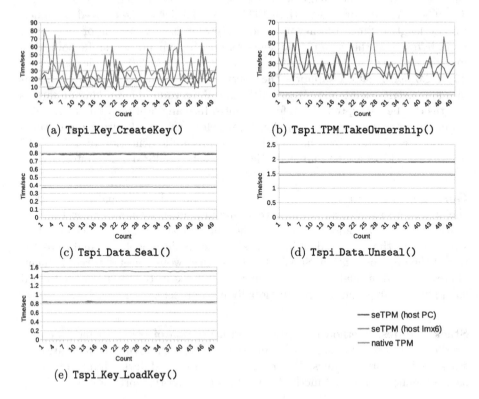

(a) `Tspi_Key_CreateKey()`

(b) `Tspi_TPM_TakeOwnership()`

(c) `Tspi_Data_Seal()`

(d) `Tspi_Data_Unseal()`

(e) `Tspi_Key_LoadKey()`

— seTPM (host PC)
— seTPM (host Imx6)
— native TPM

Fig. 6. Evaluation of TPM 1.2 commands. The high-level TSPI commands internally invoke the associated TPM commands.

perform primality tests. A random number that is not a prime must be rejected and regenerated.

- The invocation of the TPM_TakeOwnership command as well indicates a non-linear timing behavior of both seTPM setups in Fig. 6(b). Interestingly, the native TPM takes constant time to perform the command. The seTPM creates an asymmetric SRK on every TPM_TakeOwnership invocation. Thus, seTPM needs to perform primality tests, as described above. We assume that the native TPM computes the SRK in advance, right after the TPM has been reset, thus reducing the execution time.
- The execution of the command TPM_LoadKey performs better in both seTPM setups than the native TPM, as shown in Fig. 6(e). The reason for this is that symmetric cryptography is faster than asymmetric cryptography. As being discussed in Sect. 5.1, our prototype implements a modified version of TPM_CreateWrapKey: seTPM generates an asymmetric key pair, which is encrypted with the symmetric KEK instead of the asymmetric SRK. Ergo, TPM_LoadKey on the seTPM requires less time to decrypt the wrapped key.
- In both seTPM setups, the TPM commands TPM_Seal and TPM_Unseal perform slower than the native TPM, as shown in Fig. 6(c) and (d). Naturally, this is the accumulation of various factors, such as the bus transmission rate and different CPU rates of the native TPM and seTPM.

The mean time of the evaluated TSPI commands is shown in the first part of the Table 3. The table opposes the performance of the native TPM and the two seTPM implementations with different hosts. Except for Tspi_Key_CreateKey(), the table shows a minor variation between both seTPM setups, indicating a host-independent behavior. Consequently, our prototype can achieve similar results even on very resource-constrained devices.

We conclude our evaluation with a short demonstration of the functional extensibility of seTPM: The TPM_Extend command is responsible for updating specified PCR register values with integrity measurements provided by the host. This process concatenates a PCR register value with the provided measurement and subsequently generates a SHA-1 hash over the concatenated

Table 3. Mean time in ms of evaluated commands.

TSPI command	seTPM (PC)	seTPM (i.MX6)	TPM
Tspi_TPM_TakeOwnership	26555,50	27845,42	2399,94
Tspi_Key_CreateKey	17667,39	26894,09	29689,12
Tspi_Key_LoadKey	831,10	833,84	1509,60
Tspi_Data_Seal	782,27	788,77	371,90
Tspi_Data_Unseal	1900,04	1909,89	1451,96
TPM command	seTPM (PC)	seTPM (i.MX6)	TPM
TPM_Extend (SHA-1)	55,69	55,76	11,79
TPM_Extend (Keccak)	5775,32	5810,56	–

string. The resulted hash value is stored within the specified PCR register: $PCR_{new} = SHA1(PCR_{old}||measurement)$. The second part of the Table 3 presents the mean time required for the TPM_Extend command on both seTPM implementations as well as on the native TPM. One can observe that our implementation performs slightly slower that the native TPM. However, according to the data transfer overhead of contactless secure elements, our implementation requires about 40 ms to transfer 25–50 byte to and back from the seTPM. Consequently, our implementation would be able to almost keep up with the performance of a native TPM, when connected, e.g., through an internal card reader. In addition, Table 3 shows performance results of the TPM_Extend command using the KECCAK hash algorithm. Obviously, a software implementation cannot keep up with a hardware accelerated SHA-1 implementation. However, this shows that our goal concerning functional extensibility has been met.

6   Conclusion

In this paper, we presented the architecture and design of seTPM, a secure element based Trusted Platform Module. To face current compatibility issues, we introduced an architecture of a hybrid system combining the TPM 1.2 and TPM 2.0 standards, the concepts of which may be implemented in the future. Our prototype implementation comprises 20 of the most important TCG specified TPM 1.2 commands as a framework that can be easily extended to finally introduce hardware supported Trusted Computing to mobile devices. The architecture dependent parts of seTPM have been implemented for Linux-based systems and can be easily ported to Android. We showed with our implementation that a seamless integration into the widely deployed TSS implementation TrouSerS is feasible. Further, we provided a proof-of-concept that our design is more flexible than hardware TPM chips by exchanging the SHA-1 hash algorithm with the KECCAK algorithm. With that approach we were also able to increase the security level compared to native TPM solutions. Our evaluation showed that seTPM performs similar to a native TPM. Although some TPM commands perform slower on the seTPM in comparison to a native TPM, it still presents an attractive solution for mobile devices. In summary, we believe that seTPM is capable of eliminating lots of today's issues concerning trust in mobile devices as our approach closes the gap between Trusted Computing and GlobalPlatform specified SEs of modern smart phones.

References

1. Trusted Computing Group: TCG specification architecture overview specification, Revision 1.4, August 2007
2. Challener, D., Yoder, K., Catherman, R., Safford, D., Van Doorn, L.: A Practical Guide to Trusted Computing. Pearson Education, Indianapolis (2007)
3. Arthur, W., Challener, D., Goldman, K.: A Practical Guide to TPM 2.0. Springer, Heidelberg (2015)

4. GlobalPlatform Inc.: TEE System Architecture - Public Release v1.0. GlobalPlatform Inc., California (2011)
5. ARM Security Technology - Building a Secure System using TrustZone Technology, Prd29-genc-009492c ed. ARM Limited, April 2009
6. Trusted Computing Group: TPM 2.0 Mobile Reference Architecture Family "2.0", Level 00 Revision 142, December 2014
7. Trusted Computing Group: TPM MOBILE with Trusted Execution Environment for Comprehensive Mobile Device Security (2012)
8. Trusted Computing Group: TCG Mobile Trusted Module Specification Version 1.0, Revision 6, June 2008
9. Strasser, M., Stamer, H.: A software-based trusted platform module emulator. In: Lipp, P., Sadeghi, A.-R., Koch, K.-M. (eds.) Trust 2008. LNCS, vol. 4968, pp. 33–47. Springer, Heidelberg (2008)
10. Oracle: Java Card Platform Specification 2.2.2
11. Sailer, R., Zhang, X., Jaeger, T., Van Doorn, L.: Design and implementation of a TCG-based integrity measurement architecture. In: USENIX Security Symposium, vol. 13, pp. 223–238 (2004)
12. Trusted Computing Group: TPM Main Specification Level 2 Version 1.2, Revision 116, March 2011
13. Bertoni, G., Daemen, J., Peeters, M., Van Assche, G.: Keccak specifications version 2 (2009)
14. Costan, V., Sarmenta, L.F.G., van Dijk, M., Devadas, S.: The trusted execution module: commodity general-purpose trusted computing. In: Grimaud, G., Standaert, F.-X. (eds.) CARDIS 2008. LNCS, vol. 5189, pp. 133–148. Springer, Heidelberg (2008)
15. Zhang, D., Han, Z., Yan, G.: A portable TPM based on USB key. In: Proceedings of the 17th ACM Conference on Computer, Communications Security, ser. CCS 2010, pp. 750–752. ACM, New York (2010)
16. Akram, R., Markantonakis, K., Mayes, K.: Trusted platform module for smart cards. In: 2014 6th International Conference on New Technologies, Mobility and Security (NTMS), pp. 1–5, March 2014
17. Berger, S., Cáceres, R., Goldman, K.A., Perez, R., Sailer, R., van Doorn, L.: vtpm: virtualizing the trusted platform module. In: Proceedings of the 15th Conference on USENIX Security Symposium, ser. USENIX-SS 2006, vol. 15. USENIX Association, Berkeley (2006)
18. TrouSerS: The open-source TCG Software Stack
19. Trusted Computing Group: TSS System Level API and TPM Command Transmission Interface Specification Family "2.0", Level 00 Revision 01.00, January 2015
20. ISO, Identification cards - Integrated circuit cards - Part 4: Organization, security and commands for interchange, International Organization for Standardization, Geneva, Switzerland, ISO/IEC 7816-4:2005. ISO (2005)
21. Trusted Computing Group: TPM Library Specification Family "2.0", Level 00, Revision 01.16 (2014)
22. Montgomery, M., Krishna, K.: Secure object sharing in java card. In: Proceedings of the USENIX Workshop on Smartcard Technology, ser. WOST 1999, p. 14. USENIXAssociation, Berkeley (1999)
23. Wang, X., Yin, Y.L., Yu, H.: Finding collisions in the full SHA-1. In: Shoup, V. (ed.) CRYPTO 2005. LNCS, vol. 3621, pp. 17–36. Springer, Heidelberg (2005)
24. SHA-3 standard: Permutation-based hash and extendable-outputfunctions, National Institute of Standards and Technology Std., Rev. DRAFT FIPS PUB 202, May 2014

25. Bertoni, G., Daemen, J., Peeters, M., Van Assche, G.: Keccak, note on parameters and usage, February 2010
26. Trusted Computing Platform Alliance: TCPA Main Specification Version 1.1b, February 2002
27. Kauer, B.: Oslo: improving the security of trusted computing. In: Proceedings of 16th USENIX Security Symposium on USENIX Security Symposium, ser. SS 2007, pp. 16: 1–16: 9. USENIX Association, Berkeley (2007)
28. Winter, J., Dietrich, K.: A Hijacker's guide to the LPC bus. In: Petkova-Nikova, S., Pashalidis, A., Pernul, G. (eds.) EuroPKI 2011. LNCS, vol. 7163, pp. 176–193. Springer, Heidelberg (2012)
29. ARM: Designing with TrustZone®- Hardware Requirements

Java Card Virtual Machine Compromising from a Bytecode Verified Applet

Julien Lancia[1] and Guillaume Bouffard[2(✉)]

[1] THALES Communications and Security S.A.S, Parc Technologique du Canal,
Campus 2 – Bat.A, 3 Avenue de l'Europe, 31400 Toulouse, France
julien.lancia@thalesgroup.com
[2] Agence Nationale de la Sécurité des Systèmes d'Informations (ANSSI), 51,
Boulevard de La Tour-Maubourg, 75700 Paris 07 SP, France
guillaume.bouffard@ssi.gouv.fr

Abstract. The Byte Code Verifier (BCV) is one of the most important security element in the Java Card environment. Indeed, embedded applets must be verified prior installation to prevent ill-formed applet loading. In this article, we disclose a flaw in the Oracle BCV which affects the applet linking process and can be exploited on real world Java Card smartcards. We describe our exploitation of this flaw on a Java Card implementation that enables injecting and executing arbitrary native malicious code in the communication buffer from a verified applet. This native execution allows snapshotting the smart card memory with OS rights.

Keywords: Java card · Software attack · BCV vulnerabilities

1 Introduction

Developing smart card applications is a long and complex process. Despite existing standardization efforts, *e.g.*, concerning power supply, input and output signals, smart card development used to rely on proprietary Application Programming Interfaces (APIs) provided by each manufacturer. The main drawback of this development approach is that the code of the application can only be executed on a specific platform, thus lowering interoperability.

To improve the interoperability and the security of embedded softwares, the Java Card technology was designed in 1997 to allow Java-based applications for securely running on smart cards and similar footprint devices. Due to the resources constraints of this device, only a subset of the Java technology was retained in the Java Card technology. The trade-offs made on the Java architecture to permit embedding the Java Card Virtual Machine (JCVM) on low resource devices concern both functional and security aspects.

1.1 The Java Card Security Model

In the Java realm, some aspects of the software security rely on the Byte code Verifier(BCV). The BCV guarantees type correctness of the code, which in turn

© Springer International Publishing Switzerland 2016
N. Homma and M. Medwed (Eds.): CARDIS 2015, LNCS 9514, pp. 75–88, 2016.
DOI: 10.1007/978-3-319-31271-2_5

guarantees the Java properties regarding memory access. For example, it is impossible in Java to perform arithmetic operations on references. Thus, it must be proved that the two elements on top of the stack are bytes, shorts or integers before performing any arithmetic operation. Because Java Card does not support dynamic class loading, byte code verification is performed at loading time, *i.e.* before installing the Converted APplet (CAP) file onto the card. Moreover, most of Java Card platforms do not embed an on-card BCV as it is expensive in terms of memory consumption. Thus, bytecode verification is performed off-card, either directly by the card issuer if he controls the loading chain, or by a trusted third party that signs the application as a verification proof.

In addition to static off-card verification enforced by the BCV, the Java Card Firewall performs runtime checks to guarantee applets isolation. The Firewall partitions Java Card's platform into separated protected object spaces called contexts. Each package is associated to a context, thus preventing instances of a package from accessing (reading or writing) data of other packages, unless it explicitly exposes functionality through a Shareable Interface Object.

Despite all the security features enforced by the Java Card environment, several attack paths [1,2,4–6,10,11,13–15,19,22] have been found exploitable by the Java Card security community.

1.2 State-of-the-Art on Java Card Byte Code Verifier Flaws

The BCV is a key component of the Java Card platform's security. A single unchecked element in the CAP file, while apparently insignificant, can introduce critical security flaws in smart cards as shown in [11].

Although exhaustively testing a piece of software is a complex problem, several attempts have been made to characterize the BCV of the Java Standard Edition from a functional and security point of view. In [24], the authors rely on automatic test cases generation through code mutation and use a reference Virtual Machine (VM) implementation including a BCV as oracle. In [8], a formal model of the VM including the BCV is designed, then model-based testing is used to generate test cases and to assess their conformance to the model.

In the Java Card community, several works aim at providing a reference implementation of an off-card [16] or an on-card [3,9] Java Card BCV. These implementations are mainly designed from a formal model and can be used to test the BCV implementation provided by Oracle. As for the VM, model-based testing approaches [7,23] were used to assess on Java Card BCV implementations. As of today, no full reference implementation or model of the Java Card BCV has been proposed.

The Oracle's BCV implementation in version 2.2.2 was analyzed by Faugeron et al. [11]. In this implementation, the authors identified an issue in the branching instructions interpretation during the type-level abstract interpretation performed by the BCV. The authors exploited this issue to perform a type confusion in a local variable, undetected by Oracle's BCV. This issue in the BCV was patched by Oracle from version 3.0.3.

Since the version 3.0.3, no security flaw identification or exploitation in the Java Card BCV has been publicly signaled. In this paper, we present a new flaw discovered in the Java Card BCV from version 2.2.2 to 3.0.5 and we describe an exploitation of this flaw.

Section 2 introduces how a missing check in the Oracle's BCV implementation may allow an adversary to control a method offset and thus to trigger unverified bytecode execution. Section 3 shows how to success in exploiting this mechanism on a real Java Card product to trigger the execution of native code injected in a communication buffer. Finally, we evaluate our results on other Java Card products and propose a countermeasure to prevent the attack.

2   A Flaw in the BCV

2.1   The BCV Duty

The BCV enforces various security and consistency checks that guarantee each embedded application remains confined in its own sandbox. These verifications are performed on the CAP file, which is the binary representation of the classes that are loaded on the card. The BCV enforces two main kinds of checks: **type correctness** on the code and **structure verification** on the CAP file. The first one aims at performing an abstract interpretation of each method code in order to identify forbidden type conversion. The last one is an analysis of the CAP file structure to validate its consistency with the Java Card specification [20], and is detailed in the next section.

2.2   Verification of the CAP File Structure

The CAP file is composed of twelve different components, with internal and external dependencies, that are checked during the CAP file verification. Internal dependencies verification aims at validating the component properties as defined by the Java Card specification. External dependencies checks validate that redundant information specified in different components are compliant with each other. For example, each component has a `size` field that must be compliant with the `component-sizes` array contained in the Directory component where the sizes of every components are specified. An overview of all external dependencies between components in a CAP file are summarized in Fig. 1 borrowed from [12].

Among the twelve components stored in the CAP file, we will focus on the following components:

- the Method component stores the code of all methods in the package, concatenated as a set of bytes;
- the Constant Pool component contains an entry for each of classes, methods and fields referenced in the Method component;
- the Class component describes each classes and interfaces defined in the package, in a way that allows executing operations on that class or interface;

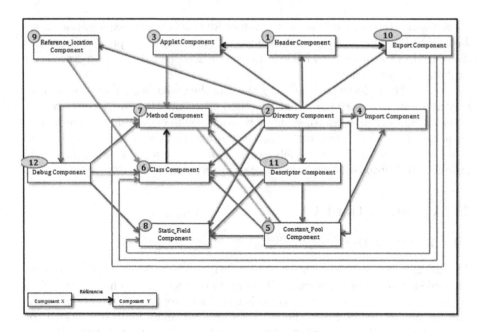

Fig. 1. External dependencies between components in a CAP file [12].

– the Descriptor component provides sufficient information to parse and verify all elements of the CAP file. This component is the main entry point for a byte code verification.

The Descriptor component is keystone of the BCV operations, but it has little or no importance for the card's processing and is therefore optionally provided during the loading of the applet.

Because of its purpose, the Descriptor component references several elements in the other components, and even provides redundant information with regards to these components. On the opposite, no component references the Descriptor component.

An analysis of the behavior of the BCV regarding the external dependency checks, and particularly the redundant information between components, brought us to identify a missing external dependency check between the Class component and the Descriptor component. We present the details of this BCV flaw and the resulting exploitation in the next sections.

2.3   Missing Check in the BCV

The missing check we have identified in the BCV involves the token-based linking scheme. This scheme allows downloaded software to be linked with API already embedded on the card. Accordingly, each externally visible item in a package is assigned a public token that can be referenced from another package. There are three kinds of items that can be assigned public tokens: classes, fields and methods. The bytecodes in the Method component refer to the items in the Constant Pool component, where the tokens required to perform the bytecode operation (*e.g.* class and method token for a method invoke) are specified.

When the CAP file is loaded on the card, the tokens are linked with the API and resolved from token form into the internal representation used by the VM. The linking process operates on the bytecode and is performed in several steps:

1. each token is an index in the Constant Pool component. The item stored at the provided index specifies the public tokens of the required items (*e.g.*, class and method token for a method invoke);
2. the tokens are resolved into the JCVM internal representation. For a method invoke, the class token identifies a `class_info` element in the Class component;
3. in the `class_info` element, the `public_virtual_method_table` array stores the methods internal representation. The method token is an index into the `public_virtual_method_table` array;
4. the element in the `public_virtual_method_table` at the method token index is an absolute offset in the Method component to the header and the bytecode of the method to execute.

The Fig. 2 summarizes the linking process for a method call.

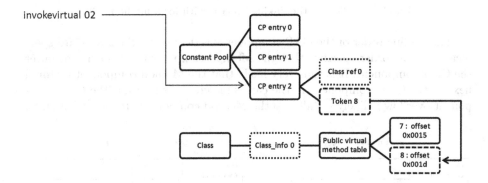

Fig. 2. Overview of the linking process for a method call.

The absolute offset in the Method component to the header and the bytecode of the method to execute is a redundant information in the CAP file as it is stored both in the `public_virtual_method_table` elements in the Class component and in the `method_descriptor_info` elements in the Descriptor component. The offset information in the Descriptor component is used exclusively by the BCV before loading, while the offset information in the Class component is used exclusively by the JCVM linker on card. Thus, any ill-formed offset information in the Class component remains undetected by the BCV checks, but is still used by the JCVM linker on card.

2.4   Exploiting the BCV Flaw

As presented so far, the BCV flaw we expose allows manipulating the method offset information in the Class component while remaining consistent with the BCV checks. The exploitation of this flaw consists in deleting an entry in the public_virtual_method_table of a class_info element in the CAP file. The resolution of the corresponding method offset during the JCVM linking leads to an overflow in the Class component, as presented in Fig. 3. This overflow brings the JCVM to interpret the content of the memory area following the Class component on card as a method index.

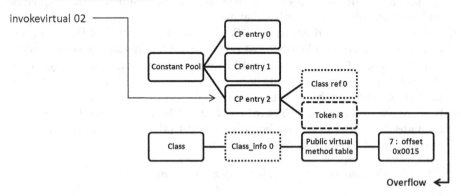

Fig. 3. Overflow in the linking process with for a method call.

The loading order of the CAP components is defined by the Java Card specification. This order specifies that the Method component is loaded right after the Class component. It is thus very likely that the Method component is stored next to the Class component in the card's memory. As a result, the Class component overflow is likely to fall into the Method component. In this eventuality,

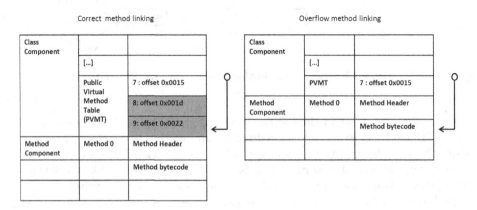

Fig. 4. Figure on left shows a successful linking in the Class component. Figure on the right shows the Class component overflow during linking when grayed out elements are deleted. Class component overflow falls into the Method component.

the offset of the method resolved in overflow is the numerical value of a byte-code in the Method component, that can be controlled by the applet developer. The Fig. 4 presents an exploitation of the Class component overflow through the Method component.

3   Code Injection from a Bytecode Verified Applet

In the previous section, we have presented, in the eventuality of a favorable memory mapping, how an attacker can exploit a BCV flaw to specify an arbitrary method offset in a BCV validated applet. In this section, we present the exploitation of this flaw on a real product that allows us to inject and execute native code in a communication buffer from a BCV validated applet.

The attack steps necessary to reach arbitrary native code on the Java platform are summed up the next sections. First, we exploit the BCV flaw presented in Sect. 2 to forge an arbitrary method header in the Method component. This arbitrary method header is then used to abuse the native method execution mechanism of the platform and thus create a buffer overflow in the native method table. Finally, this buffer overflow allows dereferencing the communication buffer address as a native function. As a consequence, the data sent to our verified applet through the communication channel are executed as native code on the JCVM.

This full attack is a proof of concept to demonstrate that the flaw discovered in the Oracle BCV may jeopardize the security of Java Card smartcards.

3.1   Native Execution in the Virtual Machine

We validate the exploitation of the BCV flaw on an open Java Card platform embedded on an ARM micro-controller. This Java Card platform was provided in the context of a security expertise, thus both the code and the memory mapping of the VM were made available.

The runtime environment of this platform provides a mechanism that allows switching execution to native implementations of Java Card API methods for performance reasons. The implementation of this mechanism is similar to the Java Native Interface (JNI) mechanism provided in classical Java VMs [18].

In the JNI approach, the native methods are identified through a dedicated flag (ACC_NATIVE) in the method header. According to the JCVM specification, the native header flag is only valid for methods located in the card mask. Therefore a native method loaded in a CAP file is not compliant with the Java Card specification, and is thus rejected by the offcard verifier.

The native method resolution in JNI relies on *interface pointers*. An interface pointer is a pointer to a pointer. This pointer refers to an array of pointers, each one itself pointing on to an interface function. Every interface function is stored at a predefined offset inside the array. Figure 5 illustrates the organization of an interface pointer. The offset inside the array where the native function pointer is to be found is provided in the body of the native method.

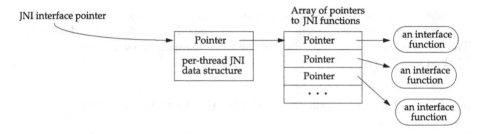

Fig. 5. JNI functions and pointers [17].

3.2   Native Execution from a Validated Applet

As presented in Sect. 2 a missing check in the BCV can cause an overflow that brings the VM to resolve the method offsets outside the Class component. In the VM implementation we use to exploit our attack, the Class component overflow falls into the Method component so the value of the method offset can be specified as the numerical value of a bytecode in the Method component.

According to the JCVM specification [20], the offset of a method must point to a method header structure in the Method component, followed by the bytecode of the method. When exploiting the BCV flaw, the offset is controlled by the developer so it can point to any portion of the Method component. This can be used to make the method offset pointing on a portion of the bytecode that can be interpreted as a method header. The iipush bytecode can be used for this purpose, as its operand is a 4-bytes constant that is not interpreted by the BCV. This 4-bytes constant is thus used to code a method header containing the ACC_NATIVE flag and the native method index. This iipush bytecode is accepted by the BCV because it forms a valid bytecode sequence, but when the operand is interpreted as a native method header (through an overflow on the Class component), the control flow switches to native execution. Figure 6 shows the attack path from the Class component overflow to the native execution of a JNI method.

We were thus able, by specifying the adequate value for the method offset, to execute any of the native methods provided by the VM in the array of JNI native function pointers.

3.3   Abusing the Native Execution Mechanism for Code Injection

The attack so far allows calling JNI native methods provided by the platform, that are stored in an array of JNI native function pointers (or *native array*). When a native method call occurs, the switch from the Java runtime environment to the native execution environment requires an index in the native array to determine the native function pointer. Experimentation on the target JCVM allowed us to determine that an overflow on the native array can be achieved by specifying the relevant index in the native method body. Thus, any memory content stored next to the native array can be exploited as a native function pointer.

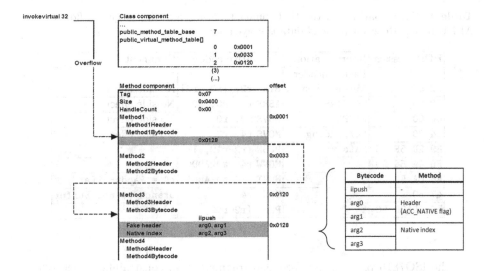

Fig. 6. Exploitation of the Class component overflow to execute a native method.

An analysis of the memory mapping of the product shows that a memory zone next to the native array contains a pointer to the communication buffer used for Host Controller Protocol (HCP) communications. The HCP protocol handles the transport layer of the Single Wire Protocol (SWP) protocol, involved in Near Field Communication (NFC) communications with smart cards. HCP messages encapsulates ISO7816 Application Protocol Data Unit (APDU) that are conveyed to the smartcard over SWP.

Using the overflow on the native array, we are able to use the HCP communication buffer pointer as native function pointer. The execution of this native function pointer leads to executing the content of the HCP communication buffer as a native assembly function.

The HCP protocol has several properties that limit the use of the HCP communication buffer as a native payload injection placeholder:

1. HCP packets are prefixed with a HCP message header and an HCP packet header. These headers are interpreted as native assembly opcodes.
2. HCP enforces fragmentation of messages, which limits packets size to 27 bytes. The entire native payload must thus be contained in 27 bytes.

In order to gain more space to inject our attack payload, we inject a minimal payload in the HCP communication buffer whose only purpose is to redirect the execution flow to the ISO7816 APDU buffer. This minimal redirection payload is presented in Table 1. Because the HCP communication buffer pointer is used as a function pointer, all the HCP buffer is interpreted as native code, including packet header, message header and encapsulated APDU header. These header bytes produce no side effect as shown in Table 1, which lets the redirection payload execute properly.

Table 1. Native payload in the HCP buffer that redirects the execution flow to the APDU buffer. Relevant payload data is grayed out.

HCP message	Interpretation	Native code	Comment
82 50	Packet header Message header	STR r2, [r0, r2]	No side effect
00 10	CLA/INS	ASRS r0, r0, #0	No side effect
00 00	P1/P2	MOVS r0, r0	No side effect
14 00	Lc/padding	MOVS r4, r2	No side effect
E9 2D 5F FC	Data	PUSH {r2-r12, lr}	
F6 4A 54 D0		MOVW r4, #0xADD0	
F6 CA 54 D1		MOVT r4, #0xADD1	r4 = &apduBuffer
47 A0		BLX r4	branch to apduBuffer
E8 BD 9F FC		POP {r2-r12, pc}	

The ISO7816 protocol has broaden fragmentation constraints, which offers sufficient space for a full native payload injection. We present in Table 2 a full payload injected in the APDU buffer that branches to a low level read/write OS function. Because the start address execution is chosen from the HCP message buffer payload, the header bytes are skipped and the native execution starts at the push instruction (Table 2, 3rd row).

The payload initializes the source parameter to the first 4 bytes of the payload (Table 2, 2nd row), such that the reading address can be selected directly in the APDU. Then, it initializes the destination address (where the read bytes are copied) to the address of the APDU buffer following the payload, such that the read bytes are immediately available for sending back through the APDU

Table 2. Native payload in the ISO7816 APDU buffer that calls an OS function to read an arbitrary memory zone and copies the result to the APDU buffer. Relevant payload data is grayed out.

	APDU	Interpretation	Native code	Comment
1	00 12 00 00 31	APDU Header		CLA/INS/P1/P2/Lc
2	B1 FA 15 00	Data		source reading address
3	2D E9 FF 5F		PUSH {r0-r12, lr}	
4	F6 4A 56 D0		MOVW r6, #0xADD0	
5	F6 CA 56 D1		MOVT r6, #0xADD1	r6 = apduBuffer
6	35 68		LDR r5, [r6,#0x00]	r5 = *apduBuffer
7	28 46		MOV r0, r5	
8	00 F1 09 00		ADD r0, r0, #0x6A	*dest: apduBuffer + 0x6A
9	D5 F8 05 10		LDR r1, [r5, #0x08]	*src: *(apduBuffer + 8)
10	4F F0 40 02		MOV r2, #0x40	length: 0x40
11	F6 4A 54 D2		MOVW r4, #0xADD2	
12	F6 CA 54 D3		MOVT r4, #0xADD3	r4 = *read_function_ptr()
13	A0 47		BLX r4	call method
14	BD E8 FF 9F		POP {r0-r12, pc}	

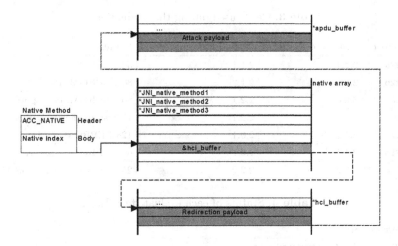

Fig. 7. Exploitation of the native array overflow to execute native code in the APDU buffer.

buffer. Finally, it branches to the low level OS function that performs the reading operation. As a result, any physical address of the card can be accessed through this native payload.

Figure 7 shows the execution flow from the native array overflow to the redirection payload in the HCP message buffer to the final attack payload in the APDU buffer. We were able to integrally dump the card memory and to reverse it using commercial reversing tools. The reversed code was identified as the code of the embedded JCVM.

4 Other Experimental Results

To evaluate the consequence of the BCV flaw on a broader range of virtual machine implementations, we tested, on different smart cards from different manufacturers, how much each of them supports the installation of an ill-formed applet. We evaluated seven cards from three distinct manufacturers (a, b and c). Each card name is associated with the manufacturer reference and its Java Card specification [20]. The list of evaluated Java Card smart cards is presented in Table 3.

None of the evaluated card implements an embedded BCV. On each card, an ill-formed applet is installed and, if the installation succeeds, the applet is executed. The ill-formed applet has a dereferenced method in the public virtual method table. Table 4 sums up the cards reactions.

As shown in Table 4, cards react differently to the ill-formed CAP file installation and execution. The cards with the symbol (✓) detect the ill-formed CAP file during the installation and reject it. On the other cards, marked with the symbol (✗), installation and execution succeed.

Table 3. Cards used during this evaluation.

Reference	Java Card Platform	GlobalPlatform Version	Details
a-22a	2.2.1	2.1.1	36 EEPROM, RSA
a-22b	2.2.2	2.1.2	80 EEPROM, RSA
a-30c	3.0.4	2.2.1	80 EEPROM, ePassport
b-30a	3.0.1	2.2.1	1 Flash memory, (U)SIM
c-21a	2.1.1	2.0.1	128 EEPROM, SIM
c-21b	2.1.1	2.0.1	64 EEPROM, RSA, AES
c-22c	2.2.2	2.2.2	256 Flash memory, (U)SIM

Table 4. Statuts of each evaluated cards.

Reference	Statut
a-22a	PCSC error: card mute. ✗
a-22b	PCSC error: card mute. ✗
a-30c	PCSC error: card mute. ✗
b-30a	No error: the card return the value 0x0701. ✗
c-21a	Global platform error: error during the loading process (*applet rejected*). ✓
c-21b	Global platform error: error during the loading process (*applet rejected*). ✓
c-22c	Global platform error: error during the loading process (*applet rejected*). ✓

Successful executions cause either unexpected card response or card mute. Unexpected card response indicates that unexpected code execution occurred. Card mute may result from infinite loop or card's reaction to illegal code, which also indicates unexpected code execution.

These behaviors proof that the control flow of the JCVM is modified. We can thus conclude that the BCV flaw presented in this article can be exploited on a range of different Java Card smartcards.

The full attack path that results in arbitrary native code execution requires information about the memory mapping and the JCVM implementation that were not available for these tests. Therefore, we did not attempt to reproduce the full attack path.

5   Conclusion, Countermeasure and Future Works

We show in this article how a missing check in the Oracle's BCV implementation can be exploited on a Java Card. We demonstrated that this BCV issue has a critical impact on smart cards security through a proof of concept exploitation on a JCVM implementation. We have successfully managed to inject and execute native code in a communication buffer, and finally gain full read/write OS privileges on the whole card memory. Finally, we evaluated on a range of different cards from different manufacturers that most of the JCVM implementations do not protect themselves against the BCV issue exploitation.

Following our responsible disclosure of the BCV issue to Oracle, we were allowed to publish this article and a new version of the BCV was released[1]. This new BCV version detects the Class component inconsistency and thus mitigate our attack. A loading process including mandatory bytecode verification step with the latest Oracle's BCV provides a valid countermeasure against the attack presented in this paper.

With the identification of a new flaw in the Oracle's BCV implementation, one sees that the BCV must be entirely verified to lower the risks of new vulnerabilities disclosure. To reach this objective, an effort should be done to specify the security and functional requirements a BCV must comply with in order to protect JCVM implementations against software attacks.

References

1. Barbu, G., Duc, G., Hoogvorst, P.: Java card operand stack: fault attacks, combined attacks and countermeasures. In: Prouff, E. (ed.) [21], pp. 297–313 (2011)
2. Barbu, G., Thiebeauld, H., Guerin, V.: Attacks on java card 3.0 combining fault and logical attacks. In: Gollmann, D., Lanet, J.-L., Iguchi-Cartigny, J. (eds.) CARDIS 2010. LNCS, vol. 6035, pp. 148–163. Springer, Heidelberg (2010)
3. Berlach, R., Lackner, M., Steger, C., Loinig, J., Haselsteiner, E.: Memory-efficient on-card byte code verification for Java cards. In: Proceedings of the First Workshop on Cryptography and Security in Computing Systems, CS2 2014, pp. 37–40. ACM, New York (2014)
4. Bouffard, G.: A generic approach for protecting Java card smart card against software attacks. Ph.D. thesis, University of Limoges, Limoges, France, October 2014
5. Bouffard, G., Iguchi-Cartigny, J., Lanet, J.: Combined software and hardware attacks on the java card control flow. In: Prouff, E. (ed.) [21], pp. 283–296
6. Bouffard, G., Lanet, J.: The ultimate control flow transfer in a Java based smart card. Comput. Secur. **50**, 33–46 (2015)
7. Calvagna, A., Fornaia, A., Tramontana, E.: Combinatorial interaction testing of a Java card static verifier. In: 2014 IEEE Seventh International Conference on Software Testing, Verification and Validation, Workshops Proceedings, March 31 - April 4, 2014, Cleveland, Ohio, USA, pp. 84–87. IEEE Computer Society (2014)
8. Calvagna, A., Tramontana, E.: Automated conformance testing of Java virtual machines. In: Barolli, L., Xhafa, F., Chen, H., Gómez-Skarmeta, A.F., Hussain, F. (eds.) Seventh International Conference on Complex, Intelligent, and Software Intensive Systems, CISIS 2013, Taichung, Taiwan, July 3–5, 2013, pp. 547–552. IEEE Computer Society (2013)
9. Casset, L.: Development of an embedded verifier for Java card byte code using formal methods. In: Eriksson, L.-H., Lindsay, P.A. (eds.) FME 2002. LNCS, vol. 2391, pp. 290–309. Springer, Heidelberg (2002)
10. Faugeron, E.: Manipulating the frame information with an underflow attack. In: Francillon, A., Rohatgi, P. (eds.) CARDIS 2013. LNCS, vol. 8419, pp. 140–151. Springer, Heidelberg (2014)

---

[1] The BCV included in the Java Card SDK 3.0.5u1 prevents the introduced attack. This version was released on 19 August 2015.

11. Faugeron, E., Valette, S.: How to hoax an off-card verifier. e-smart (2010)
12. Hamadouche, S.: Étude de la sécurité dun vérifieur de Byte Code et génération de tests de vulnérabilité. Master's thesis, University M'Hamed Bougara of Boumerdes, Faculty of Sciences, LIMOSE Laboratory, 5 Avenue de l'indpendance, 35000 Boumerdes, Algeria (2012)
13. Hamadouche, S., Bouffard, G., Lanet, J.L., Dorsemaine, B., Nouhant, B., Magloire, A., Reygnaud, A.: Subverting byte code linker service to characterize Java card API. In: Seventh Conference on Network and Information Systems Security (SARSSI), pp. 75–81, May 22rd to 25th 2012
14. Hamadouche, S., Lanet, J.: Virus in a smart card: myth or reality? J. Inf. Secur. Appl. **18**(2–3), 130–137 (2013)
15. Lancia, J.: Java card combined attacks with localization-agnostic fault injection. In: Mangard, S. (ed.) CARDIS 2012. LNCS, vol. 7771, pp. 31–45. Springer, Heidelberg (2013)
16. Leroy, X.: Bytecode verification on Java smart cards. Softw. Pract. Exper. **32**(4), 319–340 (2002)
17. Liang, S.: The Java Native Interface: Programmer's Guide and Specification, 1st edn. Addison-Wesley Professional, Reading (1999)
18. Lindholm, T., Yellin, F., Bracha, G., Buckley, A.: The Java Virtual Machine Specification: Java Series. Addison-Wesley, Reading (2014)
19. Mostowski, W., Poll, E.: Malicious code on java card smartcards: attacks and countermeasures. In: Grimaud, G., Standaert, F.-X. (eds.) CARDIS 2008. LNCS, vol. 5189, pp. 1–16. Springer, Heidelberg (2008)
20. Oracle: Java Card 3 Platform, Virtual Machine Specification, Classic Edition. No. Version 3.0.5, Oracle, Oracle America Inc, 500 Oracle Parkway, Redwood City, CA 94065 (2015)
21. Prouff, E. (ed.): CARDIS 2011. LNCS, vol. 7079. Springer, Heidelberg (2011)
22. Razafindralambo, T., Bouffard, G., Lanet, J.-L.: A friendly framework for hidding *fault enabled virus* for Java based smartcard. In: Cuppens-Boulahia, N., Cuppens, F., Garcia-Alfaro, J. (eds.) DBSec 2012. LNCS, vol. 7371, pp. 122–128. Springer, Heidelberg (2012)
23. Savary, A., Frappier, M., Lanet, J.-L.: Detecting vulnerabilities in Java-card bytecode verifiers using model-based testing. In: Johnsen, E.B., Petre, L. (eds.) IFM 2013. LNCS, vol. 7940, pp. 223–237. Springer, Heidelberg (2013)
24. Sirer, E.G.: Testing Java virtual machines. In: International Conference on Software Testing and Review, San Jose, California, November 1999

Misuse of Frame Creation to Exploit Stack Underflow Attacks on Java Card

Benoit Laugier[1]([✉]) and Tiana Razafindralambo[2]

[1] UL, Pavilion A, Ashwood Park, Ashwood Way, Basingstoke RG23 8BG, UK
benoit.laugier@ul.com
[2] Eshard, 1 Allée Jean Rostand, 33650 Martillac, France
tiana.razafindralambo@eshard.com

Abstract. Stack underflow attacks against Java Card platform attempt to access undefined local variables or operands to corrupt data that are not supposed to be accessible. Indeed, their exploitations rely on changing system data (return address, execution of context, etc.). The current attacks are restricted to the main assumption that the frame system data is located between the operand stack and the local variable area. However, Java stacks are implementation dependent and their structures are not always in the above configuration. This article presents a new attack which does not rely on the Java stack implementation model and that exploits specific countermeasure omission during frame allocation. Nevertheless the attack relies on ill-formed application that does not undergo the Bytecode Verifier. In spite of that, it is well-known that fault injection can be used to turn harmless code sequence into malicious code. We then suggest a new combined attack that allows performing several type confusions with one fault model.

1 Introduction

1.1 Java Card: An Open Platform Secure Element

Java Card is intended to run on constrained devices such as smart cards and Secure Elements (SE), components in mobile devices to provide security and confidentiality environment. This technology is used for storing secret/sensitive data and processing secure transaction in hostile environment. Most of SEs are based on open systems (interoperability and post-issuance loading capabilities) and embedded in various form factors. Therefore, they are subject to many kind of attacks that we will present later in Sect. 2.

1.2 Security in a Multi-Application Environment

The Java Card Security inherits its type safe language from Java. Additionally the Java Card technology provides a secure execution environment to host multiple applications on the same device thanks to its applet firewall and object sharing mechanism. It also provides additional security enhancements such as transaction atomicity and tamper resistant cryptographic classes.

© Springer International Publishing Switzerland 2016
N. Homma and M. Medwed (Eds.): CARDIS 2015, LNCS 9514, pp. 89–104, 2016.
DOI: 10.1007/978-3-319-31271-2_6

The Java Card Firewall plays an important role in Java Card security model. It provides applet data segregation by preventing leakage of system and non-public instance data. That is, each applet keeps its own private name-space. Indeed, the isolation is achieved with security contexts that are uniquely assigned to each applet. As a result objects can only be accessed by their owner or by the JCRE that has system privileges. However, Java Card allows specific data exchange between applets thanks to its shareable interfaces mechanism and the context switch feature.

The Java Card Virtual Machine (JCVM) consists of two-part.

The first part is executed off-card on a workstation. The Java converter, part of the Java Card Development Kit, does subset checking for the JCVM limitation and classes optimization. It takes as input all of the Java executable code (class files) and export files of imported libraries to produce a Converted APplication (CAP) file. Then the CAP file can be loaded and instantiated onto a Java Card device that implements the second part of the JCVM.

The second part is the bytecode interpreter. It is executed on-card and translates the Java bytecode into CPU instructions.

In addition to these components the ByteCode Verifier (BCV) provides means to assert that the applet to load does not compromise the integrity of the JCVM. This component can be run on the workstation or on the device. However most of currently deployed Java Card devices have no on-card BCV due to memory constraints. Their on-card component is essentially composed of the bytecode interpreter, the Java Card Runtime Environment (JCRE) and the Java Card Application Programming Interfaces (JCAPI).

GlobalPlatform provides a secure and interoperable applet management environment because it is not specified in Java Card specifications. That is, when this technology is released on Open Platform products, it did not provide a secure framework for post-issuance applet management. To compensate this, GlobalPlatform (GP) defines secure and interoperable applet management specifications. Indeed SEs involve cross-industry players where some entities may require privileges to load, install and run applications. To restrict the card content management to these entities, GP has defined security policies, secure messaging protocols and integrity/confidentiality mechanisms to protect deployment and management of multiple applications.

Nowadays the number of actors on a SE is increasing as transit, payment, loyalty and ID applets can reside on the same device. As a result, different service providers may require privileges on the card and the situation where a malevolent person gets the right to install applications could potentially arise. In that case underlying security issues may occur.

2   Context

Despite the off-card BCV from Oracle and the secure application management of the GP, the security of the card content management on SE might still be put at risk. Indeed, security has to be considered on many levels. The off-card BCV is an environment assumption and it can be difficult to assert that it has been fulfilled. In addition GP implementation might be sensitive to different kind of attacks that may overcome its implementation.

For instance, invasive techniques target the hardware layer to inject errors during the code execution. To do so, the device is monitored and subject to external interferences to change its normal behaviour. Optical fault injection described in [15] shows how faults can be injected with laser on a decapsulated IC.

Other attacks are considered as semi or non-invasive techniques. Observation attacks, such as side-channel monitoring on the device power consumption, might expose secret data handled by the devices during sensitive operations. Such attacks were first described in [9,17].

Software-based attacks aim at exploiting bugs, exotic command sequences and illegal instruction sequences. Compared to hardware and observation attacks, such attacks just need standard and cheap equipment. They are precise and deterministic as they do not rely on the physical characteristic of the device. In the context of SE hosted on connected devices, the main threat for this kind of attacks is the ability for an attacker to remotely trigger them without any physical access to the device.

All the above software based attack can be used to gain privileges on the card content management. As demonstrated at BlackHat conference 2013, Security Researcher Karsten Nohl announced discovery of vulnerabilities on some SIM cards. [12] points out the following independent problems:

- undetermined behaviour from standards regarding the Proof of Receipt introduced by the ETSI 102.225
- cryptographic checksum might use a single DES key that could be brute-forced

As a consequence of them, key confidentiality was not maintained and an attacker could use the latter to perform Over-The-Air remote applet management, an alternative way to load applet through the SIM Toolkit Application. However GP offers several secure messaging options but all of them have their intrinsic vulnerabilities regarding fault injection, observation and software attacks.

3   Contributions

A Software-Based Attack – This paper presents a software based attack that leverages the execution of ill-formed applet on Java Card device to induce an underflow that might lead to a full exploitation of the targeted platform.

A New Logical Attack Techniques – We demonstrate through different attack techniques that an exploitable flaw might exist on card Operating System (OS). This flaw can lead to data leakage and can be exploited to gain knowledge of a particular device. It potentially enables one to access or change the Java Card assets (such as code/secret data of the OS or resident applications).

We present a concrete and powerful attack that exploits potential vulnerabilities caused by the lack of runtime checks of the JCVM. This can lead to various attack scenarios with read and write access to a part of the memory.

Some Reverse Engineering Techniques – Because an embedded virtual machine is implementation-dependent, it implies some reverse engineering steps to go further in the exploitation. This paper describes briefly how we identify the system data on partial dump.

Related Exploitations – We also describe potential exploitations that can be achieved depending on the leaked data. This might enable one to threaten additional Java Card assets.

Known Limitations – One should note that this technique is only harmful to open platforms. That is, only devices with post-issuance applet management capability are prone to this attack. Besides, the ill-formed applets used in this attack do not pass the Oracle's off-card BCV and this attack has been performed only on cards that do not have on-card BCV.

4   Related Work

In this section, we briefly present some related work that are closely related to ours.

Fault Attack affects the system behaviour by injecting a physical fault, which could be voltage or system clock manipulation, external radiation (laser beam, white light, electromagnetic pulses) or temperature variation [1,14,16]. For instance, if a single bit of a secret key is flipped during a cryptographic operation and the device does not detect this fault, the faulty cryptogram with a specific pattern might be returned. By comparing this faulty cryptogram with the correct one, an adversary might be able to deduce the secret key. Moreover, an adversary may also target the execution flow in order to repeat, skip or modify inputs of certain operations.

Type Confusion Attacks are now well-known logical attacks on Java Cards and described in the literature. An overview on the general principles of such attacks is described in [18] with some examples of bytecode manipulation that enable the exploitation of Java Cards. There are several kinds of logical attacks that can be forged. Most of them rely on type confusion [1,3,7,8,11]. Type confusion is well-known in the Java world [13]. Actually, as Java is a type safe language, many known attacks are based on type confusion (e.g. CVE-2011-3521, CVE-2012-1723, CVE-2013-2423, CVE-2014-4262). There are two main ways to perform type confusion within a Java Card applet. One modifies the CAP files after convertion and the other uses fault injection to alter data at runtime to render a benign applet into a malicious one.

Frame Bound Attacks have to be considered. In addition to type safety, bound protection is also a crucial key challenge to ensure the safety of the platform. In [10] an hardware accelerated defensive VM is proposed to ensure both. They particularly explain *Frame Bound Violation Attacks* that mainly consist of Java Stack manipulation in order to overflow or underflow the current Java Frame.

In the literature, such attacks were first described in [3]. This attack uses instructions to read undefined local variable indexes to get access to data located below the operand stack. Another underflow attack was presented in [6] which relies on the *dup_x* instruction to perform the underflow. Such attacks can lead to a limited illegal access of some data contained below the Java operand stack. This kind of underflow attacks assumes that the Java stack is implemented such that the system data area is located between the operand stack and the local variables area. However, Java stack implementation is platform-dependent and thus the exploitation of those attacks is restricted to this assumption.

From another perspective, our underflow attack does not rely on such assumption and potentially works for any Java stack implementation.

5   Stack Underflow During Frame Creation

In this section, we briefly introduce the technical background of the attack concept and then we suggest different techniques to perform the attack on Java Card devices.

5.1   The Java Virtual Machine Stack

The Java virtual machine is a stack machine that uses Last-In-First-Out data structures to store data and partial results. It is common that its implementation has a stack of frames related to method execution and a stack of call-return data structures to recover the previous runtime execution variables on method completion. The memory design of the Java stack is dependent on the VM implementation. Frames and call-return structures might be stored either contiguously within the same stack thread or separately into different areas.

Frames usually store references, data and partial results related to a specific method execution. That is, each frame corresponds to a reserved area that is used by the method that owns it. Therefore, a new frame is created when a method is invoked and the frame is destroyed when the method completes. In Java card, a frame is mostly limited to a set of local variables and an operand stack.

Local variables are the variables defined within the current method block. Local variables are stored in an array in the method frame. These variables are addressed by index and the first local variable index is 0. Furthermore, the VM uses the local variable area to pass parameters. On method invocation, parameters are passed in the form of consecutive local variables.

Operand stacks are used to store constants, values from local variables, object or static fields related to the current method execution. The VM provides instructions to load temporary data to the operand stack and applies arithmetic operation to values on the top of the operand stack.

Call-return data structure saves previous method execution data. Its content is not specified, however, it usually holds data for restoring the previous frames and VM state variables. The minimum information stored in this structure is the previous execution context, the previous Java Program Counter (JPC) and the previous Java Frame Pointer (JFP). These data belongs to the system and shall not be directly accessible to Java applets running on the platform.

5.2   Compile-Time and Runtime Assignment

Compile-Time Attribution – The sizes of the local variables array ($nargs +$ max_locals) and the operand stack (max_stack) are determined at compile-time. This means the size of method frames are computed by the compiler and hard-coded into the Java bytecode for each method. That is, the Method component contains a stream of $method\_header\_info$ structures that are shown below.

```
method_header_info {                    extented_method_header_info {
    u1 bitfield {                           u1 bitfield {
        bit[4] flags                            bit[4] flags
        bit[4] max_stack                        bit[4] padding
    }                                       }
    u1 bitfield {                           u1 max_stack
        bit[4] nargs                        u1 nargs
        bit[4] max_locals                   u1 max_locals
    }                                   }
}
```

Runtime Behaviour – During the runtime the Java Card platform interprets the bytecode and dynamically allocates frames on the stack. To do so, a VM uses following registers to keep track of its execution states:

- The JPC register: contains the address of the current executed bytecode instruction. Then the bytecode interpreter loop will increment the JPC to point to the next instruction.
- The JSP (Java Stack Pointer) register: points to the top of the operand stack in the current frame. This is usually the index of the last value on the operand stack.
- The JFP register: refers to a fixed location in the current frame structure. It is common that it points to the bottom of the local variables area.
- The current execution context: keeps track of the context of the currently running application. This variable is mainly used by the Java Card firewall to verify the object access rules.
- The address of the call-return structure: is either contained in the frame or contiguous with the Java Frame stack.

Method Invocation – During a method invocation, the JPC points to the method header which has three compile-time data: The maximum size of the operand stack (max_stack), the number of local variables (max_local) and the number of arguments ($nargs$). That information are generally used to dynamically allocate a newly created frame with the right size.

5.3   Corruption of Method Frame During Invocation

The parameters passed by the caller are popped out from their operand stack after the completion of invoked method. Therefore, it is common that the parameters are pushed into a new frame consecutively to initialize the local variables of the invoked method (this case is depicted by the Fig. 1). At this point,

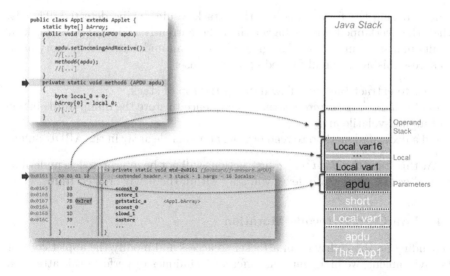

Fig. 1. Frame stacking on method invocation (**before the attack**)

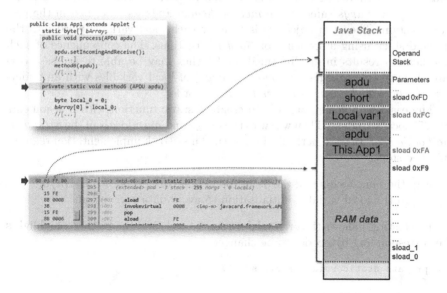

Fig. 2. Frame bound expansion after abusing the frame creation mechanism (**after the attack**)

the JFP of the newly created frame is equal to the previous JSP minus the number of argument. Therefore, by illegally extending the *nargs* value in the *method_header_info*, the frame allocation on the *invoke<>* instructions will be compromised.

This attack can be illustrated in the Fig. 2 the allocated local variables area will overlap with previous data that are outside the calling frame. If no control is done during the frame creation, the attack would not be detected. That is, when the overlapped area is bigger than the currently allocated Java stack, it results in a stack underflow that gives access to an undetermined memory area. To access this area, the ill-formed applet can use:

- *sload* to extract the underflow data on the top of stack,
- a *getstatic_a* /.../ *sastore* instruction sequence to store the dump words in one of its non-volatile array,
- and a dedicated method to read out the non-volatile array in the APDU buffer.

At this stage the *sload/aload* instructions will not be interpreted as underflow access because the local indexes will stay within the newly created frame.

5.4   Java Card Bytecode Mutation

Depending on the ability of an attacker to access and modify the applet code or its environment, we highlight four different techniques to perform this attack on a Java Card.

"nargs" **modification** First, it is possible to perform the attack by directly modifying the *nargs* value in the *method_header_info* as described in the previous section. Then the objective is to copy each local variable word into the operand stack using a sequence of *sload* instructions. The consequence of such modification results in an ill-formed applet that may be able to access a corrupted range ($max\_locals + corrupted\_nargs$) of local variables with an underflow of ($corrupted\_nargs - original\_nargs$) words.

The easiest implementation is to create a static function with 0 arguments and 255 local variables. Then we swap the *nargs* and *max_locals* in the *extended_method_header_info* to perform the attack. This attack implementation requires only two steps:

1. swap the *max_locals* and *nargs* in the *extended_method_header_info*,
2. discard the local variable initialisation to avoid data corruption.

The Listing 1 shows the original Java source code and the Listing 2 highlights the corresponding bytecodes to be changed.

```
private static void maliciousMtd()
{
    short s000 = 0, s001 = 0, // ...
          s254 = 0;
    MyStaticShortArray[0] = s000;
    MyStaticShortArray[1] = s001;
    // ...
    MyStaticShortArray[254] = s254;
}
```

Listing 1. Java source code of the malicious method

```
1    // private static void maliciousMtd
2    flags = 0; max\_stack = 3;  nargs = 0 ;  max_locals = 255
3    {
4        sconst_0                   // push zero value on the stack
5        sstore_0                   // pop the stack value and store it into s000
6        sconst_0                   // push zero value on the stack
7        sstore_1                   // pop the stack value and store it into s001
8        // ...
9        getstatic_a    XXXX   // push MyStaticShortArray reference
10       sconst_0              // push array's index (0)
11       sload_0               // load s000 on the stack
12       sastore               // pop and store s000 in MyStaticShortArray[0]
13       getstatic_a    XXXX   // push MyStaticShortArray reference
14       sconst_1              // push array's index (1)
15       sload_1               // load s001 on the stack
16       sastore               // pop and store s001 in MyStaticShortArray[1]
17       // ...
18       return
19   }
```

Listing 2. Bytecode of the malicious method

```
1    //private static void maliciousMtd
2    flags = 0; max_stack = 3;  nargs = 255 ;  max_locals = 0
3    {
4        nop                        // do nothing
5        nop
6        nop
7        nop
8
9        // ...
10       getstatic_a    XXXX   // push MyStaticShortArray reference
11       sconst_0              // push array's index (0)
12       sload_0               // load s000 on the stack
13       sastore               // pop and store s000 in MyStaticShortArray[0]
14       getstatic_a    XXXX   // push MyStaticShortArray reference
15       sconst_1              // push array's index (1)
16       sload_1               // load s000 on the stack
17       sastore               // pop and store s000 in MyStaticShortArray[0]
18       // ...
19       return
20   }
```

Listing 3. Exploitable ill-formed bytecode

The Listing 3 shows the ill-formed bytecode on *extended_method_header_info*.

This ill-formed bytecode will then copy the underflow into *MyStaticShortArray*. Designing this attack on an *extended_method_header_info* enables to read around 500 bytes below the stack. Theoretically, the attack would allow up to 256 words underflow but some are discarded as they belong to the previous frame created on the entry point method (*abstract void process(APDU apdu)* for example).

Method's Reference Modification. Another way to carry out the same attack is to forge the method signature to be invoked. This can be achieved by several different ways:

- modify the method offset in the constant pool table to redirect the call to a different private method
- modify the method token in the constant pool table to redirect the call to a different public method
- change the *invoke<>* operand to point to another method index in the constant pool.

For example if the original method signature is

```
static void myMethod1()
```

the forged method signature might be

```
static void myMethod2(short s_0, short s_1,[...] short s_255)
```

This attack technique is an improvement of the previous technique. It is preferable as it will incur less bytecode modification if the attacker wants to extract the entire underflow data. Indeed, *myMethod2* has just to carry out a sequence of *getstatic_a /.../ sastore* instructions to pull out the full underflow in a persistent array. The related Java source code is depicted by the Listing 4.

```
1  private static void myMethod2(short s_0, short s_1,[...] short s_254)
2  {
3      MyStaticShortArray[0] = s_0;
4      MyStaticShortArray[1] = s_1;
5      [...]
6      MyStaticShortArray[254] = s_254;
7  }
```

Listing 4. Java source code of a method that would carry out the full underflow attack

If *myMethod2* is successfully invoked in the place of *myMethod1*, it would have the same effect as the *nargs* modification. The *nargs* would be directly corrupted and no modification is required regarding the local variable initialisation. Then the underflow data are directly saved within the persistent array.

Token Modification on *Invokeinterface*. This technique is an extension of the previous techniques. It involves modifying the *method_token* operand on the *invokeinterface.* Indeed, this instruction takes as operands the number of passed arguments (XX), the interface class reference (YYYY) and the public method token (ZZ) as shown below:

```
invokeinterface XX YYYY ZZ
XX:       nargs,             1 byte
YYYY:     constantpool_index, 1 short
ZZ:       method_token,      1 byte
```

Those three operands are used to resolve the public method reference at runtime. That is, the device has to resolve the class reference that implements the interface and has to identify the method to be invoked with the *method_token*. When modifying the *method_token*, it is possible to redirect the *invokeinterface* to a malicious method that has a specific crafted signature. If the malicious method has more arguments than the original method, it will induce the same attack consequences and it would be possible to illegally expand the frame size for underflow accesses.

The advantage of such implementation is that it can be taken into consideration for combined attack. A fault attack can be attempted to precisely target the *method_token* or its resolution. Fault attack might set the *method_token* value to zero or corrupt the method resolution in the class component (either on *implemented_interface_info* or *public_virtual_method_table*).

Additionally, this combined attack can also be used to perform multiple type confusions at once. For example, if the interface defines the following method signatures:

```
public static void myMethod1(Object o_0, short s_0,
                             Object o_1, short s_1, ...)

public static void myMethod2(Object o_0, short s_0,
                             short s_1, Object o_1, ...)
```

the fault attack can perturb the resolution of *myMethod2* to *myMethod1*. As a result the arguments types would be interchanged between the two different signatures. Thus, it is possible to achieve as much type confusions as the number of permutation that can be defined between the two method signatures.

The Export File Modification. An export file contains all the public API linking information of classes in a given package. It is generated by the Java Card Converter tool during the CAP file generation. Class, method and field names are assigned with unique numeric tokens. Therefore, method signature forgery can also be achieved with rogue export files. In that case, the ill-formed application does not require post-compilation modification and it will behave the same as the attack described in *"Token modification"*. This technique is well-known in the literature and it has been described by different papers, such as [2, 4, 6].

6   Attacks Scenarios for Java Card

The potential attack scenarios mainly rely on the memory mapping. Depending on the nature of the dump, an attacker can get a better comprehension of the data and go further in his exploitation. To do so, a reverse engineering step is needed. As the underflow is performed on the Java stack, it is likely that the leakage data remains is the RAM area. The RAM area holds different buffers, stacks and RAM registers that can be exploited.

6.1   Underflow on Sensitive Buffers

This attack directly exploits the exposed sensitive data that can be exploited. Depending on the card memory mapping, the attack might be successful at this stage. On some Java Card, we observed that the transient memory segments were below the stack. In such implementation, an attacker is able to read and write access to the transient data directly and can potentially expose transient key or tamper application RAM data. In other cases, an attacker may access other sensitive data such as the crypto input/output buffers or system key structure.

6.2   Underflow on Runtime Data

If no asset are directly exposed, an attacker can investigate further to exploit the underflow data. On some tested cards, it turns out that we retrieve RAM registers below the stack. To have write access to this Runtime Data, an applet needs to carry out the same attack technique by implementing *sstore* instructions.

Frame Exploitation on JSP

Reverse – The JSP is an easy VM variable to reverse. One can use push instructions to increase the JSP in the current frame and observe which element of the dumped data is increased or decreased.

Consequences – Depending on the platform countermeasures, the JSP can be difficult to exploit. The attack does not grant more privileges to the attacker than direct stack overflow or underflow with *pop/push/dup_x* instructions because the interpreter still apply its security policy on each instruction. It only gives more control and flexibility on the JSP

Frame Exploitation on JFP

Reverse – The JFP can be identified by observing the JSP before the *invoke*. An easy implementation is to invoke the same fake header from different methods that have different local variable array sizes. Then, on each dump only the JFP and the JSP change.

Consequences – If an attacker manages to change the JFP value, he would shift the pointer of the fetched local variables as they usually relative to the JFP. This might allow him dumping even more memory from the corrupted JFP and the attacker has control over the address of the dump. This could enable to read the whole memory by varying the JFP from 0x00000000 to 0xFFFFFFFF.

However some hardware can limit the logical memory access range. Either the card detects the illegal reading on some range or not at all. In the latter, a full memory read can be performed. [11] describes a full memory read attack and enable the authors to identify the different memory contents (which are platform-dependent). This attack succeeded in reading out and modifying all the code and data belonging to all other applets.

Frame Exploitation on JPC

Reverse – To characterize the JPC, an applet needs to invoke several ill-formed method headers. Then on each dump, the JPC could be identified because it will be incremented according to the differences of method header offsets.

Consequences – Taking control on the JPC register would enable one to change the execution flow. As aresult, a shell code mmight be executed as demonstrated in [3].

Frame Exploitation on Execution Context. As explained in [6], an attacker can deactivate the firewall by switching the execution context to the JCRE context.

Frame Exploitation on Call-Return Structure

Reverse – The call-return structure is difficult to identify. To reverse its structure, a combination of different techniques described above should be applied when calling the ill-formed methods.

Consequences – The consequences are the same as above because the structure is supposed to store the previous VM state related to the execution of the caller method. In this case, the exploitation is only efficient when the ill-formed method completes and the VM returns into the caller method without throwing exception.

7   Discussion

7.1   Attack Assumptions

We have presented different reverse engineering method and potential exploitations. However, these attacks rely under certain assumptions:

The Verifier Checks – Applet to be installed must pass the different static checks performed by the Oracle Bytecode Verifier (see Sect. 1.2 The Java Card Virtual Machine). However as we previously pointed out, combined attacks are well-known in the Java Card security because they ecould render benign application to a malign one.

Loading Keys – The attacker needs to get the loading keys that allow him installing his malicious application onto a given Java Card. In the case of [12], the weakness resides in the SIM when using a Toolkit Application key for message integrity. However, if the SE is properly managed and configured, the exposure of such secret does not grant full installation privilege.

7.2   Reliance on Secret of Other Entities

GlobalPlatform provides security policies and authentication protocols for Card Content management. However, due to the different business and issuance models in the field, it might be difficult to assert in some cases that the secure channel keys confidentiality is fully enforced. It is true to say that GP brings the security towards by limiting the attack environment but if no efficient countermeasures have been implemented, devices may remain in the field with their vulnerabilities for several years. Moreover if the "Over The Air" (OTA) channel keys are exposed, attacks can be performed remotely without any physical access to the devices.

7.3   The Bytecode Verification

At the present, the Oracle BCV detects all the ill-formed applications that we have tested so far. It demonstrates that this tool is efficient and up to date regarding the state-of-the-art logical attacks. However, most of the verifications are based on static analysis and they do not cover attacks through bug exploitations or memory allocation mechanisms. Furthermore, most of the ill-formed bytecode sequences might be hidden behind a rogue export file. For all of these reasons, validation authorities must take the utmost care that the export files used for verification match the on-card CAP files. Even so, it is difficult to assert that all the deployed applications have undergone the Oracle BCV.

7.4   New Edition, New Vulnerabilities

Java Card products must pass through functional testing and security evaluation to gain high assurance on the overall product security. However, with the new emerging technologies, Java Card environment is evolving quickly. Since 2009, Sun released the Java Card 3.0 specification that defines a new JCVM and a new JCRE for the deployment of high end SE and USB tokens. A well detailed analysis of the vulnerabilities introduced with Java Card 3 Connected Edition can be seen in [5]. It shows that various new features have actually increased the attack surfaces.

For instances:

- Dynamic Class Loading may significantly complicate the type safety enforcement. Then reference forgery by type confusion will be more threatening than the actual type confusion attacks.
- Dynamically loaded classes may embed malicious code.
- Multithreading makes it more difficult to analyse security.
- Web-applications may introduce various code injections attacks well known in the desktop world.

8   Conclusions

In this paper, we have described different logical attacks that relies on bytecode modification to forge method headers or method signatures. They create an indirect stack underflow access by abusing the frame creation mechanism. With the proposed attacks, the number of arguments is extended to reach 255 (0xFF) words. However, the applet is ill-formed and does not pass the Oracle's off-card verifier. If a fault injection can turn the bytecode into 0xFF or 0x00 values, the attack can be performed through a well-formed application but this is out of the current paper scope. The attack enables an attacker to get access to an extended frame within which he could read up to 500 additional bytes. According to what could be read and write from this initial memory dump, different exploitations can be set. Despite the security policies, the secure authentication protocols and the bytecode verification tools, validation authorities hold a great importance in this industry area to bring safe and secure products.

References

1. Barbu, G., Thiebeauld, H., Guerin, V.: Attacks on java card 3.0 combining fault and logical attacks. In: Gollmann, D., Lanet, J.-L., Iguchi-Cartigny, J. (eds.) CARDIS 2010. LNCS, vol. 6035, pp. 148–163. Springer, Heidelberg (2010)
2. Bouffard, G.: A Generic Approach for Protecting Java Card Smart Card Against Software Attacks. PhD thesis, Université de Limoges (2014)
3. Bouffard, G., Iguchi-Cartigny, J., Lanet, J.-L.: Combined software and hardware attacks on the java card control flow. In: Prouff, E. (ed.) CARDIS 2011. LNCS, vol. 7079, pp. 283–296. Springer, Heidelberg (2011)
4. Bouffard, G., Khefif, T., Kane, I., Salvia, S.C.: Accessing Secure Information using Export file Fraudulence. In: CRiSIS, pp. 1–5, La Rochelle, France, October 2013
5. Calafato, A.: An analysis of the vulnerabilities introduced with java card 3 connected edition (2013)
6. Faugeron, E.: Manipulate frame information with an underflow attack undetected by the off-card verifie (2013)
7. Hubbers, E., Poll, E.: Transactions and non-atomic api calls in java card: specification ambiguity and strange implementation behaviours. Radboud University Nijmegen, Department of Computer Science NIII-R0438 (2004)
8. Iguchi-Cartigny, J., Lanet, J.-L.: Developing a trojan applets in a smart card. J. Comput. Virol. 6(4), 343–351 (2010)
9. Kocher, P.C., Jaffe, J., Jun, B.: Differential power analysis. In: Wiener [17], pp. 388–397
10. Lackner, M., Berlach, R., Loinig, J., Weiss, R., Steger, C.: Towards the hardware accelerated defensive virtual machine – type and bound protection. In: Mangard, S. (ed.) CARDIS 2012. LNCS, vol. 7771, pp. 1–15. Springer, Heidelberg (2013)
11. Mostowski, W., Poll, E.: Malicious code on java card smartcards: attacks and countermeasures. In: Grimaud, G., Standaert, F.-X. (eds.) CARDIS 2008. LNCS, vol. 5189, pp. 1–16. Springer, Heidelberg (2008)
12. Nohl, K.: Rooting sim cards (2013)
13. The Last Stage of Delirium Research Group: Java and java virtual machine security vulnerabilities and their exploitation techniques (2002)

14. Sere, A.A., Iguchi-Cartigny, J., Lanet, J.-L.: Evaluation of countermeasures against fault attacks on smart cards. Int. J. Secur. Appl. **5**(2), 49–61 (2011)
15. Skorobogatov, S.P., Anderson, R.J.: Optical fault induction attacks. In: Kaliski Jr., B.S., Koç, Ç.K., Paar, C. (eds.) CHES 2002. LNCS, vol. 2523, pp. 2–12. Springer, Heidelberg (2003)
16. Vetillard, E., Ferrari, A.: Combined attacks and countermeasures. In: Gollmann, D., Lanet, J.-L., Iguchi-Cartigny, J. (eds.) CARDIS 2010. LNCS, vol. 6035, pp. 133–147. Springer, Heidelberg (2010)
17. Wiener, M.J. (ed.) 19th Annual International Cryptology Conference—Advances in Cryptology - CRYPTO 1999, Santa Barbara, California, USA, August 15–19. Lecture Notes in Computer Science, vol. 1666. Springer, Heidelberg (1999)
18. Witteman, M.: Advances in smartcard security. Inf. Secur. Bull. **7**, 11–22 (2002)

Evaluation Tools

From Code Review to Fault Injection Attacks: Filling the Gap Using Fault Model Inference

Louis Dureuil[1,2,3](✉), Marie-Laure Potet[1,3], Philippe de Choudens[1,2], Cécile Dumas[1,2], and Jessy Clédière[1,2]

[1] Univ. Grenoble Alpes, 38000 Grenoble, France
{louis.dureuil,philippe.de.choudens,cecile.dumas,jessy.clediere}@cea.fr
[2] CEA, LETI, MINATEC Campus, 38054 Grenoble, France
[3] CNRS, VERIMAG, 38000 Grenoble, France
{louis.dureuil,marie-laure.potet}@imag.fr

Abstract. We propose an end-to-end approach to evaluate the robustness of smartcard embedded applications against perturbation attacks. Key to this approach is the fault model inference phase, a method to determine a precise fault model according to the attacked hardware and to the attacker's equipment, taking into account the probability of occurrence of the faults. Together with a fault injection simulator, it allows to compute a predictive metrics, the vulnerability rate, which gives a first estimation of the robustness of the application. Our approach is backed up by experiments and tools that validate its potential for prediction.

Keywords: Smartcard · Perturbation attack · Fault injection · Fault model · Vulnerability rating · Attack potential · Electromagnetic attacks

1 Introduction

1.1 Context

Secure devices (smartcards, security tokens, and in the near future mobile phones) are subject to drastic security requirements and certification processes. They must be protected against high level attack potential as described in [9] (i.e. multiple attackers with a high level of expertise, using sophisticated equipments, etc.). As a result, norms (for instance, the Common Criteria) require the vulnerability analysis to follow the state-of-the-art in terms of attacks.[1] Nowadays, a very studied class of attack is perturbation attack, which is performed using electrical glitches, focalised light [6] or electromagnetic injectors [12].[2] Progress

---

L. Dureuil—This work has been partially supported by the project SERTIF (ANR-14-ASTR-0003-01).

M.-L. Potet—This work has been partially supported by the LabEx PERSYVAL-Lab (ANR-11-LABX-0025).

[1] We target here the AVA class, dedicated to vulnerability assessment.
[2] Sometimes referred to as "EM probes".

N. Homma and M. Medwed (Eds.): CARDIS 2015, LNCS 9514, pp. 107–124, 2016.
DOI: 10.1007/978-3-319-31271-2_7

in perturbation techniques allow multiple attacks over the course of a single execution [10] (also known as high-order attacks).

Perturbation attacks typically result in fault injection, which modifies the data and/or control flow of the execution. Fault injection can be exploited to access or modify secure assets on the card and to produce faulty ciphertexts in cryptographic contexts [7]. Codes must be hardened using software countermeasures (redundant tests, integrity counters, etc.) in addition to the already mandatory hardware countermeasures. Qualifying the resulting robustness of embedded software against fault injection is a very challenging task. It is nowadays a mainly hand-crafted process that requires various skills from the implied people. Furthermore, the ever-evolving state of the art requires periodic re-evaluations of previously certified embedded software.

1.2   Perturbation Attack and Fault Model

When assessing robustness, evaluators limit the type of faults they consider to a specific fault model. Fault models vary greatly in the literature, with volatile or non-volatile bit set or reset, register corruption or modifications of a byte or a word in memory [2,6,16], and higher-level effects such as test inversion, data reassignment and instruction replacement [4,11,13]. The variability of fault models can be explained by several factors: the memory technologies used in the card, its logic circuits, the available hardware countermeasures, the equipment of the attacker and the attack parameters: for instance, in EM injectors the model depends on the angle between the injector and the plane of the card [12].

1.3   Evaluation Process

Assessing the robustness of an embedded software against fault injection spans several subprocesses. *Code analysis* aims to detect vulnerabilities in the software from the source and assembly codes and looks for attack paths using a given fault model. *Penetration tests* consist in performing perturbation attacks on the card according to the hardware technology and with some knowledge about the behaviour of the application (for instance, obtained via power consumption analysis).

Based on the results of these two processes, an *attack potential* is determined, according to a scoring grid [9]. *Attack potential* takes into account several factors such as *elapsed time*, the attacker's *expertise*, *knowledge of the target of evaluation (TOE)*, *equipment* and the *availability of open samples*. For each factor, a table establishes the correspondence between possible levels for this factor and identification and exploitability ratings. For instance, the *knowledge of the TOE* can be *public*, *restricted*, *sensitive*, *critical* or *very critical*. The final rating combines the values of identification and exploitability associated to each factor.

1.4   Open Problems

Hardening and evaluating embedded software against fault injection is a hot topic as demonstrated by the number of recent studies dedicated to this subject.

As a consequence of the first attack against RSA [7], countermeasures are proposed in cryptographic contexts [6,10], some of which are formally proved to be robust against a given fault model [8]. Unfortunately, due to the possibility for multiple fault injection, countermeasures can also be attacked [14]. Thus, adding the suitable set of countermeasures becomes a very complex task. Moreover, as pointed out by S. Mangard in his keynote at CARDIS 2014,[3] a significant part of the vulnerabilities discovered by evaluators implies non-cryptographic code.

Another research direction is the development of automated tools simulating fault injection, at the source code [3,5,13] or at the binary levels [4,11]. These tools can be combined with a proof-based approach in order to qualify the robustness of the considered applications, as shown in [3,8,13]. Fault injection simulators provide exhaustiveness and reproducibility. But, in return, these tools generally produce a very large number of potential attacks, which requires manual examination to decide if the attacks are actually a serious threat. Indeed, these tools being dedicated to some specific fault models, the attacks they detect are not necessarily achievable on a given hardware component.

1.5 Our Approach

In this paper, our contributions are the following: we propose an end-to-end approach, and tools, to respond to these challenges. The proposed approach introduces a preparatory phase designed to infer the most suitable fault model according to the considered hardware, independently of a given application. Fault models take into account the probability of occurrence of faults. The second step is fault injection simulation, which explores the consequences of the obtained fault model on the application. Lastly, we propose a predictive vulnerability rate, based on the results provided by both the inference and fault injection simulation phases, allowing us to classify attacks and to measure robustness. As we will see, this rating gives a partial measure of the attack potential, requiring no penetration testing campaign. Figure 1 summarizes the approach.

The proposed approach allows the evaluator to fine-tune the fault model in order to improve the result of fault injection simulation, and makes the fault model reusable between applications using the same card. Although an alternative method to find fault models through experiments has been proposed in [15], it is not part of an end-to-end process, which is the specificity of our approach. In particular, to our knowledge, no other attempt has been made to combine the results of a fault model deduced at the card level with fault injection simulation, with the goal of producing a vulnerability rating at the application level.

The remainder of this paper is organized as follows: Sect. 2 proposes a formalization of the fault models which can be produced by the inference phase; Sect. 3 proposes a methodology for fault model inference and illustrates it on a case study; Sect. 4 presents CELTIC, a fault injection simulator, and defines the vulnerability rate and sensibility of a location; finally, Sect. 5 presents experiments

---

[3] "The if statement that surrounds the cryptographic implementations".

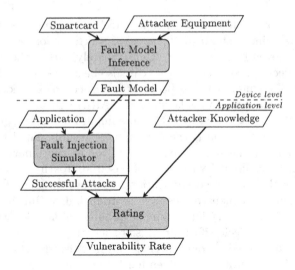

Fig. 1. The overall approach

we conducted to evaluate the vulnerability rate, and gives some future perspectives.

2 Fault Model Formalization

Fault models are a key part of our approach: they must be easy to specify as they serve as input of fault injection simulation; they must be low-level enough to be described as an output of fault model inference; lastly we aim to retain enough expressiveness to be compatible with classic fault models such as instruction skip or volatile bit (re)set.

2.1 Fault and Fault Model

With this in mind, we define a location, an instant, a fault and a fault model. The location and instant express the classic time and space characteristics of a fault.

Definition 1. *Location $\ell = (storage\_type, id)$: An abstract storage unit of type storage_type (e.g., non-volatile memory such as EEPROM, volatile memory such as RAM, registers) uniquely identified by id (an address in memory, a register name or number, etc.).*

Definition 2. *Instant i: An abstract value that identifies when a fault occurs. It can be expressed in seconds from the beginning of the execution, in numbers of loads from a given location, or number of loads/stores from any location.*

Definition 3. *Fault (i, ℓ, a, b): A replacement b of the value a returned by a load from location ℓ at the instant i.*

Definition 4. *Fault model $FM_{d,e}$: A set of sequences of faults that can actually be injected during the execution of any program on a device d with the perturbation equipment e.*

While this definition of a fault may seem restrictive, it covers classic fault models as well as combination thereof, and faults on code and data:

- *Volatile bit (re)set or byte change on code or data.* Set of faults that modify a load of the address corresponding to the code or data to the specified value.
- *Instruction skip (NOP).* In this model, instructions are skipped, i.e., replaced by NOP (no operation) instructions. The NOP fault model is a set of sequences of faults that replace the loads of the original opcodes and operands of the skipped instructions with NOP opcodes.
- *Non-volatile faults.* Set of sequences of faults that replace the original value returned by all loads from the affected location with the modified value until the next store to the affected location.

2.2   Probabilistic Fault Model

Probabilistic fault models refine fault models by adding two additional key pieces of information: The *probability of occurrence of each kind of fault* and their *relation to the attack parameters.* This way, we aim to capture the notion of plausibility of a fault.

Definition 5. *Attack Parameters p: A tuple of physical quantities that the attacker can measure and choose in a given range of values. We denote as $\mathcal{P}$ the space of the attack parameters.*

Definition 6. *Probabilistic Fault Model $\mathcal{M}_{d,e}$:*

$$Pr(F = f \mid p) \tag{1}$$

where F is a random variable valued in the domain of faults, and represents the fault injected during an attack on device d with equipment e, where f denotes a specific sequence of faults, and p the attack parameters.

In Sect. 3.2, we conduct fault model inference on a commercial, ARMv7-M, secure smartcard (denoted card A) using EM injection.[4] In EM injection, the attack parameters are a tuple $p = (\theta, x, y, z, t)$, where θ is the angle between the probe and the plane of the card, x, y and z give the spatial localization of the probe relatively to the card, and t is the delay before the EM field is applied. Table 1 presents the resulting probabilistic fault model for card A with $\mathcal{P} = \{(-90°, x_0, y_0, z_0, t_0+j\delta) \mid j \in \mathbb{N}\}$, with x_0, y_0, z_0, t_0 and δ chosen constants.

---

[4] Our EM injector is made of small copper wire loops (100 μm), driven by a 500 A current during 10 ns.

Table 1. Probabilistic fault model for card A under EM perturbation

Fault sequence	Probability
$< (i_j, \ell_j, a, 0) > \mid a \neq 0$	4.8 %
$< (i_j, \ell_j, a, b) > \mid a \neq 0 \wedge \frac{|a-b|}{a} \leq 1\%$	1.8 %
$< (i_j, \ell_j, a, b) > \mid a \neq 0 \wedge 1\% < \frac{|a-b|}{a} \leq 20\%$	1.6 %
$< (i_j, \ell_j, a, b) > \mid a \neq 0 \wedge b \neq 0 \wedge \frac{|a-b|}{a} > 20\%$	1.3 %
$< (i_j, \ell_j, a, 0), (i_{j+1}, \ell_{j+1}, a', 0) > \mid a \neq 0 \wedge a' \neq 0$	0.5 %
$< \varnothing >$ (No fault observed)	90 %

3   Fault Model Inference

Probabilistic fault model inference is performed in three steps.

Step 1. Parameter discovery: we determine a space $\mathcal{P}_0$ of attack parameters where faults occur reasonably often and whose size is small enough to carry the rest of the process.

Step 2. Raw fault model construction: we perform many perturbation attacks for each parameter $p \in \mathcal{P}_0$ on the target device running a specific program called the fault detection program.

Step 3. Fault model generalization: we manually infer a more general fault model extending parameters and values.

We detail each of these steps and illustrate them in this section. In the traditional approach, testers perform step 1 identically, while step 2 is conducted directly on the tested application and step 3 is missing, which leads to suboptimal code reviews.

3.1   Fault Detection Program

In [15], the authors propose a method called fault model extraction to establish a fault model from observations of the result of perturbation attacks on a specific test program. But in our understanding, little is done to ensure that the interpretation matches the fault that is actually injected. This is however a difficult problem, because an observation can result from various faults (for instance, a fault on data can result from a volatile bit reset in memory, or from a faulty store instruction). While the exact fault is not of interest when attacking a single application (only the success of the attack matters), it becomes crucial to eliminate context-dependent results when working at the device level.

Our specifically designed fault detection program is a first step in this direction. It directly outputs the fault injected during an execution under perturbation attack, and uses a sentinel to give us confidence that this observation matches the actual injected fault.

Listing 1.1 is an excerpt of the fault detection program, that targets an ARMv7-M architecture and aims at detecting EEPROM faults. Initially, r0 points to the start of an EEPROM buffer, r1 to the start of a RAM buffer, r2 and r3 to different parts of the output buffer. The program performs a copy of the EEPROM buffer to the output buffer and a copy of the RAM buffer to the output buffer. This program is put in RAM and ran from there. We then perform perturbation attacks to see the faults injected in EEPROM copied to the output buffer. This way, we can see how many EEPROM locations are perturbed as well as the injected values.

The copy of the RAM buffer acts as the sentinel. If the RAM copy is faulty, then it means that the attack perturbed the RAM or registers. In such case, we cannot guarantee the integrity of the code of the fault detection program, and we must discard the result.

This fault detection program can easily be adapted to other devices and architectures as long as they allow execution from RAM. Once the EEPROM fault model has been established, we can swap the roles of RAM and EEPROM in the program to establish the RAM fault model.

```
;  main_loop:
    58:    ldrb    r5, [r0, #0] ; r5 <- @EEPROM
    5a:    strb    r5, [r2, #0] ; r5 -> @IO_EEPROM
    5c:    ldrb    r5, [r1, #0] ; r5 <- @RAM
    5e:    strb    r5, [r3, #0] ; r5 -> @IO_RAM
    60:    add.w   r0, r0, #1 ; @EEPROM += 1
    64:    add.w   r1, r1, #1 ; @RAM += 1
    68:    add.w   r2, r2, #1 ; @IO_EEPROM += 1
    6c:    add.w   r3, r3, #1 ; @IO_RAM += 1
```
Listing 1.1. Fault detection program for card A

We now apply the three steps of fault model inference to card A.

3.2   Case Study/Step 1: Parameter Discovery

We tested the influence of the angle θ and the position (x, y) of the injector relatively to the surface of the chip, with z at a fixed value z_0. Regarding the influence of θ, and in accordance with the state of the art [12], we found a majority of bitset faults with the injector parallel to the card (e.g., $\theta = 0°$), and a majority of bit reset faults the injector orthogonal $(-90°)$. Figure 2 shows an overlay at (x, y) positions where faults occurred for a fixed θ angle.

3.3   Case Study/Step 2: Raw Fault Model Construction

We attacked the device running our fault detection program repeatedly. We denote as a the value in the EEPROM buffer in the fault detection program. We chose $\mathcal{P}_0 = \{(-90°, x_0, y_0, z_0, t_0 + 10k) \mid k \in \{0, \ldots, 39\}\}$, with 300 values a randomly chosen in $[0, 65535]$ (we additionally tested the special values 0 and 0xFFFF). For each pair (p, a) of parameter and input value, we performed 30 repetitions, for a total of $30 \times 40 \times 300 = 360000$ repetitions which resulted in a 10 days process. From the raw results, we generated Fig. 3, a heat map of the probability that a value a be replaced by the value b.

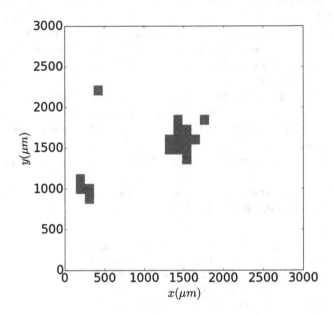

Fig. 2. (x, y) positions where an EEPROM fault is injected with $\theta = -90°$

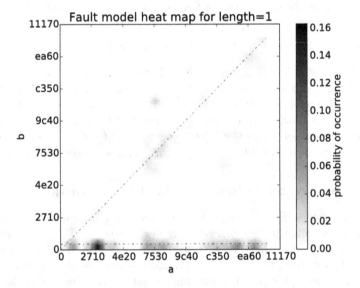

Fig. 3. Heat map of the probability of replacing a with b

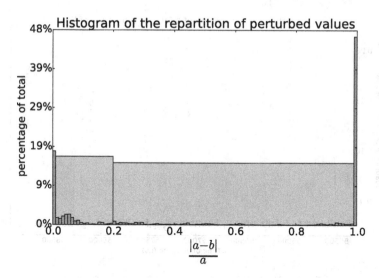

Fig. 4. Histogram of the repartition of perturbed values as a function of their distance to the original values

3.4   Case Study/Step 3: Fault Model Generalization

Fault model generalization is a necessary manual step taken to extend the fault model from the tested parameters to a bigger space of parameters and to generalize the model from our fault detection program to any application. To extend the fault model from the tested values to any value, we noticed in Fig. 3 that a majority of faults reset the original halfword a to 0, but a significant part of the faults result in slight alteration of a, i.e., the perturbed value b is such that the relative difference $d(a, b) = \frac{|a-b|}{a}$ is small.[5] We used this knowledge to build the bins of the histogram in Fig. 4, which illustrates the repartition of the probabilities of occurrence of the faults as a function of $d(a, b)$. We can see the prevalence of the zero $(d(a, 0) = 1)$, and of the smallest values of the function (when $d(a, b) < 0.01$), that match the probabilities summarized in Table 1 of Sect. 2.2.

To generalize the space of attack parameters to: $\mathcal{P} = \{(-90°, x_0, y_0, z_0, t_0 + j\delta) \mid j \in \mathbb{N}\}$, we observed the probability of fault injection as a function of time (Fig. 5) and noticed a periodicity $\delta = 720$ ns.

Moreover, we observed a relation between the position of the perturbed halfword in the EEPROM buffer and the time parameter. Specifically, if $t = t_0 + j\delta$, then the jth halfword of the buffer is perturbed. This property is essential to generalize the inferred fault model to any application under test as it ensures that there exists a range of time parameters such that any EEPROM location accessed at some point in the application can be perturbed. Although it does

---

[5] The *hamming distance* was considered, but gave seemingly less relevant results, with only 16 possible values.

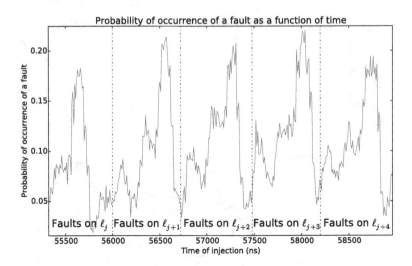

Fig. 5. Probability of fault as a function of time

not explicitly give us the correct time parameter, we see in Sect. 4.2 that only its existence is required for vulnerability rating. To our knowledge, such properties expressing the relation between the attack parameters and the space-time characteristics of the fault have not been described in the literature.

3.5   Variability of Fault Models

Table 2 summarizes the probabilistic fault model we inferred on a secure smart-card B that uses a proprietary CISC instruction set. We attacked with a laser, and chose $\mathcal{P} = \{(\text{power} = 1\text{W}, \text{spot size} = 20\,\mu m, \lambda = 980\,nm, x = x_0, y = y_0, d = 100\,ns, t = t0 + j\delta)\}$, where λ is the wavelength of the laser, and d the duration of a laser shot. Comparing the two fault models, we can notice that card B puts values at 0 with much more consistency, but can perturb between 1 and 6 consecutive bytes whereas faults in card A typically perturb a single halfword. This illustrates the variability of fault models, which is linked to the attacked hardware and to the equipment of the attacker.

4   Assessing Robustness at the Application Level

4.1   Automatic Code Analysis

The next step of our approach (see Fig. 1) consists in simulating fault injection at the application level. To do so, we designed and implemented CELTIC,[6] a simulator of native smartcard binaries, able to simulate fault injection. CELTIC was implemented in C++.

---

[6] CEsti-LeTi Integrated Circuit.

Table 2. Fault model for card B

Faults	Probability
$< (i_j, \ell_j, a, 0) >$	4.32 %
$< (i_j, \ell_j, a_0, 0), (i_{j+1}, \ell_{j+1}, a_1, 0) >$	2.93 %
$< (i_j, \ell_j, a_0, 0), (i_{j+1}, \ell_{j+1}, a_1, 0), (i_{j+2}, \ell_{j+2}, a_2, 0) >$	3.13 %
$< (i_j, \ell_j, a_0, 0), \ldots, (i_{j+3}, \ell_{j+3}, a_3, 0) >$	2.98 %
$< (i_j, \ell_j, a_0, 0), \ldots, (i_{j+4}, \ell_{j+4}, a_4, 0) >)$	6.56 %
$< (i_j, \ell_j, a_0, 0), \ldots, (i_{j+5}, \ell_{j+5}, a_5, 0) >$	2.48 %
$< \varnothing >$ (No fault injected)	77.58 %

Listing 1.2 provides a pseudo algorithm for CELTIC. The simulator starts classically with a *golden run* (variable `Xref` in Listing 1.2) of the tested native smartcard application, i.e., a run without fault injection (function `simulateWithoutFault` in Listing 1.2). The *golden run* allows to gather information which is used to identify all locations that are accessed during the execution, where faults are susceptible of being injected. CELTIC can be configured to use any probabilistic fault model $\mathcal{M}_{d,e}$ inferred following the process of Sect. 3, according to the definition given in Sect. 2.1. Each possible sequence of faults $f =< (i_0, \ell_0, a_0, b_0), \ldots, (i_k, \ell_k, a_k, b_k) >$ is generated from all sequences of accesses $< (i_0, \ell_0, a_0), \ldots, (i_k, \ell_k, a_k) >$ in the *golden run* that match the faults described by $\mathcal{M}_{d,e}$ (function `findAllFaults` in Listing 1.2). For each f, the algorithm performs an attack, i.e., a simulation where the matching sequence is replaced with the sequence $< (i_0, \ell_0, b_0), \ldots, (i_k, \ell_k, b_k) >$ (function `simulateWithFaults` in Listing 1.2). A user-provided oracle on the state of the simulated processor allows to filter the successful attacks (function `isAttackSuccessful` in Listing 1.2).[7] We denote as $\mathcal{F}_S$ (variable `successful` in Listing 1.2) the set of faults leading to successful attacks, and $\mathcal{F}$ (variable `attacks` in Listing 1.2) the set of all performed attacks. $\mathcal{F}_S$ is used as an input to compute the vulnerability rate, according to the probability attached to each kind of faults in the fault model.

```
def celtic(program, faultModel, isAttackSuccessful):
    attacks = set()
    successful = set()
    Xref = simulateWithoutFault(program)
    for f in findAllFaults(Xref, faultModel):
        attacks.add(f)
        Xfault = simulateWithFaults(program, f)
        if isAttackSuccessful(Xfault):
            successful.add(f)
    return successful, attacks
```

Listing 1.2. Pseudo-algorithm of CELTIC

---

[7] For instance, in a PIN verification one can check that the authentication token is **true** even though the provided PIN is wrong.

4.2 Vulnerability Rate

At its core, the vulnerability rate of the product describes how easy it is for the attacker to perform a successful attack. We propose the following definition:

Definition 7. *Vulnerability Rate* $\mathcal{V}$*: Let* $\mathcal{P}$ *be the space of attack parameters,* $\mathcal{M}_{d,e}$ *be a probabilistic fault model, and* $\mathcal{F}_S$ *be the set of successful attacks.*

$$\mathcal{V} = Pr(Attack \ is \ successful)$$

$$= \sum_{p \in \mathcal{P}} Pr(Attack \ is \ successful \mid p) \cdot Pr(p)$$

$$\mathcal{V} = \sum_{p \in \mathcal{P}} \underbrace{\sum_{f \in \mathcal{F}_S} Pr(F = f \mid p)}_{Fault \ Model \ \& \ CELTIC} \cdot \underbrace{Pr(p)}_{Attacker \ choice} \tag{2}$$

where $Pr(p)$ is the probability that the attacker chooses the parameters p for the perturbation attack.

Remark 1. Since we sum the space of attack parameters $\mathcal{P}$, we do not need to know the explicit attack parameters p that contribute to $\mathcal{V}$.

$Pr(p)$ depends on the attacker model. In the general case it can follow any law of probability, but we propose several typical models that suit the practice of the evaluators:

Equiprobable Attacker. An attacker without knowledge does not favor any attack, i.e., $\forall p \in \mathcal{P}, Pr(p) = \frac{1}{|\mathcal{P}|}$:

$$\mathcal{V}_{equi} = \frac{\sum\limits_{p \in \mathcal{P}} \sum\limits_{f \in \mathcal{F}_S} Pr(F = f \mid p)}{|\mathcal{P}|} \tag{3}$$

Realistic Attacker. In practice, the attacker has some knowledge of the parameters to use, for instance through side-channel information on the attacked application, and will use this knowledge to apply the equiprobable model on a reduced space $\mathcal{P}'$ of attack parameter values, that still contains the attack parameters p that contribute to $\mathcal{V}$.

All-knowing Attacker. An all-knowing, ideal attacker attacks only with the parameters p_{max} such that $\sum\limits_{f \in \mathcal{F}_S} Pr(F = f \mid p_{max})$ is maximal, which is equivalent to a degenerated equiprobable attacker where $\mathcal{P}' = \{p_{max}\}$.

Remark 2. $\mathcal{V}_{max} = \sum\limits_{f \in \mathcal{F}_S} Pr(F = f \mid p_{max}) \geq \mathcal{V}_{equi}$ for any considered $\mathcal{P}'$.

4.3 Sensibility of a Single Location

Automatic tools tend to output many vulnerabilities, some of which are less relevant than others. Therefore, existing tools [5] classically regroup successful attacks according to their location to find the most vulnerable locations. Vulnerability rate can be restricted by location for this purpose:

Definition 8. *Sensibility S_ℓ of the location ℓ: The vulnerability rate restricted to the successful sequences of faults that involve ℓ, denoted as $\mathcal{F}_S^\ell$:*

$$S_\ell = \sum_{p \in \mathcal{P}} \sum_{f \in \mathcal{F}_S^\ell} Pr(F = f \mid p) \cdot Pr(p) \tag{4}$$

5 Experimentation and Conclusion

5.1 Experimental Comparison with the Traditional Approach

Rating Comparison. We compared the vulnerability rating $\mathcal{V}$ with the rating $\mathcal{T}$ obtained in the traditional approach, using the physical success rate φ as reference. Our goal is to show the benefits in accuracy of using a probabilistic fault model obtained from fault model inference. To do so, we conducted experimental penetration tests on the cards A and B on several implementations of classic commands of various robustness.

We calculated the empirical success rate φ as the ratio of the number of physical successful attacks to the total number of performed attacks. To determine $\mathcal{V}$ we used CELTIC with the inferred fault model of Table 1. We used the *realistic* attacker model with sets of attack parameters $\mathcal{P}'$ adapted to each command. We also computed $\mathcal{T} = \frac{|\mathcal{F}_S'|}{|\mathcal{F}'|}$, the "traditional" success rate offered by existing tools [4,5], where $\mathcal{F}_S'$ and $\mathcal{F}'$ denote respectively the set of successful attacks and the set of all possible attacks found by CELTIC with an arbitrary exhaustive byte replacement fault model. We chose arbitrarily the fault model to reflect the practice of the "traditional" approach, and our choice was the exhaustive byte replacement because it model a situation with zero knowledge of the values that can be injected. Table 3 summarizes the results of the various ratings.

For all less secure implementations, our vulnerability rate $\mathcal{V}$ has the same order of magnitude as φ.

For all implementations except GetChallenge on card B, $\mathcal{T}$ predicts a much higher probability of success than φ. The difference between $\mathcal{T}$ and φ is dependent on the inconsistencies between the arbitrarily chosen fault model and the one that can actually be achieved on card. In SecureGetChallenge on card B, both $\mathcal{V} = \varphi = 0$, whereas in other secure implementations, $\varphi = 0 \neq \mathcal{V}$. The difference comes from the approximations of $\mathcal{V}$, which in turn are the results of approximations in the fault model inference process. Another source of approximation is the choice of $\mathcal{P}$, in particular the chosen range of time values in perturbation attacks are supposed to cover exactly the execution time of the code, which is difficult to ensure in practice. Lastly, φ is also approximated, in

Table 3. Rating criteria of several implementations on various cards

Card	Command	$\mathcal{V}$	$\mathcal{T}$	φ	$|\mathcal{P}'|$
A	VerifyPIN	2.35×10^{-5}	3.2×10^{-2}	3.40×10^{-5}	5883
A	SecureVerifyPIN	2.08×10^{-6}	8.5×10^{-5}	0	5000
A	GetChallenge	2.01×10^{-5}	1.75×10^{-3}	2.94×10^{-5}	6800
A	SecureGetChallenge	7.1×10^{-7}	2.74×10^{-6}	0	3000
B	GetChallenge	1.1×10^{-3}	1.2×10^{-3}	1.4×10^{-3}	231
B	SecureGetChallenge	0	2.14×10^{-4}	0	833

the sense that the individual experiments may have been too short to expose the vulnerabilities.[8]

Prediction of Elapsed Time in Attack Potential. The *elapsed time* factor of the attack potential is classically obtained as the inverse of the multiplication of the number of attacks per second s—in our case, determined experimentally at 1.27 attack·s^{-1} with EM and at 3.30 attack·s^{-1} with laser—by the empirical success rate φ: $(s \times \varphi)^{-1}$. This process requires however that the evaluator performs the physical perturbation attacks on the application. It would be interesting to predict the *elapsed time* factor using $\mathcal{V}$. We calculated $(s \times \mathcal{V})^{-1}$ and $(s \times \mathcal{T})^{-1}$ using the ratings obtained from our previous experiments. The results are summarized in Table 4, along with the score that the attack would receive according to the *elapsed time* factor (ET) in attack potential. From the results we can see that the score for $\mathcal{T}$ does not match φ, being lower in almost all cases. On the other hand, $\mathcal{V}$ has scores similar to φ, and therefore gives a good approximation of the *elapsed time* factor.

Table 4. Comparison of (expected) exploitability times

Card	Command	$(s \times \mathcal{V})^{-1}$	$\rightarrow$ ET	$(s \times \mathcal{T})^{-1}$	$\rightarrow$ ET	$(s \times \varphi)^{-1}$	$\rightarrow$ ET
A	VerifyPIN	8 hours	3	24 seconds	0	6 hours	3
A	SecureVerifyPIN	1 week	4	2.5 hours	3	> *3 days*[8]	⩾ 4
A	GetChallenge	10 hours	3	7 min	0	7.4 hours	3
A	SecureGetChallenge	2 weeks	6	3.5 days	4	> *3 days*[8]	⩾ 4
B	GetChallenge	5 min	0	5 min	0	5 min	0
B	SecureGetChallenge	unpractical	*	20 min	3	> *3 days*[8]	⩾ 4

Sensibility of the Locations. Figure 6 compares the sensibilities of the locations $\ell = (EEPROM, address)$ with $address \in [0x100030, 0x10006c]$, $\mathcal{S}_\ell$ (defined in Sect. 4.3) with the classic criteria $\mathcal{T}_\ell = \dfrac{|\mathcal{F}_S^\ell|}{|\mathcal{F}^\ell|}$ (normalized to be

---

[8] Each experiment lasted for no more than 3 days.

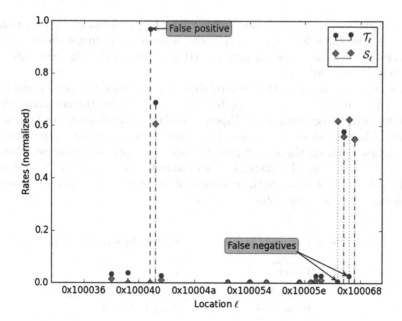

Fig. 6. Comparison of normalized $\mathcal{T}_\ell$ and $\mathcal{S}_\ell$

comparable with $\mathcal{S}_\ell$) on VerifyPIN on card A (EM injection). Our goal is to demonstrate the importance of the weight given to each fault according to a probabilistic fault model on the detection of "sensible" spots in the code. We observe a false positive at address 0x100042, where $\mathcal{T}_\ell$ is high while $\mathcal{S}_\ell = 0$. Indeed, faults at address 0x100042 are faults where the original value is $a = 0$, which we excluded in our probabilistic fault model for card A (see Table 1). Conversely, we observe two "false negatives", i.e., $\mathcal{T}_\ell \ll \mathcal{S}_\ell$ at addresses 0x100064 and 0x100066. Faults at this location have a modified value $b = 0$, which has a high probability of occurrence per the probabilistic fault model for card A. An arbitrary fault model may result in missed vulnerable spots of the code, and conversely spots may be falsely reported as vulnerable. In terms of code analysis, it may lead to vulnerabilities inexplicably difficult to patch, or to the introduction of unneeded countermeasures.

5.2 Discussion

Our approach is an end-to-end process that aims at qualifying the robustness of a smartcard product. This goal is achieved by splitting the assessment of robustness between the probabilistic fault model, that handles the faults at the device level, and the fault injection simulator that handles the consequences of the faults at the application level. The approach shifts the responsibility of performing effective perturbation attacks from the application level to the device level. For evaluators, this means an initial investment to perform the fault model inference process, which becomes worthwhile when evaluating several applications using the same device. For developers, it allows to compare the robustness of several implementations without resorting to physical tests (assuming the fault models are available).

The approach provides the vulnerability rate $\mathcal{V}$, which allows to predict the classic exploitability time factor of *attack potential* [9]. The attacker model $Pr(p)$ can be fine-tuned according to the *Expertise* and the *Knowledge of the TOE* of the attacker. The fault model $\mathcal{M}_{d,e}$ takes into account the equipment of the attacker. The relation between the *attack potential* and our approach is summarized in Table 5. We also defined a metrics $\mathcal{S}_\ell$ to compute the sensibility of individual attack paths and better assess the relevance of the vulnerable code spots detected by our fault injection simulator.

Table 5. Factors of attack potential given by our approach

Factor	$\mathcal{V}$
Elapsed Time	✓
Expertise	Partial $(Pr(p))$
Knowledge of the TOE	Partial $(Pr(p))$
Access to the TOE	✗
Equipment	Partial $(\mathcal{M}_{d,e})$
Open Samples	✗

Our approach introduces some approximations that influence the proposed vulnerability rate. Similarly to other approaches, the parameter discovery step relies on the choices of the evaluator (some interesting parameter values might be accidentally ignored). Specific to our approach is the third step of manual generalization, which can also lead to approximations in the resulting model. Since our approach also models the attacker, the choice of an unrealistic model of $Pr(p)$ also leads to approximations in $\mathcal{V}$. However, it still constitutes an improvement over the complete lack of model.

Furthermore, while our fault detection program works flawlessly with faults on the data, it cannot capture the extra mechanisms in use in microprocessors such as instruction caches or instruction pipelines, and therefore approximates faults on the code. Moreover, at the time of writing, no program is able to detect faults on registers with certainty (a sentinel is difficult to design when all instructions typically manipulates registers).

5.3   Perspectives

It would be interesting to compare our results with other fault observation means, such as fault model extraction [15]. For instance, adding their fault detection program to the fault model inference process would improve the confidence in the resulting fault model.

The inference process of Sect. 3 considers the case where a single perturbation attack occurs during the execution of the command. How should we extend this process to the now common multiple fault attacks? It is not obvious that it is possible to reuse the fault models by assuming that perturbation attacks are independent events. For instance, some extra technical difficulties can arise when synchronizing several laser shots. Further tests are required to conclude on the impact of fault model reuse in multiple fault scenarios.

Moreover, the fault injection simulator of Sect. 4.1 is not able to cope with the combinatory explosion associated with handling multiple fault attacks. Some tools propose heuristics to reduce the combinatorics by simulating the effects of the faults at a higher level [5,13], but they lose the ability to compute a vulnerability rate in the process, and they suffer from side-effects due to the compiler [1] as they work at the source level. We are currently investigating several approaches to handle the combinatorics of mutliple fault simulation while retaining the rating properties.

References

1. Balakrishnan, G., Reps, T.: WYSINWYX: what you see is not what you eXecute. ACM Trans. Programm. Lang. Syst. **32**, 23: 1–23: 84 (2010)
2. Bar-El, H., Choukri, H., Naccache, D., Tunstall, M., Whelan, C.: The Sorcerer's apprentice guide to fault attacks. In: Proceedings of the IEEE, vol. 94, pp. 370–382. IEEE (2006)
3. Barthe, G., Dupressoir, F., Fouque, P.-A., Grégoire, B., Zapalowicz, J.-C.: Synthesis of fault attacks on cryptographic implementations. In: CCS 2014: Proceedings of the ACM SIGSAC Conference on Computer and Communications Security, pp. 1016–1027. ACM, New York (2014)
4. Berthier, M., Bringer, J., Chabanne, H., Le, T.-H., Rivière, L., Servant, V.: Idea: embedded fault injection simulator on smartcard. In: Jürjens, J., Piessens, F., Bielova, N. (eds.) ESSoS. LNCS, vol. 8364, pp. 222–229. Springer, Heidelberg (2014)
5. Berthomé, P., Heydemann, K., Kauffmann-Tourkestansky, X., Lalande, J.: High level model of control flow attacks for smart card functional security. In: Seventh International Conference on Availability, Reliability and Security (ARES 2012), pp. 224–229. IEEE (2012)
6. Blömer, J., Otto, M., Seifert, J.-P.: A new CRT-RSA algorithm secure against bellcore attacks. In: CCS 2003, pp. 311–320. ACM, New York (2003)
7. Boneh, D., DeMillo, R.A., Lipton, R.J.: On the importance of checking cryptographic protocols for faults. In: Fumy, W. (ed.) EUROCRYPT 1997. LNCS, vol. 1233, pp. 37–51. Springer, Heidelberg (1997)
8. Christofi, M., Chetali, B., Goubin, L., Vigilant, D.: Formal verification of a CRT-RSA implementation against fault attacks. J. Crypt. Eng. **3**(3), 157–167 (2013)
9. JIL: Application of attack potential to smartcards. Technical report Version 2.9, Joint Interpretation Library, January 2013

10. Kim, C.H., Quisquater, J.-J.: Fault attacks for CRT based RSA: new attacks, new results, and new countermeasures. In: Sauveron, D., Markantonakis, K., Bilas, A., Quisquater, J.-J. (eds.) WISTP 2007. LNCS, vol. 4462, pp. 215–228. Springer, Heidelberg (2007)
11. Machemie, J.-B., Mazin, C., Lanet, J.-L., Cartigny, J.: SmartCM a smart card fault injection simulator. In: IEEE International Workshop on Information Forensics and Security. IEEE (2011)
12. Ordas, S., Guillaume-Sage, L., Tobich, K., Dutertre, J.-M., Maurine, P.: Evidence of a larger EM-induced fault model. In: Joye, M., Moradi, A. (eds.) CARDIS 2014. LNCS, vol. 8968, pp. 245–259. Springer, Heidelberg (2015)
13. Potet, M.-L., Mounier, L., Puys, M., Dureuil, L.: Lazart: A symbolic approach for evaluation the robustness of secured codes against control flow injections. In: Seventh IEEE International Conference on Software Testing, Verification and Validation, ICST, pp. 213–222. IEEE (2014)
14. Rauzy, P., Guilley, S.: Countermeasures against high-order fault-injection attacks on CRT-RSA. In: FDTC 2014 Workshop on Fault Diagnosis and Tolerance in Cryptography, pp. 68–82. IEEE, September 2014
15. Rivière, L., Najm, Z., Rauzy, P., Danger, J.-L., Bringer, J., Sauvage, L.: High precision fault injections on the instruction cache of ARMv7-M architectures. In: IEEE International Symposium on Hardware Oriented Security and Trust, HOST 2015, pp. 62–67. IEEE, Washington, 5–7 May 2015
16. Verbauwhede, I., Karaklajic, D., Schmidt, J.: The fault attack jungle - a classification model to guide you. In: Workshop on Fault Diagnosis and Tolerance in Cryptography (FDTC), pp. 3–8. IEEE (2011)

Comparing Approaches to Rank Estimation for Side-Channel Security Evaluations

Romain Poussier[(✉)], Vincent Grosso, and François-Xavier Standaert

ICTEAM/ELEN/Crypto Group,
Université catholique de Louvain, Louvain-la-neuve, Belgium
romain.poussier@uclouvain.be

Abstract. Rank estimation is an important tool for side-channel evaluations laboratories. It allows determining the remaining security after an attack has been performed, quantified as the time complexity required to brute force the key given the leakages. Several solutions to rank estimation have been introduced in the recent years. In this paper, we first clarify the connections between these solutions, by organizing them according to their (maximum likelihood or weak maximum likelihood) strategy and whether they take as argument a side-channel distinguishers' output or some evaluation metrics. This leads us to introduce new combinations of these approaches, and to discuss the use of weak maximum likelihood strategies for suboptimal but highly parallel enumeration. Next, we show that the different approaches to rank estimation can also be implemented with different mixes of very similar tools (e.g. histograms, convolutions, combinations and subsampling). Eventually, we provide various experiments allowing to discuss the pros and cons of these different approaches, hence consolidating the literature on this topic.

1 Introduction

Most side-channel attacks published in the literature proceed with a divide-and-conquer strategy. That is, they first extract information about independent pieces of a master key (next called subkeys), and then combine this information in order to recover their concatenation. Typical tools for the subkey information extraction include Kocher et al.'s Differential Power Analysis (DPA) [9], Brier et al.'s Correlation Power Analysis (CPA) [3], Chari et al.'s Template Attacks (TA) [4], Schindler et al.'s Linear Regression (LR) based attacks [11] and many others. As for the recombination part, two typical situations can happen. First, when the attack is close enough to succeed, *key enumeration* can be used, in order to list the most likely key candidates in decreasing order of likelihood [13]. With current computation power, this approach is typically successful when the correct (master) key is ranked up to positions 2^{40}-2^{50} in such a list. Second, when the enumeration becomes too intensive for being conducted in practice, *rank estimation* can be used [14]. In this case, one additionally requires the knowledge of the master key, hence it is only applicable in an evaluation context (while key enumeration is also applicable in an attack context). Based on the

© Springer International Publishing Switzerland 2016
N. Homma and M. Medwed (Eds.): CARDIS 2015, LNCS 9514, pp. 125–142, 2016.
DOI: 10.1007/978-3-319-31271-2_8

Table 1. Approaches to key rank estimation (*italic cases are new*).

	Sampling-based	Metric-based
wML	How: subsampling + combinations	
	What: *SR lower bound (+ subopt. parallel enumeration)*	What: SR lower bound (with limited sampling)
	Acronym: SLB, Ref. [∅]	Acronym: MLB, Ref. [5,15]
ML	How: histograms + convolutions	
	What: SR estimation (tight even for large keys)	What: *SR upper bound (with limited sampling)*
	Acronym: SE, Ref. [1,8,14]	Acronym: MUB, Ref. [∅]

value of the master key and the subkey information, rank estimation aims to efficiently approximate the correct key rank (with a given accuracy).

Rank estimation is especially useful for evaluation laboratories. Indeed, it is a tool of choice for quantifying the security of an implementation whenever it goes beyond the computing power of the evaluator (i.e. whenever an implementation is not trivially insecure). As a result, a number of works have investigated solutions to improve the original algorithm from [14]. In particular, Glowacz et al. presented a more efficient rank estimation tool at FSE 2015, that is based on a simple convolution of histograms and allows obtaining tight bounds for the key rank of (even large) keys [8]. A comparable result was developed independently by Bernstein et al. [1].[1] In parallel, Ye et al. investigated an alternative solution based on a weak Maximum Likelihood (wML) approach [15], rather than a Maximum Likelihood (ML) one for the previous examples. They additionally combined this wML approach with the possibility to approximate the security of an implementation based on "easier to sample" metrics, e.g. starting from the subkey Success Rates (SR) rather than their likelihoods, typically. Eventually, at Eurocrypt 2015 Duc et al. described a simple alternative to the algorithm of Ye et al. and provided an "even easier to sample" bound on the subkey SR, by exploiting their formal connection with a Mutual Information metric [5].

This state-of-the-art suggests the informal classification of approaches to key rank estimation in Table 1, based on whether the algorithms consider ML or wML adversaries/evaluations, and whether they are sampling-based or metric-based.[2] Looking at this table, it is clear that from the "quality of evaluation" point-of-view, the sampling-based ML approach is the most accurate. Indeed, the wML approach corresponds to a suboptimal adversary, hence can only lead to

---

[1] Their "Polynomial Rank Outlining" algorithm can be viewed as similar to the FSE 2015 one, by considering the multiplication of two polynomials as the convolution of coefficient vectors, and the coefficient in the polynomials as histogram counts.

[2] Quite naturally, metrics such as the subkey success rates also need to be sampled somehow. So the term "metric-based" only refers to the type of inputs provided to the rank estimation algorithms, to be compared with the sampling-based approach where the sampled probabilities output by a side-channel attack are used directly.

a Sampled Lower Bound (SLB). Besides, a straightfroward metric-based evaluation can only lead to a Metric-based Lower Bound (MLB), because of a Jensen
inequality (i.e. since it combines the average success rates of several subkeys
which lower bounds the average success of combined attacks against several subkeys). As a result, one can naturally question the interest of these alternative
approaches, for which we can put forward two main motivations:

1. For the wML approach, in addition to the rank estimation, it outputs an *effort
   distributor* which indicates how the enumeration effort should be spread over
   the subkeys, and therefore directly leads to a suboptimal but parallel enumeration algorithm with minimum memory requirements (which is in contrast
   with the optimal but more expensive and serial solution in [13]).
2. For the metric-based approach, the main motivation is to speed up the evaluations, i.e. to run the rank estimation once based on the subkey metrics in
   order to obtain a master key metric, rather than running it many times to
   obtain many master key rank samples to be "metrified" (e.g. averaged).

In view of this state-of-the-art, our contribution is threefold. We start by investigating two cases from Table 1 that were not experimented so far. Namely, we
first show that the simple algorithm from [5] (that exploits a combination of
subsampled metrics) naturally applies in a sampling-based setting, leading to
the previously mentioned SLB that directly suggests a suboptimal but parallel
enumaration strategy. Second, we provide a Metric-based Upper Bound (MUB)
on the SR which allows very fast security evaluations and nicely completes the
lower bound provided by the metric-based wML approach. Third and eventually, we provide an experimental evaluation of these different solutions, allowing
to comprehend their pros and cons. In particular, our experiments include an
analysis of the number of cores that would be necessary for the parallel wML
enumation to start gaining advantage over the serial approach of [13].

Related Works. Two recent works related to key enumeration and rank estimation will appear in the proceedings of SAC 2015 [2] and ASIACRYPT 2015 [10].
More precisely, they primarily contribute to key enumeration algorithms that can
be parallelized, based on simple backtracking procedures for the SAC proposal,
and by casting the enumeration problem as a knapsack for the ASIACRYPT
one. The second paper additionally proposes an alternative solution for rank
estimation, which leads to similar outcomes as the FSE 2015 algorithm.

Notations. We next use sans serif font for functions (e.g. F), calligraphic fonts
for sets (e.g. $\mathcal{A}$) and denote the ith element of a list L by $L[i-1]$.

2 Errors and Bounds

As first discussed in [14], estimating the rank of a key essentially amounts to
performing a mix of depth-first and breadth-first searches in a high-dimensional

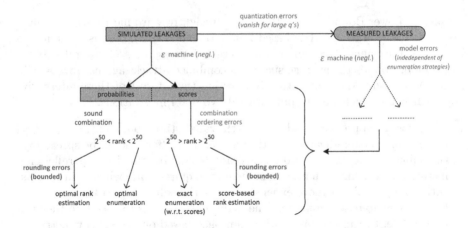

Fig. 1. Errors & bounds in key enumeration and rank estimation.

space representing the key probabilities of a side-channel attack, which turns out to be computationally hard as the key rank increases. It implies that with current computational means and knowledge, it is typically impossible to know the exact position of keys ranked beyond $2^{80} - 2^{90}$ in such high-dimensional spaces. As a result, the only solution is to estimate the rank and to bound the error on this rank estimation. Since there are in fact several types of errors that can be introduced in the course of a side-channel attack, we start this paper with a brief discussion about which are the important errors in key enumeration and rank estimation, and how they can be efficiently bounded by evaluators.

For this purpose, we summarize the main intuitions in Fig. 1, starting with "simulated leakages" (i.e. mathematically-generated ones for which we exactly know the distribution). In this case, the evaluator will start by producing a "distinguishing vector" for which there are only small numerical errors (due to the ϵ machine), that can generally be neglected. More significantly, this distinguishing vector can be made of probabilities (e.g. for TA and LR based attacks) or scores (e.g. for DPA and CPA). This is an important distinction, since in the first case the evaluator will be able to combine the information of independent subkeys on a sound basis, whereas in the second case he will potentially introduce "combination ordering errors". For example, say we have two lists of subkey probabilities $[p_1, p_2]$ and $[p_a, p_b]$ with $p_1 > p_2$ and $p_a > p_b$ (resp. scores $[s_1, s_2]$ and $[s_a, s_b]$ with $s_1 > s_2$ and $s_a > s_b$). Whereas it is clear (using both scores and probabilities) that the best-rated key corresponds to the pair $\{p_1, p_a\}$ or $\{s_1, s_a\}$ and the worst-rated one corresponds to the pair $\{p_2, p_b\}$ or $\{s_2, s_b\}$, only probabilities allow comparing the pairs $\{p_1, p_b\}$ and $\{p_2, p_a\}$ (by multiplying the probabilities). Intuitively, the key property here is that a probability of 1 for a subkey implies a success rate of 1 for this subkey, which therefore allows "guiding" the key enumeration and rank estimation algorithms.[3] Given this difference, it is then possible to enumerate optimally based on probabilities, or to enumerate exactly w.r.t. some scores, whenever the key rank is computationally reachable (e.g. when it is smaller than 2^{50} on the figure). By contrast, if the rank is too high for the keys to be enumerated, the only option is key rank estimation, where additional rounding errors will appear. Interestingly, it is shown in [1,8,10] that the errors due to this rounding can be kept small comparatively to the key rank. For example, rank estimation algorithms allow claiming that a key is rated among ranks 2^{80} and 2^{81} (or even tighter bounds) which is perfectly relevant in a side-channel evaluation context, since it indicates its remaining computational security. Admittedly, this does not mean that the rank estimation itself is perfectly accurate, since the only thing we can guarantee in our example is that the key rank is in a (large) set of size $2^{81} - 2^{80} = 2^{80}$.

Next, and when moving to the practically relevant case of measured leakages, two additional types of errors can appear. First, the measurements are typically operated with a sampling device, with 8 bits to 12 bits of accuracy, which causes quantization errors. However, the impact of these errors tends to vanish as the number of measured leakages q in the attack increases (since the cardinality of the joint leakages then increases exponentially in q, e.g. 256^q or 4096^q for our 8-bit and 12-bit cases). More importantly, model errors can be introduced, i.e. discrepancies between the true leakage distribution and the one exploited by the adversary. However, these errors are in fact independent of the enumeration strategies. So indeed, when speaking about optimal enumeration, the optimality is relative to the leakage models, which we expect to be sound in worst-case security evaluations (and can be guaranteed with leakage certification tests [6]). But for the rest, the main errors that we consider and bound in this paper are the rounding ones, that are unavoidable when estimating large ranks.

3   Algorithm Specification

3.1   Algorithms Inputs

Details on how a side-channel attack extracts information from leakage traces are not necessary to understand the following analysis. We only assume that for a n-bit master key k, an attacker recovers information on N_s subkeys $k_0, ..., k_{N_s - 1}$ of length $b = \frac{n}{N_s}$ bits (for simplicity, we assume that b divides n). The side-channel

---

[3] By contrast, one could typically imagine a scenario where the scores obtained from a CPA lead to a correlation 0.2 for a subkey that is known with high confidence and the same correlation of 0.2 for a subkey that is not know at all – because of different Signal-to-Noise Ratios. In this case, the key enumeration and rank estimation algorithms will not be able to list keys optimally. Quite naturally, it is possible to mitigate such issues by outputing the p-values of the CPA distinguisher, but this requires making additional assumptions on its distribution, and eventually corresponds to a type of profiling which would then allow evaluators to directly estimate probabilities. So in general, we believe it is advisable to directly use probability-based distinguishers for optimal key enumeration and rank estimation algorithms.

adversary uses the leakages corresponding to a set of q inputs $\mathcal{X}_q$ leading to a set of q leakages $\mathcal{L}_q$. As a result of the attack, he obtains N_s lists of 2^b probabilities $P_i = \Pr[k_i^* | \mathcal{X}_q, \mathcal{L}_q]$, where $i \in [0, N_s - 1]$ and k_i^* denotes a subkey candidate among the 2^b possible ones. As just mentioned, TA and LR based attacks directly output such probabilities. For other attacks such as DPA or CPA, one can either go for score-based rank estimation or use Bayesian extensions [13].

Based on these notations, our sampling-based approaches to rank estimation will require two additional inputs. First the lists of probabilities might be turned into lists of log probabilities, denoted as $LP_i = \log(P_i)$. Next, these lists of probabilities will also be translated into lists of cumulative probabilities as follows. First a sorted list is produced as: $SP_i = \mathsf{sort}(P_i, \text{decreasing})$. Then, the list of cumulative probabilities is derived as CP_i such that $CP_i[j] = \sum_{jj=0}^{j} SP_i[jj]$.

As for the metric-based approaches, they will require the subkey success rates of order d introduced in [12], which simply correspond to the probability that the correct subkey is rated among the first d ones by an attack. In the following, we will denote the lists of 2^b success rates of order d (with $d \in [1, 2^b]$) as SR_i. We will additionally denote the "derivative" of these success rates (i.e. the probabilities that a key is rated exactly at position d) as ΔSR_i such that $\Delta SR_i[d] = SR_i[d] - SR_i[d - 1]$ (with $SR_i[0]$ set to 0 by definition).

3.2   Toolbox

For convenience, we now introduce a number of generic tools that will be used to simplify the description of our following algorithms, and can be found (or easily developed) in most mathematical programming languages.

Linear Histograms. The function $H = \mathsf{hist\_lin}(LP, \text{bins})$ creates a standard histogram from a list of (e.g.) log probabilities LP and linearly-spaced bins bins.

Logarithmic Indexing. Given a list of (e.g.) probabilities P indexed from 1 to 2^b and a width w, the function $LI = \mathsf{index\_log}(P, w)$ groups the elements in the list by the logarithm of their indexes according to a width w. An example of such a logarithmic indexing with $w = 1$ is illustrated in the left part of Fig. 2, where we have $LI[0] = P[0]$, $LI[1] = P[1] + P[2]$ and so on. More precisely $LI[k] = \sum_{j \in \mathcal{E}_k} P[j - 1]$ with $\mathcal{E}_k = \{j \in \mathbb{N} \cap [2^{k \cdot w}, 2^{(k+1) \cdot w}[\} $ and $k \in [1, \frac{log_2(l)}{w}]$.

Linear Downsampling. Given a list of (e.g.) cumulative probabilities CP or success rates SR, the function $\mathsf{downs\_lin}(CP, N_{max})$ (resp. $\mathsf{downs\_lin}(SR, N_{max})$)

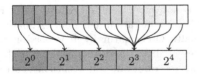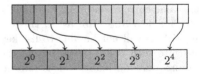

Fig. 2. Logarithmic indexing with $w = 1$ (left) and logarithmic downsampling (right).

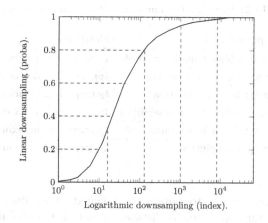

Fig. 3. Illustration of dowsampling possibilities (Color figure online).

reduces the size of CP (resp. SR) by selecting N_{max} linearly-spaced samples over the probabilities (resp. success rates). This downsampling is illustrated on the Y axis of Fig. 3, where we keep the values sampled by the blue dotted lines. *Logarithmic Downsampling.* Given a list of (e.g.) cumulative probabilities CP or success rates SR, the function downs_log(CP) (resp. downs_log(SR)) reduces the size of CP (resp. SR) by sampling logarithmically over the indexes, and selecting one sample per power of two of the keys (resp. orders). An example of this downsampling is given on the X axis of Fig. 3, where we keep the values sampled by the red dotted lines (and in the right part of Fig. 2).

Convolution. This is the usual convolution algorithm which from two histograms H_1 and H_2 of sizes n_1 and n_2 computes $H_{1,2} = \mathsf{conv}(H_1, H_2)$ where $H_{1,2}[k] = \sum_{i=0}^{k} H_1[i] \times H_2[k-i]$. It can be implemented efficiently with a FFT.

Linear Combination. Given two lists of (e.g.) cumulative probabilities CP_1 and CP_2 of sizes n_1 and n_2, the linear combination $CP_{1,2} = \mathsf{comb\_lin}(CP_1, CP_2)$ can be computed as $CP_{1,2}[k] = max\{CP_1[i] \times CP_2[j] \mid i \cdot j = k\}$ for $k \in [0, n_1 \cdot n_2 - 1]$. Such a combination assumes that the underlying relation between the indexes is multiplicative, which is the case for cumulative probabilities. As for the linear downsampling, this linear combination similarly applies to success rates.

Logarithmic Combination. Given two lists of (e.g.) cumulative probabilities CP_1 and CP_2 of sizes n_1 and n_2, the logarithmic combination $CP_{1,2} = \mathsf{comb\_log}(CP_1, CP_2)$ can be computed as $CP_{1,2}[k] = max\{CP_1[i] \times CP_2[j] \mid i + j = k\}$ for $k \in [0, n_1 + n_2 - 1]$. Such a combination assumes that the underlying relation between the indexes is additive, which is the case when a list has been previously processed by downs_log (so it again applies to success rates as well).

Effort Distributor. In general, the (linear or logarithmic) downsampling and combination procedures, output lists with reduced number of samples. But as mentioned in introduction, for sampling-based wML rank estimation, it may

Table 2. Tools used in our rank estimation algorithms.

	Sampling-based	Metric-based
wML	**Input**: subkey cumulative prob.	**Input**: subkey success rates
	Approx: log. downsampling	**Approx**: log. downsampling
	Aggreg: log. combination	**Aggreg**: log. combination
ML	**Input**: subkey log. probabilities	**Input**: subkey SR derivative
	Approx: linear histograms	**Approx**: log. indexing
	Aggreg: convolution	**Aggreg**: convolution

additionally be interesting to output a so-called effort distributor. In this case, these procedures (applied to lists of cumulative probabilities) will also input/output the indices of the retained samples, which indicates how much effort should be devoted (i.e. how many keys should be tested) for each subkey.

3.3 Preprocessing

As part of our evaluations, we will also consider the preprocessing which consists of merging m lists of probabilities P_i of size 2^b in order to generate a larger list $P_i' = \mathsf{merge}(P_0, P_1, \ldots, P_{m-1})$, such that P_i' contains the $2^{m \cdot b}$ product of probabilities of these lists. Taking again our notations where the n bits of master key are split in N_s subkeys of b bits, it amounts to split them into a $N_s' = N_s/m$ subkeys of $m \cdot b$ bits. This process is in fact similar to the previously described linear combination one. We just use the term merging and denote it as merge_m when it is used for pre-processing (to be consistent with previous works).

3.4 Overview of the Tools Used in Different Approaches

Before describing our four rank estimation algorithms in detail, Table 2 provides a quick overview of the different tools that we exploit in the different approaches. As clearly seen from the table, each of the algorithms is mainly characterized by a type of input together with an approximation and an aggregation procedure. Note that for the sampling-based ML one, we use exactly the FSE 2015 algorithm [8]. This choice is motivated by the fact that it is the fastest one published so far.[4] As for the metric-based wML approach, we use a slight variant of the EUROCRYPT 2015 heuristic [5], where we replace the linear downsampling by a logarithmic downsampling (which turns out to be more efficient).[5]

---

[4] Together with its analog in [1] which would yield very similar performances.

[5] The algorithm by Ye et al. could be used as a sightly more accurate alternative. However, as our proposal, it can only provide a lower bound on the success rate because it is based on a wML approach. We focused on the EUROCRYPT 2015 heuristic because of its simplicity and connections with the other solutions of Table 2.

3.5   Sampling-Based Rank Estimation

We use exactly the solution proposed at FSE 2015, recalled in Algorithm 1. As detailed in [8], it allows reaching tight bounds for the key ranks (for key sizes up to 1024 bits), typically setting the log of the ratio between the upper and lower bounds to less than one bit. In the following, we will consider this Sampled Estimation (SE) as a reference (i.e. our most accurate rank estimation).

Algorithm 1. Sampling-based rank estimation (SE).

Input: The log proba. of the master key lpk, lists of log proba. LP_i, and bins bins.
Output: An estimation of the master key rank.

$H_{curr} = \text{hist\_lin}(LP_0, \text{bins})$
for $i = 1$ to $N'_s - 1$ do
   $H_i \leftarrow \text{hist\_lin}(LP_i, \text{bins})$
   $H_{curr} \leftarrow \text{conv}(H_{curr}, H_i)$
end for
$rank \leftarrow log_2(\sum_{i=\text{bins}(lpk)}^{N'_s \cdot N_{bin} - (N'_s - 1)} H_{curr}[i])$
return $rank$

Note that if the evaluator's goal is to estimate a success rate of a given order for the master key (or more generally to build a security graph such as described in [14]), he will need to repeat Algorithm 1 several times in order to obtain many estimates of the key rank that he will average afterwards, i.e. a quite costly task which may motivate the use of metric-based approaches to rank estimation.

3.6   Sampling-Based Success Lower Bound

The ML rank estimation actually corresponds to an optimal enumeration strategy such as described in [13]. In this context, the adversary/evaluator produces a list of (master) key candidates in decreasing order of likelihood that he can test. Quite naturally, such an optimal enumeration implies that (most of the times) when moving from the ith most likely key to the $i + 1$th one, the indices of several subkeys will vary. In general, such an approach therefore has significant memory requirements (corresponding to the size of the lists to produce and send to the "key testing" hardware). The wML approach introduced in [15] actually corresponds to a much simpler (greedy) strategy where, when moving from the ith most likely key to the $i + 1$th one, the indices of only one subkey are modified. While obviously suboptimal, this strategy has the significant advantage that it has essentialy no memory requirements, i.e. one only needs to store the number of candidates to enumerate per subkey (i.e. the effort distributor), and is straightforward to parallelize. Its simplified version (inspired from [5] but replacing the linear downsampling and combination by logarithmic ones) is described in Algorithm 2. It outputs a SLB on the (single) attack's success together with an effort distributor. Since the combination is done using a logarithmic downsampling, any output of the effort distributor $ED[i]$ (with $i \in [0, n)$) is a N'_s-element list corresponding to an effort of 2^i, where every element of the list is a subkey effort. For simplicity, we will say that a key k is in the effort distributor $ED[i]$ if the rank of all its subkeys is lower than the corresponding subkey effort in the list $ED[i]$. As in the SE approach, estimation of a success rate thanks to this approach requires repeating attacks (and Algorithm 2) several times.

Algorithm 2. Sampling-based success lower bound (SLB).

Input: Lists of cumulative proba. CP_i and actual subkeys $k = \{k_0, ..., k_{N'_s-1}\}$.
Output: An upper bound on the master key rank.

   $CP_{curr} \leftarrow$ downs_log(CP_0)
   $ED_{curr} \leftarrow \varnothing$
   for $i = 1$ **to** $N'_s - 1$ **do**
     $CP'_i \leftarrow$ downs_log(CP_i)
     $CP_{curr}, ED \leftarrow$ comb_log(CP, CP'_i, ED_{curr})
     $ED_{curr} = ED_{curr} \cup ED$
   end for
   $log\_rank \leftarrow 0$
   while $k \notin ED[log\_rank]$ **do**
     $log\_rank \leftarrow log\_rank + 1$
   end while
   return 2^{log_rank}

3.7 Metric-Based Success Rate Lower Bound

As previously mentioned, a possible drawback of the previous sampling-based approaches is that producing success rate curves based on them requires running the rank estimation algorithms several times. One natural solution to avoid this drawback is to consider metric-based approaches, where the evaluator does not directly deal with DPA outcomes (i.e. subkey log probabilities or cumulative probabilities), but with the success rates of every subkey considered independently. Concretely, this approach highly resembles the one in the previous section (only its inputs are different). However, it does not only correspond to a suboptimal wML strategy: it also includes an additional loss of tightness due to a Jensen inequality. In the following, we refer to this strategy, described in Algorithm 3, as the Metric-based success rate Lower Bound MLB approach.

Algorithm 3. Metric-based success rate lower bound (MLB).

Input: Lists of success rates SR_i.
Output: A lower bound on the master key success rate.

   $SR_{low} \leftarrow$ downs_log(SR_0)
   for $i = 1$ **to** $N'_s - 1$ **do**
     $SR^i_{low} \leftarrow$ downs_log(SR_i)
     $SR_{low} \leftarrow$ comb_log(SR_{low}, SR^i_{low})
   end for
   return SR_{low}

3.8   Metric-Based Success Rate Upper Bound

The metric-based approach in the previous section is very convenient to manipulate (i.e. simple and efficient) but it only provides a lower bound for the success rate. This section finally brings its natural complement, i.e. an easy-to-manipulate metric-based upper bound for this success rate. For this purpose, the main technical ingredient is to replace the logarithmic downsampling of the success rate curves (where only the sample with maximum success rate is kept) by a logarithmic indexing of the derivative success rates with width w (which are then combined thanks to the convolution tool). As a result, we obtain the Metric-based success rate Upper Bound (MUB) described in Algorithm 4.

Algorithm 4. Metric-based success rate upper bound (MUB).

Input: Lists of derivative success rates ΔSR_i and bin log-width w.
Output: An upper bound on the master key success rate.

$LI_{curr} = \mathsf{index\_log}(\Delta SR_0, w)$
  for $i = 1$ to $N_s' - 1$ **do**
    $LI_i \leftarrow \mathsf{index\_log}(\Delta SR_i, w)$
    $LI_{curr} \leftarrow \mathsf{conv}(LI_{curr}, LI_i)$
  end for
$SR_{up}[0] \leftarrow \sum_{j=0}^{j=\frac{1}{w}-1} LI_{curr}[j]$
  for $i = 1$ to n **do**
    $SR_{up}[i] \leftarrow (\sum_{j=\frac{1}{w}\cdot i}^{j=\frac{1}{w}\cdot(i+1)-1} LI_{curr}[j]) + SR_{up}[i-1]$
  end for
return SR_{up}

In practice, the lower w is, the tighter the bound is. For simplicity, we will assume w is at most equal to 1 and that $\frac{1}{w}$ must fall into the integer domain (our following experiments will take $w = 0.001$). An explanation why this algorithm indeed gives an upper bound for the success rate is given in the Appendix A.

4   Experiments

In this section, we provide experiments to illustrate our four methods. For this purpose, we considered the standard case study (also used in previous evaluations of rank estimation algorithms) of a simulated AES-128 implementation, for which every encryption leaks 16 samples denoted as $l_i = \mathsf{L}(\mathsf{S}(x_i, k_i)) + N$ with $i \in [0, 15]$, where L is the leakage function, S is the AES S-box and N is a random noise following a Gaussian distribution. Concretely, we tried different L's (Hamming weight, linear, non-linear) which had no impact on our observations (as previously reported). We also tried having different L's and N's for the different subkeys with the same conclusion. So because of place constraints, we only report experiments for a single leakage function and noise level. Based on these leakages, we implemented a simple univariate TA, in order to produce the lists of probabilities defined in Sect. 3.1. For all our experiments, our evaluation metrics were obtained by launching 1000 independent attacks.

4.1   Sampling-Based Evaluations

A comparison of the (tight) rank estimation bound from FSE 2015 (using 10,000 bins) with the sampling-based lower bound of Algorithm 2 is reported in Fig. 4, for different number of measurements (hence security levels). As expected, we see that the wML approach can only provide a lower bound on the success rate. The SLB curves additionally exhibit the (positive) impact of merging the subkey probabilities prior to the evaluation for the quality of the lower bound.

Besides, and as discussed in Sect. 3.6, Algorithm 2 can also be used to provide a simple (yet suboptimal) enumeration strategy that can be parallelized. So assuming that the optimal enumeration algorithm in [13] is implemented in a purely serial fashion (which is correct as soon as generating the list of most likely keys becomes more expensive than testing them), another interesting experiment

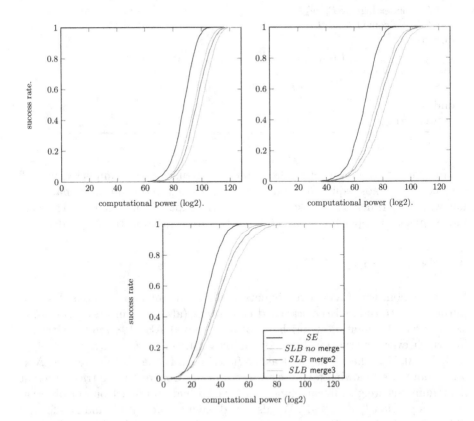

Fig. 4. Sampling-based rank estimations for different security levels. Upper left: 80-bit security level. Upper right: 65-bit security level. Bottom: 30-bit security level.

is to measure the gap between these two approaches. For this purpose, Fig. 5 shows the number of cores needed to reach the success rate of a (purely serial) ML enumeration with the suboptimal but parallel wML heuristic of Algorithm 2, for the same experiments as reported in Fig. 4. For example, we see that for the ≈ 80-bit security level (upper left plot) and assuming a merge_3 preprocessing, we can reach the same 80% success rate with both approaches assuming that the parallel enumeration exploits 2^{10} computing cores. This result is interesting since it suggests that for organized adversaries, the enumeration overheads of a wML enumeration strategy may be compensated by computing capabilities. Note that these results assume that it takes as much time for the enumeration algorithm to output a candidate as it takes to test it, which is a conservative estimate if one assumes that the testing can be performed by some dedicated hardware.

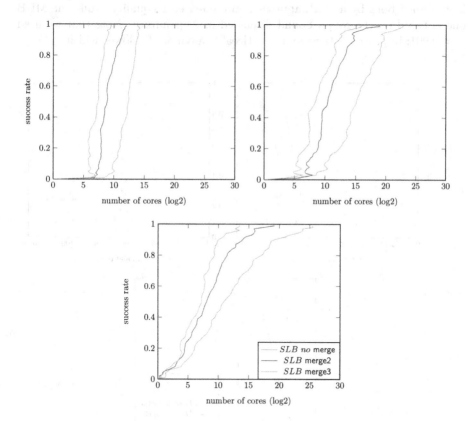

Fig. 5. Number of cores needed to reach the success rate of a (serial) ML enumeration with the suboptimal but parallel wML heuristic of Algorithm 2. Upper left: 80-bit security level. Upper right: 65-bit security level. Bottom: 30-bit security level.

4.2   Metric-Based Evaluations

We now describe the metric-based counterpart to the previous sampling-based experiments, reported in Fig. 6. We again use the estimate from Algorithm 1 as a reference, and this time compare it with Algorithms 3 and 4. Note that for comparison purposes, our subkey success rates were directly sampled (i.e. not bounded as suggested in [5]). This allows us to gauge the impact of the different enumeration strategies for similar inputs. As expected again, Algorithms 3 and 4 indeed provide lower and upper security bounds. However, while those metric-based solutions are especially convenient from an evaluation time point of view (see the following discussion in Sect. 4.3), it is also clear from the figure that none of them provides tight approximations of the security level. This is somehow expected as well since the MLB curves correspond to an adversary who is weakened both by a wML approach and a Jensen inequality, while the MUB one is based on the rough bound discussed in Appendix A. Note that we used $w = 0.001$: improvements were not noticeable anymore for lower widths.

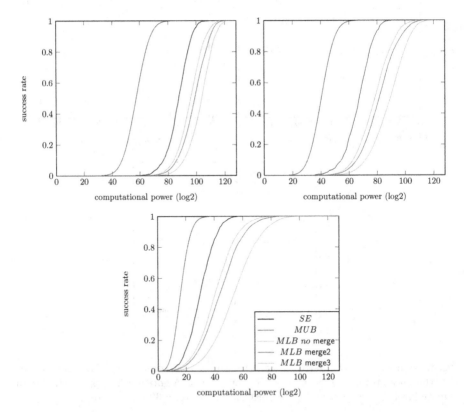

Fig. 6. Metric-based rank estimations for different security levels. Upper left: 80-bit security level. Upper right: 65-bit security level. Bottom: 30-bit security level.

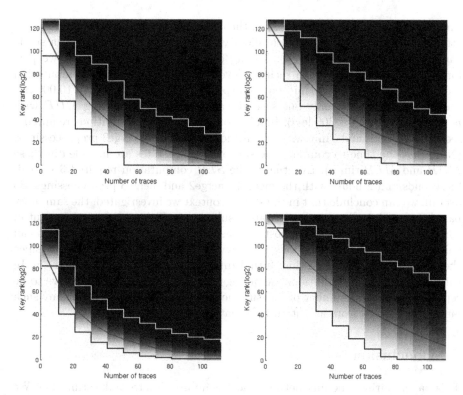

Fig. 7. Security graphs. Upper left: SE methods, upper right: MLB + merge3 pre-processing, lower left: MUB (bottom left), lower right: MLB with no merging.

Interestingly though, these conclusions are moderated when looking at the complete security graphs obtained with these different approaches, reported in Fig. 7 (i.e. plots of the success rate in function of the number of measurements and time complexity of the attacks [14]). Namely, the upper and lower security bounds that correspond to the MLB and MUB curves are not so optimistic/pessimistic from this point-of-view. This is in fact mainly due to the weaker impact of enumeration (compared to measurements) in side-channel analysis. That is, adding a new measurements reduces the security exponentially, while enumerating only does it polynomially. So overall, despite being based on relatively rough heuristics, Algorithms 3 and 4 can in fact be used to obtain a reasonable view of the security level of leaking implementation. The latter observation is in line with the experiments in [15] where the gap between the ML and wML approach appeared to be limited when looking at similar figures.

4.3   Time Complexity

In order to provide a complete view of the rank estimation problem, we finally provide a brief discussion of the time complexity of these approaches. Note that this discussion mainly makes sense in the context of an evaluation, where many attacks have to be launched in parallel (while in a real attack context, a single enumeration is usually enough). Taking our exemplary experiments, we performed 1000 attacks for each security level. In this case, the SE computation required approximatively 5 min proceed (per number of traces), with 10,000 initial bins. By contrast, only one second was needed for computing MUB with $w = 0.001$ (so a factor 300 less). In addition, the MLB computations required 1 second, 3 seconds and 5 min with the merge1, merge2 and merge3 preprocessings. (Note that the time to compute the subkeys success rates are included in these MUB and MLB times). Eventually, the SLB computation required 3 second, 38 seconds and 2 hours with the merge1, merge2 and merge3 preprocessings. So overall, we can conclude that in the simple context we investigated, the sampling-based approach leads to very accurate results in a sufficiently short time. But in contexts where the evaluation cost increases, simpler metric-based bounds can gain more interest. Such bounds are anyway useful for fast prototyping since they can be combined with the Mutual Information based evaluations in [5]. In this case, we gain the additional advantage that the analyis does not have to be repeated for several number of measurements (i.e. the success rate for any such number is derived from a Mutual Information metric).

5   Conclusion

This paper clarifies the link between various approaches to rank estimation. We divided our investigations in two parts, one sampling-based that is closer to the goals of concrete adversaries, one metric-based that is closer to evaluator's ones. We additionally discussed the interest of wML enumeration strategies in order to make this task easily parallelizable. Our experiments suggest that tight rank estimation can be efficiently implemented thanks to a simple algorithm from FSE 2015. But they also highlight that the wML and metric-based approaches can gain interest (e.g. for adversaries with high parallel computing power and to further speed up the evaluation time, respectively). In view of the efficient solutions existing for rank estimation, an important scope for further research remains to find new algorithms for optimal and parallel enumeration. First proposals in this direction can be found at SAC 2015 [2] and ASIACRYPT 2015 [10].

Acknowledgements. F.-X. Standaert is a research associate of the Belgian Fund for Scientific Research (FNRS-F.R.S.). This work has been funded in parts by the European Commission through the ERC project 280141 (CRASH).

A   Bound from the Metric-Based Maximum Likelihood

We start from the observation that if the lists of probabilities obtained for each S-box are independent, $rank(k_0) = d_0, \ldots, rank(k_{N'_s}) = d_{N'_s}$ and $rank(k) = d$, then $d \geq \prod_i d_i$. When estimating a master key success rate, it implies that:

$$\widehat{SR}[d] \leq \sum_{d_i, \prod_i d_i \leq d} \Delta SR_0[d_0] \times \cdots \times \Delta SR_{N_s'}[d_{N_s'}].$$

Algorithm 4 just computes such a sum of products of derivative success rates.

Note that the independence condition for the S-box probabilities in this bound is not the same as the usual independent leakages considered, e.g. in leakage-resilience cryptography [7], which is a purely physical condition. Here, we only need that the adversary considers the subkeys independently.

References

1. Bernstein, D.J., Lange, T., van Vredendaal, C.: Tighter, faster, simpler side-channel security evaluations beyond computing power. IACR Cryptol. ePrint Arch. **2015**, 221 (2015)
2. Bogdanov, A., Kizhvatov, I., Manzoor, K., Tischhauser, E., Witteman, M.: Fast and memory-efficient key recovery in side-channel attacks. IACR Cryptol. ePrint Arch. **2015**, 795 (2015)
3. Brier, E., Clavier, C., Olivier, F.: Correlation power analysis with a leakage model. In: Joye, M., Quisquater, J.-J. (eds.) CHES 2004. LNCS, vol. 3156, pp. 16–29. Springer, Heidelberg (2004)
4. Chari, S., Rao, J.R., Rohatgi, P.: Template attacks. In: Kaliski Jr., B.S., Koç, Ç.K., Paar, C. (eds.) CHES 2002. LNCS, vol. 2523, pp. 13–28. Springer, Heidelberg (2003)
5. Duc, A., Faust, S., Standaert, F.-X.: Making masking security proofs concrete. In: Oswald, E., Fischlin, M. (eds.) EUROCRYPT 2015. LNCS, vol. 9056, pp. 401–429. Springer, Heidelberg (2015)
6. Durvaux, F., Standaert, F.-X., Veyrat-Charvillon, N.: How to certify the leakage of a chip? In: Nguyen, P.Q., Oswald, E. (eds.) EUROCRYPT 2014. LNCS, vol. 8441, pp. 459–476. Springer, Heidelberg (2014)
7. Dziembowski, S., Pietrzak, K.: Leakage-resilient cryptography. In: 49th Annual IEEE Symposium on Foundations of Computer Science, FOCS 25–28, 2008, Philadelphia, PA, USA, pp. 293–302. IEEE Computer Society, October 2008
8. Glowacz, C., Grosso, V., Poussier, R., Schueth, J., Standaert, F.-X.: Simpler and more efficient rank estimation for side-channel security assessment. IACR Cryptol. ePrint Arch. **2014**, 920 (2014)
9. Kocher, P.C., Jaffe, J., Jun, B.: Differential power analysis. In: Wiener, M. (ed.) CRYPTO 1999. LNCS, vol. 1666, pp. 388–397. Springer, Heidelberg (1999)
10. Martin, D.P., O'Connell, J.F., Oswald, E., Stam, M.: How to enumerate your keys accurately and efficiently after a side channel attack. IACR Cryptol. ePrint Arch. **2015**, 689 (2015)
11. Schindler, W., Lemke, K., Paar, C.: A stochastic model for differential side channel cryptanalysis. In: Rao, J.R., Sunar, B. (eds.) CHES 2005. LNCS, vol. 3659, pp. 30–46. Springer, Heidelberg (2005)
12. Standaert, F.-X., Malkin, T.G., Yung, M.: A unified framework for the analysis of side-channel key recovery attacks. In: Joux, A. (ed.) EUROCRYPT 2009. LNCS, vol. 5479, pp. 443–461. Springer, Heidelberg (2009)

13. Veyrat-Charvillon, N., Gérard, B., Renauld, M., Standaert, F.-X.: An Optimal Key Enumeration Algorithm and Its Application to Side-Channel Attacks. In: Knudsen, L.R., Wu, H. (eds.) SAC 2012. LNCS, vol. 7707, pp. 390–406. Springer, Heidelberg (2013)
14. Veyrat-Charvillon, N., Gérard, B., Standaert, F.-X.: Security evaluations beyond computing power. In: Johansson, T., Nguyen, P.Q. (eds.) EUROCRYPT 2013. LNCS, vol. 7881, pp. 126–141. Springer, Heidelberg (2013)
15. Ye, X., Eisenbarth, T., Martin, W.: Bounded, yet sufficient? How to determine whether limited side channel information enables key recovery. In: Joye, M., Moradi, A. (eds.) CARDIS 2014. LNCS, vol. 8968, pp. 215–232. Springer, Heidelberg (2015)

Collision for Estimating SCA Measurement Quality and Related Applications

Ibrahima Diop[1,4(✉)], Mathieu Carbone[2], Sebastien Ordas[2], Yanis Linge[1],
Pierre Yvan Liardet[1], and Philippe Maurine[2,3]

[1] STMicroelectronics, Rousset, France
ibrahima.diop@st.com
[2] LIRMM, Université Montpellier II, Montpellier, France
[3] CEA, 880 Route de Mimet, 13541 Gardanne, France
[4] Ecole des Mines de Saint-Etienne (EMSE), Saint-Etienne, France

Abstract. If the Signal to Noise Ratio (SNR) is a figure of merit commonly used in many areas to gauge the quality of analogue measurements, its use in the context of Side-Channel Attacks (SCA) remains very difficult because the nature and characteristics of the signals are not a priori known. Consequently, the SNR is rarely used in this latter area to gauge the quality of measurements or of experimental protocols followed to acquire them. It is however used to quantify the amount of leakage in a set of traces regardless of the quality of the measures. This is a surprisingly lack despite the key role of measurements and experiments in this field. In this context, this paper introduces a fast and accurate method for estimating the SNR. Then, simple and accurate techniques are derived. They allow to process some daily tasks the evaluators have to perform in a pragmatic and efficient manner. Among them one can find the analysis of the electrical activity of Integrated Circuit (IC) or the identification of the frequencies carrying some information or leakages.

1 Introduction

In recent years, emphasis has been put on the localization of leaking content in space [4,13,14] and time [1], but also to increase our understanding of the latest or again to enhance our extraction capability [2,6,9]. Efforts have also been invested to assess the efficiency of attacks resulting in notions like the success rate and the guessing entropy.

Based on [16], one generally considers two types of evaluation metrics for assessing the leakage emitted by cryptographic devices. First, information theoretic metrics aim to capture the amount of information available in a side-channel leakage, independently of the adversary exploitation. Second, security metrics aim to quantify how this information can be exploited by adversary using the notions of Success Rate (SR) and Guessing Entropy (GE). In SCA context, these two types of metrics are clearly related but they are also surrounded by the quality of measurements for which less attention has been paid to define criteria allowing to compare experimental practices that are central.

© Springer International Publishing Switzerland 2016
N. Homma and M. Medwed (Eds.): CARDIS 2015, LNCS 9514, pp. 143–157, 2016.
DOI: 10.1007/978-3-319-31271-2_9

The Signal-to-Noise Ratio (SNR) is a simple, intuitive and relevant metric to characterize any analog phenomena, such as side channel measurements in order to gauge the quality of acquisition campaign. However the first definition of SNR [10] in the SCA context has some drawbacks making its practical use difficult given that the signal and its characteristics are a priori not known. Some workarounds have been proposed in the literature but most of them rely in converting the problem into leakage quantification or Points of Interest (PoI) detection rather than focusing the quality of the acquisition campaigns. Among these works, one may include the approach proposed in 2011 [7] that offers a method for estimating the SNR which is based on a linear model of the leakage but also on empirical considerations related to the use of Digital Sampling Oscilloscopes (DSO). However, the SNR definition considered in this work is relatively far from the standard electrical engineering definition and finally closer to that of a Leakage to Noise Ratio (LNR) concept.

This latter concept appears explicitly in [17] with an estimation method based on a modeling of the leakage in the frequency domain. Alongside the introduction of the LNR, authors in [1] propose the Normalized Inter-Class Variance (NICV). This approach based on a clever and effective use of the statistical tool of ANOVA (ANalysis Of VAriance) where the F-test allows to identify the PoI thanks to the knowledge of public information (plaintext or ciphertext) (*i.e.* allows to detect interesting time samples carrying potential leakage based on the manipulation of the inputs). Besides this important application, it is also suggested that the NICV provides an estimate of the SNR. However, again the SNR definition considered in this paper is more an estimate of the relative amount of leakage in the samples of traces that an estimate of the SNR of a measurement set.

In this context, the main contribution of this paper to the State of the Art is a method, based on signal collisions, to estimate the SNR. This method requires a small amount of measures to be applied: two in theory and up to few tens for convenient practice.

The second contribution is to show that this SNR estimate is also an effective way to gauge the quality of traces in view of the application of SCA. Additionally, it is then shown how to exploit the above technique to:

– analyze the temporal behavior of a circuit from a small amount of measures,
– distinguish the frequencies carrying information related to the signal from the frequencies essentially made up of noise.

The distinction of frequencies carrying information is crucial. Indeed, it enables, without any a priori knowledge about the characteristics of the signal, to rationally and adaptively guide the filtering procedures.

This paper is organized as follows: in Sect. 2, the meaning of the term *signal* considered in this paper, and related SNR is defined. Section 3 recalls the standard electrical engineering definition of the SNR and the corollary definition thereof in the case of zero mean signals. These definitions recalled, Sect. 4 demonstrates theoretically how to get an estimate of the SNR from signal collisions and more particularly from a bounded collision detection criterion introduced in [8]. It is then experimentally demonstrated in Sect. 5 that the obtained SNR estimate is actually a figure of merit for gauging the quality of traces in a SCA context. Similarly, Sect. 6 shows how this fast estimate method of the SNR allows analyzing SCA traces in a simple, effective and complementary way to the approaches introduced in [1,17]. Section 7 shows how to accurately distinguish with a small amount of traces the harmonics of the signal from harmonics mainly related to noise. Finally, a conclusion is drawn in Sect. 8.

2 Preamble

In this paper, the term *signal* is devoted to the deterministic evolution (repeated and measured n times with perfect equipments in the absence of any noise source, the signal is unique) of a physical quantity over time, evolving in response to an unique stimulus. For example the evolution of the magnetic field at the coordinate (X, Y, Z) above a given IC computing the cipher of a given text with a given key is a signal. The changing of one of these parameters by solely one bit gives a new signal.

In the classical literature such as [1,10,11,17], the power consumption of a measure (trace) is defined as the sum of the exploitable power consumption from an SCA point of view (P_{exp}), the power of the noise (considered in [11] as the sum of the electronic noise $P_{el.noise}$ and of the switching noise $P_{sw.noise}$) and a constant power consumption (P_{const}). In the present paper, we consider the power consumption of a measure as the sum of the power consumptions of the signal (P_S) to be measured and of the noise (P_N). P_S is considered regardless the power consumption of signal is exploitable or not. As a result, P_S includes but is not reduced to P_{exp}. This choice is done in order to evaluate the quality of the measurement protocol independently from the fact that traces contain exploitable information.

None of these meanings is preferable. They are adopted for different purposes. In our case, a paradigm shift is investigated to assess the quality of a measurement. This also allows to assess the quality of the related experimental protocol, as an alternative of quantifying the amount of leakage present in a set of SCA traces. However we make a parallel with our approach and this point later in the paper.

3 SNR Definition and the Related Problem

With the definition of the *signal* adopted in this paper, the SNR is an objective figure of merit for gauging the quality of the measurement $M(t) = [m_1, ..., m_q]$ of a signal $S(t) = [s_1, ..., s_q]$, which depends on the surrounding noise, but also of the quality of the equipments used to collect it. The standard electrical engineering definition of the SNR is the ratio between the power P_S of the signal to be measured and the power P_N of noise $N(t) = [\eta_1, ..., \eta_q]$:

$$SNR = \frac{P_S}{P_N} = \frac{\frac{1}{q} \cdot \sum_{i=1}^{q}(s_i)^2}{\frac{1}{q} \cdot \sum_{i=1}^{q}(\eta_i)^2} \quad (1)$$

If the signal and the noise are zero mean, the numerator and the denominator of Eq. 1 are the signal and noise variances, respectively. This leads, considering $S(t)$ and $N(t)$ as random variables over time (horizontal random variables or random processes), to the following compact expression of the SNR:

$$SNR = \frac{\sigma_S^2}{\sigma_N^2} = \frac{\frac{1}{q} \cdot \sum_{i=1}^{q}(s_i - 0)^2}{\frac{1}{q} \cdot \sum_{i=1}^{q}(\eta_i - 0)^2} \qquad (2)$$

with σ_S and σ_N denoting the standard deviations (measured horizontally and not vertically) of the signal $S(t)$ and noise $N(t)$, respectively. It should be noted that even if the SNR takes the form of a variance ratio, this is really a power ratio and must be perceived as it.

This SNR definition is particularly interesting in the context of SCA exploiting the Electro-Magnetic (EM) channel. Indeed, the means of the EM signals are always very close to zero, or can even be fixed to zero by forcing the usual voltage amplifiers to work in small signals or by compensating their input offset voltage. This definition is therefore considered in the rest of this paper. However, given that in the context of SCA, the signal characteristics are not known, this definition is extremely difficult to apply in this form. A solution must therefore be found to extract from measures the SNR values (Eq. 2).

4   From Collisions to SNR Estimations

If in the context of SCA the signal $S(t)$ is not known, other degrees of freedom are available to adversaries. One of these degrees of freedom is the capability to stimulate the circuit n times in the same manner to collect n measures of a same execution or calculus. However, this degree of freedom is not unlimited. Indeed, some security protocols limit to few units the possibility to repeat a same execution. In addition, if this is not the case, repeating the same execution is theoretically possible but often tedious because of misalignment of traces which implies the use of some more or less costly realignment techniques. However, it seems possible to generate few colliding traces and exploit them to estimate the SNR as explained below.

4.1   From Bounded Collision Detection Criterion to SNR

The use of signal collisions is a recognized technique to attack the implementations of symmetric [15] or asymmetric [5,18] algorithms. For this purpose, a choice of plaintexts is done in order to induce a collision between intermediate values according to the targeted secret. The adversary finally derives the secret from the occurrence or the absence of the collision. However, because in practice SCA traces are noisy, detection is not straightforward and some signal processing techniques are necessary to exploit collisions. Recently in [8], a criterion that automates the detection of collisions was proposed. This criterion, called Bounded Collision Detection Criterion (BCDC), takes values in [0,1] and is defined by:

$$BCDC(M_1, M_2) = \frac{1}{\sqrt{2}} \times \frac{\sigma_{(M_1 - M_2)}}{\sigma_{(M_1)}} \quad (3)$$

where $M_i = [m_1^i, \cdots, m_q^i]$ is a measurement, collected with a Digital Sampling Oscilloscope (DSO), representing a measure of the signal $S(t)^i$ characterized by a (horizontal) standard deviation $\sigma_{(M_i)}$. The idea behind this criterion is that in case of collision the numerator is close to zero, while in the absence of collision the BCDC is close to one.

Assuming that all samples m_j^i of these measurements (with $j \in [1, q]$) can be expressed by $m_j^i = s_j^i + \eta_j^i$, i.e. is the sum of:

- a deterministic value (s_j^i) which is a sample of $S(t)$ emitted by the Device Under Test (DUT), at time t, during its operation,
- and of the realization of the noise (η_j^i), which is a random variable, drawn in a normal distribution with zero mean and an unknown standard deviation,

it is then possible to express the difference between M_1 and M_2:

$$\Delta M = M_1 - M_2 = [\delta_{m_1}, \cdots, \delta_{m_q}] \quad (4)$$

with

$$\delta_{m_j} = m_j^1 - m_j^2 = s_j^1 + \eta_j^1 - (s_j^2 + \eta_j^2). \quad (5)$$

Considering that all terms of Eq. 5 are independent, it appears that the denominator of the BCDC, Eq. 3, can be expressed as:

$$\sigma_{(M_1 - M_2)} = \sqrt{\sigma^2([s_1^1 - s_1^2, \cdots, s_q^1 - s_q^2]) + \sigma^2([\eta_1^1 - \eta_1^2, \cdots, \eta_q^1 - \eta_q^2])}, \quad (6)$$

expression that can be re-written:

$$\sigma_{(M_1 - M_2)} = \sqrt{2 \cdot \sigma_S^2 + 2 \cdot \sigma_N^2} = \sqrt{2} \cdot \sqrt{\sigma_S^2 + \sigma_N^2} \quad (7)$$

Starting from this expression, one can calculate the asymptotic $BCDC$ value when M_1 and M_2 are two measures of the same signal, i.e. in case of a collision. Indeed, in that case, because $s_j^1 = s_j^2$ and thus because:

$$\sigma_{(M_1 - M_2)} = \sqrt{2} \cdot \sqrt{\sigma_N^2}, \quad (8)$$

Equation 3 becomes:

$$BCDC(M_1, M_2) = \frac{1}{\sqrt{2}} \frac{\sqrt{2} \cdot \sigma_N}{\sqrt{\sigma_S^2 + \sigma_N^2}} = \frac{1}{\sqrt{1 + \frac{\sigma_S^2}{\sigma_N^2}}} = \frac{1}{\sqrt{1 + SNR(M_1, M_2)}}. \quad (9)$$

As a result, the quick and pragmatic estimate of the SNR becomes possible in the context of SCA. To do this, simply collect n (> 1) traces corresponding to the

execution of the same calculus by the DUT; then calculate the $\frac{1}{2} \cdot n \cdot (n-1)$
$BCDC$ values and finally deduce as much values $SNR(M_i, M_j)$:

$$SNR(M_i, M_j) = \frac{1}{BCDC^2(M_i, M_j)} - 1 \qquad (10)$$

Finally, the SNR of a set of traces is estimated by averaging these $\frac{1}{2} \cdot n \cdot (n-1)$
$SNR(M_i, M_j)$ values (see Eq. 11). In the remainder of the paper this estimation
is denoted $\widehat{SNR}$.

$$\widehat{SNR} = \frac{2}{n \cdot (n-1)} \sum_{i=1}^{n} \sum_{j=i+1}^{n} \left(\frac{1}{BCDC^2(M_i, M_j)} - 1 \right) \qquad (11)$$

This mean value as well as the shape of the $SNR(M_i, M_j)$ distribution consti-
tute figures of merit for gauging the quality of a SCA measures and that of the
experimental protocol that has been followed to collect them: the higher $\widehat{SNR}$ is,
the better the experimental protocol is. As an illustration, typical $SNR(M_i, M_j)$
distributions are given Fig. 2c and d in Sect. 5. Next paragraphs give an illustration in a school book case.

4.2   Example

To provide practical and convincing elements about the accuracy and the simplicity of this fast SNR estimation method, which is applicable when the signal
and the data are not known, simulated traces were generated. They relate to the
measure of a sinusoidal signal of amplitude equal to 1 and with an horizontal
variance over a period of 2 ($\sigma_S = \sqrt{2}$ on a period) in an environment producing
a normal measurement noise with zero mean and standard deviation σ_N.

Table 1 gives the exact SNR value wrt σ_N as well as $\widehat{SNR}$ wrt the number of
measurements ($n = \{2, ..., 50\}$) used to estimate it with the proposed method.
One may observe that with only five colliding measures (i.e. 10 $BCDC$ and
$SNR(M_i, M_j)$ estimates) $\widehat{SNR}_{n=5}$ is really close to the exact SNR value. Indeed,
the relative absolute value is lower than 5 %. This result appears even more
accurate when σ_{SNR} is low. For $n = 50$ measures (i.e. 1275 $BCDC$ values) and
for $\sigma_N = 1.9$, $\widehat{SNR}_{n=50}$ is equal to 0.1385 and σ_{SNR} is equal to 0.0048 i.e. 3.45 %
of the exact SNR value. These results demonstrate the practicability as well the
accuracy of the proposed method.

4.3   Discussion

At this stage, a fast SNR estimation method to be applied when the signal is
not known has been introduced and its accuracy demonstrated. It is based on
the SNR definition commonly used to assess the quality of analog measures or
the quality of a communicating channel. This method is the main contribution
of this paper.

Table 1. Evolution of the mean $\widehat{SNR}$ value wrt σ_N and the number n of measurements used to estimate it

σ_N	0.1	0.3	0.5	0.7	0.9	1.1	1.3	1.5	1.7	1.9
SNR	50	5.56	2.00	1.02	0.62	0.41	0.30	0.22	0.17	0.14
$\widehat{SNR}_{n=2}$	49.38	5.58	2.03	1.00	0.64	0.41	0.28	0.24	0.17	0.16
$\widehat{SNR}_{n=5}$	49.76	5.51	1.99	1.03	0.60	0.41	0.29	0.21	0.17	0.14
$\widehat{SNR}_{n=10}$	50.41	5.56	1.99	1.02	0.62	0.41	0.29	0.21	0.18	0.14
$\widehat{SNR}_{n=20}$	49.91	5.52	2.00	1.03	0.62	0.41	0.30	0.22	0.17	0.14
$\widehat{SNR}_{n=50}$	50.08	5.56	2.01	1.01	0.62	0.41	0.30	0.22	0.17	0.14

If the definition considered in this paper is different to that adopted in [1,10,11], in which the authors aim at quantifying the amount of exploitable (with CPA) leakage in set of traces, nothing forbids to assess whether the definition considered in this paper is also an indirect measure of the amount of leakage present in traces. After all, measures of high quality are they not susceptible to convey more leakage than bad quality measurements?

This can be envisaged since the SNR definition adopted in this paper is the ratio between the signal and noise powers, and thus because the signal power is necessarily an upper bound of the exploitable leakage power Q_L, i.e. the power consumed by the cryptographic operation targeted by the adversary:

$$\frac{\sigma_S^2}{\sigma_N^2} \geq \frac{\sigma_{Q_L}^2}{\sigma_N^2} \geq 0 \tag{12}$$

If the SNR definition considered in this paper is indeed a figure of merit of SCA trace quality, the idea we propose to quantify the quality of a set of SCA traces is simple. It consists in acquiring a small amount of traces (2 to 50 for instance) of a same computational activity (or pairs of the same activity) in order to evaluate $\widehat{SNR}$ and if necessary to draw the $SNR(M_i, M_j)$ distribution. This value (or the estimated distribution law) will be considered as a quality measure of SCA traces but also of the experimental protocol applied to collect the traces.

5   Estimated SNR wrt CPA Efficiency

To assess if the SNR definition considered in this paper, dedicated to the evaluation of the quality of measures and of the experimental protocol used to obtain it, is also an indicator of the amount of leakage in a set traces of SCA and more precisely an upper bound, various experiments were conducted. One challenge was to define an experiment allowing to vary the SNR.

5.1   Experiments

In order to vary the SNR, different experimental campaigns were conducted, and different sets of EM traces, characterized by different SNR values were collected.

These campaigns have consisted in measuring the EM radiations of an AES mapped into an FPGA. The EM sensor was placed at different distances Z from the IC surface and this without changing the settings of the DSO (the vertical caliber and the time base) so that to reduce the amplitude (the power) of the signal while increasing the noise. For each considered Z value, 50 EM traces of 20000 samples corresponding to ciphering of the same plaintext were acquired to compute $\widehat{SNR}$; 5000 others traces corresponding each to the ciphering of a random plaintext were also acquired with the intent to perform CPA. This experimental procedure was defined to vary the SNR but also because measuring the EM radiations so far from the IC (when it is possible at $Z = 0$) is a really bad experimental protocol to collect EM traces.

Figure 1 illustrates the principle of these experiments and reports 25 EM measurements obtained at $Z = 0$ and $Z = 500\,\mu m$ while the AES ciphers the same plaintext. The black thick traces are the mean of the 25 measures. One can observe that the amplitudes of the measurements performed at $Z = 500\,\mu m$ are lower than the ones at $Z = 0$, but above all, that some large amplitude noises alter some traces. These spurious noises render the reading of traces less intelligible. Indeed, contrarily to measures at $Z = 0$, the rounds of the AES are less visible, and completely disappear in the noise at $Z = 4000\,\mu m$.

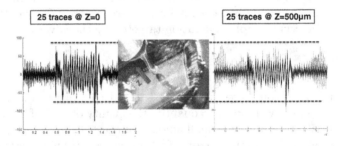

Fig. 1. 25 EM Measures EM collected at $Z = 0$ and $Z = 500\,\mu m$ above an AES mapped into an FPGA

5.2   Analysis of the Experimental Results

A CPA was applied to each set of 5000 traces collected at Z values ranging between 0 and 5 mm. Figure 2 gives the evolution with Z of σ_S and $\sqrt{SNR}$. As expected the $\widehat{SNR}$ decreases rapidly when Z increases; the distributions of the estimated $\widehat{SNR}$ values (with Eq. 2) for $Z = 0$ and $Z = 2000\,\mu m$ are given Fig. 2c and d, respectively. For measures done at $Z = 0$, $\sqrt{SNR}$ is equal to 15.11 and $\sigma_{\sqrt{SNR}}$ is equal to 4.80 while at $Z = 2000\,\mu m$, $\sqrt{SNR}$ is equal to 7.31 and $\sigma_{\sqrt{SNR}}$ to 1.64. This demonstrates that the SNR is, as expected, a measure of the quality of the experimental protocol.

Figure 2b gives the evolution of the global Guessing Entropy (gGE) with respect to $\sqrt{\widehat{SNR}}$. One can observe that the lower the $\sqrt{\widehat{SNR}}$ value is, the less efficient the CPA is. In addition, as soon as $\sqrt{\widehat{SNR}}$ is lower than 5, the CPA does not succeed in disclosing the correct key with 5000 traces and more over the gGE remains close to 128.

Nevertheless, Fig. 2b highlights the existence of a link between gGE and the SNR. The standard electrical engineering definition of the SNR (Eq. 2) is therefore a figure of merit of the quality of EM traces from an adversary point of view, as the SNR definition considered in [1,10]. The higher the $\widehat{SNR}$ associated to a set of traces is, the leakier it is expected to be. However, it should be noticed that this figure of merit does not indicate possible problems that can encounter adversaries to exploit this information. These difficulties are for instance:

– the presence or the absence of countermeasures such as masking [3],
– the choice of the adequate distinguisher [2,6],
– the identification of the accurate leakage model [11],

which are problems independent from the measurement quality.

6   Collision Criterion for Analyzing Leakage Traces

At that stage, the $BCDC$ has been used for estimating the SNR (Eq. 2). Then it has been experimentally shown that this criterion is also a figure of merit to gauge the quality of a set of EM traces with the intent to apply an SCA on it.

The BCDC can also be used to analyze the computational activity of a DUT over time. Indeed, it is quite possible to calculate BCDC values for the different time windows ($[t_i, \cdots, t_k]$ with $i \geq 1$ and $k \leq q$) constituting the traces:

$$SNR(t_i, \cdots, t_k) = \frac{1}{BCDC^2(t_i, \cdots, t_k)} - 1 \tag{13}$$

and to deduce $\widehat{SNR}$ values so that to distinguish windows characterized by different SNR values. This leads to draw the estimated $\widehat{SNR}$ evolution over time, considering that each type of electrical activity (or instruction) consumes a specific amount of power and is thus characterized by a specific SNR value.

Figure 3 gives 25 EM traces related to the ciphering of 25 random plaintexts (traces with no collision), the standard deviations of all the samples constituting the traces (thus computed with only 25 values), and finally the evolution of $\sqrt{\widehat{SNR}}$ estimated from 25 colliding traces using windows of 250 consecutive samples, i.e. of duration equal to $0.625 \times T_{CK}$, with T_{CK} the clock period of the device.

One may observe that even if the $\sqrt{\widehat{SNR}}$ is high, 25 traces do not allow to clearly localize the AES rounds, nor to interpret the behavior of the device with the vertical standard deviation. More traces are required.

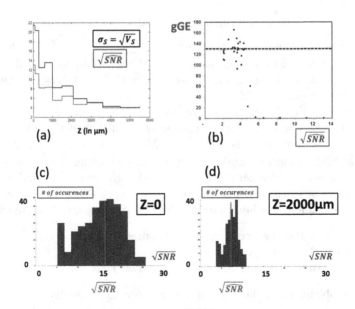

Fig. 2. (a) Evolutions with Z of σ_S and $\sqrt{\widehat{SNR}}$, (b) Evolution of the gGE wrt the $\sqrt{\widehat{SNR}}$ (c) histogram of the $\sqrt{\widehat{SNR}}$ values estimated with traces collected at $Z = 0$, (d) histogram of the $\sqrt{\widehat{SNR}}$ values estimated with traces collected at $Z = 2000\,\mu m$

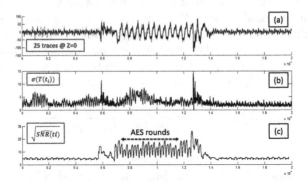

Fig. 3. (a) 25 EM traces collected @ Z=0 over an AES (b) evolution $\sigma(T(t_i))$ and (c) evolution of $\sqrt{\widehat{SNR}}$

By contrast, 25 traces are largely sufficient, by calculating the $\widehat{SNR}$, to locate and identify different phases of activity (loading of the key and the text in the registers, emissions of a trigger signal on an IO, AES computation) of the DUT assuming that each activity phase is characterized by a specific SNR value. In addition, the difference of $\sqrt{\widehat{SNR}}$ values between active phases and inactive phases is really high.

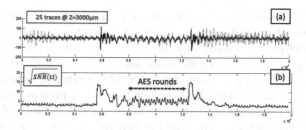

Fig. 4. (a) 25 EM traces collected @ $Z = 3000\,\mu$m over an AES (b) evolution of $\sqrt{\widehat{SNR}}$

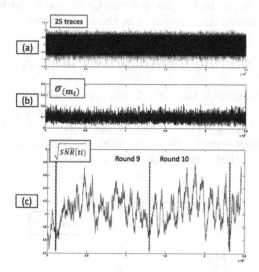

Fig. 5. (a) 25 EM traces (and their mean in black) collected above a 32bit micro-controller processing an AES (b) evolution $\sigma_{(m_i)}$ and (c) evolution of $\sqrt{\widehat{SNR}}$

This result may come from two main reasons. The first reason could be the fact that the computation of $BCDC$ values involves the calculus of standard deviations which are performed on a set of 250 consecutive samples rather than 25 values in case of the use of the vertical variance as analysis criterion. This limits the impact of noise. The second could also be related to the reduction of the impact of noise, and more particularly of the effect of outliers. Indeed, 25 traces allows computing the mean of the SNR distribution, $\widehat{SNR}$, with 300 different estimates of the SNR.

Figure 4 shows the same results than Fig. 3 for 25 traces collected at $Z = 3000\,\mu$m i.e. for traces characterized by a lower SNR value. In this condition the AES is no more visible on the mean trace (in black Fig. 4a). In addition, the transitions of a synchronization signal on an IO pad are much more visible; the EM probe is now above the related bonding.

If the results presented above, obtained on an hardware AES embedded on an FPGA, are interesting, the full effectiveness of the technique appears during the analysis of the electrical activity of a micro-controller which executes a software implementation of the AES. To illustrate this, Fig. 5 gives 25 traces EM (and their mean) corresponding to the computation of the two last rounds of the AES by a 32-bits processor (cortex M4) designed in 90 nm process technology and clocked at 40 MHz. As shown, neither the mean nor the variance of traces allow to distinguish any pattern related to the two rounds. The vertical mean and variance look like a really noisy trace. This is not the case with the evolution of $\widehat{SNR}$ on which two quite similar (but not exactly the same) patterns are visible. One can even distinguish similar shapes in the two rounds.

7   Collision Criterion for Adaptive Filtering

In the preceding paragraphs, the $BCDC$ has been exploited to analyze the evolution of the electrical activity of two DUT, an FPGA and a micro-controller, using a sliding windowing solution. Such an approach can be adopted to distinguish in the frequency domain, the frequencies carrying information related to the signal from those that convey essentially noise.

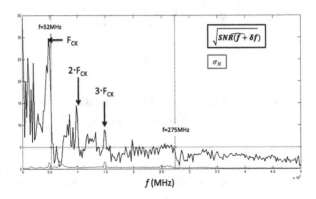

Fig. 6. $\widehat{SNR}(f)$ and $\sigma_N(f)$ computed with 8 EM traces

At that end, a frequency bandwidth, δf, is chosen. The colliding traces are then translated in the frequency domain using for example the FFT. This done, for each frequency f of the spectrum, the harmonics falling out of the frequencies bandwidth of interest $(f \pm \delta f)$ are canceled before to translate back the traces in the time domain and compute $\widehat{SNR}(f \pm \delta)$ at each frequency f of the spectrum, as in the preceding sections.

It should be noticed that δf could be set to the spectral resolution of the FFT which depends on the number of points constituting the traces. This approach with the minimal possible δf value has a larger computational cost and returns in computing $\widehat{SNR(f)}$ i.e. in keeping only one frequency in the bandwidth.

Figure 6 gives the evolution with f of $\widehat{SNR(f \pm \delta f)}$ estimated with only 8 EM traces collected above the AES mapped into the FPGA, considering a frequencies bandwidth $\delta f = 2\,\mathrm{MHz}$. The quite flat evolution of $\sigma_N(f \pm \delta f)$ is also drawn in this figure.

Contrarily to $\sigma_N(f \pm \delta f)$, $\widehat{SNR(f \pm \delta f)}$ seems to decrease following a $\frac{1}{f}$ function as indicated by the leakage model in the frequency domain introduced in [17] and as formerly observed in [12]. However, it should be noticed that peaks of $\widehat{SNR(f \pm \delta f)}$ appear at several multiples of the frequencies (50 MHz). This is probably due to the influence of the clock tree circuit, one of the largest energy consumers at these frequencies in IC.

More importantly, it should be observed that $\widehat{SNR(f \pm \delta f)}$ remains high (> 5) for $f < 275\,\mathrm{MHz}$ and particularly high for $f < 52\,\mathrm{MHz}$. It therefore seems wise to only keep harmonics below 275 MHz or even 52 MHz during SCA.

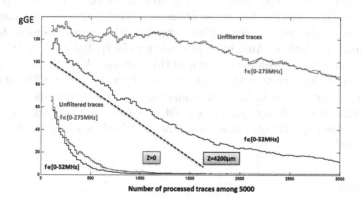

Fig. 7. Evolution of gGE with the number of processed traces (collected either at Z=0 or at $Z = 4200\,\mu\mathrm{m}$ when keeping respectively all harmonics (in blue), harmonics below 275 MHz (in red) and harmonics below 52 MHz (in black) (Color figure online).

In order to validate that $\widehat{SNR(f \pm \delta f)}$ is an interesting figure of merit allowing to adapt at best the filtering steps usually applied prior any SCA, CPA were first launched on the rough EM traces, then on these same traces after canceling of harmonics higher than 52 MHz and 275 MHz, respectively. Figure 7 gives the evolutions of the gGE for these three CPA in the case of traces collected at $Z = 0$ and at $Z = 4200\,\mu\mathrm{m}$.

Figure 7 shows that the filtering of traces characterized by a high SNR value (traces collected at $Z = 0$) has a really limited interest as it was expected. By contrast, for traces collected at $Z = 4200\,\mu\mathrm{m}$, characterized by a $\widehat{SNR}$ value lower than 3, keeping harmonics with the highest $\widehat{SNR(f \pm \delta f)}$ values allows to enhance significantly the efficiency of the CPA. Indeed, keeping only the f values lower than 52 MHz allows reaching a gGE lower than 20 after the processing of 3000 traces, value to be compared to 90 without application of any filtering procedure.

8   Conclusion

The SNR, as defined in engineering, is a key figure for gauging the quality of analogue measurements or communication channels. However, its use requires the knowledge of the signal to be measured. In the context of SCA, the nature and characteristics of the measured signals are not known. The use of the SNR is therefore particularly difficult.

In this context the paper proposes a method to estimate the SNR, when the signal is not known. This method is based on a collision detection criterion. Its advantages are its easiness of use, its accuracy, and its low computation time.

It has also been shown in this paper that the SNR is an interesting figure of merit to gauge the quality of SCA traces, to analyze the behavior of IC, or to guide rationally (and therefore in an efficient way) the filtering step commonly used as pre-processing of traces. There are also other applications of this fast SNR estimation method. Among them it use for the spatial analysis IC activity has given interesting results not shown in this paper by lack of place.

However, we believe that the main interest of the proposed SNR estimation technique is that it is a sufficiently simple, low cost and convenient technique to establish the electrical engineering SNR as a standard measure for comparing the various experimental practices of SCA of both academic and industrial laboratories.

References

1. Bhasin, S., Danger, J.-L., Guilley, S., Najm, Z.: NICV: normalized inter-class variance for detection of side-channel leakage. IACR Cryptology ePrint Archive **2013**, 717 (2013)
2. Brier, E., Clavier, C., Olivier, F.: Correlation power analysis with a leakage model. In: Joye, M., Quisquater, J.-J. (eds.) CHES 2004. LNCS, vol. 3156, pp. 16–29. Springer, Heidelberg (2004)
3. Chari, S., Jutla, C.S., Rao, J.R., Rohatgi, P.: Towards sound approaches to counteract power-analysis attacks. In: Wiener, M. (ed.) CRYPTO 1999. LNCS, vol. 1666, pp. 398–412. Springer, Heidelberg (1999)
4. Dehbaoui, A., Lomne, V., Maurine, P., Torres, L., Robert, M.: Enhancing electromagnetic attacks using spectral coherence based cartography. In: Becker, J., Johann, M., Reis, R. (eds.) VLSI-SoC 2009. IFIP AICT, vol. 360, pp. 135–155. Springer, Heidelberg (2011)
5. Fouque, P.-A., Valette, F.: The doubling attack – *why upwards is better than downwards*. In: Walter, C.D., Koç, Ç.K., Paar, C. (eds.) CHES 2003. LNCS, vol. 2779, pp. 269–280. Springer, Heidelberg (2003)

6. Gierlichs, B., Batina, L., Tuyls, P., Preneel, B.: Mutual information analysis. In: Oswald, E., Rohatgi, P. (eds.) CHES 2008. LNCS, vol. 5154, pp. 426–442. Springer, Heidelberg (2008)

7. Guilley, S., Maghrebi, H., Souissi, Y., Sauvage, L., Danger, J.-L.: Quantifying the quality of side channel acquisitions. In: COSADE (2011)

8. Diop, I., Liardet, P.-Y., Linge, Y., Maurine, P.: Collision based attacks in practice. In: CRYPTO'PUCES (2015)

9. Kocher, P.C., Jaffe, J., Jun, B.: Differential power analysis. In: Wiener, M. (ed.) CRYPTO 1999. LNCS, vol. 1666, pp. 388–397. Springer, Heidelberg (1999)

10. Mangard, S.: Hardware countermeasures against DPA – a statistical analysis of their effectiveness. In: Okamoto, T. (ed.) CT-RSA 2004. LNCS, vol. 2964, pp. 222–235. Springer, Heidelberg (2004)

11. Mangard, S., Oswald, E., Popp, T.: Power Analysis Attacks: Revealing the Secrets of Smart Cards, vol. 31. Springer Science & Business Media, New York (2008)

12. Mateos, E., Gebotys, C.H.: A new correlation frequency analysis of the side channel. In: Proceedings of the 5th Workshop on Embedded Systems Security, WESS, p. 4 (2010)

13. Réal, D., Valette, F., Drissi, M.: Enhancing correlation electromagnetic attack using planar near-field cartography. In: Design, Automation and Test in Europe, DATE 2009, pp. 628–633 (2009)

14. Sauvage, L., Guilley, S., Flament, F., Danger, J.-L., Mathieu, Y.: Blind cartography for side channel attacks: cross-correlation cartography. Int. J. Reconfig. Comput. **2012**, 360242:1–360242:9 (2012)

15. Schramm, K., Wollinger, T., Paar, C.: A new class of collision attacks and its application to DES. In: Johansson, T. (ed.) FSE 2003. LNCS, vol. 2887, pp. 206–222. Springer, Heidelberg (2003)

16. Standaert, F.-X., Malkin, T.G., Yung, M.: A unified framework for the analysis of side-channel key recovery attacks. In: Joux, A. (ed.) EUROCRYPT 2009. LNCS, vol. 5479, pp. 443–461. Springer, Heidelberg (2009)

17. Tiran, S., Ordas, S., Teglia, Y., Agoyan, M., Maurine, P.: A model of the leakage in the frequency domain and its application to CPA and DPA. J. Cryptographic Eng. **4**(3), 197–212 (2014)

18. Yen, S.-M., Lien, W.-C., Moon, S.-J., Ha, J.C.: Power analysis by exploiting chosen message and internal collisions – vulnerability of checking mechanism for RSA-decryption. In: Dawson, E., Vaudenay, S. (eds.) Mycrypt 2005. LNCS, vol. 3715, pp. 183–195. Springer, Heidelberg (2005)

Fault Attacks

Protecting the Control Flow of Embedded Processors against Fault Attacks

Mario Werner[1]([⊠]), Erich Wenger[2], and Stefan Mangard[1]

[1] Graz University of Technology, Graz, Austria
{mario.werner,stefan.mangard}@iaik.tugraz.at
[2] Infineon Technologies AG, Munich, Germany
erich.wenger@infineon.com

Abstract. During the last two decades, most of the research on fault attacks focused on attacking and securing intermediate values that occur during the computation of cryptographic primitives. However, also fault attacks on the control flow of software can compromise the security of a system completely. Fault attacks on the control flow can for example make a system branch to an administrative function directly or make it bypass comparisons of redundant computations. Security checks based on comparing redundant computations are for example commonly used to secure PIN checks and implementations of block ciphers against fault attacks.

Although control-flow integrity is of crucial importance to secure a system against fault attacks, so far there exist only very few proposals for countermeasures. This article addresses this gap and presents an efficient hardware-supported technique that allows to maintain control-flow integrity in the setting of fault attacks. The technique is based on so-called generalized path signatures, which have initially been introduced in the context of soft errors. We present a prototype implementation for a Cortex-M3 microprocessor and corresponding compiler extensions in LLVM. Our implementation, which increases the processor size by merely 6.4 %, detects *every* fault on the instruction-stream with 99.9 % probability within 3 cycles. The runtime overhead of the protected applications ranges from 2 % to 71 %.

Keywords: Control-flow integrity · Fault attacks · Countermeasures

1 Introduction

Fault attacks are a very active field of research since the seminal publication of the so-called Bellcore attack [3] in 1997. Today, there exist published fault attacks on almost all commonly used cryptographic primitives. Unless countermeasures are implemented, these attacks allow to reveal the secret key by observing only

E. Wenger—This research has been conducted while Erich Wenger was employed at Graz University of Technology.

© Springer International Publishing Switzerland 2016
N. Homma and M. Medwed (Eds.): CARDIS 2015, LNCS 9514, pp. 161–176, 2016.
DOI: 10.1007/978-3-319-31271-2_10

few outputs of faulted executions of the cryptographic primitive. A comprehensive overview of fault attacks and countermeasures for cryptographic primitives can be found in [5].

However, while most of the research on fault attacks focuses on attacking and securing cryptographic primitives, it is important to point out that securing a cryptographic primitive is not sufficient to secure a system. For example, the Xbox 360 has not been hacked because of a fault attack on a cryptographic primitive. It has been attacked successfully because it was possible to use a glitch on the reset line to make the system bypass the signature check of the loaded software [4]. In case of such attacks on the control flow of the executed software, often a single successful fault induction is sufficient to compromise the security of a system completely (e.g. by branching to an administrative function, by obtaining root privileges, or by skipping all kinds of security checks). Attacks on the control flow also allow to bypass certain countermeasures for cryptographic computations. In [12] for example, techniques for multiple fault inductions are discussed to first induce a fault in a cryptographic computation and then to bypass the comparison with a redundant computation.

So far, there exist only very few publications that address the challenge of securing the control flow of software against fault attacks. Examples of hardware-supported approaches are [2,8,9]. However, these works focus on securing basic blocks and lead to a significant overhead in terms of code size when protecting the entire control-flow graph. In [6], a software approach for securing the control flow is presented. Yet, this approach only allows to detect integrity violations at a coarse level of granularity. It does not allow detecting all modified, missing, or repeated instructions with certainty.

The present article addresses the current lack of efficient countermeasures to secure the control flow against fault attacks. We present an efficient hardware-supported technique to provide strong security for the integrity of the control flow. Our technique builds upon generalized path signature analysis that has been introduced in the context of soft errors by Wilken and Shen [10,11].

In this article, we define the requirements for fault detection in the setting of fault attacks and adapt the scheme of Wilken and Shen accordingly. Furthermore, we present an implementation of the resulting countermeasure using state-of-the-art hardware (ARM Cortex-M3) and software (LLVM compiler infrastructure). To the best of our knowledge, this work is the first to actually implement a control-flow integrity scheme based on general path signature analysis. Our prototype implementation, which increases the processor size by 6.4 %, detects *every* fault on the instruction-stream with 99.9 % probability within three cycles. The runtime overhead of the protected applications ranges from 2 % to 71 %. The overhead for implementations of cryptographic primitives is very low because such software typically has a low number of conditional branches. The handling of conditional branches causes the main part of the overhead.

The remainder of this article is organized as follows. Section 2 gives an introduction on control-flow integrity and the existing work of Wilken and Shen. We adapt the scheme to the setting of fault attacks in Sect. 3. Section 4 presents our prototype implementation and Sect. 5 the evaluation results. Finally, the work concludes in Sect. 6.

2 Control-Flow Integrity in Fault-Tolerant Computing

The detection of faults in the control flow of a program requires to include redundant information about the control flow into the program. The concept of generalized path signature analysis (GPSA) by Wilken and Shen [10,11] is a very efficient technique to add this redundancy. In the following subsections, we first define the problem of control-flow integrity and then discuss the concept of GPSA.

2.1 Control-Flow Integrity

The control flow of a program refers to the order in which its instructions, branches, loops, and function calls have to be executed. Two types of instructions can be distinguished in this context. First, there are sequential instructions, like arithmetic and memory operations, which only have indirect influence on the execution sequence. They are executed in strictly sequential order and have exactly one subsequent instruction. Second, there are control-flow instructions, like branch and call, which alter the execution sequence directly. Control-flow instructions have one or more subsequent instructions and can select which one is executed next.

A program is typically structured into code fragments which consist out of an arbitrary number of sequential instructions (zero or more) followed by up to one control-flow instruction. Such fragments are denoted as basic blocks. A basic block is a strictly sequential piece of code which can only be entered at the first and exited after the last instruction. All basic blocks of a program form the so-called control-flow graph (CFG). The edges in a CFG are always directed and visualize in which way the control flow can be transferred from one basic block to another. Ensuring control-flow integrity (CFI) during the execution of a program means that all instructions in a basic block are executed by the processor as defined in the original program (i.e. no instructions are skipped or altered) and that no new connections are added to the control-flow graph (i.e. no other branches are done than those defined at compilation time).

Control-flow integrity does not include the protection of the decision which path is taken in a CFG. This requires protecting the integrity of the data that is used for the decision. However, it is important to note that data integrity cannot be achieved without control-flow integrity. CFI is the basis for further countermeasures, like data integrity. For example multiple computations and comparisons can be done to ensure data integrity and the techniques for CFI make sure that all these operations are indeed executed by the processor.

2.2 Derived Signatures

Derived signatures are a common technique in fault-tolerant computing to detect violations of the integrity of the control flow. The basic idea of a derived signature is to add a small piece of hardware to the processor executing the software that should be protected. Upon the execution of each instruction, the hardware updates a checksum based on the executed instruction and the corresponding control signals of the decoder. In the literature on CFI in fault-tolerant computing, such a checksum is called "derived signature". It is important to note that it is not a cryptographic signature. Nevertheless, in order to be consistent with the existing literature, we also use the term derived signature to denote a checksum that is calculated in hardware based on a sequence of executed instructions.

In order to check such a derived signature when a program is executed, it is necessary to have corresponding reference values. Derived signatures depend on the executed instructions and the initial value of the signature. As both are known at compilation time, reference values can be calculated when a program is created. Typically, the reference values are embedded into the program by instrumenting the binary, either during compilation or in a post-processing step.

Derived signatures can for example be checked at the end of every basic block. This is shown in Fig. 1a. The figure shows a control-flow graph with six basic blocks, labelled %1 to %6 that include a while loop. At the end of each basic block a signature check is done and therefore a reference value for each basic block has to be added to the program. This is for example done in [2,8,9]. However, this leads to a significant overhead, which can be avoided when using generalized path signatures. Furthermore, there is no protection for the connections of the basic blocks.

2.3   Generalized Path Signature Analysis

In [7], the so-called path signature analysis (PSA) has been introduced. PSA checks the integrity not only for a basic block, but along paths through a control-flow graph. This significantly reduces the overhead. Wilken and Shen in [10, 11] extended PSA into generalized path signature analysis (GPSA) in order to optimize the overhead.

The basic idea of GPSA is to insert signature updates into the program code in such a way that independent of the used paths in a CFG, the signature value at a given instruction is always the same. This idea is illustrated in Fig. 1b. At the end of basic block %4, there is an update that makes sure that the signature at the beginning of %5 is the same independent of the fact whether it is reached via %3 or %4. The update at the end of %5 ensures that the signature at the beginning of the while loop is independent of the fact whether it is reached via %1 or %5. The values that need to be stored in the program code to do the updates are called justifying signatures [10] and they are calculated at compilation time— just like the reference values for the checks.

The concept of GPSA optimizes the number of total justifying signatures in a CFG and can also be extended to protect function calls. In case of function calls, there is an additional justifying signature necessary for each function call. For details, please refer to [10].

GPSA does not require to have a check in every basic block and allows to place signature checks at arbitrary positions in the program. These checks are denoted as vertical signature checks. At minimum, it is necessary to insert one signature check at the end of the program as it is done in Fig. 1b. Depending

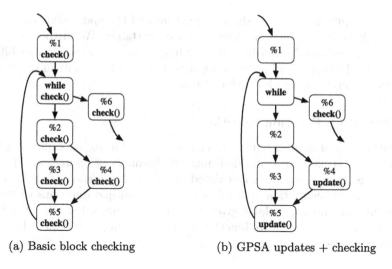

(a) Basic block checking   (b) GPSA updates + checking

Fig. 1. Signature based checking methodologies.

on the application, a trade-off has to be made between runtime and memory overhead on the one hand and the detection latency on the other hand.

2.4   Continuous-Signature Monitoring

Wilken and Shen proposed continuous-signature monitoring (CSM) as an alternative concept to the manual placement of signature checks and to solve the latency problem of vertical signature checks. The idea of CSM is to check the signature, or at least parts of it, on every executed instruction. Implementing CSM on top of GPSA is therefore as simple as checking h bits of the $|S|$ bit runtime signature on every executed instruction.

It has been proposed to use spare bits in the instruction encodings or to embed reference information into the error-correction/detection bits of the memory system. However, these approaches are not applicable to most modern processor architectures given their dense instruction encodings and the lack of error detecting memory.

3   Control-Flow Integrity in the Setting of Fault Attacks

Fault attack detection is per se very similar to the detection of soft errors. The main difference between the two is the fault model. Soft errors occur randomly at a low frequency. Fault attacks on the other hand can be very controlled. When comparing different checksums for derived signatures, it is therefore important to not only look at average detection probabilities but to also keep the worst case scenario in mind.

This section elaborates on the required properties that are needed in order to make the schemes of Wilken and Shen ready for fault attacks. We define functional requirements for both, the signature and the update function, which make single faulty instructions detectable with certainty. We further show that the actual function selection has an huge impact on the detection capabilities. The best of the evaluated functions can detect up to 7 faulty bits in the instruction stream across two cycles with certainty.

3.1   Signature Function Selection

The calculation of derived signatures can be modeled using a compression function f which is used in a Merkle-Damgård-like mode of operation. The next signature $S_{j+1} = f(S_j, I_j)$ is calculated based on the preceding signature S_j and the current instruction I_j. Collisions across multiple iterations of the signature function are unavoidable given that the signature value S has fixed size. However, choosing a signature function with specific properties can at least provide certain worst-case guarantees.

Functional Requirements. The signature function f needs the following properties in order to make a single faulty instruction $I_j \oplus \Delta_{I_j}$ detectable with certainty, independent of the actual error Δ_{I_j} and the number of faulty bits $HW(\Delta_{I_j})$.

- *Reliability*: Every error in the instruction stream $(\Delta_{I_j} \neq 0)$ has to result in a signature error $(\Delta_{S_{j+1}} \neq 0)$ given that the original signature was correct $(\Delta_{S_j} = 0)$. Note that this requirement can only be fulfilled if $|S| \geq |I|$.

$$S_{j+1} \oplus \Delta_{S_{j+1}} = f(S_j, I_j \oplus \Delta_{I_j}), \quad \forall \Delta_{I_j} \neq 0 \rightarrow \Delta_{S_{j+1}} \neq 0 \qquad (1)$$

- *Error preservation*: An error, absorbed into the signature $S_j \oplus \Delta_{S_j}$, must not be eliminated by an error-free sequence of inputs $(\Delta_{I_j} = 0)$. This requirement allows to arbitrarily delay the checking of a signature. Consequently, the number of necessary signature checks can be reduced.

$$S_{j+1} \oplus \Delta_{S_{j+1}} = f(S_j \oplus \Delta_{S_j}, I_j), \quad \forall \Delta_{S_j} \neq 0 \rightarrow \Delta_{S_{j+1}} \neq 0 \qquad (2)$$

- *Non associativity*: The order in which instructions I_j, I_k are absorbed by f must have an influence on the resulting signature value.

$$\forall I_j \neq I_k \rightarrow f(f(S_j, I_j), I_k) \neq f(f(S_j, I_k), I_j) \qquad (3)$$

- *Invertibility*: Depending on the concrete implementation of the scheme, invertibility may also be a requirement. The signature function should therefore be invertible in S given S_{j+1} and I_j. Our implementation for example uses this property to be able to place signature updates at arbitrary places along a path through the CFG. A different implementation, which enforces that signature updates are only performed at merging points in the CFG, would be able to cope without this property.

$$S_j = f^{-1}(S_{j+1}, I_j), \quad \forall S_{j+1}, \forall I_j \qquad (4)$$

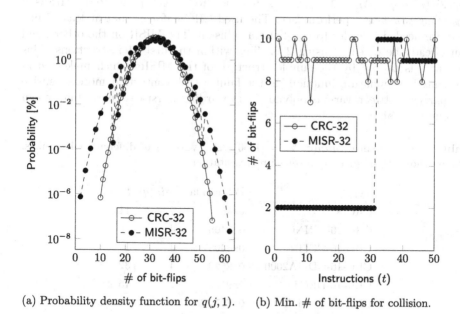

(a) Probability density function for $q(j,1)$.   (b) Min. # of bit-flips for collision.

Fig. 2. Comparison between CRC-32 and MISR-32.

Choosing the Signature Function. Classical choices for checksums in the setting of fault-tolerant computing are cyclic redundancy checks (CRCs) and multiple-input signature registers (MISRs) with various polynomials. MISRs as well as CRCs fulfill the mentioned requirements. However, they are not equally suited when fault attacks with high control over the injected fault are considered.

For the evaluation of different signature functions, we evaluated the number of bit-flips required to introduce a fault on one instruction Δ_{I_j} and to compensate it with a fault on a subsequent instruction $\Delta_{I_{j+t}}$. The sum of the bit-flips required for both faults $q(j,t) = HW(\Delta_{I_j}) + HW(\Delta_{I_{j+t}})$ is a measure for the attack complexity. The quality function q has been chosen in this way to take into account that exact knowledge of the injected fault is needed in order construct and subsequently inject the compensating fault. Average as well as worst-case performance is important when fault attacks are considered.

A comparison between the signature functions CRC-32 and MISR-32 (identical polynomial) based on the probability density function of $q(j,t)$ at $t = 1$ is shown in Fig. 2a. CRC-32 as well as MISR-32 have an expected number of bit-flips of 32. The expected value for $q(j,t)$ in general is identical to the degree of the reduction polynomial for both MISR and CRC codes. Performance in the average case is therefore identical which makes them equally suited for soft error detection.

The worst-case performance on the other hand is different. The comparison in Fig. 2b ($min(q)$ $\forall \Delta_{I_j}, \forall \Delta_{I_{j+t}}$) shows that the CRC-32 is superior to the MISR-32 regarding worst-case performance. The used CRC enforces that at least 7 bit-flips are needed in order to construct a collision. The MISR on the other hand can already be defeated using 2 bit-flips within the first 31 instructions. This weakness is caused by the simple structure of the MISRs which makes them not suited as signature functions in the fault attack context. A more extensive comparison between various polynomials regarding worst-case performance can be found in Table 1.

Table 1. Performance ($min(q)$ $\forall t = [1, 50], \forall \Delta_{I_j}, \forall \Delta_{I_{j+t}}$) of different polynomials. The polynomials are given in reversed representation.

Type	Polynomial	$min(q)$	t
CRC-8	0xAB	2	11
CRC-16-ARINC	0xD405	4	10
CRC-16-CCITT	0x8408	4	1
CRC-16-CDMA2000	0xE613	4	32
CRC-16-DECT	0x91A0	2	15
CRC-16-T10-DIF	0xEDD1	4	7
CRC-16-DNP	0xA6BC	2	9
CRC-16-IBM	0xA001	4	1
CRC-32	0xEDB88320	7	11
CRC-32C (Castagnoli)	0x82F63B78	8	2
CRC-32K (Koopman)	0xEB31D82E	6	34
CRC-32Q	0xD5828281	8	2
MISR-32	0xEDB88320	2	1

3.2 Update Function Selection

The second function which is required in GPSA and CSM implementations is the so-called update function. This function is needed in order to balance the various paths through the control-flow graph. The update function u calculates the next signature $S_{j+1} = u(S_j, J_j)$ based on the preceding signature S_j and a justifying signature constant J_j. The update function has to fulfill the following requirements in order to be usable for GPSA.

- *Full control*: All possible signature values S_{j+1} have to be constructible given an arbitrary S_j and a justifying signature J_j. Note that, the size of J must be larger or equal to S ($|J| \geq |S|$) to modify each bit in S.

$$S_{j+1} = u(S_j, J_j), \quad \forall S_{j+1}, \forall S_j, \exists J_j \tag{5}$$

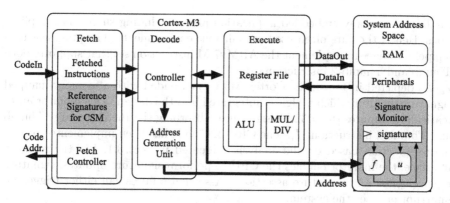

Fig. 3. Simplified Cortex-M3 architecture with grey-shaded modifications.

- *Error preservation*: An error, absorbed into the signature $S_j \oplus \Delta_{S_j}$, must not be eliminated by an error-free justifying signature ($\Delta_{J_j} = 0$). It would otherwise not be possible to arbitrarily delay the actual checking.

$$S_{j+1} \oplus \Delta_{S_{j+1}} = u(S_j \oplus \Delta_{S_j}, J_j), \quad \forall \Delta_{S_j} \neq 0 \rightarrow \Delta_{S_{j+1}} \neq 0 \qquad (6)$$

- *Invertibility*: Given S_{j+1} and S_j, it must be possible to efficiently compute the justifying signature J_j.

$$J_j = u^{-1}(S_j, S_{j+1}), \quad \forall S_j, \forall S_{j+1} \qquad (7)$$

A simple function which fulfills all those requirements is the binary xor function.

4   Prototype Implementation

We implemented GPSA and CSM on the basis of a state-of-the-art microprocessor architecture (an ARM Cortex-M3) and modern compiler technology (LLVM). The resulting implementation supports all C language features and common programming practices. Our prototype implementation is therefore not only a theoretic construct, but practically usable. The implementation supports separate compilation of C files and enables the use of static libraries. It also allows to randomize the signature values of identical programs (diversity) on different devices. This makes it harder to extend attacks against an individual towards multiple devices.

In this section, we discuss the necessary hardware modifications (which are minimal), the necessary modifications of the to-be-protected software, and elaborate on the modifications of the toolchain.

4.1   Hardware Architecture

The presented implementation is based on the ARM Cortex-M3 microprocessor architecture. Its performance-to-energy ratio makes this processor an interesting candidate for many embedded application areas, including smart-card applications. Hence, they are often used in malicious environments. The processor uses 3 pipeline stages to implement the ARMv7-M instruction set that supports both Thumb and Thumb-2 instructions.

As depicted in Fig. 3, the Cortex-M3 was extended with a memory-mapped signature monitor which is tightly integrated into the design. This monitor automatically computes $|S| = 32$-bit signatures absorbing the 16–32-bit large Thumb and Thumb-2 instructions I_j. The CRC-32C code has been implemented as signature function based on the analysis presented in Sect. 3.1. Via the memory interface, the monitor enables the CPU to perform signature updates, signature replacements, and signature assertions. Assertion failures can either trigger an interrupt or reset the system.

To support the automatic computation of derived signatures, the CPU only had to be modified to forward the currently executed instruction to the monitor. To perform continuous signature monitoring, the fetch unit of the processor was modified. The signature bits are stored in a block at the end of the program. The base address of this signature block has been embedded into the interrupt vector table, similar like the initial stack pointer. At start-up, the base address is automatically initialized. During run-time, the fetch unit always loads the instructions in combination with the reference values. An instruction is only forwarded to the decode stage, once both the instruction and the reference value are valid.

4.2   Source Code Modifications

All signature modifications are performed in software, which in turn are monitored by the derived-signature monitor in hardware. Performing the necessary software transformations manually is a challenging and error prone task. It is clearly favorable to automatically perform the transformations within the tool-chain, which makes the whole instrumentation process transparent for the programmer. Consequently, modifications of the application C source code are minimal. In the best case, a to-be-protected software does not have to be modified at all.

The programmer can insert vertical signature checks in the form of `assert_signature()` function calls into critical sections of the program. All remaining work is performed by the compiler which automatically replaces these function calls with actual signature checks. The use of function calls for the annotation has the advantage that `clang`, LLVM's C front end, can be used without any modification.

Assembly code on the other hand requires a little more work (as usual). The programmer has to place signature updates by hand when branches, loops, and function calls are encountered. However, no actual derived signature calculation has to be performed by the programmer. Additionally, if the programmer forgets a signature update, the toolchain will automatically notify her.

4.3 Software Modifications

Related work [1,8,9,13] usually performs the software transformations either during compilation or by applying a dedicated post-processing tool after linking. In this work, both techniques are combined in order to generate a protected executable. The compiler is responsible to insert signature updates based on GPSA and to insert signature assertions. A post-processing tool consecutively computes the derived signatures and patches the executable with signature update and reference values.

LLVM Compiler Modifications. The compiler has been built using the LLVM compiler infrastructure which already has great support for the targeted ARMv7-M architecture.

A machine function pass has been added to the ARM back-end in order to perform the following transformations:

- *Insertion of asserts*: Every call to the `assert_signature()` function is replaced by an actual vertical signature check. A signature check is performed as a memory-write operation of the expected signature to a certain pre-defined monitor address and is composed of three instructions. (LOAD address, LOAD value, STORE value)
- *Insertion of signature updates*: Signature updates are inserted to make the runtime signature independent of the executed path through the control-flow graph. The placement of signature updates is performed efficiently by computing the spanning tree of a function's undirected control-flow graph. Signature updates are, similar to checks, a write of the justifying signature to the memory mapped monitor.

The smart placement of the machine function pass in the optimization pipeline allows us to reuse much of the original compiler's functionality and therefore benefit from the available optimizations as well. Register allocation is for example still handled using stock LLVM functionality.

An additional component which had to be adapted is the run-time library. The compiler relies on its functions for standard operations (e.g., clearing memory) or to perform computations which are not natively supported by the processor (e.g., floating-point operation). It was therefore necessary to instrument this library with justifying signature updates in order to generate a working GPSA-hardened program.

Post Processing Tool. As a result, the compiler generates a binary with all necessary signature updates/assertions that still lacks the correct signature constants. The signature values can only be computed once the program is linked and all instructions have been finalized. The compiler never has access to this information in a traditional separate-compilation design-flow. We therefore perform the derived signature calculation using a post-processing tool.

A recursive disassembling [13] approach was used to recover the control flow and the location of the signature constants within this post-processing tool. LLVM's disassembling machinery simplifies this step considerably. Based on the control flow it is possible to identify the constant pools (aka constant islands) in the binary. Tracking the monitor's addresses using data-flow analysis techniques consecutively reveals the location of the instructions which modify the signature values.

The actual calculation of the derived signatures relies on all this recovered information. The signature values are computed by initializing each function with a random initial signature, and consequently flooding the control-flow graph of each function. As a result, all justifying signatures, assertion constants, and reference signatures for the CSM are embedded into the executable.

Another feature of the post-processing tool is its static code analysis functionality of the binary. Only correctly instrumented binaries pass the derived signature calculation. Error messages notify a programmer about wrongly instrumented assembly code.

5   Evaluation

As this is the first published, practical implementation of both GPSA and CSM in the context of fault attacks, we are excited to report performance results based on qualitative characteristics as well as practical benchmarks.

5.1   Error-Detection Coverage

Based on the previously stated requirements on the signature functions, every single fault on the instruction stream changes the runtime signature with certainty. Using vertical checks, any runtime-signature error can be detected. On the contrary, CSM checks h bits of the runtime signature per cycle. Therefore, the probability to detect an error is $1 - 2^{-h}$. As any error propagates within the signature register, the probability to detect an error is way beyond 99.9 % after 3 checks of $h = 4$ bits.

If an attacker targets two instructions, she could possibly hide the error by colliding the signature value. It was shown in Sect. 3.1 that the attacker has to flip 32 bits on average or 8 bits in his best case when a CRC-32C is used as signature function. Even using advanced attack setups, the probability for introducing a fault with precise bit-flips across multiple cycles is very low.

5.2   Error-Detection Latency

An error can only be detected at the time of the vertical signature check when GPSA is used without CSM. It is up to the programmer to insert these vertical checks next to the critical pieces of code. This allows to perform very controlled checks and consequently reduces overhead. However, it is possible that, due to bad check placement, vertical signature checks by itself detect an error once it already has been exploited.

CSM solves this problem given that it checks parts of the signature register after every executed instruction. With an increasing probability any error is detected after a few iterations.

5.3   Monitor Complexity

One of our design goals was to only introduce minimal hardware overhead. All operations beside derived signature calculation are performed entirely in software. We evaluated the monitor complexity after synthesis for UMC's 130 nm Low Leakage process using Cadence 2009 tools. The standard cell library for this process comes from Faraday. Without the monitor, our Cortex-M3 is 36,957 GE large. Adding the monitor for GPSA increases the size of the processor by only 1,469 GE, respectively by less than 4 %. Adding support for CSM additionally increases the size of the fetch unit which results in a total core size of 39,319 GE. The modifications to support GPSA and CSM therefore are minimal and account to merely 6.4 % hardware overhead.

5.4   Memory Overhead and Processor-Performance Loss

Memory overhead and processor-performance loss highly depend on the executed program. These characteristics are mainly determined by the number of branches, function calls, and vertical signature checks.

Qualitatively speaking, a single signature update costs around 10 bytes of memory and 6 cycles in our software-centered implementation. A function call costs around 14 bytes of memory and 10 cycles. Using CSM, the introduced redundancy is proportional to the size of the code within the text section of the executable. For $h = 4$ per 16-bit Thumb instruction, up to 25 % of redundant NVM has to be added.

For a quantitative, empirical evaluation, we tested multiple programs: a coremark benchmark (one iteration), an AES-256 roundtrip (encryption followed by decryption with check), and a 160-bit elliptic curve cryptography (ECC) example performing a scalar multiplication with optional assembly-optimized finite-field arithmetic. The coremark benchmark has been optimized for speed (-02) given that this yields the best performance. The crypto algorithms have been optimized for size (-0s). Additionally, link-time garbage collection (-ffunction-sections -fdata-sections and -Wl,-gc-sections) has been used to preserve only the absolutely necessary code and data segments. A synthesizeable VHDL model of the hardware, evaluated using Cadence NC Sim, has been used to execute the benchmarks.

The raw numbers and the relative overhead in terms of runtime as well as RAM and NVM size are summarized in Table 2. The evaluation was performed in two steps. First, our GPSA implementation is compared against the unmodified LLVM backend which is used as baseline. Second, CSM is compared with the GPSA version given that it extends GPSA's checking capabilities.

RAM. The RAM overhead of GPSA is below 10 % in all eveluated programs. For coremark it is even merely 3 %. This overhead is solely a side effect of the increased register pressure during function calls. The additional live variables force the compiler to spill more values and therefore slightly increase the memory usage on the stack. Using CSM on top of GPSA introduces no additional RAM overhead given that the code itself stays absolutely unchanged.

NVM. Overhead on the NVM side ranges from 29 % for the AES test case to 79 % for ECC. This overhead is composed of the actual signatures (justifying + reference) and the added code for signature updates and vertical checks. In this software-centered implementation, the majority of the overhead is code. The signatures account for 25 % NVM overhead at most.

The NVM overhead of CSM over GPSA on the other hand is purely signature based. Only minor optimization potential remains.

Runtime. The most remarkable figure in this evaluation is probably the runtime overhead. The overhead of GPSA ranges from 2 % for optimized ECC to 57 % for

Table 2. Empirical Results for GPSA and CSM regarding RAM, NVM, and runtime overhead. Additionally, the NVM overhead solely for justifying and reference signatures is given.

Program	RAM Byte	NVM Byte	Runtime Cycle	Justifying Sigatures	Reference Sigatures
Baseline					
Coremark	2,444	9,384	547,294	—	—
AES-256	248	3,212	48,581	—	—
ECC	444	4,036	4,251,697	—	—
ECC w/ ASM	400	4,824	2,836,180	—	—
Overhead of GPSA (Relative to Baseline)					
Coremark[a]	2.3 %	69.0 %	56.7 %	23.5 %	0.1 %
AES-256[b]	9.6 %	29.0 %	36.7 %	10.8 %	0.5 %
ECC[c]	9.0 %	78.9 %	33.3 %	24.5 %	0.3 %
ECC w/ ASM[c]	8.0 %	53.5 %	1.9 %	16.3 %	0.2 %
Overhead of CSM with $h = 4$ bit (Relative to GPSA)					
Coremark[a]	—	22.2 %	8.9 %	—	22.2 %
AES-256[b]	—	19.3 %	6.5 %	—	19.3 %
ECC[c]	—	21.9 %	7.6 %	—	21.9 %
ECC w/ ASM[c]	—	22.6 %	0.4 %	—	22.6 %

[a]One vertical signature check before and one after the benchmark.
[b]One vertical signature check after every round of AES.
[c]One vertical signature check after every processed bit of the scalar.

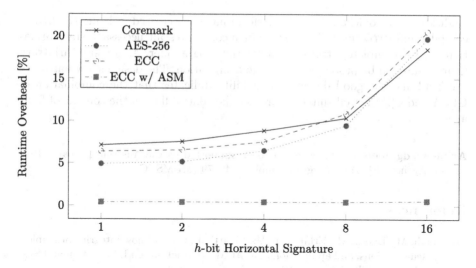

Fig. 4. Runtime overhead of CSM with different horizontal signature sizes (h-bit). (Relative to GPSA)

coremark. The software-centered approach taken in this implementation is again one of the reasons for these high values. Each GPSA operation takes between 6 and 10 cycles. Adding more hardware support could bring this values down to around 2 cycles. However, even without additional hardware much better results can be achieved. The 31.4 % difference between the ECC programs show that there is still a lot of optimization potential on the compiler side as well. Implementations of cryptographic primitives should be protectable at hardly any cost given that their control flow is typically very sequential.

Enabling CSM on top of GPSA implies an additional overhead of up to 9 %. However, this is rather low considering that horizontal signatures with 4-bit (25 % redundancy per instruction) are used. Figure 4 shows how the runtime overhead of CSM scales in dependence of the horizontal signature size h. Most astonishing is probably that the overhead is still below 21 % even at 100 % redundancy (16-bit per instruction). The processor's Harvard architecture and the combination of 32-bit bus and 16-bit instruction set makes this possible.

6   Conclusion

This work extends the CFI concepts of Wilken and Shen from the soft error to the fault attack context. To achieve this goal we not only analyzed the functional requirements for derived signature calculation, but also performed an evaluation of actual signature functions. Using a CRC with suitable polynomial, any error in a single cycle and at least 7 bit-flips, spread across two cycles, can be detected with certainty.

We further practically implemented the derived signature based GPSA and CSM techniques for a state-of-the-art processor, the ARM Cortex-M3.

Additionally, a toolchain for this platform has been created utilizing the LLVM compiler infrastructure. This toolchain incorporates all necessary transformations and is completely transparent for the programmer. As a result, arbitrary C programs can be protected by simple compilation. The design's low hardware overhead and the good detection capability indicates that the combination of GPSA and CSM is well suited to protect the control flow in the context of fault attacks.

Acknowledgements. This work has been supported by the Austrian Research Promotion Agency (FFG) under grant number 845579 (MEMSEC).

References

1. Abadi, M., Budiu, M., Erlingsson, Ú., Ligatti, J.: Control-flow integrity principles, implementations, and applications. In: ACM Transactions on Information and System Security (TISSEC), pp. 4:1–4:40, November 2009
2. Arora, D., Ravi, S., Raghunathan, A., Jha, N.: Hardware-assisted run-time monitoring for secure program execution on embedded processors. IEEE Trans. VLSI Syst. **14**(12), 1295–1308 (2006)
3. Boneh, D., DeMillo, R.A., Lipton, R.J.: On the importance of checking cryptographic protocols for faults. In: Fumy, W. (ed.) EUROCRYPT 1997. LNCS, vol. 1233, pp. 37–51. Springer, Heidelberg (1997)
4. Free60.org: (2012). http://free60.org/wiki/Reset_Glitch_Hack
5. Joye, M., Tunstall, M. (eds.): Fault Analysis in Cryptography. Information Security and Cryptography. Springer, Heidelberg (2012). No. 1619–7100
6. Lalande, J.-F., Heydemann, K., Berthomé, P.: Software countermeasures for control flow integrity of smart card C codes. In: Kutyłowski, M., Vaidya, J. (eds.) ICAIS 2014, Part II. LNCS, vol. 8713, pp. 200–218. Springer, Heidelberg (2014)
7. Namjoo, M.: Techniques for concurrent testing of VLSI processor operation. In: International Test Conference, pp. 461–468. IEEE, November 1982
8. Rodríguez, F., Campelo, J.C., Serrano, J.J.: A watchdog processor architecture with minimal performance overhead. In: Anderson, S., Bologna, S., Felici, M. (eds.) SAFECOMP 2002. LNCS, vol. 2434, pp. 261–272. Springer, Heidelberg (2002)
9. Rodríguez, F., Serrano, J.J.: Control flow error checking with ISIS. In: Yang, L.T., Zhou, X., Zhao, W., Wu, Z., Zhu, Y., Lin, M. (eds.) ICESS 2005. LNCS, vol. 3820, pp. 659–670. Springer, Heidelberg (2005)
10. Wilken, K.D., Shen, J.P.: Continuous signature monitoring: efficient concurrent-detection of processor control errors. In: New Frontiers in Testing, pp. 914–925, September 1988
11. Wilken, K.D., Shen, J.P.: Continuous signature monitoring: low-cost concurrent detection of processor control errors. IEEE Trans. Comput. Aided Des. Integr. Circuits Syst. **9**(6), 629–641 (1990)
12. van Woudenberg, J.G.J., Witteman, M.F., Menarini, F.: Practical optical fault injection on secure microcontrollers. In: Fault Diagnosis and Tolerance in Cryptography (FDTC), pp. 91–99. IEEE, September 2011
13. Zhang, M., Sekar, R.: Control Flow Integrity for COTS Binaries. In: Proceedings of the 22nd USENIX Conference on Security, pp. 337–352. SEC, USENIX Association, Berkeley, CA (2013)

Efficient Design and Evaluation of Countermeasures against Fault Attacks Using Formal Verification

Lucien Goubet[1]([✉]), Karine Heydemann[1], Emmanuelle Encrenaz[1],
and Ronald De Keulenaer[2]

[1] Sorbonne Universités, UPMC Univ Paris 06, UMR 7606, LIP6, Paris, France
{lucien.goubet,karine.heydemann,emmanuelle.encrenaz}@lip6.fr
[2] Computer Systems Lab (CSL), Ghent University, Ghent, Belgium
ronald.dekeulenaer@elis.ugent.be

Abstract. This paper presents a formal verification framework and tool
that evaluates the robustness of software countermeasures against fault-
injection attacks. By modeling reference assembly code and its protected
variant as automata, the framework can generate a set of equations for
an SMT solver, the solutions of which represent possible attack paths.
Using the tool we developed, we evaluated the robustness of state-of-the-
art countermeasures against fault injection attacks. Based on insights
gathered from this evaluation, we analyze any remaining weaknesses and
propose applications of these countermeasures that are more robust.

Keywords: Fault attack · Countermeasure · Formal proof

1 Introduction

More and more embedded systems, widely used in our everyday lives, hold information that is both personal and confidential (e.g., smartphones, IoT devices,
passports, credit cards and SIM cards). These systems are subject to physical
attacks, among which are fault attacks, that aim at disrupting the execution
of programs running on a system to further an attacker's personal gain. There
exist various means for injecting faults, such as electromagnetic or laser radiation, power or clock signal tampering, etc. [1,2]. By causing a fault with a specific
effect, an attacker can cause sensitive information to be leaked. For example, it
has been proven that the well-known RSA encryption algorithm can be broken
by differential fault analysis [3,4]. An attacker may also take control by interfering with the boot process, bypass protections to gain access to a service running
on a device, or overflow a buffer during a subroutine which is generating output, which may cause leakage of sensitive personal data. Fault injection attacks
can also aid an attacker in subverting countermeasures against Simple Power
Analysis [5], thus allowing him to perform side-channel analysis of a program.

© Springer International Publishing Switzerland 2016
N. Homma and M. Medwed (Eds.): CARDIS 2015, LNCS 9514, pp. 177–192, 2016.
DOI: 10.1007/978-3-319-31271-2_11

Many countermeasures[1] have been proposed to prevent faults from modifying a program's execution, both in hardware and in software. In any case, to provide maximum security it is necessary to combine hardware and software countermeasures. Software countermeasures have the advantage of not requiring any hardware to be manufactured again in order to provide a stronger protection. Moreover, industries such as smart card industries and mobile phone manufacturers often rely on pre-existing hardware on top of which they have to build software security solutions.

Software countermeasures can be designed at different levels, such as at an algorithmic level [6], in a high-level programming language [7–9] or at assembly level [10–12]. While higher level countermeasures may be optimized away or altered by a compiler, low-level countermeasures are compatible with existing compilers and toolchains. Also, they allow a finer study of protections since they are closer to the final code running on the chip and thus to the effect of a physical attack. Protections are designed with respect to a fault model describing a set of effects a fault can have at a certain level of abstraction [13]. For example, two well-known fault models that describe a fault at a logical level are Single Event Upset (SEU) and Multiple Event Upset (MEU). Examples of fault models that describe a fault at assembly level include instruction skip (the execution of a single instruction is skipped), instruction replacement (the execution of a single instruction is replaced by the execution of another instruction), conditional jump inversion, jump (modification of the program counter), etc.

Software countermeasures often rely on adding code and thus have an impact on code size (memory footprint) and performance (number of executed instructions) of programs. This has important consequences for both security specialists designing countermeasures and software designers applying them to their software: they both aim to maximize security while minimizing overhead. Also, it is of the utmost importance that the application of a countermeasure effectively protects code the way it is intended. However, for security specialists designing countermeasures, it is difficult to take into account every possible context in which a certain type of fault can occur, and to predict every possible effect a fault may have. Depending on the fault model taken into consideration, design complexity increases exponentially in relation to the number of instructions that have to be protected and the number of possible control flow transfers (e.g. calls or conditional branches) in the code. To truly guarantee that a software countermeasure works correctly, a formal proof is required, just as it is required to truly guarantee that a program functions the way it was intended. In practice, formally proving the correctness of software countermeasures is done only by few experts, and it is very time-consuming.

In this paper we propose a formal setting and an automated environment to check and evaluate the robustness of software countermeasures against faults by examining code fragments representing applications of those countermeasures. Using the formal framework, it is possible to guarantee that the application

---

[1] Throughout this manuscript, we will use the terms *countermeasure(s)* and *protection(s)* interchangeably.

of a countermeasure on a reference code fragment is correct and robust with respect to a given fault model. It also allows to aid in the design of new software countermeasures by exhibiting weaknesses, and can therefore help developers to test and deploy countermeasures more quickly. We illustrate the framework's use by evaluating the robustness of state-of-the-art protections, and we show how it can aid in the design of effective countermeasures.

The remainder of this paper is structured as follows: first, Sect. 2 discusses related work. The formal framework and the corresponding tool are presented in Sect. 3. Section 4 evaluates the robustness of a number of well-known existing countermeasures. In this section, we will also show how our tool can help enforce an existing countermeasure to be more robust. Finally, Sect. 5 draws conclusions.

2   Related Work

Many works have proposed software countermeasures against physical fault attacks. Software countermeasures are often based on temporal redundancy (i.e. performing the same computation multiple times) to detect or tolerate errors during computations [8,10–12]. Control flow protection requires different mechanisms to detect a modification of the execution flow [7,14]. A generic and automatic protection scheme for control flow integrity at C level has been proposed in [7]. The major drawback of this approach is its distance to the machine code: some faults, occurring at assembly level, may be impossible to model at source level due to the gap between the granularity of the fault at low level (one instruction) and at source level (one C statement). Moreover, a source-level protection may be removed by an optimizing compiler. A verification step at assembly level is necessary.

Barenghi et al. propose assembly-level countermeasures based on software redundancy and parity checking to detect instruction skips [10]. The proposed countermeasure scheme, based on instruction duplication and triplication, is claimed to be robust against any single instruction skip fault. However, it becomes difficult to determine the effectiveness of this protection against other fault models – and, more largely, of any protections on large code – without the help of formal methods. There are different means to prove (security) properties: model checking [12], SAT [15], SMT [16], taint analysis [17], rewriting rules using modular arithmetic [6], use of a proof assistant like Coq [18], etc. Moro et al. have proposed countermeasures and proved their tolerance against an instruction skip using model checking with BDD [12]. In [7] the model checking approach was used to design the generic protection scheme, without which it would have been difficult, if not impossible, to elaborate a protection that defends against all attacks for the considered fault model. However, model checking with BDD does not allow representation of larger problems, since this technique faces combinatorial explosion. Other formal methods like SAT/SMT do allow larger problems to be modeled without requiring an unreasonable amount of time for verification.

Bayrak et al. have proposed a SAT-based tool to determine which instruction of a Boolean program is sensitive to power-analysis, according to a Hamming weight uni-variate leakage model. Eldib et al. later proposed a SMT-based technique to automatically build perfectly masked Boolean programs [16]. Both methods target side channel attacks and are limited to specific assembly codes.

In his thesis [19], Moro showed that a significant percentage of faults induced by electromagnetic waves can be modeled as instruction replacements (with regard to the attacked microcontroller). This fault model remains rarely treated by countermeasures in literature, despite the fact that it can describe a large group of faults. While the countermeasure proposed by Barenghi et al. [10] should be able to detect some instruction replacement faults, the exact types of replacements are not analyzed.

Fault attacks are a powerful means to break security. Despite the need for assistance in countermeasure design, to the best of our knowledge, no study using a formal method to evaluate the robustness of assembly countermeasures against transient faults inducing instruction replacement has ever been proposed.

3   Robustness Evaluation Framework

In order to analyze the robustness of a hardened snippet of code, our framework takes two inputs: one piece of reference code, which represents a fragment of assembly code without any protection, and a hardened piece of code to be compared to the reference code. Both faulted and non faulted executions of the hardened code are considered, and compared with non faulted execution of the reference code for robustness evaluation. In the representation of the protected code, locations at which faults may occur are given, as well as the types of faults that may occur during execution at each of these locations, and the type of robustness that is globally wanted. The robustness type is either *fault tolerance* or *fault detection*. The notion 'type of fault' refers to fault models the framework is able to consider. Currently, instruction skip and a restricted version of instruction replacement (detailed in Sect. 3.1) are available.

Figure 1 shows an overview of our approach. From the inputs described above, the framework constructs a set of logical predicates whose satisfiability, which can be determined with the help of a SMT solver, answers the question: "Is the protected code robust against faults occurring during execution at the specified locations?" The framework internally represents code as interpreted automata and adds transitions that correspond to the effect of injected faults to the automaton representing hardened code. Robustness evaluation is then expressed as a logical property referring to the unfolded automata which represent the execution paths of the bounded execution of each automaton.

This process results in a SMT formulation of the robustness evaluation of hardened code with respect to its corresponding reference code. The results given by a SMT-solver determine whether the hardened code is robust, and can also be interpreted to understand any vulnerabilities still present in the code.

The following subsections detail the formal models that are used, the proof scheme, and its representation with a propositional formula whose satisfiability is checked.

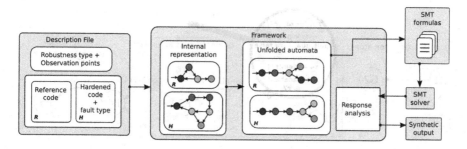

Fig. 1. Global overview

3.1   Representation of Code with Automata

The assembly code we take into consideration is ARM Thumb2 assembly (although basic operations are common to many assembly languages). Thus, the registers correspond to all user registers, among which there are the program counter, the stack pointer, the link register, and a conditional bit-wise register called `flags` that keeps the status flags. Although registers have a width of 32 bits, we have built our framework to make it possible to limit the width of registers to allow results to be calculated faster.

One way to check a property on a sequence of instructions is to model that sequence by an interpreted finite automaton. An interpreted finite automaton interferes with an external data domain by means of guarded-command transitions: the values of the data domain can restrict the firability of the transitions labelled by a guard (a Boolean expression over the data). The transition firing can modify the values of the data, by applying the action labelling the transition. In our case, each code excerpt is represented by such an interpreted automaton, interacting with a data domain (let's call it $\mathbb{D}$) containing variables representing registers (R0 – R15, flags) and addressed memory locations. Each state of the automaton refers to a position of the program counter in the code, and each transition is labelled with a couple (guard, action), representing the corresponding assembly instruction of the code. The guard establishes the data condition associated to the firability of the transition (the flag condition in case of a conditional branch for instance). The action models the effect of the execution of the instruction on the data variables. Moreover, each transition is labeled with the set of registers that are alive after that transition. This information is used to determine the attack that may affect program execution if launched at this point during execution. The representation of assembly code as an automaton, as well as the information on register liveness, can be produced by a compiler.

Let's consider a simple load from memory and its protected version with duplication and detection, given on page 12 in Listings 7 and 8 respectively. A simplified representation of the automata that correspond to both code fragments are given in Fig. 2.

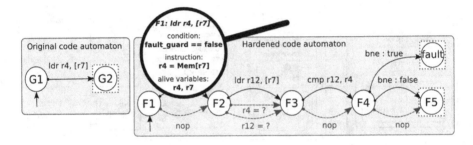

Fig. 2. Proof scheme: Automata of Listing 8 and its unhardened code

Fault Injection. Faults are represented by added transitions whose effect on variables depends on the fault model. Currently, two fault models can be specified : *Instruction Skip* and *Simplified Instruction Replacement*, respectively denoted as IS and SIR throughout the remainder of this text. In the IS fault model, the instruction may be skipped. When this happens, the data variables are not modified, but the program counter is set to the address of the next instruction. This can be seen as executing a `nop` instruction. The instruction skip fault is represented by a single transition which does not affect any register values. In the SIR fault model, an (original) instruction may be replaced by another instruction. We restrict ourselves to the case where the replacing instruction can not directly affect either the memory nor the normal control-flow. Thus, it can not be a store into memory or a jump[2]. Although this fault model does not model all possible instruction replacements, it allows to cover a significant set of possible attacks. Moreover, understanding how to build countermeasures against this simplified fault model is the first step in designing robust countermeasures against "full" instruction replacement. This fault model is represented by a set of transitions; each of them affects one register in the set of live output registers of the associated instruction. In Fig. 2, transitions that represent faults are drawn as dotted lines. In this example, every instruction of the countermeasure can be skipped (except for the second `ldr` instruction, which can be affected by the SIR fault model).

For this paper, we expect a fault to occur at most once during the execution of the hardened code snippet. However, the formal model can be easily modified to accommodate any (bounded) number of faults, at the expense of increased verification time. The number of faults restrict the firability of fault transitions: in case of one single fault, a boolean variable is added and set once a fault occurred, and all faulty transitions are guarded with a condition specifying that no fault previously occurred. Using a counter for the condition would allow to model the occurrence of several faults.

---

[2] Seeing as a fault can, however, corrupt flags and/or register contents, control-flow and memory content can be affected indirectly.

3.2   Robustness Proof Scheme

The robustness of the hardened code is formally assessed by comparing the sets of behaviors of the reference and hardened code fragments. This comparison is performed by checking dedicated properties on the set of bounded execution traces produced by the automata of both fragments (A_o and A_c for the automaton of the original code and that of the hardened code, respectively).

The properties to be verified depend on the type of robustness under consideration: in case of tolerance, one must ensure that, for any fault occurring once in any place of A_c, at given observation points, a set of variables $\mathbb{S} \subseteq \mathbb{D}$ specified by the designer have exactly the same value at these points; in case of detection, one must ensure that, for any fault occurring once in any place of A_c, either no fault is detected and the two automata end their execution in correct observation points with identical values in all variables of $\mathbb{S}$, or A_c ends in a fault detection observation point. Those states of both automata that are observation points are specified by designer. In most occasions we encountered, the observation points are the final or fault detection states of both automata. An example is given in Fig. 2, where observations points are surrounded by dotted squares.

The verification of these properties is performed in three steps: (1) Automata unfolding, (2) Automata combination and property construction, (3) Satisfiability check with the help of a SMT solver and counter-example analysis.

SMT Representation of Automata: Unfolding. From the internal representation of automata, the framework computes all possible paths from initial states to the deepest observation points. In other words, the automata are *unfolded*. In case of loops, some bounds are given to the framework to make it able to compute these paths. As an example, Fig. 3 represents the unfolded automaton of the instruction duplication countermeasure in Listing 8, along 5 steps. Notice that, because of the condition on transitions, not all paths can be taken. As an example, paths involving two faulty transitions are not possible, and thus our framework will not consider them as possible attack paths. On each possible path, a transition, faulty or not, corresponds to one execution step. The beginning of the path is at step 0 and each transition on the computed execution paths is numbered. Using the execution paths and this numbering, the framework derives a SMT formulation describing all possible evaluations of the registers, flags and memory locations (variables of $\mathbb{D}$) from an initial state.

To represent the evolution of a variable, we must declare as many logical variables as the number of the unfolding steps: a variable from a certain step i is calculated with the variables at step $i\text{-}1$ as showed by the magnifying glass above a transition in Fig. 3.

The SMT formulation is computed recursively: Let A be an automaton (either A_o or A_c), $SMT^{0..i}(A)$ the set of logical constraints related to the automaton A unfolded from step 0 to step i (i.e. expressing all execution paths of length i), and TR^{i+1} the set of logical constraints which represents all the possible

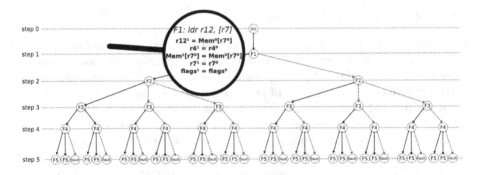

Fig. 3. Unfolded automaton of Listing 8

transitions of A at step $i+1$. The formula below shows the recursive construction of $SMT^{0..i+1}(A)$:

$$SMT^{0..i+1}(A) = TR^{i+1} \wedge SMT^{0..i}(A)$$

SMT Representation of Automata: Combination and Properties. Let n and m be the number of execution steps to reach all the observation points of A_o and A_c respectively (with respect to the specific number of iterations in case of loops). To determine if a hardened code is robust, we try to find if a weakness exists. This can be expressed with the following formula:

$$Form \ = \ SMT^{0..n}(A_o) \wedge SMT^{0..m}(A_c) \wedge \overline{prop}$$

where $prop$ expresses the properties of robustness, as explained in Sect. 3.2.

3.3   Verification and Results

The robustness property can be divided into a set of K independent sub-properties denoted $sprop_i$, each focusing on one couple of observation points of A_o and A_c and one variable of $\mathbb{S}$ whose value must be equal for both assembly codes at the observation points. The formula becomes:

$$\begin{aligned} Form \ &= \ SMT^{0..n}(A_o) \wedge SMT^{0..m}(A_c) \wedge \overline{\bigwedge_{i=0}^{K} sprop_i} \\ &= \ \bigvee_{i=0}^{K} (\ SMT^{0..n}(A_o) \wedge SMT^{0..m}(A_c) \wedge \overline{sprop_i} \ ) \end{aligned}$$

The formula can thus be divided into a set of sub-formulae, the disjunction of which defines the main formula $Form$. If one sub-formula is satisfiable, then the main formula is satisfiable. Thus, each sub-formula can be solved independently. We can further simplify the size of the sub-problems to solve by forcing a specific faulty transition in each sub-problem. Thus $Form$ can be expressed as a set of sub-formulae that each focus on a specific fault. Let $A_c^{f_j}$ be the automaton A_c where only the fault transition f_j is represented:

$$Form \ = \ \bigvee_{f_j} \bigvee_{i=0}^{K} (\ SMT^{0..n}(A_o) \wedge SMT^{0..m}(A_c^{f_j}) \wedge \overline{sprop_i} \ )$$

All sub-formula can be solved in parallel by different processors, which makes solving the problem significantly faster. Moreover, this technique enables a user to precisely know the instructions, variables of $\mathbb{D}$, and execution steps to be corrupted (this information is given by the faulty transition) in order to get an erroneous value for some variables of $\mathbb{S}$. The corrupted variables of $\mathbb{S}$ at the observation points are also known. This decomposition is therefore helpful for finding and understanding all possible attack paths to bypass the security of an assembly-level countermeasure for a given fault model.

4   Evaluating and Improving Robustness of Countermeasures

This section illustrates the usefulness of our approach by analyzing the robustness of existing protections. We show that our formal approach enables to ensure whether a certain protection is robust with regard to a specific type of fault, and that it can precisely expose any remaining weaknesses.

For each protection, we also propose an improved upon application that offers more extensive security. These improvements were developed with the aid of our formal approach. Note that we do not make any claims concerning the efficiency of these new countermeasures: we can prove that they offer superior protection, but this may come at a high overhead cost. More efficient variants offering the same amount of protection may exist.

We have chosen three existing protections for this evaluation, which are described in detail in the sections to follow.

1. *Memory store verification*, seeing as it is a very basic technique that is often used in industry.
2. *Loop iteration counter duplication*, because it attempts to guard the control flow of a loop, and uses some clever tricks to do so (e.g. inverting the condition of a branch) [20].
3. *instruction duplication*, since the principal idea behind this technique is widely applicable [12].

4.1   Memory Store Verification

A simple and well-known technique to verify whether data has been correctly written to memory, is to load that data from memory into a (free) register immediately after storing it, and comparing it to the register still holding the value that was stored. If both values are the same, then program execution can continue normally. If they differ, this indicates a fault has taken place. In the latter case, any fault handling code or mechanism may be executed to abort or possibly restore execution of the program. Note that, while this protection technique does not guarantee that data cannot be altered in memory after it has been written, it can be combined with error-correcting codes that protect the memory's integrity.

The protection technique described above was implemented (among others) by De Keulenaer et al. in a prototype link-time code rewriter [20], to show that it is possible to apply those protections automatically, and with an acceptable overhead. The technique we describe here is referred to by the authors as *memory store verification*. Listing 1 shows a sequence of instructions containing a store operation to be protected.

Listing 1. Original code

```
1      mov   r0, #imm
2      mov   r1, @data0
3      subs  r0, r0, #1
4      str   r0, [r1]
5      beq   .label
```

Listing 3. Protected code

```
1      mov   r0, #imm
2      mov   r1, @data0
3      subs  r0, r0, #1
4      str   r0, [r1]
5      ldr   r2, [r1]
6      cmp   r0, r2
7      beq   .correct
8      <fault handling code>
9  .correct :
10     cmp   r0, #0
11     beq   .label
```

Listing 2. Improved protection

```
1      mov   r0, #imm
2      mov   r0, #imm
3      mov   r1 @data0
4      mov   r1 @data0
5      subs  rx, r0, #1
6      subs  rx, r0, #1
7      str   rx, [r1]
8      str   rx, [r1]
9      beq   .label
10     beq   .label
```

Listing 3 shows a protected version of the code fragment. The countermeasure aims to protect the store instruction at line 4 in the aforementioned listing against an instruction skip. The instruction at line 10 was inserted to recompute the flags.

Both the original code fragment and the protected variant were transcribed for use by our formal verification framework. This enabled us to find vulnerabilities remaining in the protected code. They relate to the first three instructions, that determine the memory address r1 and the value of r0 which should be stored to memory. The wrong value of r0 can change the outcome of the cmp instruction (at line 10 in Listing 3), leading control flow down the wrong path. This cannot be detected by loading the value from memory again and comparing it, since the store operation itself was executed correctly. If the first or the third instruction is skipped, the memory, flags and control-flow may all become corrupted.

Moro et al. proposed a countermeasure pattern [12] which can be applied to protect the store instruction (as well as the instructions that contribute to the value in r0 and r1), and which is based on instruction duplication. Note that this scheme offers fault resilience, whereas the protection applied by De Keulenaer et al. offers fault detection. Listing 2 shows the result of applying the aforementioned countermeasure pattern proposed by Moro et al., and further optimizing it. Using our framework, we were able to prove its robustness against a single instruction skip fault. Besides protecting the store operation itself, which was already accomplished in the application of the original protection, this protection ensures that the correct value will always be written to the correct memory address. The direction of control flow at the end of the fragment is also protected.

4.2 Loop Iteration Counter Duplication

Another countermeasure implemented by De Keulenaer et al. aims to protect the number of iterations of a loop [20]. An unprotected code fragment is shown in Listing 4, whereas Listing 6 shows the same code fragment after protection.

Listing 4. Original code

```
1   .preheader :
2        mov   r2, r0
3   .body :
4        add   r2, r2, #1
5        sub   r1, r1, #1
6        cmp   r1, #0
7        bne   .body
8   .after :
```

Listing 5. Improved protection

```
1        mov   r2, r0
2        mov   r5, r1
3   .body :
4        add   r2, r2, #1
5        sub   r1, r1, #1
6        sub   r5, r5, #1
7        cmp   r1, r5
8        bne   .fault
9        cmp   r1, #0
10       cmp   r1, #0
11       bne   .body
12       bne   .body
13  .end :
14       ...
15  .fault :
16       <fault handling code>
```

Listing 6. Protected code

```
1   .preheader :
2        mov   r2, r0
3        mov   r5, r1
4   .body :
5        add   r2, r2, #1
6        sub   r1, r1, #1
7        sub   r5, r5, #1
8        cmp   r1, #0
9        bne   .check2
10  .check1 :
11       cmp   r5, #0
12       beq   .after
13       <fault handling code>
14  .check2 :
15       cmp   r5, #0
16       bne   .body
17       <fault handling code>
18  .after :
```

The loop iteration counter duplication protection was proven secure by our formal verification framework; i.e. it is able to protect the number of iterations of the loop by successfully detecting any single instruction skip, as claimed by the authors.

However, this protection does have one inherent weakness, because the counter is checked against its duplicate only when exiting from the loop. If, because of a fault, either the iteration counter or its duplicate is not decremented during a certain iteration, execution may continue for a long time before this is detected (e.g. for a high value of the counter). While it is practically

unfeasible for an attacker to prevent both the iteration counter and its duplicate from being decremented during a single loop iteration, he may be able to
prevent the iteration counter from being decremented during one iteration, and
subsequently prevent the duplicate counter from being decremented many iterations later, before either counter hits zero. If he succeeds in doing this, he has
successfully changed the number of loop iterations without this being detected.
Indeed, such an attack does imply that two faults are injected. However, given
the possibility of a large enough time-frame, we deem this to be feasible.

For this specific application of the loop iteration counter duplication, a possible improvement is shown in Listing 5. In this variant, the original loop counter
is compared to its duplicate during every iteration of the loop. This means any
modification to either the counter or its duplicate will never go undetected for
more than one iteration of the loop. By duplicating the cmp and bne instructions, we ensure that the loop will always be executed the right amount of times.
This is because it is practically unfeasible for an attacker to inject a fault in two
subsequent instructions.

4.3   Instruction Duplication

Barenghi et al. explored countermeasures and detections against fault attacks
based on software redundancy [10]. Listings 7 and 8 illustrate how these techniques can be used to protect a load instruction.

Listing 7. Original code

```
1    ldr   r4, [r7]
```

Listing 8. Protected code

```
1    ldr   r4, [r7]
2    ldr   r12, [r7]
3    cmp   r4, r12
4    bne   .fault
5    ...
6  .fault :
7      <fault handling code>
```

Listing 9. Improved protection

```
1      mov   r7, @data0
2      ldr   r4, [r7]
3      ldr   r12, [r7]
4      mov   r7, @data0
5      ldr   r12, [r7]
6      msr   apsr, #0
7      cmp   r4, r12
8      beq   .end
9      b     .fault
10  .end :
11      ...
12  .fault :
13      <fault handling code>
```

Using our framework, we were able to prove the robustness of this protection
technique against a single instruction skip fault, as claimed (but not proven)
by the authors. We also determined whether this protection technique is robust
with regard to the SIR fault model. The results are shown in Table 1.

The first column in this table shows the instruction which is modified by a
simplified instruction replacement fault. For that instruction, the second column
shows which registers are alive after the instruction has been executed, and the
third column shows how a replacement can lead to a faulty value of one of those
registers. Note that not all values of x lead to a faulty value of one of the live
registers. At this time, our tool does not yet output the complete set of values

for x that can corrupt one of the registers. While we have planned this as future work, for this manuscript we have deduced the success conditions given in the last column from the output of our tool.

Table 1. Results of the robustness evaluation: attack paths to corrupt r4

Instruction replaced	Alive variables	New instruction	Success condition
ldr r4, [r7]	r4, r7	r7 ← x	$\text{Mem}[x] = \text{r4} \wedge \text{r4} \neq \text{Mem}[\text{r7}]$
ldr r12, [r7]	r4, r12	r4 ← x	$x = \text{r12} \wedge \text{r12} \neq \text{Mem}[\text{r7}]$
cmp r4, r12	r4, flags.Z	r4 ← x	$x \neq \text{Mem}[\text{r7}] \wedge \text{flags.Z} = 1$
bne .fault	r4	r4 ← x	$x \neq \text{Mem}[\text{r7}]$

For a more detailed discussion, let's focus on the first row in the table. Registers r4 and r7 are alive after the execution of ldr r4, [r7]. Among them, only the corruption of register r7 by an address x, the contents of which must differ from memory case Mem[r7], can affect the final state of the register r4.

Table 1 shows that a simplified instruction replacement fault can bypass the security of any instruction in the protected code fragment. However, not all of these faults have the same probability of occurrence. Only one specific value of x can lead to an erroneous value of r4 if ldr r12, [r7] is attacked (if x is equal to the initial value of r12), whereas only one specific value of x will not corrupt the final state of r4 if bne .fault is attacked and r4 corrupted.

The insights we have acquired allowed us to come up with a more robust application of the instruction duplication countermeasure, one that can be used to protect the load instruction against a simplified instruction replacement fault. The improved upon application is shown in Listing 9. In this listing, the value to be loaded from memory is stored at address @data0. As we have shown earlier, register r7, which contains this address, is a sensitive register. In order to prevent r7 from getting an erroneous value which, in turn, leads r12 to have the wrong value loaded from memory, the latter had to be re-affected by @data0 (at line 4 in the aforementioned listing), between the first and second occurrence of ldr r4, [r7]. That instruction was in fact duplicated to prevent a single fault on this instruction to corrupt r4 with the initial value of r12: a fault affecting the first ldr r4, [r7] will not bypass the countermeasure since the second one will affect r12 with the correct value. The countermeasure is thus able to detect an erroneous value in r4. A fault affecting the second ldr r4, [r7] will always be detected as well, since either r4 or r12 already have the correct value.

In Listing 8, cmp r4, r12 can lead to corruption of r4 if the replacing instruction affects r4 and if the Z (zero) flag is set to true. Keeping the value true in flags.Z prevents the branch instruction from jumping to .fault. To avoid this, msr apsr, #0 was added at line 6 in Listing 9. This instruction sets all flags to false, so the branch instruction will always go to the fault detection state if r4 is corrupted.

The fourth instruction of Listing 8 is the most vulnerable one. If r4 is corrupted, only one value for x doesn't lead to an erroneous state of r4. Also, the last instruction of an application of a countermeasure is always more difficult to secure, since there is no instruction after its execution to detect the fault. One solution is to execute the last instruction (whose purpose is to branch to the fault detection state) only if a fault occurs before its execution. Otherwise, the countermeasure must have already detected that r4 has the correct value. This mechanism is implemented at lines 8 and 9 of Listing 9. This technique ensures that b .fault is executed only if a fault has already occurred. It also ensures that the control flow is subverted away from the countermeasure's basic block before it reaches the last instruction; the code that starts at label end can detect the fault.

Hence, the improved countermeasure shown in Listing 9 is robust against the simplified instruction replacement fault model. It guarantees that register r4 (and, by extension, r12) will always have the corrected value loaded from the memory address r7. Developing an improved countermeasure so quickly would have been very difficult, or even impossible, without the aid of our formal verification framework, because of the human brain's limited capacity to enumerate all vulnerabilities that are present in a fragment of assembly code.

4.4 Discussion

Seeing as the proof is divided in a set of independent sub-proofs (see Sect. 3.3), the total sequential verification time is the sum of the verification times of each sub-formula. The verification time of a sub-formula depends on the property being proved. Alos, for both the sub-proof and the proof in its entirety, the verification time is sensitive with regard to the complexity of the assembly code (register dependency, control flow, instruction mix, . . .), its length and the fault model taken into consideration. Explaining why, however, would lead us too far away from the context of this paper.

Concerning the time needed for our approach for the robustness evaluation, proving the robustness of the improved countermeasure (Listing 9) required the longest time, which was 10.7 s using a laptop computer (Intel® Core™ i3-3120M, CPU 4 × 2.50 GHz). In this case, the proof was divided into about 100 sub-proofs. The longest verification time for one such sub-proof was 90 ms. Without this decomposition, not only would the evaluation time have been at least one order of magnitude higher, but it would not have been possible to easily obtain the different attack paths in the initial version, and to construct the improved countermeasure.

For analyzing an entire code, our approach requires to decompose this code into pieces, the robustness of each piece to be analyzed separately. With the fault models considered in this paper and the robustness defined as the equivalence of the content of live registers and memory at some control points, this decomposition into small sequences of instructions enables the verification of large code.

5   Conclusions

We presented a formal verification method for evaluating the robustness of existing fault-injection countermeasures, which models code fragments as simple automata, and implemented this functionality in the form of a tool. This tool can also assist in improving existing countermeasures, as well as in the development of new countermeasures, as we have shown in this paper. Currently, the ARMv7-M (Thumb2) ISA is supported, but we estimate the porting of our tool to another assembly instruction set to be a matter of weeks. We believe the features of our formal verification framework are promising, and that there are many possible directions for this research as far as future work is concerned.

What we would like to do next, is to investigate metrics of robustness to classify countermeasures according to their strength (i.e. how robust they are against a certain type of fault). We also plan to study possible ways to reduce the verification cost for supporting a full instruction replacement fault model (which takes into account jumps and store instructions). Another research direction we are currently exploring is how we can combine the functionality of the formal verification framework with an automated code rewriting tool. This would allow to generate an automaton description representation of every single instance of an applied protection, which in turn will allow to verify whether all of the sensitive code that is to be protected, is in fact robust against a certain type of fault.

References

1. Bar-El, H., Choukri, H., Naccache, D., Tunstall, M., Whelan, C.: The sorcerer's apprentice guide to fault attacks. Proc. IEEE **94**(2), 370–382 (2006)
2. Bhasin, S., Maistri, P., Regazzoni, F.: Malicious wave: A survey on actively tampering using electromagnetic glitch. In: International Symposium on Electromagnetic Compatibility, pp. 318–321 (2014)
3. Boneh, D., DeMillo, R.A., Lipton, R.J.: On the importance of checking cryptographic protocols for faults. In: Fumy, W. (ed.) EUROCRYPT 1997. LNCS, vol. 1233, pp. 37–51. Springer, Heidelberg (1997)
4. Biham, E., Shamir, A.: Differential fault analysis of secret key cryptosystems. In: Kaliski Jr., B.S. (ed.) CRYPTO 1997. LNCS, vol. 1294, pp. 513–525. Springer, Heidelberg (1997)
5. Amiel, F., Villegas, K., Feix, B., Marcel, L.: Passive and active combined attacks: combining fault attacks and side channel analysis. In: Workshop on Fault Diagnosis and Tolerance in Cryptography FDTC, pp. 92–102 (2007)
6. Rauzy, P., Guilley, S.: A formal proof of countermeasures against fault injection attacks onCRT-RSA. J. Cryptographic Eng. JCEN **4**(3), 173–185 (2014)
7. Lalande, J.-F., Heydemann, K., Berthomé, P.: Software countermeasures for control flow integrity of smart card C codes. In: Kutyłowski, M., Vaidya, J. (eds.) ICAIS 2014, Part II. LNCS, vol. 8713, pp. 200–218. Springer, Heidelberg (2014)
8. Asghari, S., Abdi, A., Taheri, H., Pedram, H., Pourmozaffari, S.: SEDSR: soft error detection using software redundancy. J. Softw. Eng. Appl. **5**, 664 (2012)

9. Goloubeva, O., Rebaudengo, M., Reorda, M., Violante, M.: Improved software-based processor control-flow errors detection technique. In: Reliability and Maintainability Symposium, pp. 583–589 (2005)

10. Barenghi, A., Breveglieri, L., Koren, I., Pelosi, G., Regazzoni, F.: Countermeasures against fault attacks on software implemented AES: effectiveness and cost. In: 5th Workshop on Embedded Systems Security, pp. 7:1–7:10. ACM (2010)

11. Reis, G., Chang, J., Vachharajani, N., Rangan, R., August, D.: SWIFT: software implemented fault tolerance. In: International Symposium on Code Generation and Optimization, pp. 243–254 (2005)

12. Moro, N., Heydemann, K., Encrenaz, E., Robisson, B.: Formal verification of a software countermeasure against instruction skip attacks. J. Cryptographic Eng. 4(3), 145–156 (2014)

13. Verbauwhede, I., Karaklajic, D., Schmidt, J.: The fault attack jungle-A classification model to guide you. In: Workshop on Fault Diagnosis and Tolerance in Cryptography (FDTC), pp. 3–8. IEEE (2011)

14. Goloubeva, O., Rebaudengo, M., Reorda, M., Violante, M.: Soft-error detection using control flow assertions. In: 18th IEEE International Symposium on Defect and Fault Tolerance in VLSI Systems, pp. 581–588 (2003)

15. Bayrak, A.G., Regazzoni, F., Novo, D., Ienne, P.: Sleuth: automated verification of software power analysis countermeasures. In: Bertoni, G., Coron, J.-S. (eds.) CHES 2013. LNCS, vol. 8086, pp. 293–310. Springer, Heidelberg (2013)

16. Eldib, H., Wang, C.: Synthesis of masking countermeasures against side channel attacks. In: Biere, A., Bloem, R. (eds.) CAV 2014. LNCS, vol. 8559, pp. 114–130. Springer, Heidelberg (2014)

17. Potet, M.L., Mounier, L., Puys, M., Dureuil, L.: Lazart: a symbolic approach for evaluation the robustness of secured codes against control flow fault injection. In: ICST.(2014)

18. Chetali, B., Nguyen, Q.-H.: Industrial use of formal methods for a high-level security evaluation. In: Cuellar, J., Sere, K. (eds.) FM 2008. LNCS, vol. 5014, pp. 198–213. Springer, Heidelberg (2008)

19. Moro, N.: Sécurisation de programmes assembleur face aux attaques visant lesprocesseurs embarqués.Ph.D. thesis, UPMC, France (2014)

20. De Keulenaer, R., Maebe, J., De Bosschere, K., De Sutter, B.: Link-time smart card code hardening. Int. J. Inf. Secur. 1–20 (2015)

Precise Laser Fault Injections into 90 nm and 45 nm SRAM-cells

Bodo Selmke[1]([⊠]), Stefan Brummer[1], Johann Heyszl[1], and Georg Sigl[2]

[1] Fraunhofer Institute for Applied and Integrated Security, Munich, Germany
bodo.selmke@aisec.fraunhofer.de
[2] Department of Electrical and Computer Engineering,
Technische Universität München, Munich, Germany

Abstract. In the area of fault attacks, lasers are a common method to inject faults into an integrated circuit. Against the background of decreasing structure sizes in ICs, it is of interest which fault model can be met with state of the art equipment. We investigate laser-based fault injections into the SRAM-cells of block RAMs of two different FPGAs with 90 nm and 45 nm feature size respectively. Our results show that individual bit manipulations are feasible for both, the 90 nm chip and the 45 nm chip, but with limitations for the latter. To the best of our knowledge, we are the first to investigate laser fault injections into 45 nm technology nodes. We provide detailed insights of our laser equipment and the parameters of our setup to give a comparison base for further research.

Keywords: Laser-based fault injection · SRAM · High-precision · Comparing 45 nm and 90 nm

1 Introduction

Electronic devices used for information security are prone to many different attacks, like e.g. probing attacks, side-channel attacks, reverse-engineering, and fault attacks. Fault attacks aim to corrupt the intended functionality of an electronic device. Faults can be generated using many different methods [3,6]. A simple method are so-called glitching attacks, where the supply voltage or clock signal of an integrated circuit is interfered for a very short time period. This does not allow any control over the location of the injected fault since every element of the circuit could be affected. For this reason, the use of laser systems has become popular. Lasers enable the injection of highly localized faults in an integrated circuit. The generated faults can be exploited in various ways: Faults can be used to circumvent simple security checks such as password verifications, but also for highly sophisticated fault attacks against cryptographic implementations. Differential Fault Attacks (DFA) try to recover a secret key by comparing the regular output of the algorithm to a falsified one. Regardless of the actual attack method, from a designer's perspective it is important to know whether an attacker is able to perform manipulations with a sufficient precision.

© Springer International Publishing Switzerland 2016
N. Homma and M. Medwed (Eds.): CARDIS 2015, LNCS 9514, pp. 193–205, 2016.
DOI: 10.1007/978-3-319-31271-2_12

The fault model describes the properties of a fault in terms of timing, location, number of affected bits and the type of the bit-fault (bit-flip or forcing a specific value). Generic fault attacks (like e.g. Safe Error Attacks) or many early published DFAs as e.g. Giraud's attack on the AES [7] require to comply with a strict fault model. More advanced attacks require less demanding fault models, such as the DFA on AES by Saha et al. [10] which can cope with an arbitrary amount of bit faults within up to 12 bytes of the AES state in one round of the computation. In general an attack method is more powerful the lower the requirements on precision, allowing an attacker with less precise equipment to successfully mount an attack.

However, from a practical point-of-view, the capability to inject faults with a high precision is crucial for two reasons. First, it grants the flexibility to carry out a greater variety of fault attacks. Second, the presence of countermeasures in security devices ask for precise fault injections. Countermeasures against fault attacks can be divided into two classes: The direct detection of the actual fault injection by sensors (e.g. light sensors), and the detection by a redundant operation of the algorithm, e.g. using duplicated circuits to detect injected faults. In both cases, an increased precision of laser-based fault injection (LFI) is necessary to circumvent these countermeasures. Light sensors require additional space on the die and cannot be placed arbitrarily close to critical elements. Therefore they are possibly not triggered by highly localized fault injections. In order to circumvent the detection by duplicated circuit parts, with an increased precision it is more likely to inject the same fault in both parts. Therefore this topic is of special interest for the security chip industry.

In this contribution we investigate the achievable precision of fault injection into SRAM-cells using a state of the art laser system. We use two different high-volume FPGAs (Xilinx Spartan-3A and Spartan-6), and target the Block RAM (BRAM), which consists of a regular and dense array of SRAM-cells. Since SRAM-cells are composed of two cross-coupled inverters, the smallest gates used in CMOS logic, BRAMs are well-suited as test target to judge the LFI precision. The observed results are also interesting for the secure implementation of cryptographic algorithms in FPGAs, as efficient implementations make exhaustive use of available BRAMs [5]. However, in our opinion the derived conclusions are also generalizable for SRAM-cells on ASICs, fabricated in similar technologies. Our investigations show that the precision is sufficient to set single bits to specific values in the 90 nm Xilinx Spartan-3A under the condition, that focal plane and energy are precisely calibrated. On the 45 nm Xilinx Spartan-6, the precision decreases and in most fault injections single bits cannot be manipulated without affecting the adjacent memory cells. Nevertheless, single bit faults are still observable to a small extent and the capability to set a specific bit to a certain value is not limited.

Outline. After giving a summary of related work in Sect. 2, we describe our laser fault injection setup in Sect. 3. Our experimental results are based on the test devices described in Sect. 4. The results are presented and discussed in Sect. 5. Eventually, we propose considerations for secure implementations in Sect. 6.

2   Related Work

Several papers already provided information about the achievable precision of LFI so far. We extend this current state with results for smaller feature sizes of 90 nm and 45 nm. In contrast to previous publications, we specify our setup in detail to provide a solid comparison base.

Dutertre et al. show that attacks based on single-byte faults are feasible in an SRAM-memory of a microcontroller manufactured in a 350 nm process. Using the same setup and the same device, Agoyan et al. [1, 2] were able to improve this to single bit-faults. Unlike us, their results were achieved by a front-side LFI, using a wavelength of 532 nm and a spot-size of 4 μm on a chip with a much larger feature size.

Roscian et al. [9] stated that they inject single bit-faults in the memory of a microcontroller with 250 nm feature size. They use an infrared laser with 1064 nm wavelength, a spot size stated as 1 μm and a pulse length of 50 ns. In contrast, we are able to show that faults with this precision are still feasible with a larger spot size of 4 μm on devices with considerably smaller structures.

Courbon et al. [4] show that selective single-bit faults are feasible in a 90 nm microcontroller. Their setup uses a laser wavelength of 1064 nm at variable pulse lengths of down to tens of ns and a spot size of 2 μm. Though they also use a chip with 90 nm feature size, their results differ from ours in the fact that they investigate flip-flops, which consist of more transistors than SRAM cells and are therefore larger in total size. They state that the flip-flops they attacked have an approximate size of 15 μm^2, while the 90 nm SRAM-cells we attack are much smaller with a size of 3.25 μm^2. In addition they use a spot size stated as 2 μm, while we are able to show that even with a spot twice as large selective single bit faults are feasible.

Roscian et al. [8] perform a front-side fault injection with 532 nm wavelength, using very large spots of 100 μm on a 130 nm chip. They show that single-bit faults are feasible with this setup and argue that this is due to refraction of large parts of the beam. Unlike us, they do not have full control over the fault, by relying on the refraction of the metal layers.

3   Setup and Calibration

This paper examines the achievable fault injection precision in two different feature sizes. In our opinion a detailed description of the employed setup is crucial for comparable results. For this reason, we provide a detailed setup specification in this section.

3.1   Setup Overview

The experimental results in this paper are generated using a LFI-setup which is based on a diode-pumped Nd:YAG solid-state laser source, which is capable of emitting two different laser wavelengths, 532 nm and 1064 nm. An adjustable beam attenuator enables accurate control over the emitted beam energy. The pulse length of the laser source is fixed at 800 ps and supports a maximum repetition rate of 1 kHz.

In this contribution, we focus on fault injections through the backside of the die, which is common practice to avoid refraction by the metal layers of the chip. Therefore we use the 1064 nm wavelength, as it is absorbed less by the silicon substrate. To adjust the width of the collimated beam of the laser source, the beam is passed through a beam expander. By changing the beam width, the resulting spot size of the beam behind the focusing lens can be adjusted. A subsequent laser scanner supports precise and fast lateral deflection of the beam for precise control over the fault injection position. The scanner is capable of shifting the beam position within a range of ±0.25 mm on the DUT at a precision of 100 nm. Subsequently, for the visual inspection of the DUT, a digital camera is coupled in. The final element in the optical path is a 20× zoom-lens to focus the laser beam on the DUT. In order to position the DUT under the lens accurately, an xyz-table enables to move it in three spatial directions and to correct the tilt.

Total Energy Output. The total energy output of the system was measured with a laser energy sensor for the range of 1 nJ up to 5 µJ. To retrieve measurement values that include all losses in the optical system, the sensor was placed under the focusing lens. It turned out that the emitted energy is heavily dependent on the adjusted spot size. Hence, we took samples of energy versus attenuator position for each spot size we wanted to use as shown in Fig. 1. The plotted curves are averaged over 30 samples. We observed a deviation from the mean values of <10 % at maximum.

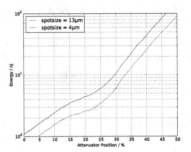

Fig. 1. Measured laser energy at DUT over attenuator settings and for two different spot-size settings

Spot Size. To measure the spot size of our laser, we used a monochrome CMOS camera sensor with a pixel size of 1.67 µm. The laser beam is focused on the surface of the sensor using the camera and pulsed with the maximum frequency of 1 kHz. Subsequently the distance of the DUT to the lens was leveled to the point where the minimum spot size was obtained.

The radius of a laser beam is physically defined by the $1/e^2$ (≈ 13.5 %) drop of the intensity, which can be measured with the sensor. Ideally the energy output is adjusted so that the beam center drives the CMOS sensor into saturation to use the full range of resolution. In Fig. 2, the sensor output for the largest and the smallest spot sizes of our setup is shown. For the small spot it was not possible to determine the size computational. We estimated the size to be about 4 µm. This is not the theoratically possible minimal spot size, which would be the size of the used wavelength.

It is important to note, that the physical spot size is not equal to the effected area on the die. Since the local energy density of the beam must reach a certain value to produce faults, the effective spot size may be larger or smaller depending on the total energy.

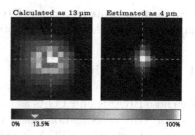

Calibration of Focal Plane. We chose to inject faults from the backside of the die. To achieve a minimal spot size in the active layers of the die, we have to set the focal plane

Fig. 2. Laser energy distribution and derived spot-size

below the surface. However, the exact thickness of the die, as well as the doping which influences the absorption in the silicon, is unknown. For this reason we empirically determined the optimal distance (z-axis) of the lens to the die.

In order to find the optimal focal plane, we used the effect in the BRAM of the FPGA as an indicator. We scanned a small area of the BRAM at different focal plane settings in a range from the surface to 150 μm below the surface. The optimal focal plane is corresponding to the maximum total number of generated bit-faults per scan. Since the roughly required energy in the focal plane was unknown, we started this procedure with the minimum energy output to avoid damaging the chip. As long as no faults were detected, the energy output was increased after each iteration.

It has to be noted, that this procedure may be unfeasible for actual attackers, since the observability of cells is usually not possible. Alternatively, an infrared camera can be used to adjust the focal plane. Figure 3 depicts the results of LFIs at different z-offsets (distance from the surface) as an example for the above described procedure: Each scan position is colored with a gray value corresponding to the number of bit-faults observed at this location. In relation these figures indicate how the total number of generated bit-faults changes with the shift of the focal plane. It can be observed that from 74 μm to 79 μm (Figs. 3a and 3b) below the surface the total number of bit-faults increases, and with an additional shift to 84 μm this number decreases again. Therefore the optimal

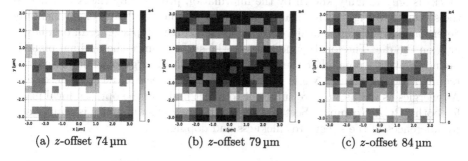

(a) z-offset 74 μm   (b) z-offset 79 μm   (c) z-offset 84 μm

Fig. 3. Spartan-6: Fault injection results for different focal planes at 1.5 nJ pulse energy and 4 μm spot-size

focal plane is located at around 79 μm. For the results shown in Sects. 5.2 and 5.3 implicitly the thus determined optimal focal planes were used.

4   Devices Under Test

We chose BRAMs on FPGAs as target for our investigation for two reasons. First, the FPGA grants full control over the memory. The BRAM blocks can be exclusively used for evaluation of the LFI because they do not hold any program data, as it might be in the case of microcontrollers. Second, SRAM-based FPGAs are manufactured in a standard CMOS process, the results should therefore be comparable to

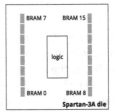 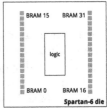

Fig. 4. Spartan-3A and Spartan-6 floorplan with location of the BRAM hard macros and placement of the logic

ASICs. We expect that the SRAM-cells within the BRAM are designed as small as possible in the respective technologies and thus the results should provide a good base for generalization. We use two Xilinx FPGAs, the Spartan-3A with a feature size of 90 nm and the Spartan-6 with 45 nm. Those features sizes are interesting since they are similar to the ones used in contemporary security chips.

On both FPGAs all available BRAM blocks are instantiated and made accessible over a serial interface to the PC. We configure the BRAMs to be organized in 2048 × 9 bits in every word and include the 9th bit, which is intended for the use as parity bit, while reading out the BRAM. Figure 4 depicts the floorplans of both FPGA dies taken from the Xilinx design tools and showing the approximate locations of the BRAM blocks. To avoid errors in the logic of the design, all elements except for the BRAM hard macros are placed in the center of the FPGA.

Locating BRAM Blocks. Since the actual location of the individual BRAM blocks is only roughly known by the information provided by the Xilinx design tools (compare Fig. 4), the exact location on the die had to be experimentally determined. This step is achieved by a coarse (20 μm step size) scan of a larger area on the die. The focal plane is set to the surface, since the optimal plane is unknown at this point. For the Spartan-3A, a pulse energy of about 10 nJ was required to inject faults, while for the Spartan-6, at least 35 nJ were necessary. As energies as low as 1 nJ are sufficient to inject faults in the optimal focal plane for both FPGAs (compare Sect. 5), we assume that this difference is mainly due to differences in the substrate thickness and doping.

BRAM Block Dimensions. Once the locations of the BRAMs were roughly known, we determined their dimensions on the die. On the Spartan-3A the

BRAM block covers an area of 300 μm×200 μm, while for the Spartan-6 the BRAM block size shrinks to 150 μm×200 μm. Thus the actual size of the BRAM shrinks only by a factor of two. Calculated from these values, the approximate size of a single SRAM cell is 3.25 μm^2 on the Spartan-3A and 1.62 μm^2 on the Spartan-6.

5 Experimental Results

For our investigation on the achievable precision of LFIs, we concentrate on a small part of the BRAM with a size of 8 μm×8 μm. The test position is varied using a step size of 200 nm. The laser spot size is set to the minimum of 4 μm with a calibrated focus level (refer to Sect. 3.1).

5.1 Test Procedure

For all following results, we use the below test procedure with two consecutive laser shots for each position during a scan:

1. Preload all BRAM bits with 0
2. Inject a single laser shot
3. Read back values and detect *set-faults*
4. Preload all BRAM bits with 1
5. Inject a single laser shot
6. Read back values and detect *reset-faults*

By preloading the BRAM with all 0 as well as all 1, we can detect both possible cases of bit faults: If bits can be *set* to 1, so-called *set-faults*, and if bits can be *reset* to 0, so-called *reset-faults*. At each scan position, we evaluate the results of comparing the preloaded to the read-back values. There are three general cases which we distinguish *for every bit and at every position*.

Fault type	Color	Description
set	red	The specified bit can be set to 1 at this position
reset	blue	The specified bit can be set to 0 at this position
toggle	green	The specified bit was set to 1 in the first shot, but also to 0 in the second

Since we are primarily interested in the ability to precisely target specific bits exclusively, the presented figures each concentrate on single specific bits and we show maps of the scan results where the results for *one specific bit* for all scan positions are plotted. To indicate, whether bits are hit *exclusively*, or whether other bits have been affected by the shot at this position, we use pale colors instead of solid ones. Additionally, grey colored positions in the figures indicate, that another bit has been affected by the fault injection, but not the targeted bit. *If an attacker aims at injecting precise set- or reset-faults into specific bits exclusively, only the positions in the scan map which are colored in solid red and blue are eligible.*

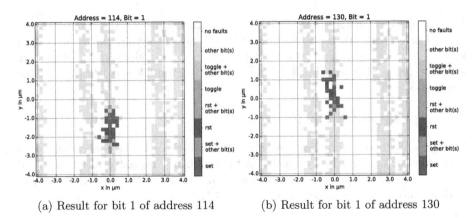

(a) Result for bit 1 of address 114   (b) Result for bit 1 of address 130

Fig. 5. 90 nm Spartan-3A: LFI into single bit at 1 nJ pulse energy (Color figure online)

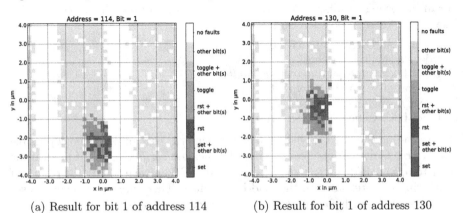

(a) Result for bit 1 of address 114   (b) Result for bit 1 of address 130

Fig. 6. 90 nm Spartan-3A: LFI into single bit at 1.5 nJ pulse energy (Color figure online)

5.2   Results on 90 nm Spartan-3A

We repeatedly carried out the test procedure described in Sect. 5.1 on the 90 nm Spartan-3A for decreasing energy outputs. In Figs. 5 and 6 the results for the energy levels of 1.0 nJ and 1.5 nJ are depicted. Thereby we evaluated the captured data for two arbitrary adjacent bits, which are located in the center of the scanned area.

Regarding the results for energy output of 1.0 nJ depicted in Fig. 5, it is observable that the fault injection achieved a very high overall precision. Almost all test locations induced only single bit faults, as indicated by the solid red and blue colors. In addition, there are specific zones that either generate a *set-fault* or a *reset-fault*. The third fault-type, toggling the bit value, does not appear. This result is in line with the results of Roscian et al. [9]. Their model-based analysis of LFI into SRAM-cells indicates, that toggling a bit is generally unfeasible.

Furthermore there are some irregularities in the distribution of the sensitive zones. By comparison of the results for both vertically adjacent bits in Figs. 5a and 5b it can be seen that the fault sensitive zones of these bits are mirrored. Horizontally adjacent bits, by contrary, are arranged in pairs with the same orientation of sensitive zones. These pairs are separated by notably wider gaps in between to neighboring pairs. These observations are probably due to layout optimizations, i.e. the sharing of doped wells and supply lines (V_{DD}, Gnd). Against the background of the research of Sarafianos et al. [11–13], who showed that NMOS transistors are more sensitive to LFI than PMOS transistors, we assume that in the wide fault insensitive gaps the PMOS transistors of the SRAM-cells are located and the energy is not sufficient to trigger them.

The results obtained at an energy output of 1.5 nJ (Fig. 6) show an increased effect area of the laser spot in comparison to the results for 1.0 nJ Unlike for the previous results, the ability to inject single-bit faults depends on the location. The sensitivity zones for vertically adjacent bits are partly overlapping, hence at most locations both bits are affected. In the results for 1.5 nJ there are some locations which induced set-faults and reset-faults (green color), however this pattern does not regularly appear. Thus we assume, the reason is a slight variation of the test position between both laser shots.

As a conclusion, we find that precision is generally higher with lower energy values as long as the energy is still sufficient for fault injection. This can be explained by the fact, that at lower energies, and if correctly focused, the effective spot-size within the active layer decreases. Regarding the Spartan-3A, it is obvious that with this setup and calibration, specific targeted bits can be set to specific values without interfering other bits.

5.3   Results on 45 nm Spartan-6

For the 45 nm Spartan-6, we carried out the same experiments with identical settings. A comparison of the results for the two different energy levels shows a similar effect as for the Spartan-3A, i.e. an improvement in precision for the lower energy of 1 nJ. Figure 7 shows the results for the energy level of 1 nJ, evaluated for two adjacent bits. Similar to the results of the Spartan-3A, we observed areas which are either *set* or *reset* sensitive and mirrored for adjacent bits. Comparing the results of the Spartan-6 with the Spartan-3A, it can be seen that significantly less single-bit faults are achieved with identical settings, as the *set*, resp. *reset* sensitive areas of adjacent bits are still overlapping. Thereby the area that has influence on a specific bit stays approximately the same size as for the Spartan-3A. We assume that further reduction of the energy would increase the precision, but could not prove this due to the limitations of our setup regarding lower energies.

As an important observation, Fig. 7a shows that for address 0, bit 0 exclusive *set-faults* are achieved more likely. This is due to the fact that this bit is located at the boarder of the BRAM and has no adjacent bit on the left side, thus it does not share its *set* sensitive area with any other bit. Analyzing the BRAM layout revealed that such a bit is existent for every second address and will either affect index 0 or 7 (1024 bits in total).

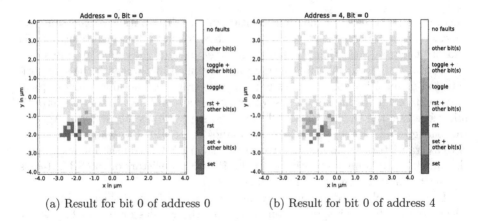

(a) Result for bit 0 of address 0   (b) Result for bit 0 of address 4

Fig. 7. 45 nm Spartan-6: LFI into single bit at 1 nJ pulse energy

5.4   LFI Precision Depending on Stored Values

In the previously described experiments, the memory cells have been preloaded with the same bit values, i.e. either all 0 or all 1 during the fault injection. Since adjacent bits have mirrored *set* and *reset* sensitive regions, this can be seen as a worst case scenario while trying to affect bits exclusively. Attackers can achieve a better precision if adjacent bits store complementary values.

We tested this in an additional experiment on the Spartan-6 and preloaded complementary values to adjacent bits. For the results shown in Fig. 8, all bits of address 0 are preloaded with 1, while all other bits are preloaded with 0. Therefore we can only observe reset-faults for bits of address 0 in the evaluation, and set-faults for all bits corresponding to other addresses.

Contrary to our previous results presented in Fig. 7, we can observe exclusive single-bit faults depicted in Fig. 8. Figure 8a concentrates on the bit with index 1 at address 0 and shows that it is *exclusively reset* at many positions which are marked as solid blue. The reason for this is that the bit shares its *reset*-sensitive zone with another horizontally adjacent bit, namely the bit with index 1 at address 4, which already contains the value 0 and is therefore not affected. Figure 8b concentrates on the bit with index 1 of address 4 and shows that it is *exclusively set* at many positions which are marked as solid red. The reason for this is that the bit shares its *set*-sensitive zone with another horizontally adjacent bit, namely the bit with index 2 at address 0, which already contains the value 1 and is therefore not affected.

As a conclusion for a feature size of 45 nm we show that single-bit faults must still be considered feasible, although the achieved precision is lower in general. This is particularly due to the observation that feasibility is dependent on the values stored in the adjacent SRAM cells.

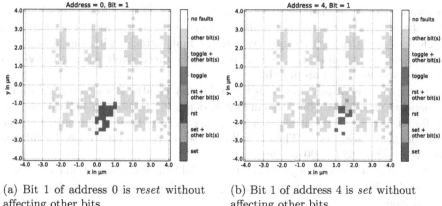

(a) Bit 1 of address 0 is *reset* without affecting other bits

(b) Bit 1 of address 4 is *set* without affecting other bits

Fig. 8. 45 nm Spartan-6: Bits are preloaded with different values before LFI into single bits at 1 nJ pulse energy (Color figure online)

6 Considerations for Secure Implementations

If an error detection or correction code is used against LFI, it should respect the specific memory layout. Cells which share common doped wells will likely be affected by faults in the same way:

- It is likely, that both cells will contain the same value after the laser injection.
- It is unlikely that both adjacent bits change their values if they had different values before.
- If adjacent cells belong to the same word, it is likely that more than one bit of a word is affected at once.

In this way, the organization of cells has a high impact on the fault model from LFI. Such information can be valuable to *design or configure efficient error correction codes* for secure implementations. Also simple redundancy measures in software can be made more effective with these considerations and the actual arrangement of the memory cells in mind.

Bits which are stored in SRAM cells that are located at the borders of BRAM hard macros will likely not share one of their sensitive regions. Therefore, an attacker will have a better chance to exclusively set them to either 0, or 1, depending on the location. *For a secure implementation, this means that data such as cryptographic keys, for whom there e.g. exist attacks based on exclusively setting some bits to certain values, should rather not be stored in such cells.*

7 Conclusion

In this work we have shown, how precise faults can be injected into the BRAM of two state-of-the-art FPGAs with feature sizes of 90 nm and 45 nm. Thereby we extend the state of publication with results for 45 nm. Our results indicate that the achievable precision is sufficient to enable the manipulation of specific single bits for 90 nm structures. As a result fault attacks with the most strict fault model are feasible. E.g. Safe-Error attacks successively setting individual bits to a specific value are feasible.

In case of the 45 nm chip, it is more difficult to attack a single bit without influencing an adjacent bit. Although it is definitely feasible to generate single-bit faults, this is only possible at a lower success rate, heavily depending on the state of the adjacent cells. The capability to set a specific bit to specific value is however equally to the 90 nm device.

In order to achieve such precision, the careful tuning of the system parameters is essential. For this reason, we thoroughly specified our setup to allow future comparison.

References

1. Agoyan, M., Dutertre, J.M., Mirbaha, A.P., Naccache, D., Ribotta, A.L., Tria, A.: Single-bit dfa using multiple-byte laser fault injection. In: 2010 IEEE International Conference on Technologies for Homeland Security (HST), pp. 113–119, November 2010

2. Agoyan, M., Dutertre, J., Mirbaha, A., Naccache, D., Ribotta, A., Tria, A.: How to flip a bit? In: 16th IEEE International On-Line Testing Symposium (IOLTS 2010), 5–7 July 2010, Corfu, Greece. pp. 235–239 (2010). http://doi.ieeecomputersociety.org/10.1109/IOLTS.2010.5560194

3. Bar-El, H., Choukri, H., Naccache, D., Tunstall, M., Whelan, C.: The sorcerer's apprentice guide to fault attacks. Proc. IEEE **94**, 370–382 (2006)

4. Courbon, F., Loubet-Moundi, P., Fournier, J.J.A., Tria, A.: Adjusting laser injections for fully controlled faults. In: Prouff, E. (ed.) COSADE 2014. LNCS, vol. 8622, pp. 229–242. Springer, Heidelberg (2014). doi:10.1007/978-3-319-10175-0_16

5. Drimer, S., Güneysu, T., Paar, C.: Dsps, brams and a pinch of logic: new recipes for AES on fpgas. In: 16th IEEE International Symposium on Field-Programmable Custom Computing Machines, FCCM 2008, 14–15 April 2008, Stanford, Palo Alto, California, USA, pp. 99–108 (2008). http://dx.doi.org/10.1109/FCCM.2008.42

6. Dutertre, J.M., Fournier, J., Mirbaha, A.P., Naccache, D., Rigaud, J.B., Robisson, B., Tria, A.: Review of fault injection mechanisms and consequences on counter-measures design. In: 2011 6th International Conference on Design Technology of Integrated Systems in Nanoscale Era (DTIS), pp. 1–6, April 2011

7. Giraud, C.: DFA on AES. In: Dobbertin, H., Rijmen, V., Sowa, A. (eds.) AES 2005. LNCS, vol. 3373, pp. 27–41. Springer, Heidelberg (2005). doi:10.1007/11506447_4

8. Roscian, C., Dutertre, J., Tria, A.: Frontside laser fault injection on cryptosystems - application to the AES' last round. In: 2013 IEEE International Symposium on Hardware-Oriented Security and Trust, HOST 2013, Austin, TX, USA, 2–3 June, 2013. pp. 119–124 (2013). http://dx.doi.org/10.1109/HST.2013.6581576

9. Roscian, C., Sarafianos, A., Dutertre, J., Tria, A.: Fault model analysis of laser-induced faults in SRAM memory cells. In: 2013 Workshop on Fault Diagnosis and Tolerance in Cryptography, Los Alamitos, CA, USA, 20 August 2013. pp. 89–98 (2013). http://dx.doi.org/10.1109/FDTC.2013.17

10. Saha, D., Mukhopadhyay, D., Chowdhury, D.R.: A diagonal fault attack on the advanced encryption standard. IACR Cryptology ePrint Archive 2009, 581 (2009). http://eprint.iacr.org/2009/581

11. Sarafianos, A., Gagliano, O., Lisart, M., Serradeil, V., Dutertre, J.M., Tria, A.: Building the electrical model of the pulsed photoelectric laser stimulation of a pmos transistor in 90 nm technology. In: 2013 20th IEEE International Symposium on the Physical and Failure Analysis of Integrated Circuits (IPFA), pp. 22–27, July 2013

12. Sarafianos, A., Gagliano, O., Serradeil, V., Lisart, M., Dutertre, J.M., Tria, A.: Building the electrical model of the pulsed photoelectric laser stimulation of an nmos transistor in 90 nm technology. In: 2013 IEEE International on Reliability Physics Symposium (IRPS), pp. 5B.5.1–5B.5.9, April 2013

13. Sarafianos, A., Roscian, C., Dutertre, J., Lisart, M., Tria, A.: Electrical modeling of the photoelectric effect induced by a pulsed laser applied to an SRAM cell. Microelectron. Reliab. 53(9–11), 1300–1305 (2013). doi:10.1016/j.microrel.2013.07. 125

Countermeasures

The Not-so-Distant Future: Distance-Bounding Protocols on Smartphones

Sébastien Gambs[1]([✉]), Carlos Eduardo Rosar Kós Lassance[2],
and Cristina Onete[3]

[1] Université de Rennes 1 - Inria / IRISA, Rennes, France
sgambs@irisa.fr
[2] Université de Rennes 1 / Télécom Bretagne, Rennes, France
cadurosar@gmail.com
[3] Inria / INSA Rennes, Rennes, France
cristina.onete@gmail.com

Abstract. In authentication protocols, a relay attack allows an adversary to impersonate a legitimate prover, possibly located far away from a verifier, by simply forwarding messages between these two entities. The effectiveness of such attacks has been demonstrated in practice in many environments, such as ISO 14443-compliant smartcards and car-locking mechanisms. Distance-bounding (DB) protocols, which enable the verifier to check his proximity to the prover, are a promising countermeasure against relay attacks. In such protocols, the verifier measures the time elapsed between sending a challenge and receiving the associated response of the prover to estimate their proximity. So far, distance bounding has remained mainly a theoretical concept. Indeed in practice, only three ISO 14443-compliant implementations exist: two proprietary smartcard ones and one on highly-customized hardware. In this paper, we demonstrate a proof-of-concept implementation of the Swiss-Knife DB protocol on smartphones running in RFID-emulation mode. To our best knowledge, this is the first time that such an implementation has been performed. Our experimental results are encouraging as they show that relay attacks introducing more than 1.5 ms are directly detectable (in general off-the-shelf relay attacks introduce at least 10 ms of delay). We also leverage on the full power of the ISO-DEP specification to implement the same protocol with 8-bit challenges and responses, thus reaching a better security level per execution without increasing the possibility of relay attacks. The analysis of our results leads to new promising research directions in the area of distance bounding.

Keywords: Distance-bounding protocol · Relay attack · NFC · Smartphone

1 Introduction

Radio Frequency IDentification (RFID) is a widespread and cost-efficient technology, currently used for applications ranging from contactless payment to

---

The authors are listed by alphabetical order.

© Springer International Publishing Switzerland 2016
N. Homma and M. Medwed (Eds.): CARDIS 2015, LNCS 9514, pp. 209–224, 2016.
DOI: 10.1007/978-3-319-31271-2_13

public transport and machine-readable identification. A fundamental cryptographic primitive that must be supported and implemented on RFID technology is *authentication*. During an authentication protocol, the device equipped with an RFID chip (also called the *prover*) interacts with a reader (called the *verifier*) to prove its legitimacy. To protect the privacy of the data stored and manipulated by RFID tags for sensitive applications, these devices must be equipped with a processor capable of performing cryptographic operations.

RFID chips may be embedded in devices such as passive tags securing items in supermarket, public transport cards as well as contactless payment smartcards. Thus, the term "RFID prover" covers a wide range of hardware, which differs in terms of characteristics such as memory, surface area, independence with respect to the verifier for energy (*i.e.*, passive versus active) and cost. However, traditional RFID provers always answer requests from the reader without asking for the user's consent. This property makes RFID technology prone to *relay attacks*. These attacks are known as mafia frauds [5] in the context of authentication, or wormhole attacks in the field of neighbourhood discovery. In a relay attack an adversary impersonates a legitimate prover by forwarding messages between him and the legitimate verifier. Relay attacks have been successfully implemented against Bluetooth [9], ISO 14443 smartcards [3,11], electronic passports [13], electronic voting schemes [19], and even access mechanisms for cars, such as Passive Keyless Entry and Start (PKES) [7].

To counter relay attacks, Brands and Chaum introduced *distance-bounding* (DB) protocols [2]. A DB protocol extends classical authentication schemes by additionally enabling the verifier to check his proximity to the prover. Most RFID tags operate according to the ISO 14443 standard, for which "proximity" is defined in the range of 10 cm. In a DB protocol, the verifier is equipped with a clock, which measures the roundtrip time of fast challenge/response rounds. As RFID communication takes place at the speed of light, such time measurements accurately reflect the communication distance, and thus can be used for proximity checking.

While the literature of DB protocols is abundant (see for instance [1,2,6,10, 16]), to the best of our knowledge only three practical implementations of RFID distance bounding currently exist. The first one is a highly-customized (and expensive) proof-of-concept implementation by Ranganathan, Tippenhauer, Singelée, Škorić and Capkun [20]. The two other solutions, namely the Proximity Check option for NXP's Mifare Plus cards and the solution of 3DB Technologies, come from industry and run with proprietary specifications and hardware.

Modern smartphones can use Near Field Communication (NFC) technology to emulate RFID tags. In this mode, the phone can behave either as an RFID prover or as a verifier, and its communication is subject to the ISO-DEP protocol specified in the ISO14443-4 standard [14,18]. Smartphones have already been used by Francis, Hancke, Mayes and Markantonakis to conduct relay attacks [8]. Their work demonstrates that any application, ranging from credit cards to electronic passports, can be attacked by using NFC phones, even if the relay attack introduced a delay of several seconds. In terms of distance, this allows the relay attacker to impersonate a prover located several hundreds of thousands of kilometers away from the verifier. However, to our best knowledge no DB protocols have so far been implemented on smartphones.

Main Contributions. In this work, we investigate the implementability of DB protocols on smartphones running in a tag-emulation mode, focusing in particular on relay attacks and mafia frauds using off-the-shelf hardware. More specifically, our countermeasures cannot compete with fast tailored hardware that can perform relays in some microseconds. Moreover, we do not consider attacks such as distance and terrorist frauds.

More precisely, we explore how DB can be implemented on Android *without* changing the design of the hardware (such as the SIM card, the phone's processor or the phone itself). In contrast to the proximity check solutions of Mifare Plus and 3DB Technologies, our implementations are public and do not require proprietary hardware. Our main objective is to evaluate how far one can implement DB protocols as a standard Android application on an existing smartphone. We do not rely on the SIM card as a cryptographic processor, nor customize its properties. Rather, we directly use the processor of the smartphone. As a consequence, our implementation is easier to adopt, but prone to side-channel and malware attacks.

We propose three proof-of-concept implementations of increasing complexity of the Swiss-Knife DB protocol [16] on Android. All these three implementations use 32 challenge-response rounds.

1. **The basic implementation.** This first implementation works at the application layer and does not require root access. While it can be used straightforwardly, our results show that the roundtrip time measurement presents a lot of variation, with a standard deviation of 4.4 ms for a distribution containing multiple clusters of values.
2. **The customized implementation.** In this second implementation, we modify the Android operating system to make the protocol run at the Hardware Abstraction Layer (HAL). We customize both the prover and the verifier to decrease the processing delays introduced by them, and reduce variations caused by propagating messages across all the layers. Our results show a normal distribution of measured roundtrip values of this implementation, with no false negatives when the protocol is implemented with an error threshold of 16 rounds and an allowed variation of 1.5 ms from the minimal observed measurement.
3. **The 8-bit implementation.** The phone follows the ISO 14443-4 standard and the ISO-DEP protocol for RFID emulation, which encodes the 1-bit challenges of the Swiss-Knife protocol as an entire byte. For our third implementation, we extended our second implementation by using the transmitted byte to exchange 8-bit challenges and responses. Our results are encouraging as the measured times present little variation while the gain in security level per execution is visible even for a proximity threshold within 1 ms of the minimum time. This last result indicates that designing DB protocols using larger challenges is a promising direction, in particular since the encoding of the message according to the ISO-DEP protocol *must* be at least the size of a byte.

This contradicts the theoretical design recommendations for DB protocols outlined in a previous work by Clulow, Hancke, Kuhn and Moore [4].

Our analysis shows how to choose the parameters for the proximity bound and for the threshold value of erroneous transmissions. In particular, choosing a proximity bound within 1.5 ms of the observed minimum time is optimal for our second implementation and reasonably good for our third implementation. By contrast, the first implementation requires a much larger variation. In terms of fault tolerance and the resulting security level, the third implementation largely outperforms the two other ones. Indeed, even when 20 out of 32 rounds are faulty, this implementation still ensures a better security level than the second implementation with 32 out of 32 rounds being correct.

We also discuss the somewhat negative result that our experimental implementations cannot detect relays at less than 1 ms if the threshold t_{max} is chosen as to provide a good tradeoff between correctness and relay-attack detection. However, all practical relay attacks necessarily introduce delays. For fast dedicated relay hardware, such as that of Hancke [11], the relay is in the order of microseconds and thus undetectable. However, other previous attacks such as [8,12] introduced delays of respectively 50 and 27 ms, which can be easily detected by our implementation. Thus, our results are encouraging in the sense that the proximity check can only be bypassed by a Man-In-the-Middle (MIM) adversary using more sophisticated technology than standard off-the-shelf mechanisms.

Outline. The paper is organized as follows. In Sect. 2, we review some preliminaries on relay attacks, DB protocols and relevant Android/RFID-emulation details. Afterwards in Sect. 3, we describe our methodology, before discussing our results in Sect. 4. Finally, in Sect. 5 we conclude by putting our work in perspective and outline future research directions.

2   Preliminaries

Relay Attack. An authentication protocol conducted between a prover $\mathcal{P}$ and a verifier $\mathcal{V}$ aims to allow the latter party to check the *legitimacy* of the former, as a prerequisite of allowing $\mathcal{P}$ access to specific privileges (*e.g.*, entering a building, using a public transportation system or unlocking a car).

In a *relay attack*, an adversary $\mathcal{A}$ authenticates as legitimate by relaying messages between an honest verifier and an honest prover located far from the verifier. The adversary "extracts" honest authentication responses from the prover by means of a *Leech* – a device acting as a verifier – and authenticates by using a *Ghost* – a second device, acting as a prover and extracting information from the verifier. If the attack is successful, then the Ghost authenticates. This attack is illustrated in Fig. 1.

Relay attacks are possible in practice and bypass usual cryptographic countermeasures like encryption and digital signatures. They are even more effective in the context of RFID authentication, since RFID tags do not require the consent of the user to transmit messages. Such tags usually require the proximity

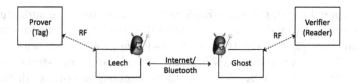

Fig. 1. A relay attack: the Ghost tries to authenticate to an honest verifier by forwarding the information received by the Leech from the honest prover.

of the verifier to transmit (being otherwise passive). However, relay attacks can contradict this assumption by "amplifying" signals (*e.g.*, using a stronger magnetic field) and by forwarding messages even from very distant provers. As a consequence, an adversary can use a far-away user's card to enter a sensitive area, or make a contactless-card payment by using a card located hundred of kilometers away from the terminal [15].

Distance-Bounding (DB) Protocols. In this work, our main focus is on implementing DB protocols on smartphones to be able to detect relay attacks (*i.e*, mafia frauds). We do not address the two other attacks usually considered in the DB literature, namely (1) the *terrorist fraud*, in which a Man-In-the-Middle adversary receives limited one-time help from a malicious prover to authenticate and (2) the *distance fraud*, in which a malicious far-away prover makes the verifier believe he is actually in his proximity.

In general, DB protocols start with an *initialization* phase, during which several protocol parameters and nonces are exchanged. Then, during the *interactive* phase, the prover and verifier run several fast rounds in which V first sends a one-bit challenge to which P responds with a single bit answer. The verifier stores the response and the measured roundtrip time. Finally, during the *verification* phase, V checks the responses sent during the fast exchanges and compares the roundtrip times to a threshold t_{max}. Based on the results obtained, the verifier authenticates (or not) the prover.

We implemented the well-known Swiss-Knife DB protocol [16], which we briefly present hereafter. In this protocol, each prover P is associated with an identity ID, stored by the verifier V together with a shared secret key sk per prover. As depicted in Fig. 2, in the initialization phase of this protocol, the prover P and the verifier V exchange two session-specific nonces N_P and N_V. Then, N_P and the key sk are used to derive two bitstrings T^0 and T^1 later used as responses in the N_c interactive challenge-response rounds. The former value corresponds to the output of a pseudo-random function (PRF) keyed with the shared key sk and given as input N_P (*e.g.*, usually this function is simply a HMAC). The second bitstring T^1 is computed as the XOR of T^0 and sk.

In each challenge-response round, V generates a random 1-bit challenge, and P responds with a bit from either T^0 or T^1 depending on the challenge. In the verification phase, P authenticates the transcript by again using a PRF. Finally, V authenticates P if and only if: (1) the responses are correct, (2) the validation of the transcript by the prover succeeds and (3) a certain number of rounds have arrived on time. Indeed, the Swiss-Knife protocol tolerates some faulty/untimely challenge-response rounds up to a predefined threshold E_{MAX}. Previous provable-security analyses [6,16] show that the Swiss-Knife protocol run with a total of N_c fast challenge-response rounds has an (approximate) mafia-fraud resistance of $2^{-(N_c - E_{\mathsf{MAX}})} + \epsilon_{\mathsf{PRF}}$, in which ϵ_{PRF} is the advantage an optimal distinguisher has in distinguishing the output of PRF from a truly random string.

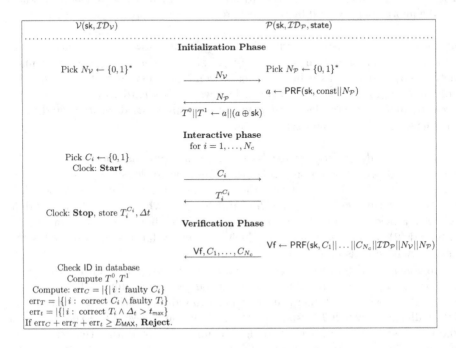

Fig. 2. The Swiss-Knife protocol with unilateral authentication.

NFC Communications on Android. NFC communications on Android smartphones are characterized by two elements: the host (the Android operating system) and the controller (usually the NFC chip communicating internally with the host and externally with other chips). The core of the NFC communications depends on the type of controller existing in the phone. For older smartphones, the controller was designed by NXP and its implementation uses the libnfc-nxp library, relying on two protocols: LLC (Logic Link Control) and HCI (Host Controller Interface). More recent controllers follow the NFC Controller Interface implementation (NCI) and use the libnfc-nci library [17]. The specific protocols used by each controller are highly relevant as they usually introduce significant delays and encode the transmissions in a way that decreases the useful information rate. Thus, in the context of distance-bounding such techniques render proximity checking more difficult.

RFID communication on a smartphone occurs via a serial port with a baud rate of 115200 using an 8-N-1 configuration. This yields $11520 * 8$ information symbols per second, which is equivalent to a constant rate of 11520 bytes per second. Thus, transferring a byte of information will take approximately 0.0868 ms. Two controllers can communicate via a peer-to-peer protocol or they can behave as reader and tag communicating via the ISO-DEP protocol [14,18] summarized in Fig. 3. We chose to implement this last option in which the controller of the prover emulates an ISO/IEC 14443-4-compliant passive NFC-A tag. For the predefined carrier frequency of 13.56 MHz, the bit duration according to the ISO/IEC 14443 protocol is 128/13.56 MHz = 9.439 µs or 75.512 µs per byte.

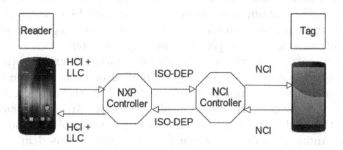

Fig. 3. Phone-to-phone communication between an NFC prover and an NCF verifier.

Older phones generally use the LLC protocol on the outer interface and the HCI protocol for the inner communication. In more recent phones, the NCI protocol functions as a token-based mechanism, which can be invoked by the controller to eliminate buffer overflows [17]. In this setting, the controller gives so-called *credits* to the host that can be used to communicate. Finally, the ISO-DEP protocol defines the format of frames exchanged between the two controllers. This format divides a frame in three blocks, each consisting of 2 bytes: the Start of Data (SoD), the Payload and the End of Data (EoD). At a per-byte duration of 75.512 µs, it takes 0.151 ms to transfer each byte from the host to the controller and back. In addition to each payload byte, the SoD and EoD blocks amount to 4 overhead bytes (*i.e.*, a 0.604 ms delay), resulting in a minimum communication time of 0.755 ms.

On Android, the data transmitted by an application to the chip must pass through all the abstraction layers provided by the operating system, from the more abstract to the more concrete: (1) the application layer, (2) the Android NFC-Service layer, (3) the Android NFC Application layer, (4) the Libnfc NXP/NCI layer, (5) the Hardware Abstraction Layer (HAL), (6) the driver/serial port, and finally (7) the NFC card layer. These abstraction layers exist to facilitate the work of the developer and to enable an easy integration of various types of hardware within Android. However, each layer also adds delays to the transmission time for both sending and receiving data. In our experiments, this delay was at least 1.5 ms for each smartphone. Circumventing these layers require root access in order to change the Android operating system or at least to install and use modified Android libraries.

3   Implementing Distance Bounding on Android

In our implementations, the verifier is a Samsung Galaxy Nexus smartphone following NXP specifications for the communication with its NFC chip. The prover (*i.e.*, tag) is implemented on an LG Google Nexus 5 running Android Lollipop (5.1) and using NCI specifications for phone-to-chip communication. The Swiss-Knife protocol was run with $N_c = 32$ challenge-response rounds and a variable tolerance threshold E_{MAX} for the maximum number of errors it can accept. An error can be a faulty challenge/response or a transmission time surpassing the threshold t_{max}. For our implementations, the threshold E_{MAX} is essential and a trade-off has to be set between reducing it and increasing t_{max} (thus permitting some relay attacks due to the spread of the response times).

Our experiments were run in 10 batches of 20 executions each, the batches themselves being separated by a random interval of time. For the computation of the pseudorandom function PRF, we relied on the implementations of HMAC_SHA1 or HMAC_SHA256 as explained below. We implemented three versions of the reader and tag. The first runs the protocol with no modification to the Android operation system (*i.e.*, the phone is used in a "normal" mode). The second one executes the protocol by changing the Android operation system so as to bypass the stack layers in the roundtrip-time estimation. Thus, we call it the "customized" implementation. Finally, the third version modifies the structure of the Swiss-Knife protocol by using 8-bit challenges and responses. Hereafter, we use the following notation for the different implementations: challengesize : verifiermode ↔ provermode, in which the prover and verifier modes are always either normal or custom, and the challenge size is either 1 or 8 bits. Thus, 1 : normal ↔ custom denotes the implementation with 1-bit challenges (as specified by the Swiss-Knife protocol), with the prover in normal mode and the verifier in custom mode.

For the custom mode, we modify the Android operating system by using the sources available on the AOSP (Android Open Source Project)[1]. For the reader protocol, we used the branch called android-4.2.2_r1, while the tag protocol uses the android-5.1.0_r3 branch. For our normal mode implementations, the reader uses the "*LMY47I*" stock version and the tag uses the *JDQ39* version[2].

When the reader runs in custom mode, it uses a fully customized Android image. In contrast, since the prover protocol is meant to be used by everyday users, we limited the tag customization to substituting the default library nfc_nci.bcm2079x.default.so with our own customized version of it. This library adds the Swiss-Knife implementation to the logic of the HAL library. To simulate a regular user environment for the prover, the smartphone implementing the tag has a number of applications installed on it and is always connected to a 3G/4G network.

---

[1] These sources can be downloaded at https://source.android.com/source/downloading.html.

[2] These versions are available at https://developers.google.com/android/nexus/images.

The fast challenge/response roundtrip time is measured starting from the moment the reader activates its sending function to the time it receives the size of the response packet. If this information was sent as soon as it was computed, then measuring the time of arrival of this first part can provide an accurate proximity estimation. However, the driver of the phone acting as a tag actually buffers all the response data before sending it to the HAL, which leads to an overhead corresponding to the full processing and computation time for the response. An additional limit is due to the granularity of the reader's clock, which can only measure with a precision of up to 30.518 µs or 5 km. While this granularity is incompatible with the precision generally required by a DB protocol, it is sufficient for our scenario, since most challenge-response time measurements are in the order of several ms.

Note that changing the models of the smartphones used could lead in a slight variation in measured times. In particular, changing the reader phone to a newer model could produce more accurate results, while changing the tag may lead to a choice of the t_{max} bound allowing a MIM adversary less time to perform a relay. Our decision of implementing the DB protocol of the phone itself, rather than on the SIM card, makes it easier to install and deploy at large scale. However, consequently our implementation is also less efficient and secure.

3.1   1 : normal ↔ normal

For the first implementation, we created a pair of Android applications (one for the prover and the other for the verifier), which execute the Swiss-Knife protocol using the development tools found in https://developer.android.com/sdk/index.html. Here, our primary objective was to implement the protocol in the simplest way possible. This implementation exchanges the necessary bytes via NFC using the standard Android API for NFC communications. This application stores the measurement obtained for each of the $N_c = 32$ challenge-response rounds. The length of the variables $N_{\mathcal{V}}$, $N_{\mathcal{P}}$, sk, the constant const and of the verification string Vf is 32 bits. The (full) challenge string and each of the two response ones are also of the same size. We rely on the HMAC_SHA1 implementation from the package javax.crypto for our PRF. This function outputs a 160-bit string, which we truncate to 32 bits. The values of sk and the constant const are generated at random and saved on the phone.

The results of the 200 measurements (in 10 batches of 20 executions) are summarized in Table 1. We recall that our main objectives were: (a) to prevent relay attacks by choosing a tight value of t_{max}, (b) to ensure correctness, thus setting a trade-off between the tightness of t_{max} and the value of E_{MAX} and (c) preventing mafia fraud by optimizing the choice of E_{MAX}. In particular, we did not consider attacks such as terrorist and distance frauds. We also did not investigate the delay induced by each abstraction layer as it would require changing the operational system in the so-called "normal" implementations, possibly altering the results due to the measurement. For the first implementation, we observed an important variation in the measured times, which range from 9.37 to 82.0 ms, with a standard deviation of 4.4 ms (which is almost half our minimum time). In practice, this means that in order to optimize correctness (objective (b)), we need either a very high value of t_{max}, which allows practical relays to be mounted, or a very high value of E_{MAX}, which would lower the mafia fraud resistance. The median time of 18.95 ms indicates that at least half the measurements are more than twice this minimal value. Thus, even having an error margin E_{MAX} as high as $\frac{1}{2}N_c = 16$ rounds still results in the adversary having a 9 ms window for mounting an attack.

3.2   1 : custom $\leftrightarrow$ custom

For our second implementation, we customized the implementation by short-circuiting some abstraction layers in the phone, which creates a trust issue. In particular, one must ensure that only NFC transmissions are spoofed during the protocol and nothing else. While this modification is not difficult to implement in a reader phone, regular users would also need to install a modified Android library for the prover (which require root access). However, since Android is open-source, there is hope that our modification could be integrated eventually in the default library. In this case, no root access would be required for the prover.

This customization shortens the measured times as the clock runs from the HAL library layer rather than at application level. This difference is visible in our results (see Table 1) showing that the minimum measured time was reduced from 9.37 to 6.26 ms. In addition, while outliers still exist (our maximal time is close to the maximum observed in the first experiment), they become unfrequent as reflected by a median of 7.11 ms and a mean of 7.30 ms. In addition, the measurements are much more uniform, with a much smaller standard deviation of 2 ms, indicating that the values are more concentrated around the mean. If we set the error threshold E_{MAX} to be $\frac{1}{2}N_c = 16$ rounds, a choice of t_{max} within 1 ms of the minimum observed time is enough to guarantee an almost perfect correctness (as explained later).

As both types of implementations are available, we also experimented by running the application between a custom reader and a normal-mode tag using a standard Android (1 : normal $\leftrightarrow$ custom). These results are also shown in Table 1. As expected the minimum value is almost the average of the 1 : normal $\leftrightarrow$ normal and 1 : custom $\leftrightarrow$ custom modes (7.69 ms). However, the standard deviation remains the same very large one as obtained in the 1 : normal $\leftrightarrow$ normal case and indeed for a particular batch we did observe an outlier as large as 200.71 ms. An in-depth analysis of the outliers obtained by this implementation revealed that only around 0.1 % of our measures where slower than 30 ms. We believe that these outliers must occur due to another process with more priority interrupting our protocol. This indicates that the variation in the measured time is actually caused by the prover's response times and not by the method the reader employs to measure time.

3.3   8 : custom $\leftrightarrow$ custom

For the 8 : custom $\leftrightarrow$ custom implementation, we modified the Swiss-Knife protocol to use 8-bit challenges and responses, but we left unchanged the *manner*

Table 1. Summary of statistics from each of our implementations (the measurement values are in milliseconds).

Implementation	Min time	Max time	Standard deviation	Median	Mean
1 : normal ↔ normal	9.37	82.00	4.40	18.95	18.27
1 : custom ↔ custom	6.25	78.80	2.00	7.11	7.30
8 : custom ↔ custom	6.29	61.03	1.95	7.35	7.83
1 : normal ↔ custom	7.69	200.71	4.45	9.68	10.20

of choosing the responses per each challenge bit. However, instead of processing the challenges one bit at a time and selecting the appropriate response, we rely on the smartphone's memory and computational power to *precompute* the responses to all possible challenges for each round. Since we did not modify the protocol itself, the mafia-fraud resistance for N_c fast interactive rounds and an error threshold of E_{MAX} rounds is about $2^{-8 \cdot (N_c - E_{\text{MAX}})} + \epsilon_{\text{PRF}}$, in which ϵ_{PRF} is the advantage of a best distinguisher to tell apart the output of PRF from a truly random string. Our modification of the protocol relies on the observation that the message encoding in the ISO14443-4 standard/ISO-DEP protocol requires that the two parties exchange bytes instead of bits.

This implementation was run with 32 fast challenge/response rounds for a customized prover and verifier, yielding an approximate mafia-fraud resistance of $2^{-256} + \epsilon_{\text{PRF}}$. Thus, we also need to ensure that both the output size of the PRF and the size of the secret key sk are at least 256 bits. Instead of HMAC_SHA1 we use HMAC_SHA256, which returns 32 bytes. The variables const, sk a, T^0, T^1, Vf, C, $N_\mathcal{V}$, and $N_\mathcal{P}$ are also 32 bytes long. The prover $\mathcal{P}$ precomputes for all 32 rounds the responses for each of the 2^8 possible challenges, and thus during the protocol he only performs a lookup to retrieve the precomputed result.

The results in Table 1 show that the minimal observed time and the standard deviation are almost the same as for the 1 : custom ↔ custom. However, this implementation has a much higher mafia-fraud resistance than the 1-bit version. This opens the door to the possibility of using less rounds and larger challenges in the future. However, we are conscious that the current scope of our analysis is currently limited and we strongly encourage a thorough investigation of its consequences as future work. In the distance-bounding literature [4], there are two fundamental reasons for requiring the challenges and responses to be single-bit only. The first reason is to reduce to a minimum the processing time for the prover during fast rounds while the second one is to prevent relay attacks in which the Leech device accelerates the tag by augmenting the magnetic field it generates when querying the honest far-away prover. The first point does not hold for our implementation since we precompute all the possible responses rather than making the prover compute the response in real time. With respect to the second strategy, we did not investigate in how far an adversary can succeed by using it in our context.

4   Comparative Analysis

In this section, we compare and analyze the results obtained for the three implementations described in the previous section. First, we investigate the distributions of the measured roundtrip times, depicted in Fig. 4 (left), and the density of those measurements (same figure on the right).

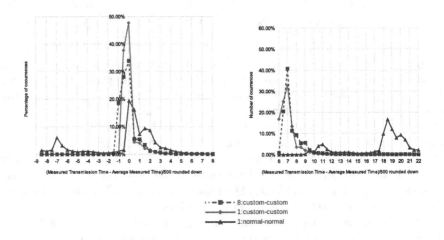

Fig. 4. Distribution of measured times around the mean (left) and density of measured times (right).

For the left plot, we first computed the mean roundtrip time $\tilde{t}$ and then the difference between each measured time and $\tilde{t}$, rounding them down to the nearest half a second. For both fully customized implementations, we observed that the values cluster in a nearly normal distribution around the mean measured time. By contrast for the 1 : normal ↔ normal case, multiple clusters of values fall outside the neighbourhood of the mean measurement. This variation implies that even honest prover-verifier authentication can only succeed if the bound t_{max} is set to be much larger than the minimal time.

The mean measurement $\tilde{t}$ is also quite far from the minimal observed time for the 1 : normal ↔ normal distribution. This is visible in Fig. 4 (right), in which the density of occurrences is shown as a percentage of the total number of measurements for each occurring value (in milliseconds). For the 1 : normal ↔ normal implementation, the minimal time is higher than for the other two implementations. Even more important, most observed times are clustered far from this minimal value. By contrast, for the 1 : custom ↔ custom and 8 : custom ↔ custom implementations, most values are close to the minimum. For the 8-bit version, there is a true peak in the measurements, with few values around the minimum, while for the 1-bit version the peak is less sharp, with multiple values around the observed minimum.

The Swiss-Knife protocol includes an error threshold E_{MAX}, such that the prover authenticates only if a number $(N_c - E_{\text{MAX}})$ of challenge-response rounds

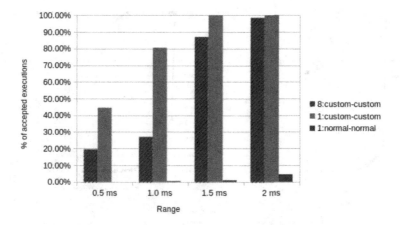

Fig. 5. Percentage of successful executions when considering $E_{MAX} = 16$ rounds.

are within the bound t_{max}. The higher E_{MAX} is chosen, the lower is the mafia-fraud resistance of the protocol, but the tighter one can set the bound t_{max}. We explore this relationship in more details in the following. Figure 5 displays the percentage of honest-prover/honest-verifier executions passing for $E_{MAX} = 16$ rounds (and $N_c = 32$ rounds), as a function of the distance between t_{max} and the minimal observed measurement. In the 1 : custom ↔ custom implementation, 45 % of the executions succeed if t_{max} is within 0.5 ms of the minimal measured time, as opposed to only 20 % for the 8 : custom ↔ custom case. Thus, a prover must run the 8 : custom ↔ custom protocol on average 5 times before authenticating. The difference between implementations is much smaller if t_{max} is within 1.5 ms of the minimal time (100 % for 1 : custom ↔ custom and 87 %

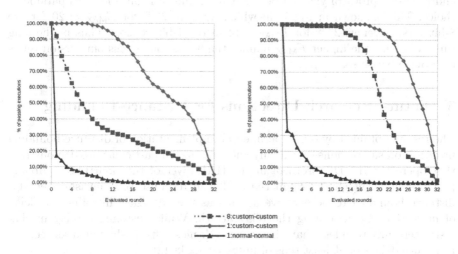

Fig. 6. Percentage of successful executions against $(N_c\text{-}E_{MAX})$, for t_{max} within 1 ms (left) and 1.5 ms of the minimum (right).

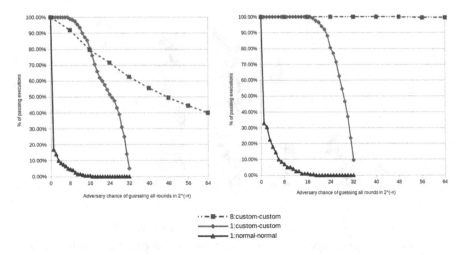

Fig. 7. Percentage of successful executions against the security level (in bits), for t_{max} within 1 ms of the minimum (left) and within 1.5 ms of the minimum (right).

for 8 : custom $\leftrightarrow$ custom). However, larger values of t_{max} lead to a higher risk of relay attacks.

We also investigated the impact of E_{MAX} on the percentage of false negatives. Figure 6 shows the results obtained when t_{max} is chosen within 1 ms and 1.5 ms from the minimal measured time. The x-axis represents the number of *evaluated* rounds, which correspond to the $(N_c - E_{MAX})$ rounds for which the measured time is compared to t_{max}. The 1 : custom $\leftrightarrow$ custom implementation always tolerates a lower value of E_{MAX} than the other versions. However, for t_{max} within 1.5 ms of the minimal measurement, the curves are closer ($E_{MAX} = 14$ versus $E_{MAX} = 20$), and the 8-bit protocol yields a better mafia-fraud resistance for this parameter choice. This is shown in Fig. 7, in which we have 2^{-96} for $E_{MAX} = 20$ for the 8-bit version versus 2^{-18} for $E_{MAX} - 14$ in the 1-bit version. Thus in the long run, even with the higher E_{MAX} bound, the 8 : custom $\leftrightarrow$ custom version tends to provide better security.

5   Future Research Directions for Distance-Bounding

The results obtained by our experimental implementation of distance-bounding protocols on smartphones are highly encouraging. In particular, we demonstrate that operating the DB protocol in the HAL layer of the smartphone already provides sufficient constancy in the challenge/response time measurement for distance bounding to be effective as long as the adversary introduces a delay of more than 1.5 ms during the relay attack. While customized relay mechanisms certainly take less than this value [11], most off-the-shelf attacks seem to introduce delays of at least tens of milliseconds [8, 12].

Another important conclusion of our work is that using 8-bit challenges rather than 1-bit ones increases the mafia-fraud resistance of the protocol in the long run. In this situation, one can leverage on the smartphone's memory to pre-compute the fast-round responses, thus lowering and stabilizing the prover's processing time. This area of research has been very little explored in the design of DB protocols thus far, thus we hope that our work will spark research towards this direction.

Another important finding of our work is that introducing a threshold for the total number of allowed errors is crucial. Indeed the variations in the measurements, even for the best executions, usually conduct to a few rounds being outside the proximity threshold. More precisely, when t_{max} is within 1.5 ms from the minimal measured time of around 6.2 ms, setting values for the thresholds of $E_{MAX} = 20$ and $E_{MAX} = 14$, respectively for the 8-bit version and the 1-bit version, are optimal.

Overall, we believe that our three implementations have only scratched the surface of the full potential of distance-bounding on smartphones. In particular, our implementations did not rely on the SIM card in any way for the computation. Investigating this possibility would make the computational time more stable while increasing the security against side-channel attacks. In the long term, if better security guarantees could be achieved against an adversary performing a relay attack, then the distance-bounding technology could have a fundamental impact by augmenting the payment possibilities of smartphones or providing new functionalities such as the construction of secure location proofs.

References

1. Avoine, G., Tchamkerten, A.: An efficient distance bounding RFID authentication protocol: balancing false-acceptance rate and memory requirement. In: Samarati, P., Yung, M., Martinelli, F., Ardagna, C.A. (eds.) ISC 2009. LNCS, vol. 5735, pp. 250–261. Springer, Heidelberg (2009)
2. Brands, S., Chaum, D.: Distance bounding protocols. In: Helleseth, T. (ed.) EUROCRYPT 1993. LNCS, vol. 765, pp. 344–359. Springer, Heidelberg (1994)
3. Carluccio, D., Kasper, T., Paar, C.: Implementation details of a multi purpose ISO 14443 rfidtool. In: Printed handout of RFIDSec 06 (2006)
4. Clulow, J., Hancke, G.P., Kuhn, M.G., Moore, T.: So near and yet so far: distance-bounding attacks in wireless networks. In: Buttyán, L., Gligor, V.D., Westhoff, D. (eds.) ESAS 2006. LNCS, vol. 4357, pp. 83–97. Springer, Heidelberg (2006)
5. Desmedt, Y.G., Goutier, C., Bengio, S.: Special uses and abuses of the fiat shamir passport protocol (extended abstract). In: Pomerance, C. (ed.) CRYPTO 1987. LNCS, vol. 293, pp. 21–39. Springer, Heidelberg (1988)
6. Fischlin, M., Onete, C.: Subtle kinks in distance bounding: an analysis of prominent protocols. In: Proceedings of WiSec 2013, pp. 195–206. ACM (2013)
7. Francillon, A., Danev, B., Čapkun, S.: Relay attacks on passive keyless entry and start systems in modern cars. In: Proceedings of NDSS 2011 (2011)
8. Francis, L., Hancke, G., Mayes, K., Markantonakis, K.: Practical relay attack oncontactless transactions by using NFC mobile phones. In: Proceedings of RFID-Sec 2010, pp. 35–49 (2010)
9. Haataja, K., Toivanen, P.: Two practical man-in-the-middle attacks on bluetooth secure simple pairing and countermeasures. Trans. Wirel. Commun. 9(1), 384–392 (2010)

10. Hancke, G., Kuhn, M.: An RFID distance bounding protocol. In: Proceedings of SECURECOMM 2005, pp. 67–73. IEEE Computer Society (2005)
11. Hancke, G.P.: A practical relay attack on ISO 14443 proximity cards. http://www.rfidblog.org.uk/hancke-rfidrelay.pdf. Accessed 9 January 2015
12. Henzl, M., Hanáček, P., Kačic, M.: Preventing real-world relay attacks on contactless devices. In: Proceedings of IEEE ICCST 2014, pp. 376–381. IEEE (2014)
13. Hlaváč, M., Tomáč, R.: A note on the relay attacks on e-passports (2007). http://eprint.iacr.org/2007/244.pdf
14. ISO/IEC-14443: Identification cards - contactless integrated circuit(s) cards - proximity cards. Technical report, International Organization for Standardization (2008)
15. Juels, A.: RFID security and privacy: a research survey. IEEE J. Sel. Areas Commun. **24**(2), 381–394 (2006)
16. Kim, C.H., Avoine, G., Koeune, F., Standaert, F.X., Pereira, O.: The swiss-knife RFID distance bounding protocol. In: Proceedings of ICISC 2008 (2008)
17. NFC Forum TM: NFC Controller Interface (NCI), version 1.1 edn. (2014)
18. NFC Forum TM: NFC Digital Protocol, version 1.1 edn. (2014)
19. Oren, Y., Wool, A.: relay attacks on RFID-based electronic voting systems. Cryptology ePrint Archive, Report 2009/442 (2009). http://eprint.iacr.org/2009/422.pdf
20. Ranganathan, A., Tippenhauer, N.O., Škorić, B., Singelée, D., Čapkun, S.: Design and implementation of a terrorist fraud resilient distance bounding system. In: Foresti, S., Yung, M., Martinelli, F. (eds.) ESORICS 2012. LNCS, vol. 7459, pp. 415–432. Springer, Heidelberg (2012)

Towards Fresh and Hybrid Re-Keying Schemes with Beyond Birthday Security

Christoph Dobraunig[1], François Koeune[2(✉)], Stefan Mangard[1],
Florian Mendel[1], and François-Xavier Standaert[2]

[1] IAIK, Graz University of Technology, Graz, Austria
{christoph.dobraunig,florian.mendel}@iaik.tugraz.at,
stefan.mangard@tugraz.at
[2] Université catholique de Louvain – ICTEAM – Crypto Group,
Louvain-la-Neuve, Belgium
{francois.koeune,fstandae}@uclouvain.be

Abstract. Fresh re-keying is a type of protocol which aims at splitting the task of protecting an encryption/authentication scheme against
side-channel attacks in two parts. One part, a re-keying function, has
to satisfy a minimum set of properties (such as good diffusion), and
is based on an algebraic structure that is easy to protect against side-
channel attacks with countermeasures such as masking. The other part, a
block cipher, brings resistance against mathematical cryptanalysis, and
only has to be secure against single-measurement attacks. Since fresh
re-keying schemes are cheap and stateless, they are convenient to use in
practice and do not require any synchronization between communication
parties. However, it has been shown that their first instantiation (from
Africacrypt 2010) only provides birthday security because of a (mathematical only) collision-based key recovery attack recently put forward
by Dobraunig et al. (CARDIS 2014). In this paper, we provide two provably secure (in the ideal cipher model) solutions to avoid such collision
attacks. The first one is based on classical block ciphers, but does not
achieve beyond-birthday CPA security (i.e. it only provably prevents
the CARDIS 2014 key recovery attack) and requires an additional block
cipher execution in the protocol. The second one is based on tweakable
block ciphers and provides tight CPA security while also being more
efficient. As a complement, we also show that our reasoning extends
to hybrid schemes, where the communication party to protect against
side-channel attacks is stateful. We illustrate this claim by describing
a collision attack against an example of a hybrid scheme patented by
Kocher, and presenting a tweak leading to beyond birthday security. We
conclude the paper by discussing the use of fresh/hybrid re-keying for
encryption and authentication, together with a cautionary note on their
side-channel resistance.

1 Introduction

Designing sound and efficient countermeasures against side-channel attacks is
a challenging problem. This is especially true in the context of applications

© Springer International Publishing Switzerland 2016
N. Homma and M. Medwed (Eds.): CARDIS 2015, LNCS 9514, pp. 225–241, 2016.
DOI: 10.1007/978-3-319-31271-2_14

with strong cost or energy constraints (e.g. RFIDs, sensor networks, pay-TV, automotive, ...). In such cases, and despite the fact that the devices are likely to be operated in a hostile environment, the direct protection of (e.g.) standard block ciphers such as the AES may be too expensive. As an illustration, the implementation of the well-known masking countermeasure for such block ciphers implies performance overheads that are (at least) quadratic in the security order [11]. Consequently, a new research path has emerged, trying to reduce the adversary's capabilities thanks to re-keying. Leakage-resilient cryptography is the most investigated representative of this trend (see, e.g. [10,18]). But unfortunately, the concrete guarantees provided by such constructions highly depend on the primitives. For stateful stream ciphers, leakage-resilience indeed delivers strong security levels at low cost. By contrast, for stateless PRFs and PRPs, the situation is less conclusive (essentially due to the fact that the latter primitives bound the number of plaintexts that an adversary can observe, rather than the number of measurements, and hence allow averaging to get noise-free measurements) [3]. Since stateless primitives are essential ingredients for the initialization of an encryption scheme, or for authentication, we are therefore left with the problem of finding good protection mechanisms in this case.

The fresh re-keying scheme proposed in [16] is a typical attempt in this direction. Here, the authors start from the observation that requiring both physical and mathematical security from a single primitive may be too challenging. Therefore, they suggest an alternative solution, where a stateless re-keying function that only has to fulfill a limited number of mathematical properties and is easy to mask is combined with a mathematically strong block cipher. In this context, hardware engineers essentially have to ensure resistance against multitrace side-channel attacks (aka DPA resistance) for the re-keying function, and resistance against single-trace side-channel attacks (aka SPA resistance) for the block cipher – the latter being an arguably easier task. While such a construction was indeed interesting from a side-channel attack point-of-view, a recent analysis by Dobraunig et al. showed that such a fresh re-keying scheme only provides birthday security against a (mathematical only) chosen-plaintext collision-based key recovery attack [9]. In this paper, we are therefore interested in improved re-keying mechanisms that provide beyond birthday security.

Our Contributions. We start by describing two new re-keying schemes – one fresh and one hybrid – with beyond birthday security against the CARDIS 2014 attack. By hybrid, we mean that one communicating party acts like in a stateful scheme, i.e. the fresh key is based on a secret internal state that is continuously updated, while the other communicating party acts stateless, i.e. the session key is always regenerated from the main secret, based on an index value communicated by the first party. In this way, the first party can be protected against side-channel analysis (as in fresh re-keying), without requiring the synchronization burden of fully stateful schemes (e.g. based on a leakage-resilient PRG). For the first scheme, we rely on a provably secure re-keying proposed by Abdalla and Bellare [1], which allows us to prove the security of our (block cipher or hash function based) re-keying in the ideal cipher model, although the bound is quite loose and does not provide beyond-birthday CPA security (i.e. it only provably prevents the CARDIS 2014 attack). For the second one, we take advantage of tweakable block ciphers to design a very efficient solution, which additionally brings CPA security and benefits from a tight security bound, assuming the existence of an ideal tweakable block cipher. We also suggest concrete instantiations for the building blocks of these schemes, including a couple of new and very efficient tweakable block ciphers based on the TWEAKEY framework [12], proposed in the context of the ongoing CAESAR competition (e.g. Deoxys, Jotlik, KIASU, and Scream) [8].

We complement these new designs with three additional contributions. First, we put forward that a similar reasoning applies to a hybrid re-keying scheme patented by Kocher [13]. That is, such a scheme is also vulnerable to collision attacks (hence only provides birthday security), and can be fixed by taking advantage of tweakable block ciphers. Second, we discuss the use of fresh/hybrid re-keying schemes in concrete applications, and underline important differences between encryption and authentication in this respect. Eventually, we conclude the paper by recalling the side-channel security guarantees of all the proposed re-keying schemes, including their grey areas regarding the interaction between the re-keying function and its underlying block cipher.

Note that resistance against fault attacks is not discussed in this paper, although all the proposed solutions inherit from the good properties of the original Africacrypt re-keying in this respect, and therefore can probably be used to rule out *differential* fault analysis (such as [5] and following works). As in [16], simple fault attacks (e.g. reducing the number of rounds) are considered out of scope, and have to be prevented by other means.

2   Background

2.1   The Africacrypt 2010 Fresh Re-Keying Scheme

The Africarypt 2010 fresh re-keying scheme [16] is pictured in Fig. 1. It is built from a block cipher BC and a re-keying function g, and essentially works in

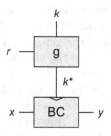

Fig. 1. Africacrypt 2010 fresh re-keying.

two steps. First, a session key k^* is produced by running the re-keying function on the master key k and a random nonce r (selected uniformly at random by the chip needing to be protected). Second this fresh key k^* is used to encrypt a (single) plaintext x with the block cipher. Note that this scheme is trivially tweaked into a hybrid re-keying by replacing the random nonce r by a counter.

2.2   Properties of the g Function

Medwed et al. [16] use g to relax the side-channel protection requirements for a block cipher. Informally, the idea is that g will be in charge of generating one-time session keys in a way resistant against side-channel attacks, whereas the block cipher will provide resistance against classical cryptanalysis, but without the need to worry about DPA, as each key is used only once. Since we will re-use the same "separation of duties" strategy and the same g function in the present paper, it is worth recalling the requirements for this function:

1. **Diffusion.** One bit of k^* shall depend on many bits of k.
2. **Stateless Communication.** The parties shall not have an inner state, which has to be kept synchronous.
3. **No additional key material.** k and k^* should have the same size.
4. **Little hardware overhead and side-channel security.** The overhead caused by the use of g (implemented in a secure way) should be small compared to fully protecting the underlying block cipher against side-channel attacks. In other words, the structure of g should make it significantly easier to protect against these attacks (e.g. via masking).
5. **Regularity.** g should have high regularity to facilitate its implementation in a full-custom design (or additional protection mechanisms).

2.3   The CARDIS 2014 Collision Attack

In this section we describe the attack presented at CARDIS 2014 [9] against the Africacrypt 2010 scheme of Sect. 2.1. We assume that the generated session keys are used to key a single block cipher encryption. This encryption is used for example in a challenge–response protocol, where the attacker is able to select the challenge x and sees the response $y_i = \mathsf{BC}_{k_i^*}(x)$. The attack can be split into two steps. The first one is the recovery of one session key k_i^*, the second one is the recovery of the master key k out of this knowledge.

The first step is independent of the generation of the session key and targets a single block encryption. In this step the attacker precalculates a list, where he stores pairs of responses (ciphertexts) y_i's and keys k_i^*'s. Those y_i's are encryptions of always the same challenge (plaintext) X for different keys k_i^*. Note that for the creation of the list, all k_i^*'s are chosen by the attacker. Next, in the online phase, the attacker queries an oracle (his target) for multiple encryptions y_i's of the same plaintext X. Since this oracle uses a fresh re-keying scheme, X is encrypted with different keys k_i^*'s and therefore, y_i varies. If such a y_i matches with a y_i in the precalculated list, the corresponding session key is recovered with high probability. For this attack, the best overall complexity of $2 \cdot 2^{n/2}$ is obtained if a list with $2^{n/2}$ entries is used and $2^{n/2}$ online queries are made (for n-bit session keys).

The second step of the attack depends on the concrete re-keying scheme. In the case of the Africacrypt 2010 proposal, $\mathbf{g}$ is a multiplication in a polynomial ring. Since we know one session key k^*, and the corresponding nonce r is invertible with a high probability, we can calculate $k = r^{-1} \cdot k^*$.

3   How to Do It Right?

A natural approach to prevent the CARDIS 2014 attack would be to change the instantiation of the $\mathbf{g}$ function and to make it non-invertible. For example, one could use a cryptographic hash function for this purpose. Unfortunately, cryptographic hash functions are not easy to protect against side-channel analysis. In order to circumvent this problem, and as already mentioned, we will use the same "separation of duties" strategy as in the Africacrypt re-keying. That is, we will try to separate the burden of side-channel protection from protection against classical cryptanalysis, but this time including collision attacks in our concerns. For this purpose, we present a fresh/hybrid scheme based on a pseudo-random function (PRF) in Sect. 3.1, and propose an instantiation thereof that is provably secure in the ideal cipher model. We then propose a more efficient solution based on tweakable block ciphers in Sect. 3.2.

The scenario we focus on in this paper is the case where one communicating party (e.g. the tag) needs re-keying as an easy and cheap protection against side-channel attacks, whereas the other (e.g. the reader) is less cost-sensitive and can be protected through other mechanisms. The re-keying nonce r will thus be randomly chosen by the cheap device and transmitted to the other party. In [15], Mewed et al. considered the scenario where multiple parties must be protected by re-keying and must thus all participate in the selection of r. Their techniques can be straightforwardly applied to our schemes.

3.1   Fresh/Hybrid Re-Keying from the Abdalla-Bellare Re-Keying

In [1], Abdalla and Bellare proved the security of a PRF-based re-keying scheme. They further suggest to instantiate their PRF with a hash function. Interestingly, such a solution is quite directly applicable in our context. We just need to prove that the combination of $\mathbf{g}$ with a well-chosen compression function C is a PRF (represented by the dotted line in Fig. 2a). As previously, the function $\mathbf{g}$ shall carry the main burden regarding side-channel protection, whereas the compression function shall prevent collision attacks. Figure 2a can thus be seen as an extension of the Africacrypt 2010 scheme. Note that here again, the scheme will be stateless if r is a random nonce, and hybrid if it is a counter.

Concretely, and since re-keying schemes are typically combined with block ciphers, we are naturally interested in block cipher-based compression functions. For this purpose, we will analyze one particular construction for C, referred to as

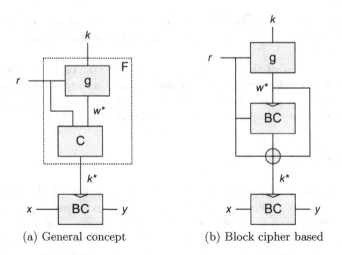

(a) General concept   (b) Block cipher based

Fig. 2. Fresh/hybrid Abdalla–Bellare re-keying

the compression function 6 in [6], which Black et al. proved to be pre-image and collision resistant in the ideal cipher model. Such a solution is pictured in Fig. 2b. However, we note that our construction would keep its security properties with any reasonable instantiation of the PRF in Fig. 2a.

We now prove that, in the ideal cipher model, the generation of k^* is a PRF provided g meets a simple requirement, namely that, for any fixed value K of its first parameter, the function $g(K, \cdot)$ is one-to-one and, for any fixed value R of its second parameter, the function $g(\cdot, R)$ is one-to-one (in other words, $g(K, \cdot)$ and $g(\cdot, R)$ are permutations of the nonce and key space, respectively). Note that the following result is independent on whether r is based on fresh nonces or a counter.

Theorem 1. *Let us define* $F(k, r) := BC_{g(k,r)}(r) \oplus r \oplus g(k, r)$. *If* $g(K, \cdot)$ *and* $g(\cdot, R)$ *are one-to-one for all values of* K, R, *then the construction* F *is a PRF in the ideal cipher model.*

Proof (sketch). Consider an adversary $\mathcal{A}$ trying to distinguish $F(k, \cdot)$ from a random function. $\mathcal{A}$ receives access to an oracle $\mathcal{O}$ corresponding to the function to test and to an oracle $\mathcal{O}'$ corresponding to the block cipher. When $\mathcal{A}$ starts, $\mathcal{O}$ tosses a coin to decide how it will behave. Depending on the result, on input r_i, $\mathcal{O}$ will:

- either output a fresh, random y_i;
- or output $y_i = BC_{g(k,r_i)}(r_i) \oplus r_i \oplus g(k, r_i)$, for a fixed value of k. In this case, $\mathcal{O}$ in turn obtains the values $BC_{g(k,r_i)}(r_i)$ by querying $\mathcal{O}'$.[1]

---

[1] As usual, we assume that both $\mathcal{O}$ and $\mathcal{O}'$ act consistently: when receiving an input corresponding to a previous query, they simply replay the previous output (when $\mathcal{O}$ implements F, its consistency is a direct consequence of the consistency of $\mathcal{O}'$).

In addition, $\mathcal{A}$ can directly query $\mathcal{O}'$ with input (k_i', r_i') to obtain $\mathsf{BC}_{k_i'}(r_i')$ or $\mathsf{BC}_{k_i'}^{-1}(r_i')$.

Consider the case where $\mathcal{O}$ implements the BC-based construction. When $\mathcal{A}$ ends, $\mathcal{O}'$ will thus have received two sets of (possibly intertwined) queries:

- Queries $\mathsf{BC}_{\mathbf{g}(k,r_i)}(r_i)$, through queries to $\mathcal{O}$: we will denote these queries and the corresponding answers as $(r_i, y_i)_{1 \leq i \leq v}$.
- Queries $\mathsf{BC}_{k_i'}(r_i')$ or $\mathsf{BC}_{k_i'}^{-1}(r_i')$, through direct calls: we will denote these queries and the corresponding answers as $(k_i', r_i', b_i', y_i')_{1 \leq i \leq v'}$, where b_i' is a bit equal to 0 (resp. 1) if the request is an encryption (resp. decryption) query.

The central point of the proof is that two queries to $\mathcal{O}'$ yield randomly and independently chosen answers provided the corresponding keys are different. We will now show that this is indeed the case, except with negligible probability.

1. If $r_i = r_j$, then it is easy to see that $y_i = y_j$ (the key is the same, but so is the plaintext too, and $\mathcal{O}'$ receives twice the same query).
2. If $r_i \neq r_j$, then, since $\mathbf{g}(k, \cdot)$ is one-to-one, $\mathbf{g}(k, r_i) \neq \mathbf{g}(k, r_j)$, as requested.
3. Since $\mathbf{g}(\cdot, r_i)$ is one-to-one, k is unknown to $\mathcal{A}$, and $\mathcal{A}$ issues only a polynomial number of requests, the probability to have $k_j' = \mathbf{g}(k, r_i)$ for some (i, j) is negligible (no value of r_i allows reducing the destination space of $\mathbf{g}(k, r_i)$).

Summarizing, if $\mathcal{O}$ implements F, then the computation of all (fresh) output values involves an XOR with $\mathsf{BC}_{\mathbf{g}(k,r_i)}(r_i)$, which, except with negligible probability, are chosen randomly and independently by $\mathcal{O}'$. On the other hand, if $\mathcal{O}$ implements a real random function, then all (fresh) output values are chosen randomly and independently. So, in all cases, all answers received by $\mathcal{A}$ are chosen randomly and independently, except with negligible probability, and none of them allows distinguishing F from a random function. $\qquad\square$

Remarks:

1. The intuition behind this proof is that, without knowledge of k, $\mathcal{A}$ cannot query $\mathcal{O}'$ with keys corresponding to one of the values w^* actually used in the scheme, so that its access to $\mathcal{O}'$ does not help $\mathcal{A}$. Note that the possibility to query $\mathcal{O}'$ with different, but related, keys is not ruled out by the structure of the function g (there could for example be a known difference between $\mathbf{g}(k, r_1)$ and $\mathbf{g}(k, r_2)$, no matter the value of k). However, this is not a problem in the ideal cipher model, where related-key attacks do not apply.
2. $\mathcal{A}$ can of course issue direct queries $(\mathsf{BC}_{k_i'}(r_{i_1}'), \mathsf{BC}_{k_i'}(r_{i_2}'))$, which will not yield independent answers. However, these will obviously not reveal any information on F, since, as shown above, they are unrelated to any query made to F.
3. It is worth noting that the properties we require from $\mathbf{g}$ are also in line with a work by Bellare and Kohno. In [4], they propose a formal treatment of related-key attacks by providing the adversary with the ability to issue related-key queries such as $E_{\phi(K)}(m)$, i.e. obtain encryptions with a function ϕ of the (unknown) target key, for a carefully defined set Φ of allowed

functions. Bellare and Kohno provide some conditions on the set Φ allowing proving resistance against related-key attacks. Interestingly, our construction can be related to theirs by defining $\phi_i(k) = g(k, r_i)$, and, with the aforementioned conditions on g, match very well the bounds of [4, Definitions 2 and 3, Lemma 1]. As our construction is slightly different, this paper provides independent proofs. Nevertheless, the fact that our re-keying function matches independently-defined conditions to avoid related-key attacks is a probable witness of the consistency of our approach.

Being able to prove that the re-keying scheme is a PRF is already of interest regarding the CARDIS 2014 collision attack. As a matter of fact, it guarantees that an attacker cannot distinguish the output of F from a random sequence, which of course also implies that he cannot recover the key k that generated this output. As a consequence, this construction is provably resistant against the collision-based key recovery attack in [9].

In addition, Abdalla and Bellare proved in [1, Theorems 1 and 3] that, if F is a PRF, $\mathcal{SE}$ is an encryption scheme and $\overline{\mathcal{SE}}$ is the associated F-based re-keyed encryption scheme, then the advantage of an adversary trying to break $\overline{\mathcal{SE}}$ can be related to that of adversaries trying to break F and $\mathcal{SE}$ as follows:

$$\mathsf{Adv}_{\overline{\mathcal{SE}}}^{\mathsf{ind-cpa}}(t, lm) \leq \mathsf{Adv}_{\mathsf{F}}^{\mathsf{prf}}(t, m) + m \cdot \mathsf{Adv}_{\mathcal{SE}}^{\mathsf{ind-cpa}}(t, l),$$

where t is the adversary's maximum running time, m is the maximum number of keys generated, and l is the maximum number of encryptions performed with each key (so $l = 1$ if we use each fresh key only once).

Unfortunately, this theoretical bound does not provide beyond birthday CPA security. As a matter of fact, an adversary trying $2^{n/2}$ keys against one single block will succeed with probability $2^{-n/2}$, so $\mathsf{Adv}_{\mathcal{SE}}^{\mathsf{ind-cpa}}(2^{n/2}, 1) \geq 2^{-n/2}$. As a consequence, the above bound for an adversary issuing $m = 2^{n/2}$ queries and having computing time $t = 2^{n/2}$ yields:

$$\mathsf{Adv}_{\overline{\mathcal{SE}}}^{\mathsf{ind-cpa}}(2^{n/2}, 2^{n/2}) \leq 1.$$

Interestingly, this bound is tight, since it corresponds to an attack similar to the CARDIS 2014 one, but breaking the CPA game rather than recovering the key. Combined with the observation that the scheme of Fig. 2b is also more expensive than the original fresh re-keying scheme, this motivates us to investigate how to overcome these drawbacks, using tweakable block ciphers.

3.2 More Efficient Solution Based on a Tweakable Block Cipher

The scheme presented in Sect. 3.1 has quite a large performance overhead because of the additional compression/block cipher call needed for a single encryption. A more efficient construction is to replace this combination by a tweakable block cipher TBC, as shown in Fig. 3. Tweakable block ciphers were introduced by Liskov et al. in [14] as a generalized version of block ciphers. In addition to the secret key, a tweakable block cipher accepts a second parameter (that can be

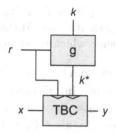

Fig. 3. Fresh/hybrid re–keying with a tweakable block cipher.

public) called the tweak. Intuitively, *"each fixed setting of the tweak gives rise to a different, apparently independent, family of standard block cipher encryption operators"* and a tweakable block cipher should remain secure even facing an adversary who has control of the tweak.

In our context, the publicly known nonce (or counter) r is used as tweak, and k^* as secret key.

This construction again follows the same separation of duties idea as the ones of Fig. 2a and b. Namely, the function g is responsible for side-channel protection, whereas the tweakable block cipher prevents the CARDIS 2014 collision attack. Therefore, the requirements for the function g stay the same.

Let us first argue why this construction defeats the aforementioned attacks. We then show it is in fact provably secure in the ideal cipher model.

First recall that the attacks on the re-keying scheme of Africacrypt 2010 exploit the fact that the same plaintext is encrypted with different session keys by the same block cipher. Let us now take into account the fact that $g(k, \cdot)$ is a permutation. Thus, we get always a different session key k^* for different nonces r. Let us also assume that we have a perfect tweakable block cipher. This means that for every different value of the tweak, we have different and independent block cipher instances. So, basically, we now just use different block ciphers with different keys, and none of them is used with multiple keys, which makes the CARDIS 2014 attack impossible to apply. Taking another viewpoint, an attacker trying to perform the first step of the attack and precalculating a list would now need to do it, not for a set of k_i^*, but for a set of pairs (r_i, k_i^*). This considerably increases the size of the list before the birthday paradox provides a non-negligible chance of success (since this pair has $2n$-bit size).

If we translate this "perfect TBC" assumption in the ideal cipher model, it simply means that each different values of the key *or* the tweak yields a different, independent permutation. We now prove that, in this model, the construction depicted on Fig. 3 is indeed a TBC (here too, note that the result is independent on whether r is based on fresh nonces or a counter).

Theorem 2. *Let* TBC *be an ideal tweakable block cipher, and let us define* TBC′ *as* $\mathsf{TBC}'_k(r, m) = \mathsf{TBC}_{g(k,r)}(r, m)$. *If* $g(K, \cdot)$ *and* $g(\cdot, R)$ *are one-to-one for all values of* K, R, *then* TBC′ *is a tweakable block cipher.*

Proof (sketch). Consider a distinguisher $\mathcal{D}$ trying to distinguish TBC'_k from a family of independent random permutations. At the beginning of the experiment, an oracle $\mathcal{O}$ tosses a coin to decide which construction it will implement.

- In the first case, $\mathcal{O}$ chooses a random key k and sets $E(r, m) := \mathsf{TBC}_{g(k,r)}(r, m)$ and $E^{-1}(r, m) := \mathsf{TBC}^{-1}_{g(k,r)}(r, m)$. In this case, $\mathcal{O}$ in turn obtains these values by querying an oracle $\mathcal{O}'$ implementing the ideal tweakable block cipher.
- In the second case, $\mathcal{O}$ chooses a family $\Pi(\cdot, \cdot)$ of independent random permutations[2] and sets $E(r, m) := \Pi(r, m)$ and $E^{-1}(r, m) := \Pi^{-1}(r, m)$.

$\mathcal{D}$ can then query $\mathcal{O}$ to obtain $E(r_i, m_i)$ or $E^{-1}(r_i, m_i)$ for values (r_i, m_i) of its choice. In addition, $\mathcal{D}$ can also directly query $\mathcal{O}'$ to obtain $\mathsf{TBC}_{k'_i}(r'_i, m'_i)$ or $\mathsf{TBC}^{-1}_{k'_i}(r'_i, m'_i)$ for values (k'_i, r'_i, m'_i) of its choice. The goal of $\mathcal{D}$ is to discover which construction $\mathcal{O}$ implements. We will denote the maximum number of (direct or indirect) queries $\mathcal{D}$ makes to $\mathcal{O}'$ as l.

Consider the case where $\mathcal{O}$ implements the TBC-based construction. When $\mathcal{D}$ ends, $\mathcal{O}'$ will thus have received two sets of (possibly intertwined) queries:

- Queries $\mathsf{TBC}_{g(k,r_i)}(r_i, m_i)$ or $\mathsf{TBC}^{-1}_{g(k,r_i)}(r_i, m_i)$, through queries to $\mathcal{O}$: we will denote these queries and the corresponding answers as $(r_i, m_i, b_i, y_i)_{1 \leq i \leq v}$, where b_i is a bit equal to 0 (resp. 1) if the request is an encryption (resp. decryption) query.
- Queries $\mathsf{TBC}_{k'_i}(r'_i, m'_i)$ or $\mathsf{TBC}^{-1}_{k'_i}(r'_i, m'_i)$, through direct calls: we will denote these queries and the corresponding answers as $(k'_i, r'_i, m'_i, b'_i, y'_i)_{1 \leq i \leq v'}$, where b'_i is a bit equal to 0 (resp. 1) if the request is an encryption (resp. decryption) query.

Observe that:

1. If $r_i \neq r_j$ (resp. $r'_i \neq r'_j$ and/or $k'_i \neq k'_j$), then y_i and y_j (resp. y'_i and y'_j) are chosen randomly and independently by $\mathcal{O}'$.
2. The same is true when $r_i \neq r'_j$: $\mathcal{O}$ is queried on different tweak values and provides independent random answers.
3. If $r_i = r_j$, then y_i and y_j are chosen randomly and independently, except that the permutation rule (i.e. different inputs yield different outputs) and consistency rule (i.e. $E(E^{-1}(r, m)) = m$) will be respected. Since Π is also a permutation, none of these limitations helps $\mathcal{D}$ guessing the construction implemented by $\mathcal{O}$.
4. The same argument applies if $(k'_i, r'_i) = (k'_j, r'_j)$.
5. Finally, if $r_i = r'_j$, then, since k is unknown and $g(\cdot, r_i)$ is one-to-one, the probability to have $k'_j = g(k, r_i)$ is only $\frac{1}{2^n}$. In all other cases, $\mathcal{O}'$ is queried on different key values and provides independent random answers. Since $\mathcal{O}'$ received a maximum of l queries, the global probability is bounded by $\frac{l}{2^n}$.

---

[2] That is, for each T, $\Pi(T, \cdot)$ is a random permutation of the message space.

It is easy to see that, in the case where $\mathcal{O}$ implements a family of independent random permutations, $\mathcal{O}$ will bear exactly the same behavior, except in one case. This only exception is that there is no corresponding to case 5 above ($k'_j = g(k, r_i)$). This difference of behavior would help discovering the behaviour of $\mathcal{O}$, but, as argued above, only occurs with probability $\frac{l}{2^n}$. In all other cases, answers received by $\mathcal{D}$ are always random, independent values consistent with a permutation.

The distinguishing advantage is thus bounded by:

$$\Pr[D^{\Pi}(t, l) = 1] - \Pr[D^{\mathsf{TBC}'}(t, l) = 1] \leq \frac{l}{2^n}.$$

$\square$

Having proved that our construction is a TBC, we can for example easily prove that encryption based on it is secure against chosen-plaintext attacks.

Theorem 3. *Let* TBC *be a tweakable block cipher and define* $\Pi = <G, E, D>$, *where* $E_k(m)$ *is performed by choosing a random* r *and returning* $E_k(m) := (r, \mathsf{TBC}_k(r, m))$. *In the ideal tweakable cipher model,* Π *provides indistinguishable encryption against a chosen-plaintext adversary.*

Proof (sketch). Consider an adversary $\mathcal{A}$ attacking Π. During the oracle query phases (both before and after the challenge phase), $\mathcal{A}$ can query an encryption oracle $\mathcal{O}$ to obtain the encryption $(r'_i, \mathsf{TBC}_k(r'_i, m'_i))$ of messages he chooses[3], under an unknown key k chosen uniformly at random. During the challenge phase, $\mathcal{A}$ outputs two messages m_0, m_1 and receives $c = (r, \mathsf{TBC}_k(r, m_b))$ from $\mathcal{O}$. His goal is to discover b. In both cases, $\mathcal{O}$ answers by querying a TBC oracle $\mathcal{O}'$. $\mathcal{A}$ can also directly query $\mathcal{O}'$ with values (m''_i, k''_i, r''_i) of its choice and obtain $E_{k''_i}(r''_i, m''_i)$ or $E_{k''_i}^{-1}(r''_i, m''_i)$. We will denote by l the maximum number of queries (both to $\mathcal{O}$ and $\mathcal{O}'$) issued by $\mathcal{A}$.
Observe that:

- As k was chosen uniformly at random, the probability to have $k = k''_i$ for some i is bounded by $\frac{l}{2^n}$. In all other cases, answers to direct queries to $\mathcal{O}'$ are independent from b (queries on different key values).
- Similarly, the probability to have $r = r'_i$ for some i is bounded by $\frac{l}{2^n}$. In all other cases, answers to queries to $\mathcal{O}$ are independent from b (queries on different tweak values).

As a consequence,

$$\mathsf{Adv}_{\Pi}^{\mathsf{ind-cpa}}(l) \leq \frac{1}{2} + \frac{2l}{2^n}.$$

$\square$

Remarks:

- The proof also holds in the stateful case. The only difference is that the case $r = r_i$ can then never happen, resulting in a slightly better bound, namely $\frac{1}{2} + \frac{l}{2^n}$.

---

[3] The tweak r'_i, however, is randomly chosen by $\mathcal{O}$.

- CPA security obviously assumes that the adversary cannot control the random nonce r used for encryption. By contrast, it is worth noting that the construction of Theorem 1 did not need to prevent this control of r by the adversary in order to achieve a PRF, and is thus slightly more general.
- Interestingly, we see that the use of a TBC brings the same advantage over block cipher-based constructions (i.e. natural beyond-birthday security) as in the context of authenticated encryption [14].

3.3   Concrete Instantiations

Instantiating the previous fresh re-keying schemes essentially requires to specify a block cipher BC, a re-keying function g, and possibly a tweakable block cipher TBC. For the block cipher, a natural choice is the AES. For the re-keying function, Medwed et al. [16] proposed this polynomial multiplication in $\mathbb{F}_{2^8}[y]$ modulo $p(y) = y^{16} + 1$:

$$g \; : \; (\mathbb{F}_{2^8}[y]/p(y))^2 \to \mathbb{F}_{2^8}[y]/p(y), \quad (k,r) \mapsto k \cdot r.$$

A polynomial multiplication globally fits our goals. Unfortunately, the choice $p(y) = y^{16} + 1$ is not suitable for our purpose[4]. As a matter of fact, this polynomial is not irreducible, which implies that the requirement that $g(K, \cdot), g(\cdot, R)$ are one-to-one is not strictly satisfied. To meet this requirement, an irreducible polynomial (e.g. $p(y) = y^{16}+y^3+y+$ "14", using the Rijndael notation for $\mathbb{F}_{2^8}$ elements) should be used instead. This impacts performance a bit, namely making shuffling and implementation in protected logic-styles slightly more expensive than in [16], but this impact is limited, and DPA-protection of this g function remains cheap. Note that the analysis of the side-channel behaviour of the polynomial multiplication has only been done for random nonces r by Medwed et al. [16]. Thus, the polynomial multiplication should only be used in this scenario. Finding instances of g that behave well in the hybrid case is an interesting scope for further research. For the tweakable block cipher, we suggest to use the efficient instances listed in introduction (i.e. Deoxys, Jotlik, KIASU, and Scream). AES-based solutions can also be exploited, by considering the block cipher-based constructions in [14]. Mennink also proposes optimal techniques to build a tweakable block cipher from a block cipher in [17].

4   Application to a Hybrid Scheme by Kocher

We now investigate another alternative to hybrid re-keying that was patented by Kocher in [13]. We first recall that this scheme can be compromised using the CARDIS 2014 collision attack. We then describe how to fix it with a tweakable block cipher.

---

[4] The authors thank Marcel Medwed for pointing this out during this paper's presentation.

4.1   The CARDIS 2014 Attack Against Kocher's Hybrid Re-Keying

Description of the Scheme. In Kocher's re-keying, and in contrast with the schemes of Sect. 2.1, the session key is not derived from a static secret master key with the help of randomly generated nonces. Instead, the secret itself is updated, changed, and used as session key. The update is based on the tree structure that is depicted in Fig. 4.

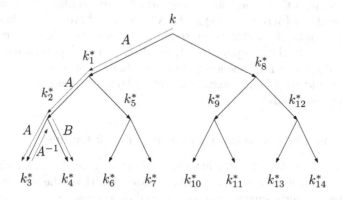

Fig. 4. Hybrid re-keying patented by Kocher [13]

The root of the tree is the secret master key k and the other vertices represent session keys k_i^*. To traverse through the tree, the functions A, B, A^{-1}, and B^{-1} are used, where A^{-1}, and B^{-1} are the inverse functions of A, and B. For instance if we want to go from k to k_1^* in Fig. 4, we calculate $k_1^* = A(k)$. If we want to go from k to k_8^*, we calculate $k_8^* = B(k)$. The number of usable session keys k_i^* is determined by the depth of the tree, which has to be fixed in advance.

We assume for this scheme a similar use-case as supposed for the Africacrypt 2010 scheme. Thus, one party (e.g. the tag) needs easy and cheap protection against side-channel attacks, whereas the other party (e.g. the reader) has to be protected by other mechanisms. To realize this, the tag strictly follows the tree, which means that it uses the session keys in the strict order given in Fig. 4 ($k_1^*, k_2^*, \ldots k_n^*$). The tag tells the other party (the reader) the index i of the currently used session key k_i^*, and the reader calculates the session key k_i^* starting from the root k.

Note that other variants of this scheme are possible. For instance, session keys corresponding to internal vertices can be used three times (every time a vertex is visited). By doing so, the number of transitions for the tag can be limited to one. In other words, this reuse of session keys allows the tag to perform only one of the operations A, B, A^{-1}, or B^{-1} per change of the session key.

Collision Attack. As already hinted by Dobraunig et al. [9], the CARDIS 2014 collision attack also applies to re-keying schemes like Kocher's one. For simplicity, we make the same assumptions as in Sect. 2.3 (i.e. each session key is used in a single block cipher execution, and the attacker can choose the plaintext which is encrypted). In addition, we assume that the concrete instance of Kocher's scheme only uses every session key once.

The first step of the CARDIS 2014 attack described in Sect. 2.3 is to recover one session key: this step goes exactly as before, i.e. building (offline) a database of encryptions of the same plaintext with various keys, then relying on the birthday paradox to obtain collisions with (online) encryptions of the same plaintext. Next, and as far as the second step is concerned, if we additionally assume that the used operations (permutations) A, B, A^{-1}, and B^{-1} are publicly known, one recovered session key k_i^* and the corresponding index i are enough to recover the master key k. Note that keeping the A, B, A^{-1}, and B^{-1} permutations secret would typically mean implementing them as a block cipher with secret (fixed) key, which would then be a potential target to DPA (i.e. lead to a chicken and egg problem, essentially).

4.2 Efficient Fix Based on a Tweakable Block Cipher

To get rid of the CARDIS 2014 attack, we propose a fix for Kocher's scheme based on a tweakable block cipher similar to Sect. 3.2. Here, the session key k_i^* – generated by Kocher's scheme (Fig. 4) – is used as a secret key for the tweakable block cipher, and the index i of the key is used as tweak, as illustrated in Fig. 5. The collision attack does not work in this case, for the same reasons as described in Sect. 3.2 (namely, different tweaks, and so virtually different block ciphers, are used with different keys).

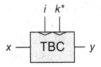

Fig. 5. Hybrid re–keying with a tweakable block cipher.

5 Encryption vs. Authentication Issues

Our discussion so far dealt with the generic problem of designing a secure and side-channel resistant re-keying scheme. Since they originally borrow from Abdalla and Bellare, our solutions typically lead to secure encryption per se. However, it is worth mentioning that additional security issues might arise when dealing with other uses of this re-keying scheme. In particular, although we ruled out key recovery attacks by ensuring that the master key cannot be recovered from a session key, it should be pointed out that, in some contexts such as authentication, even the recovery of one single session key might already be a serious threat.

Consider a simple challenge–response protocol carried out between two parties. In this scenario we have a tag that acts as prover and a reader that acts as verifier. So in the first step, the reader sends the challenge x_i to the tag. The tag encrypts the challenge and responds with $y_i = E_{k_i^*}(x_i)$. We assume that a re-keying scheme is used, which changes the key k_i^* for every new call of the encryption. As before, one of the n-bit session keys k^* can be recovered with a complexity of about $2 \cdot 2^{n/2}$, regardless of the re-keying scheme actually used.

Now examine the implications of one session key recovery in this scenario, for actual re-keying schemes. If the Africacrypt 2010 scheme is used to generate the session key k^*, the tag (prover) decides alone of the nonce value r. So an attacker does not necessarily need the master key. It is already enough to have one session key to pass the challenge–response protocol, since the attacker can force the use of a single recovered session key. Concretely, the attacker would first select a plaintext value X and build off-line a DB of encryptions of X with random keys. He would then play the role of a reader and query a genuine tag with challenge X. Finally, having recovered one session key, he would be able to impersonate the tag by always using r as nonce. The same attack would also succeed against the tree-based session key generation scheme of Sect. 4.1.

This attack cannot be prevented by making g not invertible. In fact, this attack always applies to every re-keying scheme, as long as a block cipher is re-keyed for every encryption and the prover can determine the session key to be used. This means that this attack might be also applicable to schemes where the CARDIS 2014 attack does not work. Belaïd et al. [2] presented such a scheme, where the re-keying function g of the Africacrypt 2010 scheme is replaced by a non-invertible function. However, the applicability of the session key replay attack depends on the actual method to determine the nonce, which is not specified by Belaïd et al.

In general, there exist two countermeasures against such a session key replay attack. The first one is to have both parties contributing to the selection process of the session key, as is already done in the CARDIS 2011 scheme [15]. The other one is to prohibit the recovery of the session key in the first place. Interestingly, the constructions using tweakable block ciphers we propose in Sects. 3.2 and 4.2 do prevent this recovery. Indeed, as discussed in Sect. 3.2, changing the value of r will not only result in a different session key k^*, but also in a different tweak value and hence – assuming a perfect tweakable block cipher – virtually in a different block cipher. As a consequence, the collision attack to recover session keys is not applicable any more in this case.

6 Conclusion: Side-Channel Security

We conclude this paper with a cautionary note regarding the exact security improvements brought by fresh re-keying regarding side-channel attacks. For this purpose, the first positive observation is that if the adversary targets the re-keying function and the block cipher independently, the resulting security guarantees are well understood. That is, the implementation will be secure as long as g resists DPA and BC (or TBC) resists SPA. But quite naturally, security arguments and proofs also indicate what are the potential weak points of a construction, and this is clearly the case for fresh re-keying. Looking at Figs. 1, 2a and b, this potential weak point is indeed the interaction between the re-keying function and the block cipher. That is, if some leakage about k^* (in Fig. 1) or w^* (in Fig. 2a, b) is obtained by the adversary (e.g. when recombining the shares after the masked execution of g), attacks combining mathematical cryptanalysis and leakage (e.g. the algebraic SPA described in [15]) are likely to be very powerful to accumulate partial information on the master key k and finally recover it. This is why fresh re-keying crucially relies on the SPA security of the block cipher, and a secure implementation should recombine the shares of the fresh keys in a sufficiently secure, i.e. typically shuffled, manner (as clearly mentioned in [15] as well). Note that this observation does not annihilate the interest of fresh re-keying which still significantly reduces the adversary's attack paths (compared to the straightforward execution of a block cipher). Interestingly, a very similar situation can be found for the SPRING primitive discussed in [7], which also aims at an informal separation between the parts of the primitive that are easy to mask, and those that are not (and therefore need to be carefully shuffled). Besides, such an issue does not directly apply to Kocher's hybrid scheme which does not make use of a g function. Indeed, combining small leakage on the session keys would require to go through the permutations A and B (and their inverses), which may not be easy if they are implemented with fixed key block ciphers. But this comes at the cost of a slightly more expensive key update mechanism. Besides, and more importantly, it makes any attempt to secure both the encrypting/proving and the decrypting/verifying parties of a protocol much more challenging, since the tree-based construction in Fig. 4 has to be stateless. In other words, it does not benefit from the malleability of the g function which is exploited for this purpose in multi-parties fresh re-keying [15], which gives a typical application of the "no free lunch" theorem.

Acknowledgments. The authors thank Christophe Petit for useful advice. This work has been supported in part by the Austrian Science Fund (project P26494-N15), by the Austrian Research Promotion Agency (FFG) under grant number 845589 (SCALAS), by the Brussels Region Research Funding Agency through the program Secur'IT and by the European Commission through the ERC project 280141 (CRASH) and the COST Action CRYPTACUS. F.-X. Standaert is a research associate of the Belgian Fund for Scientific Research (FNRS-F.R.S.).

References

1. Abdalla, M., Bellare, M.: Increasing the lifetime of a key: a comparative analysis of the security of re-keying techniques. In: Okamoto, T. (ed.) ASIACRYPT 2000. LNCS, vol. 1976, pp. 546–559. Springer, Heidelberg (2000)
2. Belaïd, S., De Santis, F., Heyszl, J., Mangard, S., Medwed, M., Schmidt, J., Standaert, F., Tillich, S.: Towards fresh re-keying with leakage-resilient PRFs: cipher design principles and analysis. J. Cryptographic Eng. **4**(3), 157–171 (2014)

3. Belaïd, S., Grosso, V., Standaert, F.: Masking and leakage-resilient primitives: one, the other(s) or both? Crypt. Commun. **7**(1), 163–184 (2015)

4. Bellare, M., Kohno, T.: A theoretical treatment of related-key attacks: RKA-PRPs, RKA-PRFs, and applications. In: Biham, E. (ed.) EUROCRYPT 2003. LNCS, vol. 2656, pp. 491–506. Springer, Heidelberg (2003)

5. Biham, E., Shamir, A.: Differential fault analysis of secret key cryptosystems. In: Kaliski Jr., B.S. (ed.) CRYPTO 1997. LNCS, vol. 1294, pp. 513–525. Springer, Heidelberg (1997)

6. Black, J., Rogaway, P., Shrimpton, T., Stam, M.: An analysis of the blockcipher-based hash functions from PGV. J. Cryptology **23**(4), 519–545 (2010)

7. Brenner, H., Gaspar, L., Leurent, G., Rosen, A., Standaert, F.-X.: FPGA implementations of SPRING. In: Batina, L., Robshaw, M. (eds.) CHES 2014. LNCS, vol. 8731, pp. 414–432. Springer, Heidelberg (2014)

8. Competition, C. http://competitions.cr.yp.to/caesar-submissions.html

9. Dobraunig, C., Eichlseder, M., Mangard, S., Mendel, F.: On the security of fresh re-keying to counteract side-channel and fault attacks. In: Joye, M., Moradi, A. (eds.) CARDIS 2014. LNCS, vol. 8968, pp. 233–244. Springer, Heidelberg (2015)

10. Dziembowski, S., Pietrzak, K.: Leakage-resilient cryptography. In: FOCS 2008, pp. 293–302. IEEE Computer Society (2008)

11. Grosso, V., Standaert, F., Faust, S.: Masking vs. multiparty computation: how large is the gap for AES? J. Cryptographic Eng. **4**(1), 47–57 (2014)

12. Jean, J., Nikolic, I., Peyrin, T.: Tweaks and keys for block ciphers: the TWEAKEY framework. In: Sarkar, P., Iwata, T. (eds.) ASIACRYPT 2014, Part II. LNCS, vol. 8874, pp. 274–288. Springer, Heidelberg (2014)

13. Kocher, P.C.: Leak-resistant cryptographic indexed key update. US Patent 6,539,092 (2003)

14. Liskov, M., Rivest, R.L., Wagner, D.: Tweakable block ciphers. In: Yung, M. (ed.) CRYPTO 2002. LNCS, vol. 2442, pp. 31–46. Springer, Heidelberg (2002)

15. Medwed, M., Petit, C., Regazzoni, F., Renauld, M., Standaert, F.-X.: Fresh re-keying II: securing multiple parties against side-channel and fault attacks. In: Prouff, E. (ed.) CARDIS 2011. LNCS, vol. 7079, pp. 115–132. Springer, Heidelberg (2011)

16. Medwed, M., Standaert, F.-X., Großschädl, J., Regazzoni, F.: Fresh re-keying: security against side-channel and fault attacks for low-cost devices. In: Bernstein, D.J., Lange, T. (eds.) AFRICACRYPT 2010. LNCS, vol. 6055, pp. 279–296. Springer, Heidelberg (2010)

17. Mennink, B.: Optimally secure tweakable blockciphers. In: Leander, G. (ed.) FSE 2015. LNCS, vol. 9054, pp. 428–448. Springer, Heidelberg (2015). http://dx.doi.org/10.1007/978-3-662-48116-5_21

18. Yu, Y., Standaert, F., Pereira, O., Yung, M.: Practical leakage-resilient pseudorandom generators. In: Al-Shaer, E., Keromytis, A.D., Shmatikov, V. (eds.) CCS 2010, pp. 141–151. ACM (2010)

On the Security of Balanced Encoding Countermeasures

Yoo-Seung Won[1,2], Philip Hodgers[2], Máire O'Neill[2], and Dong-Guk Han[1,3(✉)]

[1] Department of Financial Information Security, Kookmin University, Seoul, Korea
mathwys87@kookmin.ac.kr
[2] Center for Secure Information Technologies, Queen's University, Belfast, UK
p.hodgers@qub.ac.uk, m.oneill@ecit.qub.ac.uk
[3] Department of Mathematics, Kookmin University, Seoul, Korea
christa@kookmin.ac.kr

Abstract. Most cryptographic devices should inevitably have a resistance against the threat of side channel attacks. For this, masking and hiding schemes have been proposed since 1999. The security validation of these countermeasures is an ongoing reserach topic, as a wider range of new and existing attack techniques are tested against these countermeasures. This paper examines the side channel security of the balanced encoding countermeasure, whose aim is to process the secret key-related data under a constant Hamming weight and/or Hamming distance leakage. Unlike previous works, we assume that the leakage model coefficients conform to a normal distribution, producing a model with closer fidelity to real-world implementations. We perform analysis on the balanced encoded PRINCE block cipher with simulated leakage model and also an implementation on an AVR board. We consider both standard correlation power analysis (CPA) and bit-wise CPA. We confirm the resistance of the countermeasure against standard CPA, however, we find with a bit-wise CPA that we can reveal the key with only a few thousands traces.

Keywords: Balanced encoding · Bit-wise CPA · PRINCE block cipher

1 Introduction

With the advent of the Internet of Things, an increasing number of cryptographic devices enter our daily lives. Most of these devices are accessible, and therefore, cannot avoid the threat of side channel attacks [1]. Thus, it is essential that these devices are protected with side channel countermeasures, such as masking and/or hiding [14,17,19,20,24,28]. From the point of view of a software implementation, masking countermeasures aim to break the relationship between the power leakages and the intermediate variables. However, masking is still vulnerable to higher-order attacks [31]. Hiding countermeasures, on the other hand, aim to reduce the statistical linkage between the trace samples and the intermediate variables. In general, the cost of a hiding countermeasure is lower than that of a

© Springer International Publishing Switzerland 2016
N. Homma and M. Medwed (Eds.): CARDIS 2015, LNCS 9514, pp. 242–256, 2016.
DOI: 10.1007/978-3-319-31271-2_15

masking countermeasure. Due to the complementary security features of these countermeasures, their combination is often regarded as advantageous compared to the implementation of either in isolation.

In order to improve protection against side channel analysis, the idea of producing a constant leakage for any intermediate variables in software implementations was first proposed by Hoogvorst *et al.* [23], suggesting the concept of Dual-rail with Precharge Logic [5,7,10–12,21]. However, their work did not include an implementation for security evaluation. Subsequently, Maekawa *et al.* [26] proposed an improved scheme in terms of memory-cost, referred to as Symbolic Representation. Similarly they did not evaluate the security of their proposal in terms of implementation. That is, nobody knows for sure whether the implementation of the constant leakage countermeasure is secure or not. Recently, these approaches have been re-proposed with a security validation by Servant *et al.* [32], claiming that their scheme is resistant to side channel analysis. More precisely, they showed that the leakage of the constant Hamming weight countermeasure remains fixed for constant weighting coefficients of a polynomial leakage function, regardless of the variation of intermediate variables. Thus, this countermeasure appears to be more secure than other previously proposed countermeasures. In support of this, they showed that the success rate for key recovery was less than $10\,\%$, when performing correlation power analysis (CPA) [8] from a simulated leakage model.

Most prior works, which deal with constant weight countermeasures, only consider the Hamming weight model. However, some leakage of the Hamming distance between intermediate variables is still a possibility, even when a cryptographic algorithm is implemented in software. Ideally, a scheme should provide resistance against both Hamming distance and Hamming weight leakage. Recently, Chen *et al.* [30] proposed such a scheme for the first time, calling it balanced encoding. They showed that their scheme was not vulnerable to first-order CPA in an AVR microcontroller board. They also claimed that their scheme ensures security against linear and balanced leakage models.

In this paper, we conduct a security evaluation for the balanced encoding countermeasure proposed in [30]. For this, we employ the polynomial of higher degree leakage model as with previous works. The coefficients of leakage model in [29,32] are regarded as 0 or 1. However, since these ideal values may be difficult to realize in practice, we therefore consider a leakage model where the coefficients deviate from purely constant values. For this purpose, we assume that the coefficients comform to a normal distribution. We therefore develop a balanced and imbalanced leakage model of the PRINCE block cipher [25], performing CPA on both simulated and real traces obtained from an 8-bit AVR microcontroller implementation. This is the same environment as prior work [30], allowing for a direct comparison. Crucially, we will show that the leakage of a balanced encoding countermeasure is not constant in simulated and implemented environments, when analyzed with a bit-wise CPA, demonstrating that the countermeasure in [30] is not secure against standard side channel analysis techniques.

The remainder of this work is structured as follows: The balanced encoding countermeasure is summerized in Sect. 2. The leakage model and the result of the security evaluation for simulated traces are reported in Sect. 3. Section 4 presents the result of the security evaluation for real traces implemented on an AVR microcontroller board, with our conclusions in Sect. 5.

2   Related Works

This section provides an overview of the constant leakage countermeasure for the balanced encoded PRINCE block cipher.

2.1   Dual-Rail with Precharge Logic

Dual-rail with precharge logic, which has been proposed as a hardware-based countermeasure, is a combination of dual-rail logic and precharge logic. In contrast with single-rail logic, where each wire carries a single bit-value, dual-rail logic uses two wires to carry each bit. Furthermore, in precharge logic all signals in the circuit are set to a precharge value of either 0 or 1. In a software implementation, each bit of an intermediate variable is replaced with either 01 or 10. The purpose of this concept is to retain a constant Hamming weight value. If either 00 or 11 is selected, this rule will be broken.

2.2   Balanced Encoding Countermeasure for PRINCE Block Cipher

In this section, we introduce the balanced encoding countermeasure for PRINCE, proposed in [30]. The purpose of all such encoding schemes is to produce constant weight bytes by inserting the relevant complementary bits for any position. Figure 1 shows part of a balanced encoding scheme for the PRINCE block cipher. The two columns on the left-hand-side of Fig. 1 show the Hamming weight and Hamming distances of the states. Because the unencoded state of PRINCE is 4-bits (nibble), the balanced encoded state is a byte. In Fig. 1, the basic encoding scheme is called Encode I, and additionally, in order to perform the **S-layer** operation, Encode II and III are also required.

The first state nibble can be simply extended to one byte without inserting complementary bits. That is, $x_3x_2x_1x_0 \rightarrow x_3x_3x_2x_2x_1x_1x_0x_0$. The **Key Addition** operation is then calculated after K_0 is encoded with Encode I. The other round key and round constant values are likewise extended to one byte without inserting complementary bits, retaining a consistant encoding representation. Encode I cannot be applied to **S-layer** and therefore Encode II, whose encoding operation is given in the lower right-hand side of Fig. 1, is applied. That is, $EncII[S(x_3x_2x_1x_0)] = S'(EncI[x_3x_2x_1x_0])$ where $S(\cdot)$ and $S'(\cdot)$ represent the S-box and the new S-box, respectively. In this way, a constant Hamming weight and Hamming distance value is preserved. In order to input the **M-layer** (**MixColumns**) we need to go back to Encode I. However, Encode III is required since it is not possible to go directly from Encode II to Encode I

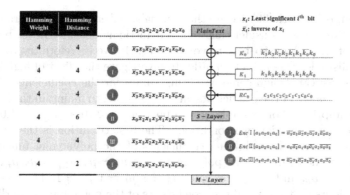

Fig. 1. Part of the structure for the balanced encoding of PRINCE

as this would generate a non-constant Hamming distance value. The scheme is described in further detail in [30]. The above explanation of Encode I, Encode II, and Encode III is just one example of a balanced encoding scheme and there are other potential ways to design such a scheme.

We now turn out attention to the security of the balanced encoding countermeasure of [30].

3   Security Evaluation Based on Polynomial Leakage Model

In this section, we conduct a security evaluation with a simulated leakage model. By performing standard and bit-wise CPA, we can examine whether the balanced encoding ensures security under both analysis methods or not. First, however, we need to define the leakage model. As with prior works [29, 32], we assume that the leakage function follows a polynomial form as Eq. (1).

$$L(X) = \sum_i a_i \cdot x_i + \sum_{i,j} b_{i,j} \cdot (x_i \cdot x_j) + \sum_{i,j,k} c_{i,j,k} \cdot (x_i \cdot x_j \cdot x_k) \qquad (1)$$

where x_i indicates the ith bit of the sensitive value X and a_i, $b_{i,j}$ and $c_{i,j,k}$ are some weighting coefficients, and $a_i \sim \mathcal{N}(\mu_i, \sigma_i)$, $b_{i,j} \sim \mathcal{N}(\mu_{i,j}, \sigma_{i,j})$ and $c_{i,j,k} \sim \mathcal{N}(\mu_{i,j,k}, \sigma_{i,j,k})$, where μ_i and σ_i denote mean and variance respectively.

The difference between our model and prior works [29, 32] is that we assume the coefficient follows a normal distribution. We make this assumption to create a more realistic model. Also, we consider that the mean of the coefficients should be close to one, because most cryptographic devices conform to a Hamming weight model when implemented in software. In other words, we consider that each distribution of coefficients will likely be equal or very similar.

Previous work [32] has modeled coefficients of leakage following $\mathcal{N}(1, \sigma)$ and as such we consider the case which satisfies $\mu_i = \mu_{i,j} = \mu_{i,j,k} = 1$. Under this assumption, prior work [30] declare that the balanced encoding countermeasure is secure. But we do not consider this to be a realistic model since in the real-world the value of μ_i is **close to but never exactly** 1. We therefore try to consider a more realistic leakage model. In order to investigate the effect of higher degree coefficients, we can assign some weighting values for the coefficients. However, we limit the change of the coefficients on a small scale, to maintain the Hamming weight assumptions. For example, $\mu_i = 1.00 < \mu_{i,j} = 1.01 < \mu_{i,j,k} = 1.02$.

We therefore consider two conditions. The first condition is the fundamental approach where the weighting coefficients of the polynomial functions are **identical** for the degree of the polynomial, *i.e.* $\mu_i = \mu_a, \mu_{i,j} = \mu_b, \mu_{i,j,k} = \mu_c$, $\sigma_i = \sigma_a, \sigma_{i,j} = \sigma_b$, and $\sigma_{i,j,k} = \sigma_c$, and $\mu_a \approx 1, \mu_b \approx 1, \mu_c \approx 1$. The second condition considers that the weighting coefficients of the polynomials are **different from each other**. These models are called balanced and imbalanced leakage models, respectively. Also, these approaches are used to evaluate the balanced encoded PRINCE traces generated from a simulation tool such as Matlab.

To assess their security, we target the sensitive value X from the **S-layer** output of the encoding scheme in Fig. 1. We focus on Encode II in this work because it is directly applied to the output of the **S-layer**. That is, $O = L(EncII(X))$. We apply both standard CPA and bit-wise CPA during the security evaluation of the balanced encoding countermeasure. We now briefly introduce standard and bit-wise CPA.

3.1   Standard and Bit-Wise CPA

In order to perform a CPA, after predicting the leakage model, the adversary will calculate the correlation between the acquired traces and the guessed intermediate variables. However, in case of a balanced encoding countermeasure, the guessed intermediate variables are constant (assuming a perfect Hamming weight model). We therefore wish to consider bit-wise CPA to find the leaked information from the balanced encoding countermeasure. When performing standard CPA, we denote the guessed intermediate variable including the Hamming weight leakage model $H(\cdot)$ and the intermediate variable X as $H(X)$. In the PRINCE block cipher, it is obvious that $H(X)$ is represented as the Hamming weight value of the nibble. And, when performing bit-wise CPA, we denote that X_i is the least significant i^{th} bit, and can use $H(X_i)$, corresponding to the guessed intermediate variable ($i = 0, 1, 2, 3$).

3.2   Security Metrics

Before we conduct the security evaluation for the balanced encoding countermeasure, and in order to quantify the effectiveness of our attack with a security metric, we employ guessing entropy [13,16]. Let $\mathbf{g}_q$ be the vector including the key candidates sorted according to the evaluation result, after side channel analysis has been performed: $\mathbf{g}_q := [g_1, g_1, \ldots, g_{|S|}]$ (S denotes the set of key candidates), and $\mathbf{L}_q$ be the random vector of the observations generated with q queries to the target physical device, and $\mathbf{l}_q = [l_1, l_2, \ldots, l_q]$ be a realization of this vector.

We define the index of a key class s in side channel analysis as: $\mathsf{I}_s\,(\mathbf{g}_q) = i$ such that $g_i = s$. The guessing entropy is then the average position of s in this vector, as shown Eq. (2):

$$\mathbf{GE}_S = \mathop{\mathbf{E}}_{s}\mathop{\mathbf{E}}_{\mathbf{1}_q}\mathsf{I}_s(\mathbf{g}_q) \qquad (2)$$

Intuitively, the guessing entropy means the average number of key candidates required for successful evaluation after the side channel analysis has been performed. Additionally, guessing entropy will be averaged over 1,000 trials in this work.

3.3   Security Evaluation for Balanced Leakage Model

We conduct the security evaluation for the balanced encoding countermeasure when assuming the fundamental approach. Because Sect. 4 will present the results of performing CPA for the real traces, the guessing entropy is adopted as the security metric. We consider some specific cases for assessing the security as follows.

- Case 1 : $\mu_c = \mu_b = \mu_a > 0, \sigma_c = \sigma_b = \sigma_a > 0$
- Case 2 : $\mu_c > \mu_b > \mu_a > 0, \sigma_c = \sigma_b = \sigma_a > 0$
- Case 3 : $\mu_c = \mu_b = \mu_a > 0, \sigma_c > \sigma_b > \sigma_a > 0$
- Case 4 : $\mu_c > \mu_b > \mu_a > 0, \sigma_c > \sigma_b > \sigma_a > 0$

In Case 1, the mean and variance are constant, reflecting the approach of previous works [29,32]. The main purpose of Case 2 is to examine the variation of the means, and Case 3 to examine the variation of the variances, of the coefficients in Eq. (1). Case 4 is a combination of Case 2 and Case 3. The cases consider that the mean and the variance of the coefficients of the leakage functions are non-zero in the real world and we assume that the leakage model conforms to the Hamming weight model, where $\mu_a \approx 1, \mu_b \approx 1, \mu_c \approx 1$, and $\mu_a \neq \mu_b \neq \mu_c$. In other words, the above cases are more realistic in practice than previous works [29,32]. We give a high weighting to coefficients of higher degree since they exhibit higher mean and variance values. Without variance in the coefficents there would be no leakage and therefore in pursuit of a more realistic model, it is an inevitable parameter to select.

Figure 2 represents the result of security evaluations for the balanced encoding countermeasure. Against our expectations, all cases have a similar result. That is, the leakage of information is independent of the mean and variance of the leakage distribution when assuming a balanced leakage model. However, we feel that it is hard to perfectly conceal sensitive variables from the balanced encoding countermeasure, since the guessing entropy has under 6 candidates when performing bit-wise CPA.

In Fig. 2, all cases seem to be secure, since guessing entropy is between 10 or 12 when performing standard CPA. Like prior work [30], the balanced encoding countermeasure is shown to resist standard CPA. The complexity of an exhaustive attack of the PRINCE round key is about 32 bit or 41 bit, if we consider

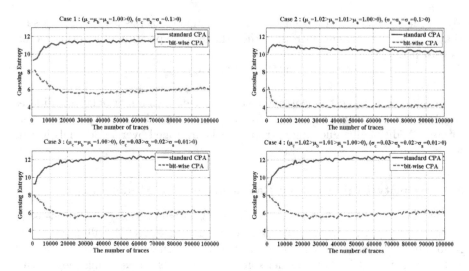

Fig. 2. The result of security evaluations for the balanced encoding countermeasure when assuming a balanced leakage model

guessing entropy 4 or 6. In other words, the round key complexity can be reduced by about 50 % because the round key is 64 bit.

There is of course a tolerance against basic side channel analysis when properties of the device significantly conform to the assumption. We consider, however, that there are few cryptographic devices which would have these ideal properties. Therefore, in the next subsection, we introduce a more realistic assumption than the just considered fundamental approach.

3.4   Security Evaluation for Imbalanced Leakage Model

We now consider the scenario of an imbalanced leakage model. As previously mentioned, we assign a different-weight for the coefficients of a polynomial leakage function. However, we only control the first degree of the polynomial, since this is enough to create a more realistic model, although higher degree coefficients could be considered. That is, $b_{i,j} = c_{i,j,k} = 0$. We therefore adopt a linear model, however, we expect that it can reflect a more realistic model, because the distributions of the coefficients are different from each other. Likewise as per the balanced leakage model, we assume that $\mu_i \approx 1$, but $\mu_i \neq \mu_j$.

For investigation of the security, we make the assumption that only a few bits have a biased distribution. For example, if only signal bit has a biased distribution, $\mu_0 = 1.01, \mu_i = 1.00$, with i not equal to zero. The reason why we set this distribution is to examine the security of the balanced encoding countermeasure, when the leakage model is extremely biased. Additionally, we cannot handle all cases, because there would be too many to consider. In this work, we therefore only examine two cases, namely a single biased bit and two biased bits.

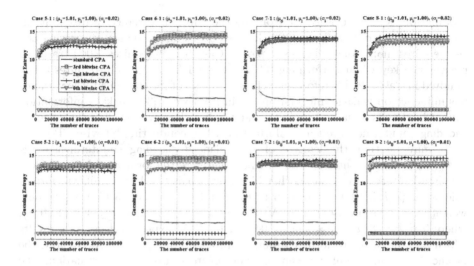

Fig. 3. The result of security evaluation for the balanced encoding countermeasure when assuming single bit-weighted imbalanced leakage model

Because the state of unprotected PRINCE is represented as a nibble, it is possible to insert a biased distribution for at most 4 positions of the state for the balanced encoding countermeasure in the case of a biased single bit. Since $EncII[x_3x_2x_1x_0]$ is represented as $x_0\bar{x}_2x_1x_3\bar{x}_1x_2\bar{x}_0\bar{x}_3$, we can insert a biased distribution for any position. But when inserting a biased distribution for x_i or $\bar{x}_i$, the same result is expected. Therefore, we have to select the position for insertion of the biased distribution; the original bit or complementary bit. In this work we choose the complementary bit. Then, we can find matching bits between the pre-conversion nibble and the post-conversion byte. For instance, pre-conversion bit x_3 is matched with post-conversion least significant 0th bit. That is, a_0 only has a different distribution: $a_0 \sim \mathcal{N}(\mu_0, \sigma_0)$, $a_i \sim \mathcal{N}(\mu, \sigma)$, where $i \neq 0$. Also, we assign different variances for all cases, in order to investigate the effect of variance.

The result of performing standard CPA and bit-wise CPA is illustrated in Fig. 3. Also, the mean of the distribution of coefficients is set to **almost 1**. As previously mentioned, our premise is that the real model almost follows the Hamming weight model. That is, $a_i \sim \mathcal{N}(1.01, \sigma)$, $a_j \sim \mathcal{N}(1.00, \sigma)$, where $0 \leq j \leq 8$, $i \neq j$, $\sigma = 0.01$ or 0.02. As explained earlier, we consider that i is 0 or 1 or 3 or 6. As expected, the sensitive variables is not concealed for all cases when performing bit-wise CPA. However, excluding Case 8, it seems to be secure when performing standard CPA. It is hard to explain the result of Case 8^1. In any case, another countermeasure is required as all other cases exposed the key

---

[1] It is still not sure the cause of result. However the result slightly depends on the correlation between data. $Corr(x_3x_2x_1x_0, x_3) \approx 0.87$ but other cases are lower than 0.5. ($Corr(A, B)$: correlation coefficient between A and B).

information. More precisely, we examine the effect of variance of distribution. For this, we set σ to 0.01 or 0.02. In case of a large variance, recovering the key requires more traces. For example, in Case 5-1, it requires 5,000 traces to recover the key when performing 0th bit-wise CPA, but it only requires a few hundred in Case 5-2. Therefore, as well as the mean of the coefficient, the variance has influence on leakage information. As in prior work [30], leakage information cannot be detected via performing standard CPA. However, we find the balanced encoding countermeasure leaks information when conducting bit-wise CPA.

It may be that the leakage of the balanced encoding countermeasure is revealed, thanks to the constrained rule. Therefore the former rule is extended. As already stated, we examine that biased-weight is two bits. Similar to former rule, when (i, j) is $(0, 1)$ or $(0, 3)$ or $(0, 6)$ or $(1, 3)$ or $(1, 6)$ or $(3, 6)$, we give some weightings. More precisely, $a_i \sim \mathcal{N}(0.99, \sigma)$, $a_j \sim \mathcal{N}(1.01, \sigma)$, $a_k \sim \mathcal{N}(1.00, \sigma)$, where $0 \leq k \leq 8$, $i \neq j \neq k$, $\sigma = 0.01$ or 0.02. As expected, this gives results which are analogous to former results as provided in Appendix A. Namely, the balanced encoding countermeasure cannot ensure security in any situation. The success of the attack may be a natural result because we give some weightings for the distribution. However, surprisingly, it fails to recover the key when performing standard CPA for all cases. It means that it cannot guarantee security for bit-wise CPA, only for performing standard CPA.

Therefore, it is important that future constant leakage countermeasures should be resilient against both standard and bit-wise CPA. We note that as the variance of the distribution of the coefficient increases so does its resistance.

4   Experimental Results for an AVR Implementation

In this section, we conduct a security evaluation for the balanced encoding countermeasure on an AVR microcontroller board. For this, the power consumption of the AVR microcontroller chip has been measured using a 1 GHz LeCroy WaveRunner 104MXi 8-bit digital-storage oscilloscope. For all experiments, we used a sampling rate of 500MS/s. The target of attack is the output of S-layer, and a total of 500,000 power traces with random plaintext inputs were acquired. Additionally, for calculating the guessing entropy, many power traces are required.

We performed CPA on unprotected and balanced encoded PRINCE. As mentioned earlier, in order to compare between standard CPA and bit-wise CPA, we only consider the single output of the S-box. The results are represented in Fig. 4. As authors of prior work claimed [30], the correlation between power traces and assumed leakage model is significantly reduced in the balanced encoding countermeasure. Again, the correlation of unprotected PRINCE has about 0.6 in Fig. 4(a), but one of balanced encoded PRINCE has about 0.2 in Fig. 4(c). That is, the correlation is reduced by a third. However, in case of the result of performing bit-wise CPA, the key is directly revealed although there is not much change in correlation. In fact, when comparing between Fig. 4(a) and (b), bit-wise CPA doesn't allow a better result than standard CPA. The result represented as Fig. 4

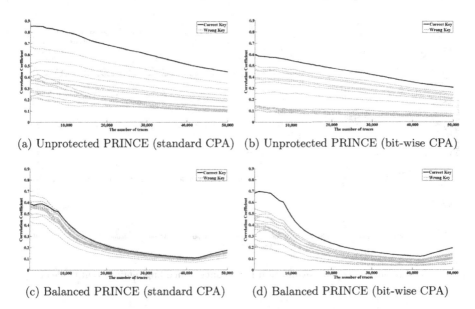

(a) Unprotected PRINCE (standard CPA)   (b) Unprotected PRINCE (bit-wise CPA)

(c) Balanced PRINCE (standard CPA)   (d) Balanced PRINCE (bit-wise CPA)

Fig. 4. The standard and bit-wise CPA results for the unprotected PRINCE (a), (b), and balanced encoding PRINCE (c), (d), respectively. The y-axis indicates the absolute correlation coefficient, and the x-axis indicates the number of real traces used.

shows that the balanced encoding countermeasure is definitely more vulnerable to bit-wise CPA. As stated in Sect. 3, it directly reveals the vulnerability if the real power model tends to be slightly biased-weight at any bit location. Figure 5 illustrates how vulnerable the balanced encoding countermeasure is.

When performing bit-wise CPA, we can get the sensitive information using only a few thousand power traces. However, it's not enough to get sensitive information when only performing standard CPA. As seen in Table 1, in order to get satisfactory guessing entropy, many power traces are required. However, the guessing entropy for a few thousand power traces is not much different than for one requiring thousands. For example, in case of standard CPA, the guessing entropy ranges from 3.75 to 3 in Fig. 5. In conclusion, it allows us to easily retrieve round key candidates which are included in correct round key.

Note that the result is analogous to our simulated leakage model. In comparision with single-weighted leakage model, the trend of guessing entropy has some similarity with the result of Case 5 in Fig. 3. In other words, the guessing entropy is very poor when performing standard CPA. Additionally, it is vulnerable when performing 0th bit-wise CPA. But, some parts do not match with the result of simulation; the result of 2nd and 3rd bit-wise CPA. Also, some parts are analogous to Case 9 of Figs. 6 and 7 in Appendix A; the result of 0th and 1st bit-wise CPA. Nevertheless, real traces revealed the sensitive information when conducting bit-wise CPA. However, assuming the balanced leakage model, it doesn't perfectly reveal the sensitive information, even when performing bit-wise CPA.

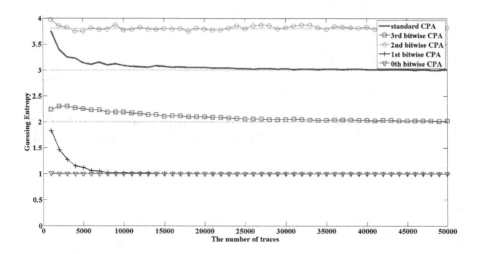

Fig. 5. The result of security evaluation for balanced encoding against real traces in an AVR board

Table 1. The result of security evaluation for the balanced encoding against real traces in an AVR board. In order to get asymptotic guessing entropy, it illustrates the minimum number of traces.

Attack	The minimum number of traces	Asymptotic guessing entropy
Standard CPA	45,000	3
3rd bit-wise CPA	50,000	2
2nd bit-wise CPA	4,000	3.8
1st bit-wise CPA	15,000	1
0th bit-wise CPA	2,000	1

It means that the balanced leakage model is not matched with the real model. As mentioned earlier, the security is ensured if the real model is matched with a balanced leakage model.

5   Conclusion and Future Work

This work conducts a security evaluation of a balanced encoding countermeasure. Before we can examine whether the countermeasure is effective, it is necessary to build simulated leakage models; balanced and imbalanced leakage models. Unlike prior works [29,32], in accordance with Hamming weight model, we assume that the coefficients of polynomial obey a normal distribution. In all cases, it allows us to identify the leak of the balanced encoding countermeasure from the simulated leakage model. Also, we demonstrate that it reveals the vulnerability of the balanced encoding countermeasure from real traces. In conclusion, from both simulated traces and real traces, we can detect the sensitive information when only using a basic side channel analysis approach.

In [32], it was suggested that the balanced encoding scheme could be combined with masking and/or randomization countermeasures, since they are independent from each other. However, this combination of countermeasures needs to be re-examined in light of this work.

Acknowledgements. This research was supported by Basic Science Research Program through the National Research Foundation of Korea(NRF) funded by the Ministry of Education (NRF-2013R1A1A2A10062137). The authors would like to thank Dooho Choi at ETRI for supporting us with SCARF boards (http://www.k-scarf.or.kr/). The SCARF boards were supported by the KLA-SCARF project, the ICT R&D program of ETRI.

A The Result of Security Evaluation for the **Balanced Encoding** Countermeasure when Assuming Multiple Bit-Weighted Imbalanced Leakage Model

Figures 6 and 7 represent the result of conducting standard CPA and bit-wise CPA when assuming imbalanced leakage model. As previously stated, we assume that two bits of the coefficients have some weighted-value. That is, (i, j) is $(0, 1)$ or $(0, 3)$ or $(0, 6)$ or $(1, 3)$ or $(1, 6)$ or $(3, 6)$. For example, in case of $(i, j) = (0, 1)$, $\mu_0 = 0.99, \mu_1 = 1.01, \mu_i = 1.00$ $(i \neq 0, 1)$.

Also, in order to examine the effect of variance of leakage model, variance is considred as 0.01 or 0.02. In more detail, it does not conceal the key information when performing 0th and 1st bit-wise CPA at Case 9-1 in Fig. 6 and Case 9-2 in Fig. 7. The success of the attack may be a natural result because we give some weight for distribution of a_3 and a_1. Additionally, when the value of variance is 0.02, resistance strength to standard CPA is stronger. That is, the slope in Fig. 6 gentle. Anyhow, this countermeasure doesn't have a resistance to basic side channel analysis any more. Additionally, in all cases, standard CPA doesn't work. Note that it seems to be secure when only conducting standard CPA. In conclusion, if the real leakage model obeys roughly Hamming weight model (the coefficients **nearly equal to 1**), the vulnerability of this countermeasure is revealed. Most devices may be difficult to conform perfectly Hamming weight model. Thus, our assumption is not unrealistic.

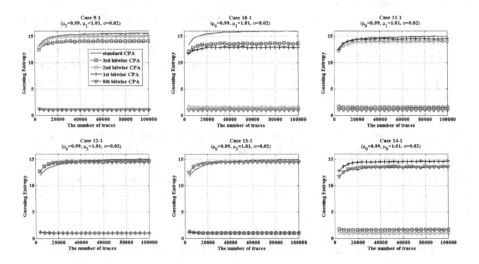

Fig. 6. The result of security evaluation for the balanced encoding countermeasure when assuming multiple bit-weighted imbalanced leakage model ($\sigma=0.02$)

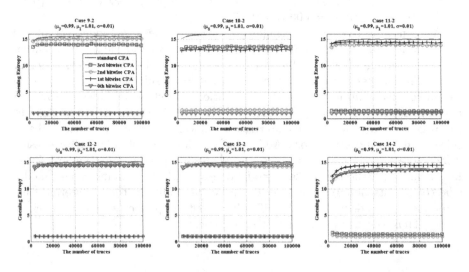

Fig. 7. The result of security evaluation for the balanced encoding countermeasure when assuming multiple bit-weighted imbalanced leakage model ($\sigma=0.01$)

References

1. Kocher, P.C., Jaffe, J., Jun, B.: Differential power analysis. In: Wiener, M. (ed.) CRYPTO 1999. LNCS, vol. 1666, pp. 388–397. Springer, Heidelberg (1999)
2. Satoh, A., Morioka, S., Takano, K., Munetoh, S.: A compact Rijndael hardware architecture with S-box optimization. In: Boyd, C. (ed.) ASIACRYPT 2001. LNCS, vol. 2248, pp. 239–254. Springer, Heidelberg (2001)
3. Bévan, R., Knudsen, E.W.: Ways to enhance differential power analysis. In: Lee, P.J., Lim, C.H. (eds.) ICISC 2002. LNCS, vol. 2587, pp. 327–342. Springer, Heidelberg (2003)
4. Messerges, T.-S., Dabbish, E.-A., Sloan, R.-H.: Examining smart-card security under the threat of power anlaysis attacks. IEEE Trans. Comput. **51**, 541–552 (2002)
5. Tiri, K., Verbauwhede, I.: Securing encryption algorithms against DPA at the logic level: next generation smart card technology. In: Walter, C.D., Koç, Ç.K., Paar, C. (eds.) CHES 2003. LNCS, vol. 2779, pp. 125–136. Springer, Heidelberg (2003)
6. Ishai, Y., Sahai, A., Wagner, D.: Private circuits: securing hardware against probing attacks. In: Boneh, D. (ed.) CRYPTO 2003. LNCS, vol. 2729, pp. 463–481. Springer, Heidelberg (2003)
7. Sokolov, D., Murphy, J., Bystrov, A., Yakovlev, A.: Improving the security of dual-rail circuits. In: Joye, M., Quisquater, J.-J. (eds.) CHES 2004. LNCS, vol. 3156, pp. 282–297. Springer, Heidelberg (2004)
8. Brier, E., Clavier, C., Olivier, F.: Correlation power analysis with a leakage model. In: Joye, M., Quisquater, J.-J. (eds.) CHES 2004. LNCS, vol. 3156, pp. 16–29. Springer, Heidelberg (2004)
9. Waddle, J., Wagner, D.: Towards efficient second-order power analysis. In: Joye, M., Quisquater, J.-J. (eds.) CHES 2004. LNCS, vol. 3156, pp. 1–15. Springer, Heidelberg (2004)
10. Tiri, K., Verbauwhede, I.: A logic level design methodology for a secure DPA resistant ASIC or FPGA implementation. In: Proceedings of the Conference on Design, automation and Test in Europe, pp. 246–251. IEEE Computer Society, Washington (2004)
11. Popp, T., Mangard, S.: Masked dual-rail pre-charge logic: DPA-resistance without routing constraints. In: Rao, J.R., Sunar, B. (eds.) CHES 2005. LNCS, vol. 3659, pp. 172–186. Springer, Heidelberg (2005)
12. Suzuki, D., Saeki, M.: Security evaluation of DPA countermeasures using dual-rail pre-charge logic style. In: Goubin, L., Matsui, M. (eds.) CHES 2006. LNCS, vol. 4249, pp. 255–269. Springer, Heidelberg (2006)
13. Standaert, F.-X., Malkin, T.G., Yung, M.: A Unified Framework for the Analysis of Side-Channel Key Recovery Attacks. Cryptology ePrint Archieve, Report 2006.139 (2006)
14. Schramm, K., Paar, C.: Higher order masking of the AES. In: Pointcheval, D. (ed.) CT-RSA 2006. LNCS, vol. 3860, pp. 208–225. Springer, Heidelberg (2006)
15. Mangard, S., Oswald, E., Popp, T.: Power Analysis Attacks: Revealing the Secrets of Smart Cards. Springer, New York (2007)
16. Standaert, F.-X., Gierlichs, B., Verbauwhede, I.: Partition vs. comparison side-channel distinguishers: an empirical evaluation of statistical tests for univariate side-channel attacks against two unprotected CMOS devices. In: Lee, P.J., Cheon, J.H. (eds.) ICISC 2008. LNCS, vol. 5461, pp. 253–267. Springer, Heidelberg (2009)

17. Rivain, M., Dottax, E., Prouff, E.: Block ciphers implementations provably secure against second order side channel analysis. In: Nyberg, K. (ed.) FSE 2008. LNCS, vol. 5086, pp. 127–143. Springer, Heidelberg (2008)

18. Pan, J., den Hartog, J.I., Lu, J.: You cannot hide behind the mask: power analysis on a provably secure S-Box implementation. In: Youm, H.Y., Yung, M. (eds.) WISA 2009. LNCS, vol. 5932, pp. 178–192. Springer, Heidelberg (2009)

19. Fumaroli, G., Martinelli, A., Prouff, E., Rivain, M.: Affine masking against higher-order side channel analysis. In: Biryukov, A., Gong, G., Stinson, D.R. (eds.) SAC 2010. LNCS, vol. 6544, pp. 262–280. Springer, Heidelberg (2011)

20. Rivain, M., Prouff, E.: Provably secure higher-order masking of AES. In: Mangard, S., Standaert, F.-X. (eds.) CHES 2010. LNCS, vol. 5086, pp. 127–143. Springer, Heidelberg (2010)

21. Guilley, S., Sauvage, L., Flament, F., Vong, V.N., Hoogvorst, P., Pacalet, R.: Evaluation of power constant dual-rail logics countermeasures against DPA with design time security metrics. IEEE Trans. Comput. **59**, 1250–1263 (2010)

22. Goubin, L., Martinelli, A.: Protecting AES with Shamir's secret sharing scheme. In: Preneel, B., Takagi, T. (eds.) CHES 2011. LNCS, vol. 6917, pp. 79–94. Springer, Heidelberg (2011)

23. Hoogvorst, P., Duc, G., Danger, J.-L.: Software implementation of dual-rail representation. In: COSADE 2011, pp. 73–81 (2011)

24. Kim, H.S., Hong, S., Lim, J.: A fast and provably secure higher-order masking of AES S-Box. In: Preneel, B., Takagi, T. (eds.) CHES 2011. LNCS, vol. 6917, pp. 95–107. Springer, Heidelberg (2011)

25. Borghoff, J., et al.: PRINCE – A low-latency block cipher for pervasive computing applications. In: Wang, X., Sako, K. (eds.) ASIACRYPT 2012. LNCS, vol. 7658, pp. 208–225. Springer, Heidelberg (2012)

26. Naekawa, A., Yamashita, N., Tsunoo, T., Minematsu, K., Suzuki, T., Tsunoo, Y.: Tamper-resistance techniques based on symbolic implementation against power analysis. In: SCIS 2013, pp. 73–81 (2013)

27. Tunstall, M., Whitnall, C., Oswald, E.: Masking tables – an underestimated security risk. In: Moriai, S. (ed.) FSE 2013. LNCS, vol. 8424, pp. 425–444. Springer, Heidelberg (2014)

28. Coron, J.-S., Prouff, E., Rivain, M., Roche, T.: Higher-order side channel security and mask refreshing. In: Moriai, S. (ed.) FSE 2013. LNCS, vol. 8424, pp. 410–424. Springer, Heidelberg (2014)

29. Grosso, V., Standaert, F.-X., Prouff, E.: Low entropy masking schemes, revisited. In: Francillon, A., Rohatgi, P. (eds.) CARDIS 2013. LNCS, vol. 8419, pp. 33–43. Springer, Heidelberg (2014)

30. Chen, C., Eisenbarth, T., Shahverdi, A., Ye, X.: Balanced encoding to mitigate power analysis: a case study. In: Joye, M., Moradi, A. (eds.) CARDIS 2014. LNCS, vol. 8968, pp. 49–63. Springer, Heidelberg (2015)

31. Ding, A.A., Zhang, L., Fei, Y., Luo, P.: A statistical model for higher order DPA on masked devices. In: Batina, L., Robshaw, M. (eds.) CHES 2014. LNCS, vol. 8731, pp. 147–169. Springer, Heidelberg (2014)

32. Servant, V., Debande, N., Maghrebi, H., Bringer, J.: Study of a novel software constant weight implementation. In: Joye, M., Moradi, A. (eds.) CARDIS 2014. LNCS, vol. 8968, pp. 35–48. Springer, Heidelberg (2015)

Implementations

Higher-Order Threshold Implementation
of the AES S-Box

Thomas De Cnudde[1]([⊠]), Begül Bilgin[1], Oscar Reparaz[1],
Ventzislav Nikov[2], and Svetla Nikova[1]

[1] KU Leuven, ESAT-COSIC and iMinds, Leuven, Belgium
{thomas.decnudde,begul.bilgin,oscar.reparaz,
svetla.Nikova}@esat.kuleuven.be
[2] NXP Semiconductors, Leuven, Belgium
venci.nikov@gmail.com

Abstract. In this paper we present a threshold implementation of the
Advanced Encryption Standard's S-box which is secure against first-
and second-order power analysis attacks. This security guarantee holds
even in the presence of glitches, and includes resistance against bivariate
attacks. The design requires an area of 7849 Gate Equivalents and 126
bits of randomness per S-box execution. The implementation is tested
on an FPGA platform and its security claim is supported by practical
leakage detection tests.

Keywords: Higher-order · Threshold implementations · AES · S-box ·
Masking

1 Introduction

Side-Channel Analysis (SCA) and more specifically Differential Power Analysis
(DPA) [12] are considered to be powerful methods which can be used to extract
secrets, e.g. keys or passwords, from cryptographic implementations running on
embedded devices. The wide usage of these devices demands strong yet practical
methods to mitigate this problem. A sound and popular such method is masking
[6,11]. Masking works by splitting every intermediate variable that depends on
the secret into several shares such that knowledge of any share does not provide any information about the intermediate variable. This splitting breaks the
dependency between the average instantaneous power consumption and the sensitive intermediates handled by the implementation, and thus thwarts first-order
DPA attacks.

In theory, however, a masked implementation can always be broken by
a higher-order attack. Higher-order attacks consider information from several
shares simultaneously and are increasingly difficult to mount as the order
increases, both in terms of number of traces [6] and computational complexity.
Nonetheless, second-order attacks have been shown to be practical to mount
[14,19,20,24,27,28] and hence its protection is of importance. Higher-order

© Springer International Publishing Switzerland 2016
N. Homma and M. Medwed (Eds.): CARDIS 2015, LNCS 9514, pp. 259–272, 2016.
DOI: 10.1007/978-3-319-31271-2_16

masking schemes provide security guarantees against higher-order DPA attacks under specific assumptions, and up to a certain order.

When implemented in hardware, masking can lead to insecure designs due to glitches. Standard CMOS gates can glitch, and these glitches can cause the power consumption to depend on unmasked variables. This behavior degrades the security claims. For instance, Mangard et al. [13] present first-order attacks against masked implementations in hardware exploiting this idea.

Threshold Implementation (TI) [17,18] is a specific masking approach that provides security even in the presence of glitches in the hardware. First-order TIs of the Advanced Encryption Standard (AES) have been shown to being practically feasible as well as being secure [2,4,16]. The theory of TI has recently been extended to provide higher-order security by Bilgin et al. [3].

Prouff and Roche's Higher-Order Glitches Free Implementation (HOGFI) [21] provides an alternative approach to TI. A first-order secure HOGFI of the AES S-box has been presented [15]. However, a higher-order extension has not yet been put into practice for AES. To our knowledge, the only higher-order implementation of this method is applied to PRESENT [9].

Contribution. We provide the first higher-order threshold implementation of the AES S-box. Our design shows up to second-order security (including bivariate attacks) in the presence of glitches. This paper is, to our knowledge, the first one to show this security in practice within the context of TI. Additionally, we discuss several trade-offs between randomness and area that can be considered.

Organization. Section 2 introduces our notation, the necessary background information regarding higher-order TI and Canright's decomposition of the AES S-box on which we base our implementation. In Sect. 3, we present our hardware design of which the implementation costs are given in Sect. 4. Discussions of these results by comparing them with other glitch resistant implementations of the AES S-box and by investigating trade-offs in area and randomness through different design decisions are also given in the same section. We detail our measurement setup and the results of the side-channel analysis in Sect. 5. Finally, the conclusion is drawn in Sect. 6.

2   Preliminaries

In this section, we first introduce our notation, then provide a brief description of the threshold implementation technique to produce higher-order masked hardware implementations, and finally we end with the description of a compact (unmasked) implementation of the AES S-box that will serve as a basis of our masked implementation.

2.1   Notation

We use lower-case characters to denote elements in $GF(2^n)$. A function f is defined from $GF(2^n)$ to $GF(2^m)$ and can be considered as an m-tuple of Boolean functions $(f^1(x), \ldots, f^m(x))$, where $x \in \mathrm{GF}(2^n)$. Similarly, $x \in \mathrm{GF}(2^n)$ can be denoted as $(x^1, \ldots, x^n)$, where $x_i \in \mathrm{GF}(2)$. We use $\oplus$ for XOR and $\otimes$ for multiplication in a given field. If the multiplication is bit-wise, we drop $\otimes$.

In order to perform a masked computation, a secret variable x should be split into s_x shares x_i. In this paper, we consider Boolean masking for this initial split which is described as follows: without loss of generality, the shares $x_1, \ldots, x_{s_x - 1}$ are drawn from independent and uniform random distributions and the share x_{s_x} is calculated s.t. $x = \bigoplus_i x_i$ holds. A shared vector (sharing) (e.g. $(x_1, \ldots, x_{s_x})$) is denoted by bold characters (e.g. $\mathbf{x}$). A sharing is a uniform masking if for each value x, the corresponding vectors with masked values occur with the same probability.

In order to perform operations in the masked domain, the function f is also split in shares f_i which are called component functions. The sharing of f is denoted by $\mathbf{f}$.

2.2   Threshold Implementations

Threshold implementation (TI) is a masking method which provides security against higher-order DPA (hence the name higher-order TI). It diverges from many other masking schemes since it can provide security when non-ideal, glitchy cells are used given the following property:

> $d^{th} - order\ non\text{-}completeness.$ Any combination of up to d component functions f_i of $\mathbf{f}$ must be independent of at least one input share x_i.

This property enforces the combination of leakages from the calculation of d component functions to be independent of the sensitive variable x given a uniform sharing $\mathbf{x}$. We refer the reader to [3] for details. In addition, it has been shown that there always exists a dth-order non-complete sharing of a degree t function f with $s_{in} \geq td + 1$ input shares [3]. This naturally implies that the required number of shares for a given security increases together with the degree of the function.

In [3], a method for generating the component functions with $s_{in} = td + 1$ input and $s_{out} = \binom{s_{in}}{t}$ is provided. Hereon, we refer $\mathbf{f}$ with s_{in} input and s_{out} output shares as (s_{in}, s_{out}) sharing.

Uniform Sharings vs. Refreshing. As stated in Sect. 2.2, the computation of a sharing $\mathbf{f}$ requires the input $\mathbf{x}$ to be uniform. However, the fact that $\mathbf{x}$ is uniform does not automatically ensure that $\mathbf{y}$ is uniform. The lack of uniformity of $\mathbf{y}$ poses a problem if this variable is plugged into another sharing $\mathbf{g}(\mathbf{y})$, since the input $\mathbf{y}$ should also be uniform for $\mathbf{g}$ to be secure. By careful selection of the shared function $\mathbf{f}$, it is possible to guarantee the uniformity of $\mathbf{y}$ given a uniform input $\mathbf{x}$. We refer to such a sharing $\mathbf{f}$ as a uniform sharing. This uniformity allows an elegant composition mechanism: uniform sharings can be composed freely[1]

---

[1] We mean strict composition as $g \circ f$. If g sees the concatenation of two functions f_1, f_2, one should make sure that the input to g stays uniform. This does not automatically happen even if f_1 and f_2 are independently uniform [4].

without using further randomization, and still provide first-order security for the whole circuit [18]. If one cannot find uniform sharings, it is always possible to resort to refreshing the sharing **y** prior to applying **g**. This refreshing produces a uniform output at the cost of additional randomness.

The situation in higher-order threshold implementations is more subtle. It has been shown in [23] that the composition of uniform sharings without refreshing is not necessarily higher-order secure; the composition can be made higher-order secure by introducing a refreshing block. Thus, in our design, we refresh the output of each non-linear function to provide higher-order security.

2.3 Canright's Very Compact AES S-Box

The AES S-box is an 8-bit permutation composed of a multiplicative inversion in $GF(2^8)$ followed by a $GF(2)$-affine transformation [8]. Side-channel resistant implementations of this S-box are commonly based on subfield arithmetic as proposed by Rijmen [25] and explored by Canright [5]. This approach typically produces low-area circuits. It takes its name from the recursive decomposition of the S-box into computations in smaller fields. Namely, the $GF(2^8)$ inversion is first decomposed into arithmetic operations in $GF(2^4)$; and in turn the nonlinear operations are performed in the subfield $GF(2^2)$. The resulting computation is composed of a $GF(2)$-linear (LM) and inverse $GF(2)$-linear map (ILM), several $GF(2^2)$ multiplications, bitwise XORs and multiple instantiations of linear operations in $GF(2^2)$ (l_i). For a detailed description of the individual operations, we refer to the original work [5].

3   Hardware Implementation

This section gives an overview of the choices we made during the design of the second-order threshold implementations of the AES S-box.

3.1   Redefining the S-Box Decomposition

Converting the Canright S-box to a threshold implementation can be achieved on several levels. Each individual block can be composed with the neighbouring blocks or decomposed into smaller sub-blocks to attain different trade-offs between area, speed and randomness. We acknowledge the fact that randomness requirements also (indirectly) affect the area requirements. Hence, we strive for a compact, low-area implementation, and at the same time we try to keep the randomness requirements as low as possible.

For the discussion of our shared AES S-box, we rely on Fig. 1. We choose to implement the square scale and multiplication operations in $GF(2^4)$ as done by Bilgin et al. [2]. This adaptation requires less randomness and clock cycles than sharing their subfield functions in $GF(2^2)$ since some of the refreshing and registering that must follow the nonlinear operation is avoided. The inversion in $GF(2^4)$ is of algebraic degree three. Since no small second-order non-complete

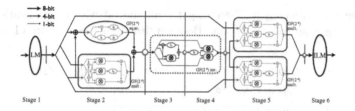

Fig. 1. Unmasked S-box based on Canright (Color figure online)

sharing of such a function has been yet proposed, we share its subfield decomposition, which is contained of a linear operation and three multiplications in $GF(2^2)$. Although, this increases the number of clock cycles by one, it keeps the area and randomness contained.

We decompose the calculation of the S-box into 6 pipeline stages. All stages are separated by registers, indicated by the vertical blue lines in Fig. 1, in order to satisfy the non-completeness property within pipeline stages as explained in Sect. 2.2. Note that the register after the linear map and the register preceding the inverse linear map can be merged with the AES state or key registers.

3.2 Sharing the Nonlinear Operations

The $GF(2^4)$ and $GF(2^2)$ multipliers are the only nonlinear operations of our S-box. For the second-order threshold implementation we need a sharing with second-order non-completeness. There are two known sharings with $s_{in} \geq td + 1$ input shares and fulfilling the non-completeness condition for a function of the form $f(x, y) = xy$, with $x, y \in GF(2)$ [1,3]. One uses $s_{in} = 5$ input shares and results in $s_{out} = 10$ output shares, the other one accepts $s_{in} = 6$ input shares and outputs $s_{out} = 7$ shares. We choose the $(6, 7)$-sharing for the multiplications with the following observations in mind:

- To achieve higher-order security, all nonlinear sharings need refreshing of all their output shares as noted in Sect. 2.2. Hence, we remask the outputs of all the multiplications. The details of how this refreshing is done is described in Sect. 3.4. The lower s_{out}, the lower the consumed randomness is. By using only 7 output shares, the required randomness can be decreased by 30 % in comparison to using 10 output shares.
- The $(5,10)$-sharing requires 20 XOR gates, 25 AND gates and 10 output registers per bit. For one bit of the $(6,7)$-sharing, 29 XOR and 36 AND gates are needed while 7 output registers suffice. Taking 5.66 Gate Equivalents (GE) per register bit, 1.33 GE per AND gate and 2 GE per XOR gate, this boils down to 12 % increase when using 6 instead of 5 input shares. These GE numbers are obtained from the NanGate 45 nm Open Cell Library.

With our choice of the $(6, 7)$-sharing over the $(5, 10)$-sharing we pay a slightly larger area for a substantial reduction of the required randomness.

We use the following $(6,7)$-sharing for all the bit-wise multiplications $a = f(x,y) = xy$ that occur in the Boolean function description of the field multipliers.

$$a_1 = x_2y_2 \oplus x_1y_2 \oplus x_2y_1 \oplus x_1y_3 \oplus x_3y_1 \oplus x_3y_2 \oplus x_2y_3$$
$$a_2 = x_3y_3 \oplus x_3y_4 \oplus x_4y_3 \oplus x_3y_5 \oplus x_5y_3$$
$$a_3 = x_4y_4 \oplus x_2y_4 \oplus x_4y_2 \oplus x_2y_6 \oplus x_6y_2$$
$$a_4 = x_5y_5 \oplus x_1y_4 \oplus x_4y_1 \oplus x_1y_5 \oplus x_5y_1$$
$$a_5 = x_2y_5 \oplus x_5y_2 \oplus x_4y_5 \oplus x_5y_4$$
$$a_6 = x_6y_6 \oplus x_3y_6 \oplus x_6y_3 \oplus x_4y_6 \oplus x_6y_4$$
$$a_7 = x_1y_1 \oplus x_1y_6 \oplus x_6y_1 \oplus x_5y_6 \oplus x_6y_5$$

For convenience, we provide the Boolean functions descriptions of the field multipliers for which we denote each element with its most significant bit on the left-hand side. $GF(2^4)$ multiplication $(a^1, a^2, a^3, a^4) = (x^1, x^2, x^3, x^4) \otimes (y^1, y^2, y^3, y^4)$:

$$a^1 = x^1y^1 \oplus x^3y^1 \oplus x^4y^1 \oplus x^2y^2 \oplus x^3y^2 \oplus x^1y^3 \oplus x^2y^3 \oplus x^3y^3 \oplus x^4y^3 \oplus x^1y^4 \oplus x^3y^4$$
$$a^2 = x^2y^1 \oplus x^3y^1 \oplus x^1y^2 \oplus x^2y^2 \oplus x^4y^2 \oplus x^1y^3 \oplus x^3y^3 \oplus x^2y^4 \oplus x^4y^4$$
$$a^3 = x^1y^1 \oplus x^2y^1 \oplus x^3y^1 \oplus x^4y^1 \oplus x^1y^2 \oplus x^3y^2 \oplus x^1y^3 \oplus x^2y^3 \oplus x^3y^3 \oplus x^1y^4 \oplus x^4y^4$$
$$a^4 = x^1y^1 \oplus x^3y^1 \oplus x^2y^2 \oplus x^4y^2 \oplus x^1y^3 \oplus x^4y^3 \oplus x^2y^4 \oplus x^3y^4 \oplus x^4y^4$$

$GF(2^2)$ multiplication $(a^1, a^2) = (x^1, x^2) \otimes (y^1, y^2)$:

$$a^1 = (x^1 \oplus x^2)(y^1 \oplus y^2) \oplus x^1y^1$$
$$a^2 = (x^1 \oplus x^2)(y^1 \oplus y^2) \oplus x^2y^2$$

3.3 Sharing the Linear Operations

Linear operations are well-known to be easy to mask. The linear computation is performed on each share independently. This works for the following functions:

- Square scale in $GF(2^4)$
- l_1 and l_3 in $GF(2^2)$
- Linear map and inverse linear map

In our implementation, we chose to instantiate $s_{in} = 6$ copies for each of these functions.

The affine operations are performed in parallel with the multiplication in Stages 2 and 3. The output of the affine operation is added to the output of the multiplication; the novelty here is that we can add them *before* storing them in the register, and thus only store the result of the addition. In this way we use less registers and hence a lower area. This addition has to be performed carefully. We have to ensure that the output of the addition still satisfies non-completeness. For instance one wire can carry the value $a_1 \oplus A(x^2, y^2)$ instead of a_1, where A symbolizes an affine operation. This process can be alternatively seen as the sharing of a single function $f' = x \otimes y \oplus A(x,y)$.

3.4 Mask Refreshing and Compression

Apart from the initial sharing, extra randomness is required in the refreshing blocks to attain second-order security. We use a ring structure for this refreshing as proposed in [23]. An advantage of this method is that the sum of the fresh masks does not need to be saved in an extra register. Since we operate on six input shares in each stage, we need to *compress* the seven preceding output shares into six shares. Figure 2 shows how the mask refreshing and the compression are performed over register boundaries after each nonlinear operation. The points where these refreshing and compression layers occur are depicted in Fig. 1 by red circles.

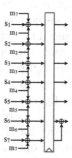

Fig. 2. Ring refreshing and compression

4 Implementation Cost and Trade-Offs

In this section, we elaborate on the implementation cost of our design and the impact of possible trade-offs. We use Xilinx ISE version 12.2 to verify the functionality of our design and Synopsys 2010.03 with the NanGate 45 nm Open Cell Library when providing area estimations.

4.1 Implementation Cost

Table 1 shows the summary of the implementation cost for our S-box design. This is compared to previous first-order secure TIs of the AES S-box. We now briefly discuss these figures.

Area Requirements. From Table 1 we can see that our design uses ×1.84 more area when compared to the first-order TI from [16], or ×3.53 more area when compared to the more compact first-order secure design of [4]. Both figures for the synthesis options "compile" and "compile ultra" are provided[2]. This is the price we pay in area to go from first-order security to second-order security.

---

[2] Special attention is paid so that these options optimize within, but not across, block boundaries. Otherwise, the non-completeness property could be destroyed by the synthesis tool.

Table 1. Implementation cost of different TIs of the AES S-box

S-box	Area [GE]*	Randomness [bit]	Clock cycles	Security
[16]	-/4244	48	5	1st-order
[2]	3708/3003	44	3	1st-order
[4]	2835/2224	32	3	1st-order
This Paper	11174/7849	126	6	2nd-order

*:Using `compile` / `compile_ultra` synthesis option

Table 2 lists the contribution in area of the several components from a single S-box. Note that the l_3 operation, which is the inversion in $GF(2^2)$, is merely a swapping of wires and has therefore no contribution to the area. Also listed are the numbers for the second-order TI of the full AES based on [16]. As in [4], we use $d + 1$ shares in the key and state array. The registers that hold the randomness are not included in the figures. Note that the full AES was not tested in practice. In addition, Table 2 also lists the results of the synthesis for a Virtex 5 FPGA. We provide these figures for future comparison, following the HOGFI design from [15]. Currently, it is hard to discuss the impact of scaling from first-order to second-order security for HOGFI. An extrapolation factor of ×1.667 could be used[3], but may be too optimistic, e.g. for the PRESENT S-box, the factor of area increase was shown to be ×2.3 in [9]. Furthermore, the area of the second-order PRESENT S-box implementation amounts to 8338 GE, which is larger than our second-order design.

Randomness Requirements. Our design requires four ring refreshing on seven shares. Two on 4 bit shares, one on 2 bit shares and one on 8 bit shares. This results in 126 bits of randomness per S-box execution. For a full AES execution we require 3.814 kB, this includes the initial sharing and the randomness needed to increase the three shares of the state and key arrays to the six input shares of the S-box.

When compared to other TIs that provide first-order security, our implementation requires ×2.6 more randomness than [16] or ×3.9 more than [4].

For the first-order HOGFI implementation [15], 432 bits are consumed per S-box execution. This increases to 1440 bits for the second-order HOGFI of the AES S-box[4]. Thus, our implementation consumes ×11.4 less randomness than a second-order HOGFI S-box.

Clock Cycle Requirements. Our S-box currently evaluates in six clock cycles. This is one more than [16] and three clock cycles more than the fastest TI [4]. In Sect. 4.2, we show that our S-box can easily be modified to achieve an evaluation speed of only four clock cycles. For the S-box implemented with HOGFI, 132

---

[3] This is because the size of a HOGFI circuit grows, very roughly, with the number of shares $2d + 1$.

[4] This number is obtained by applying the HOGFI theory [21].

Table 2. Area of different functions of the masked S-box

	Area [GE]	
	Compile	Compile Ultra
Linear Map	22.3	22.3
Inverse Linear Map	17.6	17.6
$GF(2^4)$ Square Scale	11.2	11.2
$GF(2^2)$ l_1	4.8	4.8
$GF(2^2)$ l_3	0	0
$GF(2^4)$ Multiplier	2189.0	1117.7
$GF(2^2)$ Multiplier	408.8	248.6
Registers	1937.77	1937.77
Control S-box	799.6	797.2
Total S-box	11173.57	7849.27
AES Key &State Array	7204.8	6807.75
AES Control	223.2	215.2
Total AES	18601.57	14872.22
Virtex 5 FPGA		
Total S-box [FFs]	691	
Total S-box [LUTs]	3696	
Total S-box [Slices]	1925	

*:These numbers are for the full, untested AES

clock cycles are required for the first-order implementation. This scales to 220 cycles for the second-order implementation. This is substantially larger than our design.

4.2 Directions for Optimizations

We now list several trade-offs we can make to reduce the area and their effect on the randomness.

– We can reduce the area by changing the number of instances of the linear functions to $d + 1 = 3$. This was done in the *nimble version* of [4]. The required randomness is not changed by this modification.
– The registers for the output of the linear map and the input of the inverse linear map can be bypassed. This was shown in [2,4,16]. This bypass will not lead to a reduction in the randomness cost. The execution speed will however be improved by two clock cycles, making a whole AES encryption with this S-box as fast as the implementation of [16]. Note that in a full AES implementation, these two Stages do not add an area overhead, as these registers can be merged with the State and Key Arrays.
– As previously mentioned, the (5,10)-sharing of [3] can be used to save area, but this will increase the required randomness to 180 bits.

5   Side-Channel Analysis Evaluation

For the purpose of evaluating the security claims of our approach, we implemented the design on a Virtex-II xc2vp7-fg456-5 FPGA on a SASEBO-G board. We generate the required randomness prior to the S-box execution on the control FPGA on board. We silence all activity on the board except the S-box lookup during the lookup itself. The design is clocked at 3.072 MHz and the instantaneous power consumption is acquired with a Tektronix DPO 7254C oscilloscope at 500 MS/s. The platform is very low noise.

Methodology. We pursue the following steps to test that the soundness of our setup and masking. First, we switch off the randomness source. This effectively disables the masking countermeasure, thus the design is expected to be vulnerable. Nevertheless, the analysis is first performed in this setting to show that the setup is sound. Then, we repeat the analysis with the randomness source switched on. Any gain in resistance shown in the analysis is then exclusively due to masking.

Security Claims. We claim security against first- and second-order power analysis attacks. That is, the adversary is bounded in the statistical order that he can use in the attacks. Note that since higher statistical moments are increasingly more difficult to estimate in the presence of noise, higher-order attacks beyond our security claims requires considerably more traces to work on and thus are deemed more impractical.

There is an orthogonal classification dividing attacks into uni- or multivariate ones according to the number of different time samples considered jointly in the analysis. This distinction is relevant in practice since multi-variate attacks can be more cumbersome to mount. Here, our second-order claims also include the bi-variate case as the variables considered can be evaluated in different times.

Leakage Detection. We use leakage detection to test our security claims [7, 10, 26]. A basic leakage detection to test the univariate first-order security claim is as follows. Two sets of measurements are acquired corresponding to a lookup of either a fixed value or a random value. A statistical test is applied to test the null hypothesis "the means of the two trace distributions are the same". We use Student's t-statistic and compare it against a threshold of ± 5 corresponding to a confidence level $>99.999\%$. If the statistic surpasses the threshold, there is a statistically significant difference in the means, and thus the means carry some information on the handled value. The test is failed in this case and passed otherwise.[5]

Higher statistical orders are tested in a similar fashion by first pre-processing the traces with an appropriate function. In our case, we use the centered

---

[5] Usual precautions should be taken when mounting the test. For instance, in order to assure that no environmental factor creates an undesired balance between the sets, we interleave the lookups from each set in a random manner.

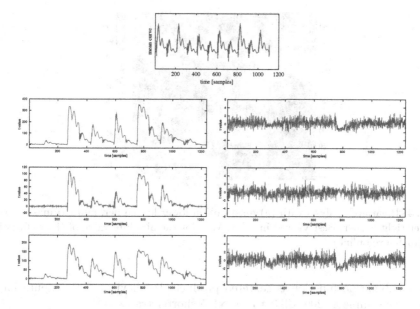

Fig. 3. Univariate analysis. Top Figure: power trace of one S-box execution, Lower Figure: top to bottom, left to right. (a) first-order analysis, masks off (b) second-order analysis, masks off (c) third-order analysis masks off (d) first-order analysis, masks on (e) second-order analysis, masks on (f) third-order analysis, masks on. Note that although the S-box evaluates in 6 cycles, we raise the trigger 1 cycle before the actual computation.

product [6]. If no observable leakage is detected, classical key-recovery attacks will not succeed.

5.1 Univariate Analyses

Masks off. In Fig. 3, we plot the t-statistic when the masks are switched off. We used 500 000 traces to produce plots with clear leakage which was more than the required amount of traces for detecting leakage. We can see clear excursions of the statistic beyond the specified threshold of ±5. The same behavior can be observed for the second and third moment. Hence, all three tests fail. This is expected and means that the measurement setup is sound.

Masks on. When the randomness is switched on, the implementation passes the leakage detection tests for first and second order using up to 100 million traces. This supports the claim of univariate first- and second-order univariate security of the implementation.

5.2 Bivariate Analysis

The previous analysis can be straightforwardly generalized for multivariate statistics. Each time sample is centered before combined with all other timesamples.

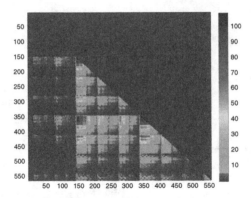

Fig. 4. Bivariate analysis with (a) masks off in lower left corner, and (b) masks on in upper right corner. Best viewed in color. We plot the absolute value of the t-statistic. (Color figure online)

The combination function is centered product. To alleviate the computational effort, we sample at 200 MS/s to get ×2.5 shorter traces.

Masks off. Figure 4 shows the result of the bivariate second-order test when the masks are off using 100 000 traces. Clear excursions above ±5 are seen, both in the diagonal (squaring) and off the diagonal (centered product of two different time samples). This serves as confirmation that our approach is sound, in particular, the change in the sampling rate did not have a significant effect on the magnitude of the t-statistic.

Masks on. We repeated the same test when the randomness is switched on. The implementation shows resistance when using up to 70 million measurements. No excursion beyond the threshold were detected, and thus the test is passed.

6   Conclusion

In this work, we presented the first higher-order threshold implementation of AES S-box with second-order univariate and bivariate security in the presence of glitches. We directed our attention to the S-box specifically as it is the hardest part to secure due to its nonlinearity. Our design was implemented on an FPGA and was shown to achieve our claimed security by resisting leakage detection tests with 70 million traces.

A total area of 7849 Gate Equivalents is covered by our design. One S-box execution consumes 126 bits of randomness, which is largely required to achieve the bivariate security. We discussed the scaling of area, speed and randomness when increasing the order of security. Exactly how these costs scale for TI is our first direction for future research, while optimizing the randomness cost provides a second direction.

Acknowledgements. This work was supported in part by the Research Council KU Leuven: GOA TENSE (GOA/11/007). In addition, this work was partially supported by the Research Fund KU Leuven, OT/13/071, and by European Union's Horizon 2020 research and innovation programme under grant agreement No 644052 HECTOR. Begül Bilgin was partially supported by the FWO project G0B4213N. Oscar Reparaz is funded by a PhD fellowship of the Fund for Scientific Research - Flanders (FWO). Thomas De Cnudde is funded by a research grant of the Institute for the Promotion of Innovation through Science and Technology in Flanders (IWT-Vlaanderen).

References

1. Bilgin, B.: Threshold implementations, as countermeasure against higher-order differential power analysis. Ph.D. thesis, University of Twente, Enschede, May 2015
2. Bilgin, B., Gierlichs, B., Nikova, S., Nikov, V., Rijmen, V.: A more efficient AES threshold implementation. In: Pointcheval, D., Vergnaud, D. (eds.) AFRICACRYPT. LNCS, vol. 8469, pp. 267–284. Springer, Heidelberg (2014). http://dx.doi.org/10.1007/978-3-319-06734-6_17
3. Bilgin, B., Gierlichs, B., Nikova, S., Nikov, V., Rijmen, V.: Higher-order threshold implementations. In: Sarkar, P., Iwata, T. (eds.) ASIACRYPT 2014, Part II. LNCS, vol. 8874, pp. 326–343. Springer, Heidelberg (2014). http://dx.doi.org/10.1007/978-3-662-45608-8_18
4. Bilgin, B., Gierlichs, B., Nikova, S., Nikov, V., Rijmen, V.: Trade-offs for threshold implementations illustrated on AES. IEEE Trans. CAD Integr. Circ. Syst. **34**(7), 1188–1200 (2015). doi:10.1109/TCAD.2015.2419623
5. Canright, D.: A very compact S-box for AES. In: Rao and Sunar [22], pp. 441–455. http://dx.org/10.1007/11545262_32
6. Chari, S., Jutla, C.S., Rao, J.R., Rohatgi, P.: Towards sound approaches to counteract power-analysis attacks. In: Wiener, M. (ed.) CRYPTO 1999. LNCS, vol. 1666, pp. 398–412. Springer, Heidelberg (1999)
7. Cooper, J., DeMulder, E., Goodwill, G., Jaffe, J., Kenworthy, G., Rohatgi, P.: Test vector leakage assessment (TVLA) methodology in practice. In: International Cryptographic Module Conference (2013). http://icmc-2013.org/wp/wp-content/uploads/2013/09/goodwillkenworthtestvector.pdf
8. Daemen, J., Rijmen, V.: The design of rijndael: AES - the advanced encryption standard. In: Information Security and Cryptography. Springer, Berlin (2002). doi:10.1007/978-3-662-04722-4
9. De Cnudde, T., Bilgin, B., Reparaz, O., Nikova, S.: Higher-order glitch resistant implementation of the PRESENT S-box. In: Ors, B., Preneel, B. (eds.) Balkan-CryptSec 2014. LNCS, vol. 9024, pp. 75–93. Springer, Heidelberg (2015)
10. Goodwill, G., Jun, B., Jaffe, J., Rohatgi, P.: A testing methodology for side-channel resistance validation. In: NIST Non-Invasive Attack Testing Workshop (2011). http://csrc.nist.gov/news_events/non-invasive-attack-testing-workshop/papers/08_Goodwill.pdf
11. Goubin, L., Patarin, J.: DES and differential power analysis. In: Koç, Ç.K., Paar, C. (eds.) CHES 1999. LNCS, vol. 1717, pp. 158–172. Springer, Heidelberg (1999)
12. Kocher, P.C., Jaffe, J., Jun, B.: Differential power analysis. In: Wiener, M. (ed.) CRYPTO 1999. LNCS, vol. 1666, pp. 388–397. Springer, Heidelberg (1999)
13. Mangard, S., Pramstaller, N., Oswald, E.: Successfully attacking masked AES hardware implementations. In: Rao and Sunar [22], pp. 157–171. http://dblp.uni-trier.de/db/conf/ches/ches2005.html#MangardPO05

14. Messerges, T.S.: Using second-order power analysis to attack DPA resistant software. In: Paar, C., Koç, Ç.K. (eds.) CHES 2000. LNCS, vol. 1965, pp. 238–251. Springer, Heidelberg (2000)
15. Moradi, A., Mischke, O.: On the simplicity of converting leakages from multivariate to univariate. In: Bertoni, G., Coron, J.-S. (eds.) CHES 2013. LNCS, vol. 8086, pp. 1–20. Springer, Heidelberg (2013)
16. Moradi, A., Poschmann, A., Ling, S., Paar, C., Wang, H.: Pushing the limits: a very compact and a threshold implementation of AES. In: Paterson, K.G. (ed.) EUROCRYPT 2011. LNCS, vol. 6632, pp. 69–88. Springer, Heidelberg (2011)
17. Nikova, S., Rechberger, C., Rijmen, V.: Threshold implementations against side-channel attacks and glitches. In: Ning, P., Qing, S., Li, N. (eds.) ICICS 2006. LNCS, vol. 4307, pp. 529–545. Springer, Heidelberg (2006)
18. Nikova, S., Rijmen, V., Schläffer, M.: Secure hardware implementation of nonlinear functions in the presence of glitches. J. Cryptology 24(2), 292–321 (2011). doi:10. 1007/s00145-010-9085-7
19. Oswald, E., Mangard, S., Herbst, C., Tillich, S.: Practical second-order DPA attacks for masked smart card implementations of block ciphers. In: Pointcheval, D. (ed.) CT-RSA 2006. LNCS, vol. 3860, pp. 192–207. Springer, Heidelberg (2006)
20. Peeters, E., Standaert, F., Donckers, N., Quisquater, J.: Improved higher-order side-channel attacks with FPGA experiments. In: Rao and Sunar [22], pp. 309–323. doi:10.1007/11545262_23
21. Prouff, E., Roche, T.: Higher-order glitches free implementation of the AES using secure multi-party computation protocols. In: Preneel, B., Takagi, T. (eds.) CHES 2011. LNCS, vol. 6917, pp. 63–78. Springer, Heidelberg (2011)
22. Rao, J.R., Sunar, B. (eds.): CHES 2005. LNCS, vol. 3659. Springer, Heidelberg (2005)
23. Reparaz, O., Bilgin, B., Nikova, S., Gierlichs, B., Verbauwhede, I.: Consolidating Masking Schemes. In: Gennaro, R., Robshaw, M. (eds.) CRYPTO 2015. LNCS, vol. 9215, pp. 1–20. Springer, Heidelberg (2015)
24. Reparaz, O., Gierlichs, B., Verbauwhede, I.: Selecting time samples for multivariate DPA attacks. In: Prouff, E., Schaumont, P. (eds.) CHES 2012. LNCS, vol. 7428, pp. 155–174. Springer, Heidelberg (2012)
25. Rijmen, V.: Efficient implementation of the rijndael S-box. http://www. researchgate.net/profile/Vincent_Rijmen/publication/2621085_Efficient_ Implementation_of_the_Rijndael_S-box/links/0912f50f7a7be367d7000000? origin=publication_detail
26. Schneider, T., Moradi, A.: Leakage assessment methodology. In: Güneysu, T., Handschuh, H. (eds.) CHES 2015. LNCS, vol. 9293, pp. 495–513. Springer, Heidelberg (2015)
27. Standaert, F., Peeters, E., Quisquater, J.: On the masking countermeasure and higher-order power analysis attacks. In: International Symposium on Information Technology: Coding and Computing (ITCC 2005), vol. 1, pp. 562–567. IEEE Computer Society, Las Vegas, Nevada, USA, 4–6 April 2005. doi:10.1109/ITCC.2005. 213
28. Waddle, J., Wagner, D.: Towards efficient second-order power analysis. In: Joye, M., Quisquater, J.-J. (eds.) CHES 2004. LNCS, vol. 3156, pp. 1–15. Springer, Heidelberg (2004)

Compact Implementations of Multi-Sbox Designs

Begül Bilgin[1]([✉]), Miroslav Knežević[2], Ventzislav Nikov[2], and Svetla Nikova[1]

[1] ESAT-COSIC and iMinds, KU Leuven, Leuven, Belgium
{begul.bilgin,Svetla.Nikova}@esat.kuleuven.be
[2] NXP Semiconductors, Leuven, Belgium
miroslav.knezevic@nxp.com, venci.nikov@gmail.com

Abstract. Implementations of cryptographic algorithms using several different Sboxes by design are typically considered burdensome. The first reason is that unlike single-Sbox designs, serialized implementations of such cryptographic algorithms require instantiations of all Sboxes which prohibits the desired reduction of area. The second reason is that applying countermeasures such as masking causes an undesired increase in area due to the amount of different nonlinear blocks in the algorithm. In this paper, we propose a novel method to implement multi-Sbox designs using as few nonlinear blocks as possible. We exemplify our finding on DES algorithm of which the Triple-DES variant is still widely used in practice. With this method, it is possible to implement the DES substitution layer, which is composed of eight 6×4 Sboxes, using only three 4-bit nonlinear and several affine 4-bit permutations. Our investigation shows that such an implementation requires less area than the state-of-the-art. Moreover, it opens up the possibilities for compact implementations with countermeasures.

1 Introduction

Technological developments in the field of low-end devices are proceeding at a rapid pace; preserving, however, never ending implementation challenges. Driven by the very fierce constraints, two of those are of utmost importance: silicon area and energy consumption. Based on economical and technical limitations these two constraints remain the key factors in today's evolution of low-cost devices. Due to the linear relationship between silicon area and chip manufacturing costs on one side, and the billions of devices produced every year on the other side, the total production cost is naturally a limiting factor.

To overcome the mentioned challenge, there have been many new lightweight block ciphers coming out of the academic research [2,7,14,16,20,28,29]. In practice, however, there are still billions of devices in the field carrying standardized ciphers such as Advanced Encryption Standard (AES) [13], Data Encryption Standard (DES) [24] and the Russian block cipher standard GOST [1] which are not necessarily considered lightweight. The reason for the former block cipher is mainly its high-degree 8-bit Sbox. There has been recent progress [8,15,17,22] in

© Springer International Publishing Switzerland 2016
N. Homma and M. Medwed (Eds.): CARDIS 2015, LNCS 9514, pp. 273–285, 2016.
DOI: 10.1007/978-3-319-31271-2_17

optimizing implementations of AES and its Sbox. However, a very little improvement has been made on the lightweight implementations of DES and GOST. To our knowledge, [20] provides the most significant improvement when lightweight implementation of DES is considered. The mentioned implementation is serialized with 6-bit data-path. The authors emphasize that the cost of the Sboxes is significant and suggest to use one single alternative Sbox. In general, many multi-Sbox designs such as Lblock [30], mCrypton [21], the Advanced Encryption Standard candidates SERPENT [3] and TwoFish [27] share the same faith with DES by lacking lightweight implementations.

Due to the usage of these algorithms in devices, such as ID cards, smart cards, payment cards, the implementations of these algorithms are subject to implementation attacks. The most common implementation attack, namely differential power analysis (DPA), is based on observing the power consumption of the device [19]. Countermeasures, such as masking are suggested for secure implementations [4,9,18,26]. Some masking schemes even provide security under the probing model in addition to DPA. Masking-like countermeasures have the advantage to perform efficiently when affine functions are considered. However, their implementation cost increases together with the degree of the nonlinear function to be protected. Therefore, it is desired to implement a cryptographic algorithm with minimum number of nonlinear functions. Even though there has been ongoing research on minimizing the field multiplications per S-box [11,12], there has been no progress done on minimizing the number of nonlinear permutations of a cryptographic algorithm by looking at the full substitution layer. This also explains the lack of research on masking of multi-Sbox designs.

Contribution. In this work, we propose a method, based on decompositions of permutations, to reduce the number of nonlinear permutations of existing multi-Sbox designs for efficient hardware implementations. This method not only decreases the area of the unprotected implementation, but also creates a significant advantage for implementing masking-like countermeasures. We illustrate the proposed method on DES. We acknowledge that DES is considered insecure for many applications nowadays due to its 56-bit key length. However, this implementation can be used during the implementation of its successor Triple-DES (which essentially applies the DES algorithm three times with different keys to each input data block). Triple-DES, also denoted as 3DES or TDEA, is still massively used in the electronic payment industry. When the three consecutive instances of DES are applied using three different 56-bit keys, Triple-DES provides effective 112 bits of security. In addition, we provide implementation results and suggest design ideas to cryptographers.

Organization. We introduce the DES algorithm by detailing its sub-functions in the following section. Our method inherits ideas from the affine equivalence relation between the permutations and possible decompositions of them. An introduction to these subjects are also given in Sect. 2. The details of our method and its instantiation on DES Sboxes are provided in Sect. 2.3. We discuss our hardware implementation in Sect. 3 which is followed by the conclusion.

2   Preliminaries

We denote an $m \times n$ Sbox with m input bits and n output bits (from $\mathrm{GF}(2^m)$ to $\mathrm{GF}(2^n)$) as $S(x_1, \ldots, x_m) = (y_1 \ldots, y_n)$ and equivalently $S(x) = y$. Alternatively, we also use $S = .$ where $.$ stands for table look-up of the Sbox. We use calligraphic letters to denote a set (e.g. $\mathcal{A}$) and $|.|$ (e.g. $|\mathcal{A}|$) to denote its cardinality.

2.1   Data Encryption Standard (DES)

A single iteration of DES (Fig. 1) takes as input a 64-bit plaintext together with a 56-bit key in order to output a 64-bit ciphertext. It is a balanced Feistel network where only 32 bits of the state are updated per round. The round function RF which takes a 32-bit input and a 48-bit round key follows the steps below:

Expansion. The 32-bit input is divided into eight 4-bit chunks. Each chunk is extended to 6 bits by inheriting the first (resp. last) bit from its adjacent chunk on the right (resp. left). Hence this operation duplicates half of the input bits to generate a 48-bit output.

Key Mixing. The 48-bit round key is mixed with the expanded 48 bits by means of XORs.

Substitution. The 48-bit output of key mixing is split into eight 6-bit chunks. Each 6-bit chunk is substituted to a 4-bit block using a different 6×4 Sbox. Hence, the substitution layer is composed of eight different Sboxes. These Sboxes are designed so that they can be represented as four 4-bit permutations (hereto mini-Sboxes). The outer bits (x_1, x_6) are used to select which mini-Sbox is used whereas the inner bits (x_2, x_3, x_4, x_5) are responsible for the look-up.

Permutation. The 32-bit output of the substitution layer is bit-wise permuted using a special permutation matrix.

Key Schedule. It is used to generate 48-bit round keys from the 56-bit master key. This generation is simply rotation and selection.

We refer to [10] for more detailed description.

2.2   Affine Equivalence Relation

For our efficient implementation, we mainly consider the 4-bit mini-Sboxes. Since these Sboxes are permutations, we focus on some properties of permutations in this section.

The set of all n-bit permutations form the symetric group $\mathcal{S}_{2^n}$. This set can be split using the affine equivalence relation between Sboxes as defined below:

Definition 1. *Two permutations $S_1(x)$ and $S_2(x)$ are affine equivalent if there exists a pair of affine permutations $A(x)$ and $B(x)$, such that $S_1 = B \circ S_2 \circ A$.*

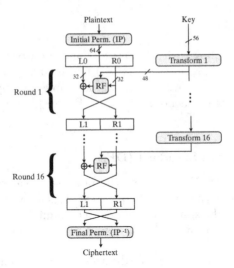

Fig. 1. DES block cipher

Each group of n-bit permutations that are affine equivalent form a class. Hence, all the Sboxes in a class can be represented with a designated representative Sbox from the same class. Every Sbox in the same class has the same algebraic degree. Moreover, every Sbox in a class are either in the Alternating group $\mathcal{A}_{2^n}$ or not. Being in $\mathcal{A}_{2^n}$ implies that the Sbox can be represented with even number of transpositions. The set of non-Alternating permutations are denoted by $\mathcal{S}_{2^n} \setminus \mathcal{A}_{2^n}$.

Following the notation in [6], we represent linear, quadratic and cubic affine equivalence classes of 4-bit permutations as $\mathcal{A}_i$, $\mathcal{Q}_i$ and $\mathcal{C}_i$ where i stands for the class number when classes are ordered lexicographically. We refer to [6] for the list of all 302 affine-equivalence classes' representatives of 4-bit permutations.

It has been shown in [6] that there exist one affine, six quadratic and 295 cubic classes of 4-bit permutations. It is well known that all the affine permutations are in $\mathcal{A}_{16}$. Moreover, all the quadratic 4-bit permutations are shown to be in $\mathcal{A}_{16}$. From the remaining cubic permutations, only 144 of them are in $\mathcal{A}_{16}$. For the representatives of these specific classes, we refer the reader to [6].

2.3 Decomposition

Decomposition of a cubic Sbox S into two quadratic Sboxes S_1 and S_2, such that $S = S_1 \circ S_2$ is first proposed in [25] for the 4-bit PRESENT Sbox to ease the application of a countermeasure. Later in [5,6] this idea has been generalized to all 4-bit permutations with sometimes more than two Sboxes in decomposition ($S = S_1 \circ S_2 \circ \ldots \circ S_s$) as follows.

Let $\mathcal{M}$ define the set of all six quadratic permutation classes $\{\mathcal{Q}_{004}, \mathcal{Q}_{012}, \mathcal{Q}_{293}, \mathcal{Q}_{294}, \mathcal{Q}_{299}, \mathcal{Q}_{300}\} = \mathcal{M}$. It has been shown that all permutations in $\mathcal{A}_{16}$ can be decomposed using permutations from $\mathcal{M}$. Note that the possibility to decompose some cubic Sboxes to quadratics but not all can be described with the fact that all 4-bit quadratic permutations are in $\mathcal{A}_{16}$ as do the cubic classes with quadratic decomposition. The decomposition length of these cubic classes, which is defined as the minimum number of quadratic permutations used in such decompositions varies between two and four. Naturally, it is also possible to decompose these cubic Sboxes into one cubic and one quadratic permutation from $\mathcal{A}_{16}$.

The rest of the cubic permutations, which are in $\mathcal{S}_{16} \setminus \mathcal{A}_{16}$, can be represented using one cubic ($\in \mathcal{S}_{16} \setminus \mathcal{A}_{16}$) and one or more quadratic permutations ($\in \mathcal{A}_{16}$). In [5,6], such decompositions are generated using the cubic permutations from a certain set of Sboxes, namely $\mathcal{N} = \{\mathcal{C}_{001}, \mathcal{C}_{003}, \mathcal{C}_{013}, \mathcal{C}_{301}\}$. It has been shown that the permutations in $\mathcal{N}$ have special properties that are advantageous when masking is considered. Even though we do not explicitly use these properties, we choose to use these classes when permutations form $\in \mathcal{S}_{16} \setminus \mathcal{A}_{16}$ are required.

Section Decomposition to Simplify Multi-Sbox Designs Even thought there exists prior applications of particular Sboxes using decomposition, it is the first time that such a method is applied in order to reduce the implementation overhead of multi-Sbox designs and obtain a compact implementation on hardware. Here, we mainly describe our method on DES for easy understanding and provide implementation results for it. However, this method can be applied to other designs such as GOST [1], SERPENT [3] TwoFish [27], Lblock [30] and mCrypton [21].

2.4   Methodology

As mentioned in Sect. 2.1, DES comprises of eight different 6×4 Sboxes, which can be represented as 32 different 4×4 mini-Sboxes. This presents a challenge for a compact hardware implementation, since all of them need to be implemented (instantiated) separately.

Idea. In order to minimize the cost of several different Sboxes, we aim to decompose them such that minimum number of nonlinear permutations is used to jointly describe all mini-Sboxes. Therefore, we search for one or more decompositions of the mini-Sboxes that hold for as many Sboxes as possible.

Possible Decompositions. It is known that the 32 mini-Sboxes of DES belong to 21 different affine equivalent classes [6]. Nine of these classes are in $\mathcal{A}_{16}$, specifically they are from the set $\{\mathcal{C}_{046}, \mathcal{C}_{073}, \mathcal{C}_{085}, \mathcal{C}_{086}, \mathcal{C}_{148}, \mathcal{C}_{184}, \mathcal{C}_{221}, \mathcal{C}_{254}, \mathcal{C}_{281}\} = \mathcal{K}$. As described in Sect. 2.3, being in $\mathcal{A}_{16}$ implies that an Sbox in $\mathcal{K}$ can be decomposed into a permutation from $\mathcal{M}$ and a permutation from $\mathcal{A}_{16}$. Given the affine equivalence relation, one can search for a solution of the form

$$S_{\mathcal{K}} = C \circ F \circ B \circ G_{\mathcal{K}} \circ A \qquad \text{(left decomposition)}$$
$$S_{\mathcal{K}} = C \circ G_{\mathcal{K}} \circ B \circ F \circ A \qquad \text{(right decomposition)} \qquad (1)$$

for the mini-Sboxes in $\mathcal{K}$. Here, $S_{\mathcal{K}}$ is the representative of the targeted mini-Sbox, $G_{\mathcal{K}}$ is a quadratic permutation from one of the classes in $\mathcal{M}$, F is a permutation from $\mathcal{A}_{16}$, and A, B, C are affine permutations.

The remaining 12 mini-Sboxes are in $\mathcal{S}_{16} \setminus \mathcal{A}_{16}$, specifically from the set $\{C_{059}, C_{069}, C_{079}, C_{098}, C_{117}, C_{137}, C_{139}, C_{166}, C_{204}, C_{220}, C_{257}, C_{279}\} = \mathcal{L}$. Similar to the previous case, one can search for a solution of the form

$$S_{\mathcal{L}} = C \circ F \circ B \circ G_{\mathcal{L}} \circ A \qquad \text{(left decomposition)}$$
$$S_{\mathcal{L}} = C \circ G_{\mathcal{L}} \circ B \circ F \circ A \qquad \text{(right decomposition)} \qquad (2)$$

where $S_{\mathcal{L}}$ is the representative of the targeted mini-Sbox, $G_{\mathcal{L}}$ is a permutation from $\mathcal{N}$, F is a permutation from $\mathcal{A}_{16}$, and A, B, C are affine permutations. Note that it is possible to find solutions where $G_{\mathcal{L}}$ is a permutation from $\mathcal{S}_{16} \setminus \mathcal{A}_{16}$ but not strictly from $\mathcal{N}$. Here, we ignore such decompositions for reasons described in Sect. 2.3.

Goal. We aim to find F in $\mathcal{A}_{16}$ such that it satisfies Eqs. (1) and (2) and is the same for all these mini-Sboxes.

Algorithm to Achieve the Goal. We propose the following algorithm (we are considering thereafter the left decomposition only since for the right decomposition the method is similar):

1. Take one representative permutation $S_{\mathcal{K}}$, $S_{\mathcal{L}}$, $G_{\mathcal{K}}$ and $G_{\mathcal{L}}$ for each class in $\mathcal{K}$, $\mathcal{L}$, $\mathcal{M}$ and $\mathcal{N}$ respectively.
2. Compute $D_{\mathcal{K}} = S_{\mathcal{K}} \circ (A)^{-1} \circ (G_{\mathcal{K}})^{-1}$ and $D_{\mathcal{L}} = S_{\mathcal{L}} \circ (A)^{-1} \circ (G_{\mathcal{L}})^{-1}$ for all possible affine permutations A, i.e. for all permutations in class $\mathcal{A}_{000}$ where $|\mathcal{A}_{000}| = 322,560$. Since $|\mathcal{K}| = 9$ and $|\mathcal{M}| = 6$, there exists $9 \times 322,560 \times 6$ solutions for $D_{\mathcal{K}}$. Similarly, $|\mathcal{L}| = 12$ and $|\mathcal{N}| = 4$ provides $12 \times 322,560 \times 4$ solutions for $D_{\mathcal{L}}$. In total, we get $9 \times 322,560 \times 6 + 12 \times 322,560 \times 4 = 32,901,120$ solutions for this left decomposition. We cluster them in $9 \times 6 + 12 \times 4 = 102$ groups each containing 322,560 solutions.
3. Cluster the groups in super groups of $9 + 12 = 21$ in total, i.e. for each mini-Sbox class.
4. Search for a class from $\mathcal{A}_{16}$ which is present in all these super groups (recall that $\mathcal{A}_{16}$ contains 151 classes).
5. If such a class exists, find $F \in \mathcal{A}_{16}$, which satisfies the relation $D_{\mathcal{K}} = C \circ F \circ B$ (and correspondingly $D_{\mathcal{L}} = C \circ F \circ B$), and hence Eqs. (1) and (2).

Note that we abuse the notation for A, B, C constantly which is certainly different for all mini-Sbox representatives $S_{\mathcal{K}}$ and $S_{\mathcal{L}}$.

2.5   Results

Applying the algorithm in Sect. 2.4, we found 12 solutions for the left decomposition and another 12 for the right decomposition – so in total 24 solutions.

The found common class where F lies is one of $\{C_{158}, C_{159}\}$. In Table 1, we summarize our solutions. It can be observed that by fixing C_{158} or C_{159} , we get 4 or 8 solutions respectively for left decomposition (alternatively 8 or 4 solutions respectively for right decomposition).

Table 1. Possible solutions for decomposing DES mini-Sboxes.

	Left Decomp.	Right Decomp.
$\mathcal{K}$	$C_{158} \times Q_{293}$	$Q_{012} \times C_{158}$
	$C_{158} \times Q_{299}$	$Q_{293} \times C_{158}$
	$C_{159} \times Q_{012}$	$Q_{294} \times C_{158}$
	$C_{159} \times Q_{293}$	$Q_{299} \times C_{158}$
	$C_{159} \times Q_{294}$	$Q_{293} \times C_{159}$
	$C_{159} \times Q_{299}$	$Q_{299} \times C_{159}$
$\mathcal{L}$	$C_{158} \times C_{013}$	$C_{013} \times C_{158}$
	$C_{158} \times C_{301}$	$C_{301} \times C_{158}$
	$C_{159} \times C_{013}$	$C_{013} \times C_{159}$
	$C_{159} \times C_{301}$	$C_{301} \times C_{159}$

However, note that we only considered the *representatives* of the DES mini-Sboxes so far. In order to obtain the final solution for each of the 32 mini-Sboxes, we take into account that they are affine equivalent to the representative $S_{\mathcal{K}}$ (or $S_{\mathcal{L}}$), i.e. $S = C' \circ S_{\mathcal{K}} \circ A'$ (or $S = C' \circ S_{\mathcal{L}} \circ A'$), where S is one of the 32 mini-Sboxes, C' and A' are affine permutations (i.e. from class $\mathcal{A}_{000}$).

Therefore the representation for S becomes $S = C' \circ C \circ F \circ B \circ G_{\mathcal{K}} \circ A \circ A'$ (or $S = C' \circ C \circ G_{\mathcal{K}} \circ B \circ F \circ A \circ A'$) if $S \in \mathcal{A}_{16}$ and $S = C' \circ C \circ F \circ B \circ G_{\mathcal{L}} \circ A \circ A'$ (or $S = C' \circ C \circ G_{\mathcal{L}} \circ B \circ F \circ A \circ A'$) if $S \in \mathcal{S}_{16} \setminus \mathcal{A}_{16}$. Obviously, $C' \circ C$ and $A \circ A'$ can be replaced by one single affine permutation. For simplicity we represent this compositions with C and A respectively and reach the final decomposition for all 32 mini-Sboxes given in Eqs. (1) and (2) correspondingly.

Hereon, we refer to the jth mini-Sbox of the ith DES Sbox as S^{ij}, where $1 \le i \le 8$, $0 \le j \le 3$. As described in Eqs. (1) and (2), these mini-Sboxes belong to either of the two defined cases (denoted hereafter with S^{ij}_{left} and S^{ij}_{right}). Furthermore, each of these mini-Sboxes can be represented as explained in the previous section as a composition of two higher-degree (quadratic or cubic) and three affine vectorial boolean functions (permutations). In other words:

$$S^{ij}_{left} = \begin{cases} C^{ij} \circ F \circ B^{ij} \circ G_{\mathcal{K}} \circ A^{ij}, & \text{if } (i,j) \in \{(1,*),(5,1),(5,2),(5,3), \\ & (6,1),(6,2),(7,3),(8,3)\} \\ C^{ij} \circ F \circ B^{ij} \circ G_{\mathcal{L}} \circ A^{ij}, & \text{if } (i,j) \in \{(2,*),(3,*),(4,*),(5,0), \\ & (6,0),(6,3),(7,0),(7,1),(7,2),(8,0), \\ & (8,1),(8,2)\} \end{cases}$$

$$
S_{right}^{ij} = \begin{cases} C^{ij} \circ G_{\mathcal{K}} \circ B^{ij} \circ F \circ A^{ij}, & \text{if } (i,j) \in \{(1,*),(5,1),(5,2),(5,3), \\ & \quad (6,1),\ (6,2),\ (7,3),\ (8,3)\} \\[2mm] C^{ij} \circ G_{\mathcal{L}} \circ B^{ij} \circ F \circ A^{ij}, & \text{if } (i,j) \in \{(2,*),(3,*),(4,*),(5,0), \\ & \quad (6,0),\ (6,3),\ (7,0),\ (7,1),\ (7,2),\ (8,0), \\ & \quad (8,1),\ (8,2)\} \end{cases}
$$

where $G_{\mathcal{K}}$ is quadratic, and $G_{\mathcal{L}}$ and F are cubic vectorial Boolean functions and A^{ij}, B^{ij}, C^{ij} are affine. As we can see, F, $G_{\mathcal{K}}$, and $G_{\mathcal{L}}$ can be shared for all the mini-Sboxes and therefore make the whole implementation considerably smaller.

Due to page limitations, we provide only one possible tuple $(F, G_{\mathcal{K}}, G_{\mathcal{L}})$ out of 24 tuples that satisfy the solution for the DES Sbox (12 solutions for S_{left}^{ij} and 12 for S_{right}^{ij}) in Table 2. For each tuple, the affine vectorial Boolean functions A^{ij}, B^{ij}, C^{ij} are then uniquely determined. The representations in Table 2 are in the form of lookup tables. The others solutions are equivalent and trivial to derive.

3   Hardware Implementation

We consider a serialized structure for our lightweight implementation which uses one-Sbox block that can calculate all DES Sboxes. The smallest DES implementation known so far, presented in [20] is an example of such a serialized structure. For compatibility, we inherit the mentioned implementation together with the same 6-bit input 4-bit output behavior of the S-box layer in our implementation.

Our implementation does not possess any countermeasures against physical attacks. However, we emphasize that this one-Sbox structure, which only has three nonlinear permutation blocks F, $G_{\mathcal{K}}$, $G_{\mathcal{L}}$, is highly advantageous when countermeasures such as masking are considered. This is due to the fact that implementing a nonlinear function in masked domain is very challenging whereas a linear function can be implemented in a straight-forward way. Moreover, it has been shown in [4] that the required number of shares for linear functions is smaller than that of nonlinear functions.

3.1   Instantiation of the Multi-Sbox Design

We focus on the specific solution suggested in Table 2 out of the 24 equivalent choices. Figure 2 represents a block diagram of our DES Sbox architecture. The input of the Sbox consists of 6 bits of which the two outer bits will be used together with the 3-bit clock counter of one round in order to decide which mini-Sbox calculation operation is followed. We denote this selection bits as sel. The remaining 4 bits of the input are sent to the first affine permutation layer. Depending on the calculated mini-Sbox, and hence the value of sel, the input of the nonlinear function $G_{\mathcal{K}}$ or $G_{\mathcal{L}}$ is selected from the outputs of A^{ij}. The output of $G_{\mathcal{K}}$ (resp. $G_{\mathcal{L}}$) is used as input to the second affine permutation layer. Similar to the previous step, the input of the nonlinear permutation F is chosen

Table 2. DES Sbox decomposition (one of the 24 possible representations).

F	0123458A6BCF7D9E	$G_{\mathcal{K}}$	0123457689CDEFBA	$G_{\mathcal{L}}$	0123456789CDEFBA
A^{10}	43DA8F169E0752CB	B^{10}	0145ABEFCD896723	C^{10}	6B0D94F21C7AE385
A^{11}	EDB874213065A9FC	B^{11}	0145ABEFCD896723	C^{11}	618FDA349E7025CB
A^{12}	43168FDA9ECB5207	B^{12}	0145ABEFCD896723	C^{12}	5E92A16DB07C4F83
A^{13}	7F6E2A3B8091D5C4	B^{13}	0514AFBE9C8D3627	C^{13}	B4691EC378A5D20F
A^{20}	2156DEA90374FC8B	B^{20}	02318AB94675CEFD	C^{20}	971F5BD34AC2860E
A^{21}	78D23C96F05AB41E	B^{21}	57021346ECB9A8FD	C^{21}	79F1E0683DB5A42C
A^{22}	7C1AE583294FB0D6	B^{22}	BFC8EA9D26517304	C^{22}	EAD926158CBF4073
A^{23}	D7A0C6B15F284E39	B^{23}	5261E9DA7043CBF8	C^{23}	9E2561DA70CB8F34
A^{30}	E079B52CA43DF168	B^{30}	5F0A4E1BC693D782	C^{30}	F27AD058E36BC149
A^{31}	52BC709EDA34F816	B^{31}	8F439E5261AD70BC	C^{31}	06357142BD8ECAF9
A^{32}	F30C956A48B72ED1	B^{32}	BFC8EA9D26517304	C^{32}	9A12ED658B03FC74
A^{33}	E68091F74C2A3B5D	B^{33}	1A29380BF4C7D6E5	C^{33}	A0E46C285F1B93D7
A^{40}	8FAD0725E9CB6143	B^{40}	5261E9DA7043CBF8	C^{40}	2FC1D03E947A6B85
A^{41}	89AB2301EFCD4567	B^{41}	5261E9DA7043CBF8	C^{41}	8F3470CB61DA9E25
A^{42}	5270DAF83416BC9E	B^{42}	5261E9DA7043CBF8	C^{42}	8F3470CB61DA9E25
A^{43}	5270DAF83416BC9E	B^{43}	5261E9DA7043CBF8	C^{43}	295ED6A1F4830B7C
A^{50}	EA7326BF049DC851	B^{50}	5F0A4E1BC693D782	C^{50}	7AF258D03EB61C94
A^{51}	A8B975643120ECFD	B^{51}	021346578A9BCEDF	C^{51}	AF0514BE72D8C963
A^{52}	7EA3D40918C5B26F	B^{52}	0123456789ABCDEF	C^{52}	7F3BD5914C08E6A2
A^{53}	AE40FB158C62D937	B^{53}	0167EF89CDAB2345	C^{53}	72BEFA369C5014D8
A^{60}	28F56CB10AD74E93	B^{60}	EBC963412705AF8D	C^{60}	A41F972CE05BD368
A^{61}	EFAB1054DC982367	B^{61}	01236745EFCD89AB	C^{61}	C70B834F5E921AD6
A^{62}	A578F02DC31E964B	B^{62}	04152637BFAE9D8C	C^{62}	8CBF4073EAD92615
A^{63}	B9CE46318AFD7502	B^{63}	02318AB94675CEFD	C^{63}	8FADBC9E34160725
A^{70}	F719D53B806EA24C	B^{70}	8F439E5261AD70BC	C^{70}	DEB8A9CF30564721
A^{71}	E284C0A6593F7B1D	B^{71}	8C37AE1504BF269D	C^{71}	BA103298FE5476DC
A^{72}	027564138AFDEC9B	B^{72}	5261E9DA7043CBF8	C^{72}	9E70618F43ADBC52
A^{73}	AC8E1735BD9F0624	B^{73}	02468ACE9BDF1357	C^{73}	E6193BC4A25D7F80
A^{80}	C74F921A38B06DE5	B^{80}	B8FC03471256A9ED	C^{80}	896754BACD2310FE
A^{81}	2A6E91D5B3F7084C	B^{81}	831A29B07CE5D64F	C^{81}	B193280AC6E45F7D
A^{82}	905CF63AE72B814D	B^{82}	BF73AE628C409D51	C^{82}	086E91F7C4A25D3B
A^{83}	56A912EDCF308B74	B^{83}	0167CDAB2345EF89	C^{83}	0437C8FBAE9D6251

from the outputs of B^{ij} with the help of *sel*. The output of F is sent to the final layer of affine permutations C^{ij}. The correct output of the DES Sbox is chosen from the outputs of C^{ij} using the *sel*. There are no registers in this implementation.

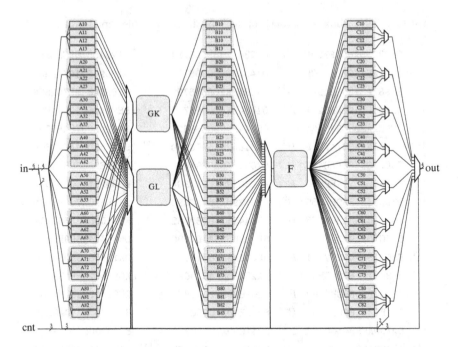

Fig. 2. Substitution layer of DES composed of 8 Sboxes (equivalently 32 mini-Sboxes).

Table 3. List of affine permutations that are equal.

$A^{42} = A^{43}$
$B^{10} = B^{11} = B^{12}$
$B^{40} = B^{41} = B^{42} = B^{43} = B^{23} = B^{72}$
$B^{22} = B^{32}$
$B^{50} = B^{30}$
$B^{63} = B^{20}$
$B^{70} = B^{31}$
$C^{41} = C^{42}$

Please note that several affine permutation blocks, specifically $A^{43}, B^{11}, B^{12}, B^{32}, B^{40}, B^{41}, B^{42}, B^{43}, B^{50}, B^{63}, B^{70}, B^{72}$ and C^{32} (i.e. 13 in total) are represented with dotted lines and they are not connected. This is due to the fact that these permutation blocks are equivalent to other permutation blocks (Table 3) which can be reused to obtain even smaller footprint.

3.2   Synthesis Results

We implemented the proposed method and all eight 6 × 4 Sboxes of DES for a fair comparison (i.e. we assumed 6-bit input and 4-bit output including the final multiplexer which is also depicted in Fig. 2). We described both options as their corresponding Boolean function representation and let our synthesis tool (Synopsys Design Vision D-2010.03-SP4) optimize these functions using the compile_ultra command. Synthesis results show 40 % decrease of hardware (1017 GE vs. 603 GE) area when 45 nm NanGate standard cell library is used [23].

Moreover, we also implemented DES in a serialized manner as suggested in [20] by replacing the Sbox with ours. The synthesis with the mentioned settings yields 2089 GE. Since our library and the library used by [20] are different as well as the synthesis tools, we can not directly compare the exact GE values. In [20], it has been stated that 32 % of the area is consumed by the Sboxes. Following this metric, we conclude that our Sbox which employs 28 % of the area is smaller.

We repeated the same analysis with Cadance RTL Compiler RC14.22 and the same library since the performance of the optimization can vary depending on the synthesis tool. We got similar results.

Note that the variety of the affine permutations which also increases the amount of the multiplexers consume a big ratio of the area. We emphasize that it is possible to minimize such cost with careful selection of Sboxes during the design process.

4   Conclusion

We discuss a novel method to describe many permutations of the same size with high degree using fewer smaller degree permutations using the affine equivalence relation between their decompositions. We exemplified our method on DES algorithm for which we used only one quadratic, two cubic 4-bit permutations instead of 32 cubic 4-bit permutations or equivalently eight degree five functions. We leave other instantiations of this work to the reader. Moreover, the mentioned method not only has the advantage of resulting with smaller implementations, but also leads to possible low-cost implementations with countermeasures since it minimizes the number of nonlinear elements in the description.

Acknowledgments. This work has been supported in part by the Research Council of KU Leuven (OT/13/071) and by GOA (tense). B. Bilgin was partially supported by the FWO project G0B4213N and she is a Postdoctoral Fellow of the Research Foundation - Flanders (FWO).

References

1. Gost, gosudarstvennyi standard 28147–89. Cryptographic Protection for Data Processing Systems, Government Committee of the USSR for Standards (1989)
2. Beaulieu, R., Shors, D., Smith, J., Treatman-Clark, S., Weeks, B., Wingers, L.: The SIMON and SPECK families of lightweight block ciphers. In: eprint.iacr.org/404, 2013 (2013)

3. Biham, E., Anderson, R., Knudsen, L.R.: Serpent: a new block cipher proposal. In: Vaudenay, S. (ed.) FSE 1998. LNCS, vol. 1372, p. 222. Springer, Heidelberg (1998)
4. Bilgin, B., Gierlichs, B., Nikova, S., Nikov, V., Rijmen, V.: Higher-order threshold implementations. In: Sarkar, P., Iwata, T. (eds.) ASIACRYPT 2014, Part II. LNCS, vol. 8874, pp. 326–343. Springer, Heidelberg (2014)
5. Bilgin, B., Nikova, S., Nikov, V., Rijmen, V., Stütz, G.: Threshold implementations of all 3 ×3 and 4 ×4 s-boxes. In: Prouff, E., Schaumont, P. (eds.) CHES 2012. LNCS, vol. 7428, pp. 76–91. Springer, Heidelberg (2012)
6. Bilgin, B., Nikova, S., Nikov, V., Rijmen, V., Tokareva, N., Vitkup, V.: Threshold implementations of small S-boxes. Cryptograph. Commun. 7(1), 3–33 (2015)
7. Bogdanov, A.A., Knudsen, L.R., Leander, G., Paar, C., Poschmann, A., Robshaw, M., Seurin, Y., Vikkelsoe, C.: PRESENT: an ultra-lightweight block cipher. In: Paillier, P., Verbauwhede, I. (eds.) CHES 2007. LNCS, vol. 4727, pp. 450–466. Springer, Heidelberg (2007)
8. Canright, D.: A very compact s-box for AES. In: Proceedings of 7th International Workshop on Cryptographic Hardware and Embedded Systems - CHES, Edinburgh, UK, pp. 441–455, 29 August–1 September 2005
9. Carlet, C., Goubin, L., Prouff, E., Quisquater, M., Rivain, M.: Higher-order masking schemes for s-boxes. In: Canteaut, A. (ed.) FSE 2012. LNCS, vol. 7549, pp. 366–384. Springer, Heidelberg (2012)
10. Coppersmith, D.: The data encryption standard (DES) and its strength against attacks. IBM J. Res. Dev. 38(3), 243–250 (1994)
11. Coron, J.-S., Roy, A., Vivek, S.: Fast evaluation of polynomials over binary finite fields and application to side-channel countermeasures. In: Batina, L., Robshaw, M. (eds.) CHES 2014. LNCS, vol. 8731, pp. 170–187. Springer, Heidelberg (2014)
12. Coron, J.-S., Roy, A., Vivek, S.: Fast evaluation of polynomials over binary finite fields and application to side-channel countermeasures. J. Cryptograph. Eng. 5(2), 73–83 (2015)
13. Daemen, J., Rijmen, V.: Aes proposal: Rijndael (1998)
14. De Cannière, C., Dunkelman, O., Knežević, M.: KATAN and KTANTAN — a family of small and efficient hardware-oriented block ciphers. In: Clavier, C., Gaj, K. (eds.) CHES 2009. LNCS, vol. 5747, pp. 272–288. Springer, Heidelberg (2009)
15. Feldhofer, M., Wolkerstorfer, J., Rijmen, V.: AES implementation on a grain of sand. IEE Proc. Inf. Securi. 152(1), 13–20 (2005)
16. Guo, J., Peyrin, T., Poschmann, A., Robshaw, M.: The LED block cipher. In: Preneel, B., Takagi, T. (eds.) CHES 2011. LNCS, vol. 6917, pp. 326–341. Springer, Heidelberg (2011)
17. Hämäläinen, P., Alho, T., Hännikäinen, M., Hämäläinen, T.D.: Design and Implementation of low-area and low-power AES encryption hardware core. In: Euromicro Conference on Digital System Design, pp. 577–583. IEEE Computer Society (2006)
18. Ishai, Y., Sahai, A., Wagner, D.: Private circuits: securing hardware against probing attacks. In: Boneh, D. (ed.) CRYPTO 2003. LNCS, vol. 2729, pp. 463–481. Springer, Heidelberg (2003)
19. Kocher, P.C., Jaffe, J., Jun, B.: Differential power analysis. In: Wiener, M. (ed.) CRYPTO 1999. LNCS, vol. 1666, pp. 388–397. Springer, Heidelberg (1999)
20. Leander, G., Paar, C., Poschmann, A., Schramm, K.: New lightweight DES variants. In: Biryukov, A. (ed.) FSE 2007. LNCS, vol. 4593, pp. 196–210. Springer, Heidelberg (2007)
21. Lim, C.H., Korkishko, T.: mCrypton – a lightweight block cipher for security of low-cost RFID tags and sensors. In: Song, J.-S., Kwon, T., Yung, M. (eds.) WISA 2005. LNCS, vol. 3786, pp. 243–258. Springer, Heidelberg (2006)

22. Moradi, A., Poschmann, A., Ling, S., Paar, C., Wang, H.: Pushing the limits: a very compact and a threshold implementation of AES. In: Paterson, K.G. (ed.) EUROCRYPT 2011. LNCS, vol. 6632, pp. 69–88. Springer, Heidelberg (2011)

23. NanGate. The NanGate 45nm Open Cell Library. http://www.nangate.com

24. Data Encryption Standard. U. S. Department of Commerce, Washington, DC, USA (1977)

25. Poschmann, A., Moradi, A., Khoo, K., Lim, C.-W., Wang, H., Ling, S.: Side-channel resistant crypto for less than 2,300 GE. J. Cryptol. **24**(2), 322–345 (2011)

26. Prouff, E., Rivain, M.: Masking against side-channel attacks: a formal security proof. In: Johansson, T., Nguyen, P.Q. (eds.) EUROCRYPT 2013. LNCS, vol. 7881, pp. 142–159. Springer, Heidelberg (2013)

27. Schneier, B., Kelsey, J., Whiting, D., Wagner, D., Hall, C., Ferguson, N.: The Twofish Encryption Algorithm: a 128-bit Block Cipher. Wiley, New York (1999)

28. Shirai, T., Shibutani, K., Akishita, T., Moriai, S., Iwata, T.: The 128-bit block-cipher CLEFIA (extended abstract). In: Biryukov, A. (ed.) FSE 2007. LNCS, vol. 4593, pp. 181–195. Springer, Heidelberg (2007)

29. Suzaki, T., Minematsu, K., Morioka, S., Kobayashi, E.: Twine: A lightweight, versatile block cipher. In: ECRYPT Workshop on Lightweight Cryptography, pp. 146–169 (2011)

30. Wu, W., Zhang, L.: LBlock: a lightweight block cipher. In: Lopez, J., Tsudik, G. (eds.) ACNS 2011. LNCS, vol. 6715, pp. 327–344. Springer, Heidelberg (2011)

Author Index